T0211587

Lecture Notes in Computer Science　　10451

Commenced Publication in 1973
Founding and Former Series Editors:
Gerhard Goos, Juris Hartmanis, and Jan van Leeuwen

More information about this series at http://www.springer.com/series/7409

Yuhua Luo (Ed.)

Cooperative Design, Visualization, and Engineering

14th International Conference, CDVE 2017
Mallorca, Spain, September 17–20, 2017
Proceedings

 Springer

Editor
Yuhua Luo
University of the Balearic Islands
Palma, Mallorca
Spain

ISSN 0302-9743 ISSN 1611-3349 (electronic)
Lecture Notes in Computer Science
ISBN 978-3-319-66804-8 ISBN 978-3-319-66805-5 (eBook)
DOI 10.1007/978-3-319-66805-5

Library of Congress Control Number: 2017951435

LNCS Sublibrary: SL3 – Information Systems and Applications, incl. Internet/Web, and HCI

Printed on acid-free paper

This Springer imprint is published by Springer Nature
The registered company is Springer International Publishing AG
The registered company address is: Gewerbestrasse 11, 6330 Cham, Switzerland

Preface

This year our conference, CDVE 2017, came back home to Mallorca, Spain, following conferences held in Australia, Asia, and North America. The conference was initiated as a European research exchange forum for the field of cooperative design, visualization, and engineering. As the research community has grown, it has become more and more global.

This year, we had submissions from the major European countries. We also had submissions from North and South America, Asia, Africa, and Australia. This means that the conference is now truly global with authors from all the continents in the world. We welcome researchers from all the continents to join our community. As was the initial goal of this conference, we still tried to maintain the core theme of cooperative working since this has become increasingly important over the years.

This year, the focus of the submissions was evenly spread between the areas of cooperative design, visualization, and engineering. The cooperative applications cover wider areas among the submitted papers.

In the field of cooperative applications, we do not only have cooperation among people and working teams, we also see new research results in the cooperation of robots, and cooperation between robots and humans. This reflects a major trend in our current technological world, where artificial intelligence is playing an increasingly important role. On the topic of cooperative editing, there is some fine research work presented on handling disturbance and awareness of concurrent updates in collaborative editors. User interface is a very important part of cooperative applications. We are happy to see that in this volume authors presented some exciting solutions for flexible user interfaces using the Internet of Things–IoT.

There is a lot of research activity in the field of cooperative visualization, as we can see. It has been applied to a very broad area of applications. Cooperative visualization is combined with other techniques such as virtual reality and augmented reality, which has led to better visualization and visual analytics. Applications include e-learning, decision making, data analysis, etc. Cooperative visualization can also increase social welfare, user experience, and visual comprehension such as in disaster prediction, virtual tourism, etc.

In the field of cooperative engineering, a couple of papers discuss the architecture, engineering, and construction (AEC) industry and its new challenges such as management of knowledge. How to tailor existing tools and standards, such as BIM, to use them as collaborative platforms and tools is the subject of a couple research papers. At the same time, cloud manufacturing is still a major research area for cooperative engineering researchers working in mechanical engineering and related fields. In this area, knowledge management also plays a critical role.

In the field of cooperative design, sustainability of user commitment is a topic that attracts researchers' attention. In a group of papers about cooperative design, authors approach different stages of design from very different perspectives. There are a couple papers discussing issues such as cooperative sketching, story telling, etc.

The papers published in this volume reflect some substantial progress in our research field. We can see the hard work and continuous effort of our community, leading to better and better technological solutions. As the editor of this volume, I would like to express my sincere thanks to all the authors for submitting their papers to the CDVE 2017 conference and sharing their research results with the community.

I sincerely thank all our volunteer reviewers, Program Committee members, and Organization Committee members for their continuous support to the conference. My special thanks go to my colleague, the Organization Committee chair Dr. Sebasitá Galmes, for his enthusiasm about this conference. I would also like to thank my university, the University of the Balearic Islands, Spain, for its constant support and sponsorship of this conference. The success of this year's conference would not have been possible without their generous support.

September 2017   Yuhua Luo

Organization

Conference Chair

Yuhua Luo   University of the Balearic Islands, Spain

International Program Committee

Program Chair

Dieter Roller   University of Stuttgart, Germany

Members

Jose Alfredo Costa	Ursula Kirschner	Manuel Ortega
Peter Demian	Jean-Christophe Lapayre	Niko Salonen
Carrie Sturts Dossick	Francis Lau	Fernando Sanchez
Susan Finger	Pierre Leclercq	Weiming Shen
Sebastia Galmes	Jang Ho Lee	Ram Sriram
Halin Gilles	Jaime Lloret	Chengzheng Sun
Shuangxi Huang	Moira C. Norrie	Thomas Tamisier
Tony Huang	Kwan-Liu Ma	Xiangyu Wang
Claudia-Lavinia Ignat	Mary Lou Maher	Nobuyoshi Yabuki

Reviewers

Belqais Allali	Tony Huang	Guofeng Qin
Ramón Barber	Claudia-Lavinia Ignat	Dieter Roler
Yang Chengwei	Jean-Christophe Lapayre	Niko Salonen
Dariusz Choinski	Pierre Leclercq	Fernando Sanchez
Jose Alfredo Costa	Jang Ho Lee	Weiming Shen
Steve Cutchin	Jaime Lloret	Chengzheng Sun
Peter Demian	Agnieszka Mars	Thomas Tamisier
Sylvia Encheva	Agustina Ng	Piotr Skupin
Leman Figen Gul	Quang Vinh Nguyen	Nobuyoshi Yabuki
Susan Finger	Manuel Ortega	Li-Nan Zhu
Sebastia Galmes	Eva Pajorova	
Halin Gilles	Kriengsak Panuwatwanich	

Organization Committee

Chair

Sebastia Galmes   University of the Balearic Islands, Spain

Members

Pilar Fuster
Tomeu Estrany
Alex Garcia
Takayuki Fujimoto
Guofeng Qin
Jaime Lloret

Contents

New Results on Possibilistic Cooperative Multi-robot Systems

Pilar Fuster-Parra[✉], José Guerrero, Javier Martín, and Óscar Valero

Universitat Illes Balears, Carr. Valldemossa km. 7.5, Palma de Mallorca, Spain
{pilar.fuster,jose.guerrero,javier.martin,o.valero}@uib.es

Abstract. This paper addresses one of the main problems to solve in a multi-robot system, allocating tasks to a set of robots (multi-robot task allocation-MRTA). Among all the approaches proposed in the literature to face up MRTA problem, this paper is focused on swarm-like methods called response threshold algorithms. The task allocation algorithms inspired on response threshold are based on probabilistic Markov chains. In the MRTA problem literature, possibilistic Markov chains have proved to outperform the probabilistic Markov chains when a Max-Min algebra is considered for matrix composition. In this paper we analyze the system behavior when a more general algebra than the Max-Min one is taken for matrix composition. Concretely, we consider the algebra $([0,1], S_M, T)$, where S_M denotes the maximum t-conorm and T stands for any t-norm. The performed experiments show how only some well-known t-norms are suitable to allocate tasks and how the possibility transition function parameters are related to the used t-norm.

Keywords: Multi-robot · Possibility theory · Swarm intelligence · Task allocation · Triangular conorm · Triangular norm

1   Introduction

Systems with two or more autonomous robots with a common objective, from now on referenced as multi-robot systems, provide a great number of advantages compared to systems with only one robot: robustness, parallelism, efficiency and so on. In order to take these advantages several problems must be addressed. This paper will be focused on one of them called Multi-Robot Task Allocation problem (MRTA for short) which consists on selecting the best robot or group of robots to carry out a task. Although its significance, MRTA is still an open problem in real systems and, therefore, a lot of efforts have been made to propose suitable methods [5,7]. These methods can be grouped into two main paradigms: swarm like approaches and negotiation methods. The latter paradigm is based on explicit negotiation communication between robots with complex protocols that limits the number of the robots in the system. In contrast, swarm approaches [10], inspired by insect colonies behaviour, are more scalable and require simpler robots. Several swarm like algorithms have been proposed but, nowadays, those

© Springer International Publishing AG 2017
Y. Luo (Ed.): CDVE 2017, LNCS 10451, pp. 1–9, 2017.
DOI: 10.1007/978-3-319-66805-5_1

based on the so-called Response Threshold Method (RTM for short) are probably the most broadly used. In RTM methods each robot has a value, called stimulus, associated to each task to execute and a threshold value. The stimulus indicates how much attractive is the task for the robot and determines its probability to transit from its current task (state) to a new one. Since the transition probability only depends on the current robot's state, the evolution of the system can be modeled as a probabilistic Markov process. The applicability of the probabilistic Markov approach to real missions is limited due to two main issues. On the one hand, the transition probabilities from one state to the other are not a probability distribution (the sum of all of them is not necessarily 1). On the other hand, the probabilistic processes, in general terms, converge to a stationary stage asymptotically, i.e., the number of steps is not bounded in general.

In the light of the aforementioned problems, possibilistic Markov chains raise as a very promising alternative approach for MRTA real problems. In [6] previous theoretical results showed that possibilistic Markov chains converge to a stable state taken a very few number of steps when the algebra $([0,1], S_M, T_M)$ is used for matrix composition (T_M stands for the minimum t-norm). Of course we assume the reader is familiar with the basic notions about triangular norms and fuzzy sets (our main reference for the aforesaid topics is [9]). The aim of this work is to extend the work in [6]. Thus, we consider more general algebras $([0,1], S_M, T)$, where S_M denotes the maximum t-conorm and T any t-norm on $[0,1]$. Taking into account that the finite convergence conditions discussed in [6] (see also [4]) are also satisfied when the algebra $([0,1], S_M, T_M)$ is replaced by $([0,1], S_M, T)$ (T any t-norm), a great number of simulations with several t-norms have been conducted in order to calculate the number of iterations needed to converge to a stationary state. The experiments show that T_M provides very stable results with respect to the parameters. Moreover, our study demonstrates that the t-norms, Lukasiewicz T_L, Product T_P, Drastic T_D and Schweizer-Sklar T_λ^{SS} are only useful for allocating tasks under certain conditions.

The remainder of the paper is organized as follows: Sect. 2 reviews the basics of the MTRA problem and redefine the classical RTM as a probabilistic Markov chain. Section 3 shows the experiments carried out and, finally, Sect. 4 presents the conclusions and future work.

2   Multi-robot Task Allocation Problem: Response Threshold

This section will review the main concepts related to the multi-robot task allocation problem and Response Threshold methods. Firstly, we will explain the classical probabilistic approach and then these concepts will be adapted to the possibilistic framework.

2.1   Probabilistic Approach

Following [2], the classical response threshold method defines for each robot r_i and for each task t_j, a stimulus $s_{r_i, t_j} \in \mathbb{R}$ that represents how suitable t_j is for r_i (by $\mathbb{R}$ we denote the set of real numbers). The most common way to allocate tasks is assign to each robot r_i a value θ_{r_i} ($\theta_{r_i} \in \mathbb{R}$). The robot r_i will select a task t_j to execute with a probability P_{r_i, t_j} according to a probabilistic Markov decision chain. Although there are a lot of alternatives for the transition probability P_{r_i, t_j}, this paper will be focused on one of the most widely used (see [3]) which is given by:

$$P_{r_i, t_j} = \frac{s_{r_i, t_j}^n}{s_{r_i, t_j}^n + \theta_{r_i}^n}, \qquad (1)$$

where $n \in \mathbb{N}$ ($\mathbb{N}$ stands for the set of non-negative integer numbers).

In general, $\sum_{j=1}^m P_{r_k, t_j} = 1$ does not hold and, hence, the transition probabilities do not meet the axioms of the probability theory. Moreover, the convergence to a stationary state can only be guaranteed asymptotically.

2.2 Possibilistic Method

According to [11] a possibility Markov (memoryless) process can be defined as follows: let $S = \{s_1, \ldots, s_m\}$ ($m \in \mathbb{N}$) denote a finite set of states. If the system is in the state s_i at time τ ($\tau \in \mathbb{N}$), then the system will move to the state s_j with possibility p_{ij} at time $\tau + 1$. Let $x(\tau) = (x_1(\tau), \ldots, x_m(\tau))$ be a fuzzy state set, where $x_i(\tau)$ is defined as the possibility that the state s_i will occur at time τ for all $i = 1, \ldots, m$. Given a general algebra $([0,1], S_M, T)$, where T stands for any t-norm, the evolution of the possibilistic Markov chain in time is given by

$$x_i(\tau) = S_M{}_{j=1}^m \left(T(p_{ji}, x_j(\tau - 1)) \right).$$

The preceding expression admits a matrix formulated as follows:

$$x(\tau) = x(\tau - 1) \circ P = x(0) \circ P^\tau, \qquad (2)$$

where $P = \{p_{ij}\}_{i,j=1}^m$, $\circ$ and $x(\tau) = (x_1(\tau), \ldots, x_m(\tau))$ denote the possibilistic transition matrix, the matrix composition in the algebra $([0,1], S_M, T)$ and the possibility distribution at time τ, respectively. Taking into account the preceding notions, a possibility distribution $x(\tau)$ of the system states at time τ is said to be stationary, or stable, whenever $x(\tau) = x(\tau) \circ P$.

In [4], Duan provided conditions that guarantee that a possibilistic Markov chain converges to a stationary state in a finite number of steps. It is not hard to check that the prossibilistic response threshold method that will be introduced in the following paragraphs meets these conditions.

In order to introduce a possibilistic response threshold method, we will assume that the stimulus only depends on the distance between the robot and the task. Consider the position space endowed with a distance (metric) d. Then, denote by $d(r_i, t_j)$ the distance between the current position of r_i and the position of t_j. It is assumed that when a robot is assigned to a task the position of this task and the robot's position are the same and therefore, the distance between the task and the robot is 0. Following the standard RTM notation [1,2], define the stimulus of the robot r_k to carry out task t_j as follows:

$$s_{r_k,t_j} = \begin{cases} \frac{U_{t_j}}{d(r_k,t_j)} & \text{if } d(r_k,t_j) \neq 0 \\ \infty & \text{if } d(r_k,t_j) = 0 \end{cases}, \tag{3}$$

where U_{t_j} denotes the utility of the task j.

The stimulus s_{r_k,t_j} allows us to obtain, by means of (1), the following possibility response function:

$$p_{r_k,ij} = \frac{U_{t_j}^n}{U_{t_j}^n + d(r_k,t_j)^n \theta_{r_k}^n}. \tag{4}$$

In [6], the authors showed that the response function given in (4) meets the conditions provided in [4] to guarantee the finite convergence in at most $m-1$ steps when the algebra $([0,1], S_M, T_M)$ is used for matrix composition. Similar reasoning to that given in [6] remains valid to prove that the response function given in (4) meets the conditions provided in [4] to guarantee the finite convergence in at most $m-1$ steps when the algebra $([0,1], S_M, T)$ is used for matrix composition (where T is any t-norm). Notice that the t-conorm under consideration must be always S_M.

3   Experimental Results

In this section we will explain the experiments carried out in order to compute the number of steps required to converge to stationary stage using possibilistic Markov chains with several t-norms. It will be considered that a fuzzy Markov chain converges in k steps if $P^k = P^{k+1}$, where P is the possibility transition matrix.

3.1   Experimental Framework

During the experiments the tasks were randomly placed in an environment following a uniform distribution. The dimensions of all these environments were always the same and were equal to 600×600 units. All the experiments have been executed using MATLAB with 500 different environments and with different number of tasks: 50 and 100 ($m = 50, 100$). As stated in [8], the θ_{r_k} must depend on the environment dimensions. Thus, θ_{r_k} follows the following expression: $\theta_{r_k} = \frac{nTH}{d_{max}}$, where $d_{max} = 800.5$ units is the maximum distance between two tasks and nTH is a parameter of the system. In order to analyze how the threshold value impacts on the system performance, several values of nTH have been tested. Moreover, the possibility response function (see (4)) has been executed with two different values of the power $n = 1, 2$. In the sake of simplicity, we have assumed that all tasks have the same utility, i.e., $U_{t_j} = 1$ for all $j = 1, \ldots, m$.

3.2 Convergence Results and the Basic t-Norms

In this section we will study the impact of considering the matrix composition algebra $([0,1], S_M, T_l)$ on the number of steps needed to converge with $l \in \{M, L, P, D\}$. As pointed out in Subsect. 2.2, the t-conorm must be always the maximum S_M.

In all cases the number of steps are considered as the mean number of steps to converge. When the power value n is equal to 1, the power matrices obtained from the algebras $([0,1], S_M, T_l)$ with $l \in \{M, L, P, D\}$ converge in only 2 or 3 steps for all the values of the parameter nTH. In spite of this low number of steps, the resulting matrix after iterating is either equal to or very similar to the original one. In contrast, when the t-norm T_M is used the system requires a higher number of iterations to converge (15.8 with 50 tasks and 23.8 with 100 tasks on average), but the transition matrix obtained after iterating is quite different from the initial one. A more detailed description of the results for T_M can be found in [6]. From these results, it follows that with $n = 1$, except for T_M, the use of the tested t-norms do not produce an evolution of the system and, hence, they are not suitable for multi-robot task allocation.

Figure 1 shows the number of steps (iterations) needed to converge to a stationary state with different vales of nTH ($nTH = 1, 4, 8, 12, 16$), 50 tasks ($m = 50$), the power value $n = 2$ and when the t-norms T_M, T_L, T_P are used. Each bar represents the mean number of iterations over 500 different environments. As can be seen, the use of the t-norm T_M always provides a system convergence in a same number of steps (15.85). Therefore, the convergence to an stationary state with T_M only depends on the environment characteristics and is not affected by the parameters of the possibility transition function (see (3)). Obviously, the values of the final transition matrix obtained after iterating changes according to alterations of the parameter values (see (3)). In contrast, the iterations number when the t-norms T_L and T_P are used for matrix composition depends on the nTH parameter values. In general, the number of iterations decreases as the nTH increases. Future work will analyse how well the matrix obtained after iterating meets the expected system characteristics.

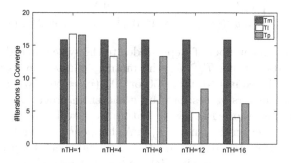

Fig. 1. Number of iteration required to converge with 50 tasks, $n = 2$, $nTH = 1, 4, 8, 12, 16$, and the t-norms: minimum (TM), Lukasiewicz (TL) and product (TP).

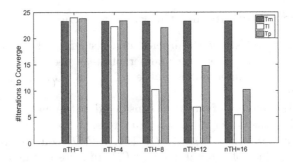

Fig. 2. Number of iteration required to converge with 100 tasks, $n = 2$, $nTH = 1, 4, 8, 12, 16$, and the t-norms: minimum (TM), Lukasiewicz (TL) and product (TP).

Figure 2 shows the number of steps needed to converge to a stationary state with 100 tasks under the same conditions as the experiments with 50 tasks whose results are in Fig. 1. As can be seen, the results obtained by the new experiments are similar to those obtained with 50 tasks. In fact, the results for T_M do not depend on the parameters and, again, the number of iterations decreases as nTH increases for T_L and T_P.

In all cases (both 50 and 100 tasks), the use of the t-norm T_D generates a final matrix equals to the original one, and therefore it is not an appropriate t-norm for the tested environments. Due to this fact, its results are not showed in the aforementioned Figs. 1 and 2.

3.3 Convergence Results and Schweizer-Sklar t-Norms

In this section we will analyze the utility of a family of celebrated t-norms, the so-called Schweizer-Sklar t-norms. Such a family, given by (5), has been chosen because it retrieves all the basic t-norms as a particular case.

$$T_\lambda^{SS}(x,y) = \begin{cases} T_M(x,y) & \text{if } \lambda = -\infty \\ T_P(x,y) & \text{if } \lambda = 0 \\ T_D(x,y) & \text{if } \lambda = \infty \\ (max((x^\lambda + y^\lambda - 1), 0))^{\frac{1}{\lambda}} & \text{if } \lambda \in (-\infty, 0) \cup (-\infty, 0) \end{cases} \quad . \quad (5)$$

Figure 3 shows the number of steps needed to the system in order to converge to a stationary state using T_λ^{SS} for the matrix composition as t-norm, with the number of tasks equals to either 50 or 100 ($m = 50, 100$), $nTH = 4$ and $n = 2$. These parameters values have been chosen in order to perform similar experiments as those showed in Fig. 3. Future work will analyse the impact of nTH and n parameter on the t-norm T_λ^{SS}. As happened during the experiments for the basic t-norms, the results are the mean number of steps to converge after executing the simulations with 500 randomly generated environments. The behaviour of the system strongly depends on the parameter λ, as it can be shown in Fig. 3. Figure 3(a) shows the number of steps decreases as the λ value

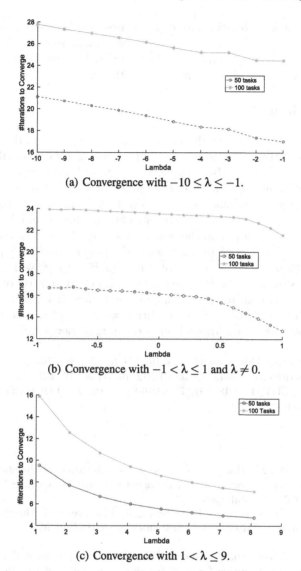

(a) Convergence with $-10 \leq \lambda \leq -1$.

(b) Convergence with $-1 < \lambda \leq 1$ and $\lambda \neq 0$.

(c) Convergence with $1 < \lambda \leq 9$.

Fig. 3. Number of steps for Schweizer-Sklar t-norms with several values of λ.

increases when $\lambda \in (-\infty, -1]$ (we have only drawn the results for the values $-10 \leq \lambda \leq -1$, however, the behavior is the same for the remainder values in $(-\infty, -1]$). Figure 3(b) shows the same experiments but with $\lambda \in (-1, 1]$. In this case the number of steps decreases very slowly if $\lambda < 0.5$, and that number starts to decrease quickly when $\lambda \in (0.5, 1]$. Finally, Fig. 3(c) shows the results with $\lambda \in (1, \infty)$ (we have only drawn the results for the values $\lambda \in (1, 9]$, however, the behavior is the same for the remainder values in $(1, \infty)$). It follows that in all cases the number of iterations needed to converge is inversely proportional to the λ value. As a consequence, for the Schweizer-Sklar t-norms changes in the parameter values have high impact on the system behaviour. Moreover, the final iterating matrix is quite different from the initial one.

4   Conclusions

This new work extends the results in [6] where the algebra $([0, 1], S_M, T_M)$ was considered for matrix composition when implementing a RTM possibilistic algorithm. Concretely more algebras $([0, 1], S_M, T)$ have been considered, where T is one of the following t-norms: T_M, T_L, T_P, T_D and T_λ^{SS}. The number of steps needed to converge to stationary state for T_M does not depend on the possibility function parameters. In contrast, the results obtained for T_L and T_P are affected by the threshold value (θ_{r_k}) and the power n (see Eq. (4)). T_L, T_P and T_λ^{SS} show that can be useful for MRTA problem when the power value n is equal to 2 but T_L, T_P not with $n = 1$. The effects of n and nTH for T_λ^{SS} will be studied in a future work. Moreover, the resulting transition matrix (matrix obtained after iterating) for T_D is equal to the original one and, thus, it is not appropriate to model the evolution of the system. As future work, we plan to study in depth the system convergence conditions from a theoretical viewpoint.

Acknowledgement. This research was funded by the Spanish Ministry of Economy and Competitiveness under Grants DPI2014-57746-C03-2-R, TIN2014-53772-R, TIN2014-56381-REDT (LODISCO), TIN2016-81731-REDT (LODISCO II) and AEI/ FEDER, UE funds.

References

1. Agassounon, W., Martinoli, A.: Efficiency and robustness of threshold-based distributed allocation algorithms in multi-agent systems. In: AAMAS 2012, Bolonia, Italy, pp. 1090–1097, July 2002
2. Bonabeau, E., Theraulaz, G., Deneubourg, J.: Fixed response threshold threshold and the regulation of division labour in insect societes. Bull. Math. Biol. **4**, 753–807 (1998)
3. Castello, E., Yamamoto, T., Libera, F.D., Liu, W., Winfield, A.F.T., Nakamura, Y., Ishiguro, H.: Adaptive foraging for simulated and real robotic swarms: the dynamical response threshold approach. Swarm Intell. **10**(1), 1–31 (2016)
4. Duan, J.: The transitive clousure, convergence of powers and adjoint of generalized fuzzy matrices. Fuzzy Sets Syst. **145**, 301–311 (2004)
5. Gerkey, B.P., Mataric, M.: A formal analysis and taxonomy of task allocation in multi-robot systems. Int. J. Robot. Res. **23**(9), 939–954 (2004)
6. Guerrero, J., Valero, Ó., Oliver, G.: A first step toward a possibilistic swarm multi-robot task allocation. In: Rojas, I., Joya, G., Catala, A. (eds.) IWANN 2015. LNCS, vol. 9094, pp. 147–158. Springer, Cham (2015). doi:10.1007/978-3-319-19258-1_13
7. Heap, B., Pagnucco, M.: Repeated sequential single-cluster auctions with dynamic tasks for multi-robot task allocation with pickup and delivery. In: Klusch, M., Thimm, M., Paprzycki, M. (eds.) MATES 2013. LNCS, vol. 8076, pp. 87–100. Springer, Heidelberg (2013). doi:10.1007/978-3-642-40776-5_10

8. Kalra, N., Martinoli, A.: A comparative study of market-based and threshold-based task allocation. In: Gini, M., Voyles, R. (eds.) DARS, pp. 91–102. Springer, Tokyo (2006). doi:10.1007/4-431-35881-1_10
9. Klement, E.P., Mesiar, R., Pap, E.: Triangular Norms. Kluwer Academic Publishers, Dordrecht (2000)
10. Navarro, I., Matía, F.: An introduction to swarm robotics. ISRN Robotics (2013)
11. Zadeh, L.: Fuzzy sets as a basis for a theory of possibility. FSS **1**, 3–28 (1978)

Standard-Based Bidirectional Decision Making for Job Seekers and Employers

Chakkrit Snae Namahoot[1,2(✉)] and Michael Brückner[3]

[1] Department of Computer Science and Information Technology,
Faculty of Science, Naresuan University, Phitsanulok, Thailand
chakkrits@nu.ac.th
[2] Center of Excellence in Nonlinear Analysis and Optimization,
Faculty of Science, Naresuan University, Phitsanulok, Thailand
[3] Department of Educational Technology and Communication,
Faculty of Education, Naresuan University, Phitsanulok, Thailand
michaelb@nu.ac.th

Abstract. In this research we designed and developed an ontology-driven decision support system (DSS) for (1) electronic recruitment processes in organizations operating in Thailand and for (2) job seekers trying to find appropriate employment in the country. The database holding the job profiles has been designed in accordance with the standards of the Department of Employment (Ministry of Labour, Thailand), and it is used to mutually match the required criteria with the offered properties. For this, a score is calculated from the required properties that gives a percentage based fit rate harnessing the statistical part of the ontology. The DSS can also be used for staffing project teams or preparing for succession through channeling employees to appropriate positions within the company by matching the required and the offered profile data.

Keywords: Content-based recommender system · Online job seeking · E-recruitment · Statistical ontology · Decision support system

1 Introduction

Recent years have seen a growing trend to electronic recruitment, mainly based on Internet activities of organizations, for which the typical recruitment process consists of four phases: (1) writing a job offer, (2) publishing the job offer, (3) pre-selecting the job applications, and (4) finding the best candidates for interviews. Whereas step (1) is an inter-departmental activity between the operating department and the human resource management department and typically supported by text processing software, step (2) is mainly the task of the human resource management and carried out online or as conventional advertisements. Steps (3) and (4) offer the best opportunities online job offers to make the whole process more efficient.

Another use scenario that focuses on the opposite direction involves a job seeker who has a set of requirements and wants to find an appropriate job. The task of finding a job that best meets all the requirements is a huge one, and this direction of the task has not been studied in great detail [1]. The recommendation task dealt with in this

© Springer International Publishing AG 2017
Y. Luo (Ed.): CDVE 2017, LNCS 10451, pp. 10–20, 2017.
DOI: 10.1007/978-3-319-66805-5_2

paper uses the tuple <user profile, desired characteristics> and maps them to the value of a rating function R: $[u_i, d_j] \rightarrow r_k$. User profiles refer to employers and job seekers and are used in the respective scenarios, whereas desired characteristics are used to identify job seekers and employers. It is important to understand that simple Boolean search strategies do usually not lead to satisfactory results because quite often the d_j contain mandatory as well as optional items. This may be accounted for by introducing weights to the d_j, whether they come from the employer's or from the job seeker's side. One of the earliest approaches for that matter was introduced by Färber et al. [2], who implemented a probabilistic recommender system for employer and job seekers. This system relied on collaborative filtering (for more recent developments, see [3, 4]) as well as content-based filtering [5] and, therefore, represents an example of a hybrid recommender system.

An effective recommender system needs to take into account the diversity of data from those user groups (job seekers and recruiters) and has to handle those data appropriately. Human resource management (HRM) systems typically rely on database management systems or data warehouses (Enterprise Resource Planning). In recent years ontologies have been introduced into the systems to improve precision of the search results within the HRM system. Statistical ontologies (as proposed in [6]) allow for the easy calculation of similarity measures of reference skills and candidate skills in order to find the best quartile among the candidates for follow-up job interviews.

The Department of Employment in the Ministry of Labor (Thailand) has set up a complex catalog of skills and competencies together with a questionnaire that candidates have to fill in before they can apply for a job. On the other hand, every job is categorized with regard to necessary skills and competencies [7]. There are quite a few ontologies available that relate to human resource management, but they do not reflect the standards of the Department of Employment (Ministry of Labour, Thailand); see for example Mochol et al. [8], who applied German, European and North American standards of job classification to build the ontology. Unfortunately, the majority of the literature does not reveal or is not based on practical standards but relies on ad-hoc solutions for ontology building.

2 Job Ontology Design for Recruitment Criteria

Ontology-based methods can be used to reduce problems that content-based recommender systems are known to suffer from. These problems concern the way the systems analyze the content they recommend, the way they retrieve the content, and the way they treat heterogeneously represented content [9]. Our job ontology is designed based on the International Standard Classification of Occupations [10], which is structured using codes for profession terms and definitions of professions. Ontologies are used to cover the semantics of a domain, and in our case this requires the discovery of the similarity of content of pairs of more or less structured texts on occupational matters, i.e. the resume of the job seekers and the job description of the employer.

The job ontology (Fig. 1) is designed to group recruitment criteria with weights as follows:

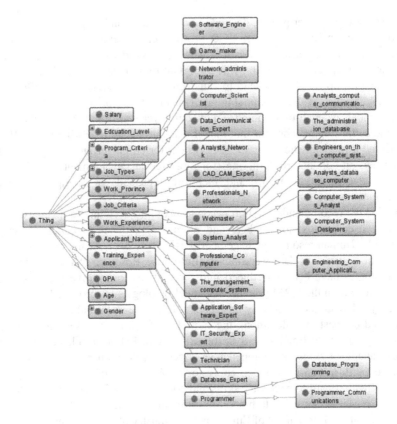

Fig. 1. Design of the job ontology

1. Criteria of job (professional occupations): covers the career classification based on relationships to the same career group with hierarchical weight identification by department of labor staff. For example, a career group such as system analyst and designer consists of seven professional careers: system analyst, application software expert, data communication expert, database expert, IT security expert, software engineer, and CAD/CAM expert.

2. Criteria of Program/Field of study: covers the semantics related to areas of study in the same group, because the job application usually contains questions related to the fields of study. If the candidate's fields of study are related to the required areas they will be assigned a weighted score of 1. If not, the candidates will be assigned a weighted score of 0.

3. Level of education is used for determining suitable educational criteria that meet the qualifications required by the employer. For example, a company seeks a data communication expert with bachelor degree and finds two applicants who match the criteria. If the first candidate has a bachelor degree and the second one has a master degree, the system will check the criteria and give the same score to both candidates. On the other hand, if the notification of the master degree application is

required, the candidates with bachelor degree or less will be considered less qualified and get a score of zero for this.

4. Work experience criteria: used for considering the required candidate's experience relevant to the position. The criteria of work experience can be weighted as 1, 0.5,0.25, and 0, which represents the work experience as the most relevant, moderately relevant, little relevant, and not relevant to the job, respectively. Applicants must choose the relevant level and attach a file work regarding their experience with evidence via the system. If employers detect and found that the evidence submitted by the applicants do not meet the claim, then those applicants are considered to be unqualified.

5. Training experience criteria: used for considering the candidate's experience relevant to the job or placements position. The criteria of training experience can be weighted as 1, 0.5,0.25, and 0 which represent the training experience has the most relevant, moderate relevant, little relevant, and not relevant to the job respectively. Similar to work experience, applicants must choose the relevant level and attach a file regarding their training experience with evidence via the system.

6. Working province criteria: used for employers who need local employees or ones living nearby. The system can locate the employer province and cluster neighboring provinces by calculating distances using the methods of the Department of Highways. The criteria of working province are weighted as 1, 0.5 and 0, which represents that the working province is the same as employer required, nearby, and neither the same nor nearby, respectively.

7. Criteria of job types can be identified with three job types: full time, part time and independent. If candidates select to meet job requirements for these job types, then they will be assigned a weighted score of 0.5. If not, the candidates are assigned a weighted score of 0.

8. Age criteria: specified by employers as age span such as 25–30 years. If the age of the applicant is matched, the system gives weighted score of 0.5, and if not, the applicant is assigned a weighted score of 0.

9. Gender criteria: specified by employers as male, female, and no specified. If the gender of the applicant is matched, the system gives weighted score of 0.5, and if not the applicants is assigned a weighted score to 0.

10. GPA (Grade Point Average) is specified by employers as starting grades or grade ranges such as >3.25 or between 2.50–3.00 etc. If the grade of the applicant is matched, the system assigns a weighted score of 0.2, and if not the applicant is assigned a weighted score to 0.

11. Salary criteria is specified by employers as starting salary or salary ranges such as >12,000 baht or between 15,000–20,000 baht etc. If the salary of the applicant is matched, the system gives weighted score of 0.2, and if not, the applicants is assigned a weighted score to 0. The system skips score calculation, if the employer does not specify these criteria.

3 System Architecture Design

The user interface of system architecture comprises three levels (Fig. 2), which are organized according to user roles:

1. Applicants/job seekers: register and fill out forms with all necessary details

   - System extracts and matches recruitment by taking applicant information and matches with employer requirements. Then, the system calculates the suitability of candidates and matches the right job to applicants.
   - System allows the applicants to be able to get the result of suitable job.

2. Employers: post vacancy with criteria ranking, e.g. give "the most important" level to job and field of study criteria but give "not important" level to gender criteria.

   - System allows employers to choose applicants for job interview from result of suitable candidates based on high or highest marks. Also the employers can check validity of attachments from applicants.

3. Department of labor staff/administrators can add, delete and modify information about recruitment data.

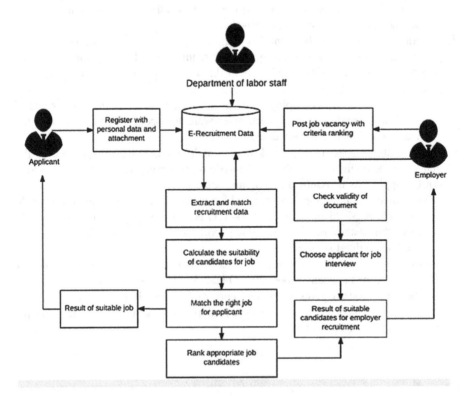

Fig. 2. Bidirectional decision support system for online recruitment processes

There are three databases used in the system for online recruitment processes; candidate database stores features of the job applicants; employer database stores job requirements which defined by employees; and career database stores features careers standards of the Department of Employment, Ministry of Labour.

4   System and Testing Process

This section explains the system process that uses sample data from both employer and applicants to calculate the suitable jobs for candidates according to employer recruitment. There are three main components: employer score, applicant score and the suitability score.

1. Employers announce job requirements and define and rank weight of job features which can be classified into 5 levels: 5, 4, 3, 2, 1 and 0 represent the most important, very important, important (moderate), less important, least important, and not important, respectively. For example, Table 1 shows that the employer defines the criteria of job and field of study as "the most important" levels, thus these two criteria have the maximum points (max_i) of 5 and the employer score (Emp_i) of both criteria equal to 10. The calculation for employer score uses Eq. (1):

$$\text{Employer score} = \sum_{i=1}^{n} (Emp_i) = \sum_{i=1}^{n} (W_i \times Max_i) \tag{1}$$

where Emp_i is employer score in each criteria i to n (number of recruitment criteria), w_i is weight of criteria i defined by employers, and max_i is maximum point of each criteria i defined by employers. An example of the Emp_i calculation of eleven criteria according to group occupations with statistical criteria in department of labor (i = 11) and the sum of Emp_i can be presented in Table 1.

Table 1. An example of recruitment criteria with employer score

	Recruitment criteria	w_i	max_i	Emp_i
1.	Job	2.00	5	10
2.	Field of study	2.00	5	10
3.	Degree level	2.00	4	8
4.	Work experience	1.00	3	3
5.	Training experience	0.50	2	1
6.	Working province	0.50	1	0.5
7.	Job type	0.50	1	0.5
8.	Age	0.50	1	0.5
9.	Gender	0.50	0	0
10.	GPA	0.20	3	0.6
11.	Salary	0.20	2	0.4
	Sum of Emp_i			34.5

Table 1 shows an example of the eleven recruitment criteria with employer scores for each criterion and the total score. As can be seen, the employer gives the highest weights criteria to job, field of study and degree level ($w_i = 2.00$) and these three criteria are ranked in the following levels: "the most important", "the most important", and "very important" levels with max_i equal to 5, 5, and 4 respectively. Therefore these three criteria earn high scores (28 points) and total of employer score is 34.5 according to the calculation using Eq. (1). Apart from that, the gender criterion is not important in the recruitment criteria.

2. Applicants register and fill out personal data for job requirement interface with necessary attachment. Then system matches applicant information with recruitment data and calculates the suitable job for applicant using statistical ontology of criteria described above. Both the applicant score (App_i) and the score of suitability of applicants for the job are calculated using Eqs. (2) and (3) respectively.

$$\text{Applicant score} = \sum_{i=1}^{n} (App_i) = \sum_{i=1}^{n} (Emp_i \times Wsm_i) \tag{2}$$

$$\text{Suitability} = \left(\frac{\sum_{i=1}^{n} Emp_i}{\sum_{i=1}^{n} App_i} \right) \times 100 \tag{3}$$

where Emp_i is employer requirement score in each criteria i and wsm_i is weight score matched of each employer criteria i. An example of the App_i calculation of eleven criteria, the sum of App_i of two applicants and the score of the suitability can be presented in Table 2.

Table 2. Applicant score with suitability

	Recruitment criteria	Emp_i	Applicant 1		Applicant 2	
			wsm_i	App_i	wsm_i	App_i
1.	Job	10	1	10	1	10
2.	Field of study	10	0	0	1	10
3.	Degree level	8	0	0	1	8
4.	Work experience	3	1	3	0	0
5.	Training experience	1	0.5	0.5	0	0
6.	Working province	0.5	1	0.5	1	0.5
7.	Job type	0.5	0	0	1	0.5
8.	Age	0.5	1	0.5	1	0.5
9.	Gender	0	0	0	0	0
10.	GPA	0.6	0	0	1	0.6
11.	Salary	0.4	1	0.4	1	0.4
	Total score of applicant (sum of App_i)			14.90		30.50
	The score of suitability			43.19		88.41

Table 2 shows that the two applicants have the score of suitability 43.19% (14.90/34.5) and 88.41% (30.5/34.5) respectively. Therefore the applicant 2 is very keen to be chosen for job interview because of the highest score of suitability. As can be seen, the Emp_i of recruitment criteria is taken from Table 1 for matching and calculating applicant score and suitability. For example, the two applicants have the same weight score matched (wsm_i) in job criteria described in Sect. 2 (statistical ontology design for recruitment criteria) which are 1. This means that both applicants have the same career group related to the recruitment criteria and the applicant scores (App_i) for both applicants of the job criteria are 10 according to the Eq. (2). Similarly to other criteria such as gender, the App_i is equal 0, since the employer defined in the recruitment criteria as "not important". Thus in this criteria both applicants have got score of zero. However, in the criteria of field of study, the applicant 1 has got zero point but the applicant 2 has got 10 points. This mean that the applicant 2 has the field of study related areas of recruitment while the applicant 1 does not. In addition, the applicant 1 has App_i zero point in degree level whereas the applicant 2 has 4 points of App_i. This due to the wsm_i of applicant 1 does not match the recruitment criteria of employer but the applicant 2 does match. Other criteria calculations are based on the features covered in Sect. 2 (statistical ontology design for recruitment criteria).

5 Testing and Results

The user interface provides the description of the application process. The System Interface consists of two parts: employer and applicant interfaces. The design of the employer part can post detailed information about the job vacancy with criteria ranking (Fig. 3) and the result of suitable candidates for employer recruitment which can be described as follows (Fig. 4).

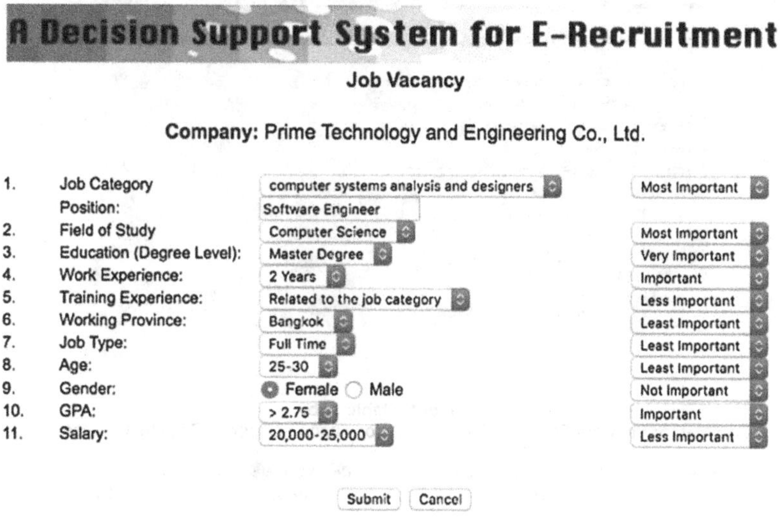

A Decision Support System for E-Recruitment

Job Vacancy

Company: Prime Technology and Engineering Co., Ltd.

1.	Job Category	computer systems analysis and designers	Most Important
	Position:	Software Engineer	
2.	Field of Study	Computer Science	Most Important
3.	Education (Degree Level):	Master Degree	Very Important
4.	Work Experience:	2 Years	Important
5.	Training Experience:	Related to the job category	Less Important
6.	Working Province:	Bangkok	Least Important
7.	Job Type:	Full Time	Least Important
8.	Age:	25-30	Least Important
9.	Gender:	● Female ○ Male	Not Important
10.	GPA:	> 2.75	Important
11.	Salary:	20,000-25,000	Less Important

Submit   Cancel

Fig. 3. Employer part for job vacancy

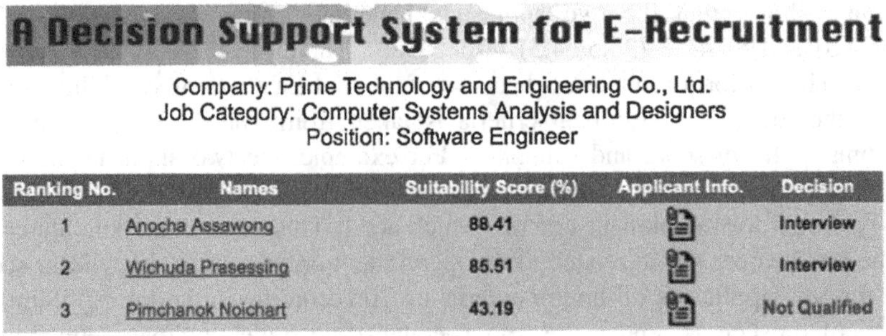

A Decision Support System for E-Recruitment

Company: Prime Technology and Engineering Co., Ltd.
Job Category: Computer Systems Analysis and Designers
Position: Software Engineer

Ranking No.	Names	Suitability Score (%)	Applicant Info.	Decision
1	Anocha Assawong	88.41		Interview
2	Wichuda Prasessing	85.51		Interview
3	Pimchanok Noichart	43.19		Not Qualified

Fig. 4. The result of suitable candidates for employer recruitment

Figure 3 shows job vacancy with weight ranking, e.g., Job category and field of study are the most important, degree level is very important, training experience, working province and job type are the least important, and gender is not important of this recruitment criteria posted by the Prime technology and Engineering Company. The system takes the weight ranking and changes into weight levels (max_i) 5, 4, 3, 2, 1 and 0 (Table 1). The system then calculates the employer score (Emp_i) using Eq. (1) and the results are exactly the same as Table 1.

Figure 4 the result of suitable candidates for employer recruitment. The system takes applicant data, e.g. from Fig. 5 to calculates the suitability scores of applicants and return result with score ranking. As can be seen, Pimchanok Noichart and Anocha Assawong have the suitability scores 43.19 and 88.41, respectively, which are the

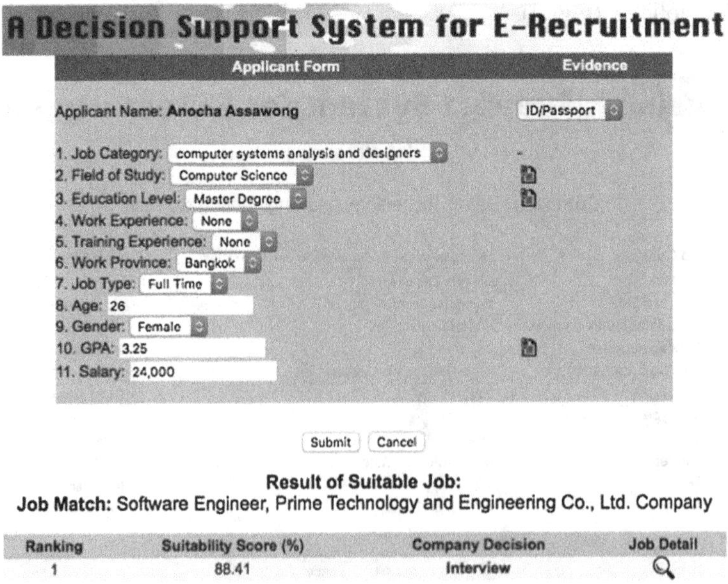

A Decision Support System for E-Recruitment

Applicant Form		Evidence

Applicant Name: Anocha Assawong   ID/Passport

1. Job Category: computer systems analysis and designers   -
2. Field of Study: Computer Science
3. Education Level: Master Degree
4. Work Experience: None
5. Training Experience: None
6. Work Province: Bangkok
7. Job Type: Full Time
8. Age: 26
9. Gender: Female
10. GPA: 3.25
11. Salary: 24,000

Submit   Cancel

Result of Suitable Job:
Job Match: Software Engineer, Prime Technology and Engineering Co., Ltd. Company

Ranking	Suitability Score (%)	Company Decision	Job Detail
1	88.41	Interview	Q

Fig. 5. Applicant form and result of suitable job.

sample described in Table 2 (the applicant 1 and 2). The employer (Prime Technology and Engineering Company) can check the validity of applicant documents from "Applicant info" before making the decision to notify the applicants as "interview" or "not qualified".

Figure 5 shows that after applicant has filled the applicant form with evidence, e.g. ID card or passport number, degree certificate, and the system calculates the suitability using Eqs. (2) and (3) as described in Table 2: applicant 2. The result of suitable jobs tells Anocha Assawong that the highest ranking is gained by the software engineer position, Prime technology and Engineering Company. The result shows that this candidate is invited for an interview.

6 Conclusions

This paper reports on the development of a Decision Support System (DSS) for matching job offers to the qualifications and characteristics of job applicants in the computer industry of Thailand. The resulting system employs a novel component to DSS, namely a statistical ontology used for clustering and matching data derived from the general characterization of job descriptions maintained by the Department of Labor (Thailand) and specific data delivered by employers seeking employees with computer background and job applicants. The clustering and matching is done by labeling the characteristics with weights, which are then used in the ontology and the matching component. The testing of the system has shown the suitability of the DSS. Further work is necessary: the system should be able to cluster employer criteria of the Thai provinces first, so that the candidate can choose an appropriate region before filling in personal data. The system should update the recruitment data after the candidates have been recruited from the employer, e.g. certificates earned and job experiences gained through the work period.

References

1. Domeniconi, G., Moro, G., Pagliarani, A., Pasini, K., Pasolini, R.: Job recommendation from semantic similarity of LinkedIn users' skills. In: 5th International Conference on Pattern Recognition Applications and Methods (ICPRAM), pp. 270–277, Rome, Italy (2016)
2. Färber, F, Weitzel, T, Keim, T.: An automated recommendation approach to selection in personnel recruitment. In: Proceedings of AMCIS, AISeL, Tampa, FL, USA (2003)
3. Bobadilla, J., Serradilla, F., Bernal, J.: A new collaborative filtering metric that improves the behavior of recommender systems. Knowl.-Based Syst. **23**, 520–528 (2010)
4. Bernardes, D., Diaby, M., Fournier, R., Fogelmann-Soulie, F., Viennet, E.: A social formalism and survey for recommender systems. SIGKDD Explor. **16**(2), 20–37 (2013)
5. Giordano, D., Kavasidis, I., Pino, C., Spampinato, C.: Content based recommender system by using eye gaze data. In: ETRA 2012, pp. 369–372, Santa Barbara, CA (2012)
6. Marchionini, G., Hass S., Plaisant, C., Shneiderman, B, Heart, C.: Towards a statistical knowledge network. In: Proceedings of the 2003 Annual National Conference on Digital Government Research, pp. 1–6. Boston, MA, USA (2003)

7. Department of Employment, Ministry of Labour. Career information. In: Bpit Printing Company Ltd., Bangkok (2006)
8. Mochol, M., Oldakowski, R., Heese, R.: Ontology based recruitment process. In: Workshop: Semantische Technologien für Informationsportale INFORMATIK 2004, Ulm, Germany (2004)
9. Ruotsalo., T.: Methods and applications for ontology-based recommender systems. Doctoral dissertation Helsinki 2010, TKK Dissertation 222 (2010)
10. ILO Homepage. http://www.ilo.org/public/english/bureau/stat/isco/isco08/. Accessed 20 Feb 2017

A Comparative Analysis of Indistinguishability Operators Applied to Swarm Multi-Robot Task Allocation Problem

José Guerrero$^{(\boxtimes)}$, Juan-José Miñana, and Oscar Valero

Mathematics and Computer Science Department, Universitat de les Illes Balears,
Carr. Valldemossa km. 7.5, Palma de Mallorca, Spain
{jose.guerrero,jj.minana,o.valero}@uib.es

Abstract. One of the main problems to solve in multi-robot systems is to select the best robot to execute each task (task allocation). Several ways to address this problem have been proposed in the literature. This paper focuses on one of them, the so-called response threshold methods. In a recent previous work, it was proved that the possibilistic Markov chains outperform the classical probabilistic using a celebrated possibility transition function. In this paper we use a new possibility transition function and we make several experiments in order to compare both, the new one and the tested before. The experiments show that the number of steps that a possibilistic Markov chain needs to converge does not depend on the response function used. This paper also emphasizes that these possibility transition functions are indistinguishably operators.

Keywords: Indistinguishability operator · Markov chain · Multi-robot · Possibility theory · Swarm intelligence · Task allocation

1 Introduction

Multi-robot systems, and in general multi-agent systems, are defined as systems with two or more robots (or agents) that perform the same mission or task. These systems provide several advantages compared to single-robot systems, for example: robustness, flexibility and efficiency. To make its benefits several problems have to be addressed. This paper focuses on the problem commonly referred to as "Multi-robot Task Allocation" (MRTA for short) which consists in selecting the best robots to execute each one of the tasks that must be performed.

MRTA is still an open problem and due to its significance, a lot of research has been done to solve this problem in the last years (see [6]). Some of the proposed solutions are based on swarm intelligence, where the cooperative behaviour emerges from the interaction of very simple behaviours running on each robot. Due to its simplicity, scalability and robustness, several swarm like algorithms have been proposed but, nowadays, those based on the so-called Response Threshold Method (RTM for short) are probably the most broadly used. In these methods, each involved robot has associated a task response threshold and a task

© Springer International Publishing AG 2017
Y. Luo (Ed.): CDVE 2017, LNCS 10451, pp. 21–28, 2017.
DOI: 10.1007/978-3-319-66805-5_3

stimuli. The task stimuli value indicates how much attractive is the task for the robot. When the task stimuli, associated to a task, takes a value greater than a certain threshold, the robot starts its execution following a probability function. This is a Markov process, where the probability of executing a task only depends on the current task (state). This probabilistic approach presents a lot of disadvantages: problems with the selection of the probability function when more than two tasks are considered, asymptotic converge, and so on.

In the light of the above-mentioned inexpedient associated to the probabilistic RTM for task allocation, in [5] a new possibilistic theoretical formalism for a RTM was proposed and its utility for the MRTA problem was also proved. In this case, the RTM is implemented considering transitions possibilities instead of transitions probabilities and this fact implies that in the intrinsic decision process, the possibilistic Markov chains (also known as fuzzy Markov chains), play the role of the probabilistic ones. The theoretical and empirical results demonstrated that fuzzy Markov chains applied to task allocation problem require a very few number of steps to converge to a stable state. In all cases the transition possibility from one task to another one was modeled by a widely accepted response function (see (1)). This paper extends our previous work about RTM and studies the impact of other kind of transition possibilistic functions, concretely the exponential one. An extensive number of experiments has been carried out with different threshold values and several kind of tasks distributions using Matlab. These experiments show that the convergence time does not depend on the possibility transition function (response function) used. However, it depends on the distribution of the tasks in the environment and, thus, it differs when each aforesaid response functions are under consideration. It must be stressed that theses possibility transition functions are both indistinguishably operators in the sense of [8] and, thus, that indistinguishability operators could be useful in the modelling of response functions in Swarm Multi-Robot Task Allocation Problem.

The remainder of the paper is organized as follows: Sect. 2 reviews the basics of the MTRA problem. Section 3 shows the experiments carried out to validate our approach and, finally, Sect. 4 presents the conclusions and future work.

2 Multi-robot Task Allocation

This section introduces the main concepts about multi-robot task allocation and the RTM approaches and review the previous works made in this field.

2.1 Probabilistic Response Threshold Methods

As pointed out in Sect. 1, the response threshold methods are a very promising approach in order to face up realistic tasks in a decentralized way. According to [1], the classical response threshold method defines for each robot r_i and for each task t_j, a stimuli $s_{r_i,t_j} \in \mathbb{R}$ that represents how suitable t_j is for r_i, where $\mathbb{R}$ stands for the set of real numbers. When s_{r_i,t_j} exceeds a given threshold θ_{r_i}

$(\theta_{r_i} \in \mathbb{R})$, the robot r_i starts to execute the task t_j. To avoid relying on the threshold value to an excessive degree, the task selection is usually modeled by a probabilistic response function. Thus, a robot r_i will select a task t_j to execute with a probability $P(r_i, t_j)$ according to a probabilistic Markov decision chain. There are different kind of probabilities response functions that define a transition, but one of the most widely used (see [3,10]) is given by

$$P(r_i, t_j) = \frac{s_{r_i,t_j}^n}{s_{r_i,t_j}^n + \theta_{r_i}^n}, \tag{1}$$

where $n \in \mathbb{N}$, where $\mathbb{N}$ stands for the set of natural numbers. It must be pointed out that the preceding response function has been also used in [5]. In this paper we test another transition function that presents similar characteristics to the given in (1) and which is given by:

$$P(r_i, t_j) = e^{-\frac{\theta_{r_i}^n}{s_{r_i,t_j}^n}} \tag{2}$$

It is not hard to check that the above-mentioned transitions functions are indistinguishably operators whenever s_{r_i,t_j} only depends on the distance between the robot and the task as follows:

$$s_{r_i,t_j} = \frac{1}{d(r_i, t_j)}.$$

We refer the reader to [8] for the definition of this kind of operators. Moreover, in general for both response functions, the equality $\sum_{j=1}^{m} P(r_k, t_j) = 1$ does not hold and, hence, the transition does not meet the axioms of the probability theory. In order to avoid this disadvantage normalization processes can be introduced although they imply to impose system modifications with possible implications in the behavior of the system.

2.2 Possibilistic Markov Chains: Theory

As has been proven in [5], possibilistic Markov chains provide a lot of advantages and outperform its probabilistic counterpart. This section summarizes the main theoretical concepts of possibilistic Markov chains and the new aforementioned (possibility) exponential transition response function is introduced.

Following [2,11] we can define a possibility Markov (memoryless) process as follows: let $S = \{s_1, \ldots, s_m\}$ $(m \in \mathbb{N})$ denote a finite set of states. If the system is in the state s_i at time τ $(\tau \in \mathbb{N})$, then the system will move to the state s_j with possibility p_{ij} at time $\tau + 1$. Let $x(\tau) = (x_1(\tau), \ldots, x_m(\tau))$ be a fuzzy state set, where $x_i(\tau)$ is defined as the possibility that the state s_i will occur at time τ for all $i = 1, \ldots, m$. Notice that $\bigvee_{i=1}^{m} x_i(\tau) \leq 1$ where $\vee$ stands for the maximum operator on $[0, 1]$. In the light of the preceding facts, the evolution of the fuzzy Markov chain in time is given by

$$x_i(\tau) = \bigvee_{j=1}^{m} p_{ji} \wedge x_j(\tau - 1),$$

where $\wedge$ stands for the minimum operator on $[0, 1]$. The preceding expression admits a matrix formulated as follows:

$$x(\tau) = x(\tau - 1) \circ P = x(0) \circ P^{\tau}, \tag{3}$$

where $P = \{p_{ij}\}_{i,j=1}^{m}$ is the fuzzy transition matrix, $\circ$ is the matrix product in the max-min algebra $([0, 1], \vee, \wedge)$ and $x(\tau) = (x_1(\tau), \ldots, x_m(\tau))$ for all $\tau \in \mathbb{N}$ is the possibility distribution at time τ.

Taking into account the preceding matrix notation and following [2], a possibility distribution $x(\tau)$ of the system states at time n is said to be stationary, or stable, whenever $x(\tau) = x(\tau) \circ P$.

One of the main advantages of the possibilistic Markov chains with respect to their probabilistic counterpart is given by the fact that under certain conditions, provided in [4], the system converges to a stationary state in a finite number of steps.

2.3   Possibilistic Response Threshold

In this section we will see an example of how to use possibilistic Markov chains for developing a RTM in order to allocate a set of robots to tasks. We will assume that the tasks are randomly placed in an environment and the robots are initially randomly placed too. Furthermore, we will assume that each robot allocation, that is the stimulus, only depends on the distance between the robot and the task. Consider the position space endowed with a distance (metric) d. Then, denote by $d(r_i, t_j)$ the distance between the current position of r_i. It is assumed that when a robot is assigned to a task the position of this task and the robot's position are the same and therefore, the distance between the task and the robot is 0. Following the RTM notation, define the stimulus of the robot r_k to carry out task t_j as follows:

$$s_{r_k, t_j} = \begin{cases} \frac{U_{t_j}}{d(r_k, t_j)} & \text{if } d(r_k, t_j) \neq 0 \\ \infty & \text{if } d(r_k, t_j) = 0 \end{cases}. \tag{4}$$

This stimulus s_{r_k, t_j} allows us to obtain, by means of (1), the following possibility response function,

$$p_{r_k, ij} = \frac{U_{t_j}^n}{U_{t_j}^n + d(r_k, t_j)^n \, \theta_{r_k}^n}. \tag{5}$$

If the same stimulus s_{r_k, t_j} is used in (2), then the following exponential possibility response function is obtained:

$$p_{r_k, ij} = e^{-\frac{\theta_{r_k}^n \, d(r_k, t_j)^n}{U_{t_j}^n}}. \tag{6}$$

For convenience to our subsequent discussion we will reference the response function given by (6) as Exponential Possibility Response Function (EPRF for short) and the response function given by (5) as Original Possibility Response Function (OPRF for short). As stated in Sect. 2.1, both possibility response functions are also indistinguishably operators. Therefore, we will use interchangeably the concepts of indistinguishably operator and possibility response/transition functions when we reference the former.

In [5], it was demonstrated that the response function given by (5) fulfills smooth conditions (column diagonally dominant and power dominant) that guarantee the finite convergence (see [4] for a detailed description of such notions) provided that all tasks have the same utility U_{t_j}. Therefore, fixed $r_k \in R$, the possibilistic Markov chain obtained by means of the OPRF converges to a stationary non-periodic state in finite time (exactly in at most $m - 1$ steps). Following similar arguments to those given in [5] one can prove easily that the possibilistic Markov chain obtained by means of EPRF also converges to a stable state in at most $m - 1$ steps.

3 Experimental Results

In this section we will explain the experiments performed to compare the number of steps required to converge to a stationary state using probabilistic and possibilistic Markov chains induced from the indistinguishability operators given in (5) and (6).

3.1 Experimental Framework

The experiments have been carried out under different conditions: position of the objects (placement of tasks), parameters of the possibility response functions (θ_{r_k} and n) and number of tasks. All the experiments have been carried out using MATLAB with different synthetic environments following a uniform distribution to generate the position of the tasks. Figure 1 represents a set of experiments where the task have been placed randomly in the environment, where each blue dot is a task. Furthermore, all the environments have the same dimension (width $= 600$ units and high $= 600$ units). In the shake of simplicity, we assume that all the tasks have the same utility, i.e., $U_{t_j} = 1$ for all $j = 1, \ldots, m$.

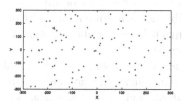

Fig. 1. Kind of environments with 100 task randomly placed. Blue dots represents the position of the tasks or objects. (Color figure online)

Following the reasoning made in [7], the θ_{r_k} must depend on the environment conditions. During the performed experiments the θ_{r_k} will depend on the maximum distance between tasks as follows:

$$\theta_{r_k} = \frac{nTH}{d_{max}}, \tag{7}$$

where d_{max} is the maximum distance between two objects and nTH is a parameter of the system. Due to the above-mentioned environment dimensions, d_{max} is constant and equals to 800.5 units. For the first time, the nTH parameter has been introduced with respect to previous papers (see [7]) in order to analyze how the threshold value impact on the system performance. All the experiments have been performed with 500 different environments, with different number of tasks ($m = 50, 100$) and different values of the power n in the expression of possibility response functions (see (5) and (6)). The threshold θ_{r_k} values under consideration are obtained from (7) setting $nTH = 2, 4, 8$.

Whichever possibility response function is used, the given by either (5) or (6), the possibilistic transition matrix, P_{r_k}, must be converted into a probabilistic matrix, in order to be comparable the possibilistic and probabilistic Markov chain results. To make this conversion we use the transformation proposed in [9], where each element of P_{r_k} is normalized (divided by the sum of all the elements in its row) meeting the conditions of a probability distribution.

Figure 2 shows some results obtained with 100 randomly placed tasks using OPRF given by (5), and EPRF given by (6). Figure 2(a) shows the percentage of experiments that with the probabilistic Markov process does converge. If the process does not converge after 10,000 iterations we assume that it will never converge. As can be seen, in all probabilistic cases around 50% of experiments converges. Although it is not graphically represented, the experiments that converges need 256.8 steps on average to do it. Figure 2(b) shows the mean number of steps required to converge using fuzzy Markov chains. Let us recall that, all fuzzy Markov chains under consideration converge. As can be seen, there are no significance differences between the experiments that use OPRF (Original labeled bars) and those that use EPRF (Exponential labeled bars). Moreover, the nTH parameter or the power value n do not have any impact on this results. Therefore, we can conclude that when the tasks are randomly placed in the environment, both possibility response functions provide similar results on average and both seems not to be affected by its parameters nTH or n. Moreover, the possibilitics Markov chains, whichever possibility response functions is used, needs much lower number of steps to converge compared to their probabilsitic counterpart.

Table 1 shows the standard deviation, σ, of the number of steps required to converge with 100 tasks when fuzzy Markov chains are considered. Thus, this table represents the standard deviation of the results given in Fig. 2(b). From these results, we can state that in most cases the use of EPRF produces a decrease of the standard deviation compared to the values of σ obtained when ORPF is used. Similar results, regarding mean and standard deviation, have been obtained after performing experiments with 50 tasks ($m = 50$).

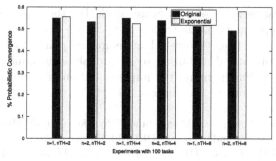

(a) Percentage of experiments that, using probabilistic Markov process, do converge.

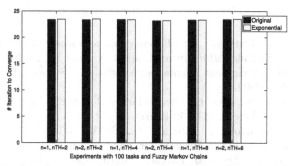

(b) Number of steps required to converge with fuzzy Markov chains

Fig. 2. Experimental results with 100 tasks.

Table 1. Standard deviation (σ) of the number of steps required to converge with fuzzy Markov chains.

Function	n = 1, nTH = 2	n = 2, nTH = 2	n = 1, nTH = 4	n = 2, nTH = 4	n = 1, nTH = 8	n = 2, nTH = 8
OPRF	3.59	3.48	3.56	3.58	3.7	3.52
EPRF	3.58	3.6	3.35	3.57	3.47	3.47

4   Conclusions and Future Work

This paper has presented an empirical comparative analysis of two indistinguishability operators (or possibility response function) applied to the convergence of possibilistic Markov chains where the goal of the system is to allocate tasks to a colony of robots using response-threshold methodologies. As was proved in [5], possibilistic Markov chains outperforms its probabilistic counterpart when they are used to model response-threshold multi-robot systems. This paper extends the aforementioned work. In addition, it shows how the use of the aforementioned possibility response functions in modeling fuzzy Markov chains provides similar results and they are very robust with respect to their parameters. In the light of the obtained results a lot of new challenges, problems and improvements must be addressed as future work. For the time being, we focus on providing a deeper analysis about how the position of the tasks impacts the convergence time, both from theoretical and empirical point of view. Other conversions from possibilistic distribution to its probabilistic counterpart are also under consideration. Furthermore, the implementation of these methods using real robots is carrying out by the authors.

Acknowledgments. This research was funded by the Spanish Ministry of Economy and Competitiveness under Grants DPI2014-57746-C03-2-R, TIN2014-53772-R, TIN2014-56381-REDT (LODISCO), TIN2016-81731-REDT and AEI/FEDER, UE funds.

References

1. Agassounon, W., Martinoli, A.: Efficiency and robustness of threshold-based distributed allocation algorithms in multi-agent systems. In: 1st International Joint Conference on Autonomous Agents and Multi-agents Systems, Bolonia, Italy, pp. 1090–1097, July 2002
2. Avrachenkov, K., Sanchez, E.: Fuzzy Markov chains and decision making. Fuzzy Optim. Decis. Making **1**, 143–159 (2002)
3. Castello, E., Yamamoto, T., Libera, F.D., Liu, W., Winfield, A.F.T., Nakamura, Y., Ishiguro, H.: Adaptive foraging for simulated and real robotic swarms: the dynamical response threshold approach. Swarm Intell. **10**(1), 1–31 (2016)
4. Duan, J.: The transitive clousure, convegence of powers and adjoint of generalized fuzzy matrices. Fuzzy Sets Syst. **145**, 301–311 (2004)
5. Guerrero, J., Valero, Ó., Oliver, G.: A first step toward a possibilistic swarm multi-robot task allocation. In: Rojas, I., Joya, G., Catala, A. (eds.) IWANN 2015. LNCS, vol. 9094, pp. 147–158. Springer, Cham (2015). doi:10.1007/978-3-319-19258-1_13
6. Guerrero, J., Oliver, G., Valero, O.: Multi-robot coalitions formation with deadlines: complexity analysis and solutions. PLoS ONE **12**(1), 1–26 (2017)
7. Kalra, N., Martinoli, A.: A comparative study of market-based and threshold-based task allocation. In: 8th International Symposium on Distributed Autonomous Robotic Systems, Minneapolis, USA, pp. 91–102 (2006)
8. Recasens, J.: Indistinguishability Operators: Modelling Fuzzy Equalities and Fuzzy Equivalence Relations. Springer, Heidelberg (2010)
9. Vajargah, B.F., Gharehdaghi, M.: Ergodicity of fuzzy markov chains based on simulation using sequences. Int. J. Appl. Math. Comput. Sci. **11**(2), 159–165 (2014)
10. Yang, Y., Zhou, C., Tin, Y.: Swarm robots task allocation based on response threshold model. In: 4th International Conference on Autonomous Robots and Agents, Wellington, New Zealand, pp. 171–176 (2009)
11. Zadeh, L.: Fuzzy sets as a basis for a theory of possibility. Fuzzy Sets Syst. **1**, 3–28 (1978)

Sustainability of Users' Commitment to Collaborative Design Tasks: An Exploratory Research

Catherine Elsen[1(✉)], Lara Vigneron[2], Alessandro Acconcia[2], and Pierre Leclercq[1]

[1] LUCID-ULg, University of Liège, Liège, Belgium
catherine.elsen@ulg.ac.be
[2] WeLL, Wallonia e-health Living Lab, Liège, Belgium

Abstract. This paper investigates why end-users sometimes find difficult to fully invest themselves in a Living Lab initiative, at least on the long run. The paper builds insights on the basis of users' feedback about four projects currently managed by the Wallonia e-health Living Lab (WeLL) and paves the way for renewed models of collaboration that could lead to sustainable satisfaction and long-term commitment of end-users.

Keywords: Living lab · End-users' commitment · End-users' satisfaction · Community

1 Context of the Research

As any other health care complex system, the Belgian one faces multiple and intertwined problems that require innovative solutions [1]. According to the Organization for Economic Co-operation and Development annual report, Belgium has spent in 2013 10.2% of its GDP in healthcare, that is 1.3% above the OECD average of 8.9% [2]. Most of these costs (78%) are supported by the public authorities, and yet Belgian patients rank high in the European barometer for self-supporting another 17.9% of the remaining costs. Confronted to these excessive expenses, the Belgian healthcare system is slowly undertaking major reforms such as progressive decrease of hospital beds, or decrease in the average length of hospital stay.

In response to these challenges, the Walloon government launched in 2015 the first living lab concerned with health and e-health and called it the "WeLL" (for "Wallonia e-health Living Lab"). The Living Lab methodologies and ecosystem were chosen as the most promising path to deal with these challenges, mainly because of the involvement of end-users that would, supposedly, enrich the point of view of healthcare expert stakeholders and lead to more adequate, socially acceptable solutions. This hypothesis had been since supported by research done by Vanweerbeek et al. [3] that looked into the specificities of 20 Living Labs around the world, and showed that the living lab approach is indeed particularly valuable for projects aiming at creating social value and acceptability (in contrast with those aiming at creating rather economic value). The WeLL, in operation for almost two years and a half, today gathers a

Y. Luo (Ed.): CDVE 2017, LNCS 10451, pp. 29–38, 2017.
DOI: 10.1007/978-3-319-66805-5_4

community of around 700 members active in 13 on-going projects. This paper builds on four of these projects and focuses on one of the key issues of managing a Living Lab that is insuring community satisfaction and its long-term commitment.

2 State of the Art

2.1 Innovation in the Health and Care System

Aside from the expenditure issues mentioned above, Herzlinger summarized the most blatant challenges health-care systems have to deal with worldwide [1]. In her research, she points out that health-care systems are highly complex systems involving many stakeholders, each with their own sphere of influence and personal agenda. These stakeholders often gather in closed groups and disciplines that sometimes pursue competing interests, especially when it comes to get a hold on funding and/or demarcating new-generation medical devices. Considering the management of change inside such structures, one has to observe that the multiplicity of policies and government regulations sometimes aids innovation, but most of the time hinders it, and that growing interest for ethics and privacy, especially when it comes to consumers' data, adds to the overall complexity of sharing experiences at a national scale.

As a concluding remark, Herzlinger suggests that health-care "consumers" are more and more engaged and in control of their personal health record (far from the "passive patient" that increasingly becomes an anachronistic model), and that solutions might lie in the empowerment of those patients. Research in various disciplines indeed points out the fact that customers and end-users are no longer willing to undergo a whole process simply as external observers. Considering themselves as "part of a team" where professionals no longer hold positions of omniscient experts, these always better-informed users expect to have their say all along the collaborative decision-making process. This "client-led revolution" testifies of how increasingly users want part of the control on the process, how they don't hesitate anymore to lead radical changes and decisions [4] and what kind of active role they are ready to tackle, by suggesting new ideas for instance, all along the process [5]. As Heylighen and Bianchin already underlined for the field of design, qualitative assessment of a design process is nowadays related to a "deliberative cooperation between designers and users", where "stakeholders will not just happen to converge in their attitude, but come to converge by virtue of the justification they get through dialogue" ([6], p. 14).

2.2 Living Labs as a New Model of Innovation

In response to this pressing need to involve and empower end-users, most design, engineering or related disciplines have progressively introduced notions or methodologies such as "co-design" or "open innovation". These models of innovation anchor in practice in two ways: either in an institutionalized way or in a "horizontal" way. The institutionalized way calls for end-users that consciously decide to integrate and take part to participative, bottom-up initiatives organized for instance by their government or local communities' representatives [7]. The horizontal way, on the other hand, is the sole innovative consequence of practical problems end-users decide to tackle by their own means [8].

The Living Lab approach somehow navigates in between: end-users indeed consciously decide to take part to it, but in the meanwhile the Living Lab also stimulates and supports bottom-up innovations in response to in situ observations of problematic situations end-users face in their real living or working environments. Considering the specific challenges end-users encounter in the context of their own private health, the Living Lab consequently, and adequately, provides both institutionalized, multidisciplinary creative guidance as well as space for self-creative exploration.

More specifically, the "Living Lab" concept often refers to "both the methodology and the instrument or agency that is created for its practice", be it physical or immaterial [9]. Living Labs provide structure, governance and creative methodologies to support user participation in the collaborative innovation process [10], considering end-users as co-creators of artefacts, side by side with actors from the public or private sectors [11–14], artefacts that will be experimented in real-world settings.

3 Users' Involvement as One of the Key Challenges

Stahlbröst et al. lately researched how users' motivation, as well as the perceived usability of social software to maintain connection between these users, might impact productivity and creativeness [15]. In terms of motivational factors, they found that interest in innovation was a better predictor of co-creativeness than implicit benefits of the study (i.e. desire to be socially engaged, stimulated, recognized) or explicit benefits of the study (i.e. rewards such as study incentives).

Aside from fully involving users *while* they take part to workshops, the WeLL more importantly experiences difficulties in users' long-term engagement and commitment. While online community management and social software certainly are ways to sustain interest, this paper investigates additional underlying reasons for users' involvement or non-involvement to such long-term collaborative process. What are the various factors impacting participants' return rate? Do users value their participation? And if they do, in which terms?

4 Design, Methodology and Approach

The methodology consisted first in confronting our research gap to Living Labs experts' point of view, and later to reach out to Living Labs' participants to test factors of (un)involvement. We organized our research in three steps. We first interviewed members of the WeLL consortium, experts in Living Labs' methodologies, in order to grasp what they thought the more pressing challenges were. We then analysed the satisfaction surveys each participant was asked to fill-in directly after each WeLL's workshop. We finally conducted phone interviews with some of the participants wishing to keep contributing weeks after their participation to a workshop.

For the first step, we interviewed 10 experts gathered during the first WeLL consortium meeting (around 6 months after the launch of the living lab). This panel was composed of a various profiles (academics, private and public sectors experts) and various backgrounds (lawyer, business consultant, health professional, researcher, marketer,...). Those experts have various degrees of implication in the living lab (from day to day work to focused interventions) and all develop specific work/research related to living labs' ecosystems (IP challenges, living lab business models,...). These interviews lasted around 40 min. and were primarily focused on the difficulties related to innovation in an e-health living lab environment.

For the second step, we collected the satisfaction surveys that participants were asked to fill-in after every workshop organized during the first year of the living lab (from January 2015 to December 2015). The Table 1 below presents the repartition of participants by project. In total, we gather data issued from 13 workshops, either organized in the context of 3 main projects or organized as one-shot projects.

Table 1. Name, number of workshops organized and number of participants for each project.

Projects	Workshops' names				Participants
Happy mum	Happy mum with mothers	Happy mum with fathers	Happy mum professional	Happy mum co-design	24
Doctors without borders	MSF Idéematon 1	MSF Idéematon 2	MSF 3D printing		16
Mens sana	Mens sana exploration	Mens sana co-design			25
One-shot projects	Idéematon 1	Idéematon 2	"Image and me"	Hospitals	93

They were two different surveys with different questions. The first survey was used during the first 6 months of the living lab while the other was used after that. The change occurred because the living lab wanted to focus on a more qualitative feedback in order to better understand why the participants decided to take part to these workshops. The first survey was used on 53 participants and was primarily composed of quantitative questions, while the second one was used on 105 participants and consisted mostly of qualitative questions. From the first one we compiled figures about a detailed appreciation of the workshop on several criteria (usefulness, originality, appropriateness of the form, appropriateness of the content, willingness to come back and willingness to recommend the WeLL and its activities to friends). From the second survey, we collected and analyzed answers to some of the open questions that are meaningful to the context of this specific paper (e.g. do you think you'll keep in touch with some participants and, if yes, how many? what did you learn during this workshop (about the project, the technology or the methodology)?).

Regarding the third step, we asked the participants by mail if they were available for an additional phone interview, in order to collect a more in-depth feedback. The interview consisted of 10 open questions distributed in three main categories: "workshop", "project" and "living lab". We tried to understand how participants perceived their contributions during the workshop (e.g., what would you say about the workshop after several weeks?), as a whole for the project (e.g., what did you learn? did you feel you really contributed to the project?) and if they feel involved in the living lab (e.g., have you talked about the living lab? Have you met again some participants later on?). Out of the 158 participants, only five answered the contact email and out of these five persons, only four eventually answered the interview. Two of those participants went to the same workshop. Each interview lasted from 20 to 35 min.

5 Main Findings

5.1 Step 1: Testing Our Hypothesis with Experts

The experts interviews enabled us to identify obstacles considered as the main bottlenecks of the current living lab model, seen here both as an ecosystem for collaborative innovation and as a methodology. We clustered these obstacles in 6 main categories: valorization, field, users, technology, process and relevance.

Valorization is directly related to intellectual property questions: what happens to ideas created by users and who owns them? The experts (mainly lawyers) were questioning the intellectual property strategy that the living lab should adopt in order to provide a fair space for the participants, the project leader and the living lab itself. *Field* incorporates all uncertainties specific to the WeLL that is the relationship to the health and e-health sector. The main questions were mainly about ethics, such as "how can a living lab be profitable to the health sector while being respectful of patients, for instance in regard to future involvement with a specific insurance system?". *Users* refers to user involvement in the short and long-term, and questions their interest in the living lab process: what should a living lab do to keep them involved in the long run? *Technology* refers to the paradox between user-centered innovation and the fact that most of the "e-health" innovations often tend to reduce the implication of human being in favor of the technology. It also appears that the cost of the technology is a point of concern, especially because of the WeLL willingness to make each technology as affordable as possible. *Process* is about the difficulty to involve end-users in complex research and development fields. For example, which role can end-users play in the field of pharmaceutical industry? Experts mainly questioned the suitability of the living lab approach given various types of innovation fields. Finally, *relevance* refers to all the questions related to the quality of the innovation produced using living lab methodologies, and in particular in regard to potential impact for our society. These questions were mostly related to innovation in general and to the capacity for a living lab to keep producing considerable and continuous innovation in the long term.

Beside concerns related to the specific field of e-health, experts underlined challenges directly related to end-users, be it respecting their rights as co-creators or considering their input hand-in-hand with high-level, technological developments. More importantly, experts spontaneously underlined users' involvement and long-term commitment as one of the concerns for Living Labs' sustainability, this way confirming our starting hypothesis as valid from a global point of view.

5.2   Step 2: Evaluating Users' Satisfaction Through Short Surveys

The first survey, used during the first six months, was composed of seven questions: four questions were based on a five-points Likert scale, two were fixed-alternative questions and the last one was open. The first four questions were: did you find the workshop useful? original? were the format and the content appropriate? Out of the 53 surveys, the "usefulness" mean level was assessed at 3.94 (out of the 5 points of the Likert scale), while the "originality" mean level was 4.06, "appropriateness of the format" mean level was 4.32 and the "appropriateness of the content" mean level was 4.34. Most of the participants therefore considered the workshops as meaningful for the project, original in its methodologies and appropriate both in form and content.

The first of the two fixed-alternative question was "Would you come back to a future workshop?". It is worth noticing that although 94.34% (50 out of 53) of the participants answered yes, only one came back to another workshop. The second one was "Would you recommend a workshop to your friend?". Here again, although 98.11% (52 out of 53) said yes, none of the later participants mentioned recommendation by friends as the reason for their participation.

The second survey, distributed to 105 participants in total, consisted mostly in open questions concerning the workshop and the living lab (did you learn something in terms of methodology, technology or about the project?, did you feel you could participate and express yourself freely? with how many participants do you think you will keep in touch? to whom would you recommend a workshop?, would you like to tell us something?). The single five-points Likert scale question aimed at evaluating global appreciation about the workshop in general.

Table 2 summarizes the number of participants that at least answered one word to each of the open questions. The first question was about whether participants would keep in touch with other participants (and possibly, how many). About 60% of the participants answered they would maintain contact with at least another participant. To the question "did you learn something during this workshop about technology/ methodology and/or the project?", 76% of the participants answered positively. Most of them underlined learning about the creative methodology used during the workshop and a few pointed out learning something about the project. None of the comments concerned technology. The third question asked them if they feel they could express themselves enough and freely during the workshop. 92% of the participants considered they could express themselves as freely as wished and mostly, in their opinion, because of the animation method and the workshop atmosphere. The next question was about whether the participants would like to recommend the living lab's workshops. Only 29% of the participants wrote one or several names for the staff to contact for future workshops. The vast majority (60%) didn't answer the question. Regarding the final question, it is interesting to notice that most open comments were related to the continuation of the project and the materialization of the workshop's results (e.g., "*What is the follow up of the project?*", "*What will be the tangible results of this workshop?*", "*Interesting but now we wanna see what this workshop will result in*",...).

Finally, it is worth noticing that the return rate was again quite limited. Out of the 105 surveys distributed, only seven participants came back to another workshop. All seven came back in a follow-up workshop for the project they primarily came for, in

Table 2. Proportion of participants answering at least one word by open question.

	Keep in touch?	Learn something?	Freedom to participate	Further recommendation?
Yes	60%	76%	92%	28.6%
No	11%	14%	6%	7.6%
Maybe				3.8%
No answer	29%	10%	2%	60%

other words none of the returning participants came for a workshop dedicated to another project or topic.

5.3 Step 3: In-Depth Phone Interviews for Feedback and to Test Long-Term Commitment

Out of the 158 participants contacted by email for in-depth interviews, only four eventually agreed to answer our questions and give some feedback.

They were asked to express again their global appreciation of the workshop they took part to, sometimes up to several months earlier. Their appreciation didn't change, even after several months. One of the participants explained: *"I think I gave it a 4 or a 5. And no it didn't change, I keep good memories. I even contacted the WeLL regarding a* [personal, editor note] *project I'd like to develop"*.

When asked what they thought they brought to the project, they mostly felt like they contributed thanks to their experience and expertise, especially when the workshop was related to technological matters. One participant comments: *"I think I brought the experience of what is more important and less important. My experience as a user, but also the experience and the needs of others that I hear about"*.

Participants essentially kept in touch with the project through the WeLL newsletter. None of them contacted the WeLL nor any project leader to have an update about the project they took part to. Neither did they try to find information on the internet: *"I read your newsletter. I read something like 15 days later that the project leader explained what she did since the workshop but nothing more. However, if there is a final report I would gladly read it"*. Regarding the living lab itself, the newsletter seems to be their main source of information. They all read it frequently but not thoroughly. They were a bit more interested by the project they contributed to, but found the rest of the information relevant and interesting: *"Yes, from time to time. Depending on my workflow and on my time. I may take a deeper look at some subjects"*; *"If, for instance, from time to time there is a project you don't mention, it doesn't matter. I'm more in a passive consumer mode"*.

When asked about what the living lab should undertake to make them want to come back, none of the participants gave a specific answer. They were all quite happy with the experience, and didn't find it lacked something in particular in terms of feedback or community follow-up. They mostly pointed out the lack of time for the main reason not to take part to another workshop: *"It's not like there is something missing. I lack time. If there were more users, we could rotate. Everyone has his own calendar. It could be 4 or 5 persons who would agree on coming, and we could come in alternately to give our opinions"*.

Finally, they recognized they never really talked about the living lab after the workshop, and when they did it was to a very strict number of people (close friends or colleagues). Moreover, one of the participants told us she wouldn't come back because she thought she would stop bringing fresh information if she came too often: *"I wonder if a newcomer isn't more suited than someone that already came several times. If it's always the same people who work on the projects, the solutions might end up looking alike"*. It is worth noticing that during these interviews, the participants all agreed that diversity in profile is beneficial for the project although it can lead to various problems (such as users having difficulties to keep an open mind when it comes to their own field of expertise). These results are in accordance with Berger [16] who found that the integration of different profiles is key to the user engagement.

6 Discussion

We see that the experts pointed users' involvement as one of the main concerns for the effective and sustainable operation of a living lab. Indeed, the community surrounding a living lab is one of its most precious value but also one its most intricate aspect. Out of the six categories experts referred to, the last four directly relate to end-users' involvement into the Living Lab model and how the Living Lab can lead to ideas and propositions that will really impact end-users' everyday life while remaining respectful of ethical aspects.

As shown by the surveys, users often express their willingness to keep participating to workshops. They do believe these workshops provide value to the projects. In practice, however, we observe quite the opposite. The two main causes identified are the time participants accept to invest to such workshops, and the perception of their own usefulness in regard of a specific subject. Our research suggests that users need to feel relevant in order to be willing to participate in projects led by a living lab methodology.

Our in-depth phone interviews revealed another possible explanation: some participants believed that if they come too often, the effectiveness and creativity of the final solutions would be impacted. Of all people, one could believe that users involved in a living lab process would understand and appreciate the necessity of feedbacks. It is important to note that we deliberately chose to make only one mailing in order to assess the primary interest of the WeLL community in such an in-depth feedback interview. The fact that, out of the 158 participants, only four agreed to the phone interviews is a quite revealing indication that the WeLL community is currently not yet fully involved in the living lab philosophy.

7 Conclusion

This study first reveals that the form and content of the workshop, although considered appropriate, are not enough to convince users to participate to further living lab collaborative workshops. Living labs, more fundamentally, should keep informing their community of users very specifically on how they contributed and could continue contributing to their projects. They should be clear on what is expected from the users, from one project to another. As underlined by Bergvall-Kareborn and Stahlbröst: "inherent in being a partner, from an end-user perspective, is the power of choice. People always can choose if, when and to what extent they want to participate" ([17], p. 367). But to give them the power to choose, the living labs must first provide them with options to choose from. This can be achieved in being accurate about what is expected from participants, what are the profiles needed and why these profiles are fundamental to the project. Our research reveals that if users don't feel they are relevant enough to be useful to the project, or feel they don't have the adequate profile (anymore), their willingness to come reduces accordingly.

Secondly, most of the users interviewed in this sample didn't adopt a proactive stance when it comes to innovation in a living lab environment, even when it was related to projects they already participated to. If they didn't receive information about upcoming workshops, they would not likely search it by themselves. It appears that most of the time they were expecting to be asked to come back by the living lab itself, and didn't feel integrated in the innovation process as a whole. Once again the key remains in the hands of the living lab staff: it is its responsibility to constantly reach out and keep the users in the loop of on-going processes.

When it comes to the perception of their own value to the collaborative innovation process, this research eventually shows that most of the participants perceive their involvement as positive for the project. However, our results also underline that this perception seems insufficient to make them want to keep contributing to other workshops. The main reason preventing them from being part to a recurring pool of participants seems to be the time available for such events. A renewed model of interaction, as suggested by one of the participants, might be to organize sub-groups of participants that would rotate and take part alternately to the workshops, while remaining connected and aware of the project current state of progress.

One of the limitations of this study is the small amount of phone interviews granted by the participants. Further in-depth feedback should be collected to confirm our preliminary results, even though the single fact that such a few number of people agreed to such an interview by itself reveals the state of involvement of the community.

Aside from collecting feedback from a larger range of participants, further research could expand towards the reasons why participants initially decided to take part to their first WeLL workshop. A better understanding of these reasons might increase their return rate, long-term commitment as well as interest of newcomers.

References

1. Herzlinger, R.E.: Why Innovation in Health Care is so Hard? Harvard Business Review. Harvard Business School Publishing Corporation, Brighton (2006). 11 p.
2. OECD (2015). OECD Health Statistics 2015. Country Note: how does health spending in Belgium compare? http://www.oecd.org/belgium/Country-Note-BELGIUM-OECD-Health-Statistics-2015.pdf. Accessed 05 Apr 2016
3. Vanmeerbeek, P., Antoine, M., Delvenne, P., Rosskamp, B., Vigneron, L.: Involvement of end-users in innovation process: toward a user-driven approach of innovation. A qualitative analysis of 20 Living Labs. Unpublished report - CRIDS (University of Namur) & SPIRAL (University of Liège) (2015)
4. Cole-Colander, C.: Designing the customer experience. Build. Res. Inf. **31**(5), 357–366 (2003)
5. Luck, R., McDonnell, J.: Architect and user interaction: the spoken representation of form and functional meaning in early design conversations. Des. Stud. **27**, 141–166 (2005)
6. Heylighen, A., Bianchin, M.: How does inclusive design relate to good design? Designing as a deliberative entreprise. Des. Stud. **34**(1), 93–110 (2013)
7. Chesbrough, H., Vanhaverbeke, W., West, J.: Open Innovation: Researching a New Paradigm. Oxford University Press, Oxford (2006)
8. Cardon, D.: Innovation par l'usage. In: Ambrosi, A., Peugeot, V., Pimienta, D. (eds.) Enjeux de mots. Regards multiculturels sur les sociétés de l'information. C&F Editions, Caen (2005)
9. Almirall, E., Lee, M., Wareham, J.: Mapping living labs in the landscape of innovation technologies. Technol. Innov. Manag. Rev. **2**(9), 12–18 (2012)
10. Almirall, E.: Living labs and open innovation: roles and applicability. Electron. J. Virtual organ. Netw. **10**, 21–46 (2008). Special Issue in Living Labs
11. Kristensson, P., Gustafsson, A., Archer, T.: Harnessing the creative potential among users. J. Prod. Innov. Manag. **21**(1), 4–14 (2004)
12. Vargo, S.L., Lusch, R.F.: Evolving to a new dominant logic for marketing. J. Mark. **68**, 1–17 (2004)
13. Lusch, R.F.: The small and long view. J. Macromark. **26**, 240–244 (2005)
14. Dubé, P., Sarrailh, J., Billebaud, C., Grillet, C., Zingraff, V., Kostecki, I.: Le livre blanc des Living Labs, 1st edn. Umvelt, Montréal (2014)
15. Stahlbröst, A., Bertoni, M., Fölstad, A., Ebbesson, E., Lund, J.: Motivational factors influencing user co-creativeness in living labs. In: Proceedings of the 4th ENoLL Living Lab Summer School in Manchester (2013)
16. Berger, W.: CAD Monkeys, Dinosaur Babies, and T-shaped People: Inside the World of Design Thinking and How it can Spark Creativity and Innovation. Penguin group, London (2010). 352 p.
17. Bergvall-Kareborn, B., Stahlbröst, A.: Living lab: an open and citizen-centric approach for innovation. Int. J. Innov. Reg. Dev. **1**(4), 356–370 (2009)

Handling Disturbance and Awareness of Concurrent Updates in a Collaborative Editor

Weihai Yu[1]($\boxtimes$), Gérald Oster[2,3,4], and Claudia-Lavinia Ignat[2,3,4]

[1] University of Tromsø - The Arctic University of Norway, Tromsø, Norway
weihai.yu@uit.no
[2] Inria, 54600 Villers-lès-Nancy, France
[3] Université de Lorraine, LORIA, UMR 7503, 54506 Vandoeuvre-lès-Nancy, France
[4] CNRS, LORIA, UMR 7503, 54506 Vandoeuvre-lès-Nancy, France

Abstract. When people work collaboratively on a shared document, they have two contradictory requirements on their editors that may affect the efficiency of their work. On the one hand, they would like to know what other people are currently doing on a particular part of the document. On the other hand, they would like to focus their attention on their own current work, with as little disturbance from the concurrent activities as possible. We present some features that help the user handle disturbance and awareness of concurrent updates. While collaboratively editing a shared document with other people, a user can create a focus region. The user can concentrate on the work in the region without being interfered with the concurrent updates of the other people. Occasionally, the user can preview the concurrent updates and select a number of these updates to be integrated into the local copy. We have implemented a collaborative editing subsystem in the GNU Emacs (https://www.gnu.org/software/emacs) text editor with the described features.

Keywords: Data replication · Concurrency control · CRDT

1 Introduction

When people work collaboratively on a shared document or artifact, two contradictory aspects may affect the efficiency of their work. On the one hand, a person would like to know what the other people are currently doing with the document, so she can avoid duplicating the same work or working unnecessarily on conflicting ideas. On the other hand, the person would like to be as concentrated as possible on her current work without the interference of concurrent work of other people, particularly when her current work requires deep thinking and involvement.

One commonly applied practice is that people work independently (offline) on their own copies of the document. They are able to concentrate completely on their work, but have no idea what the other people are currently doing with the document. They must use some additional communication channels, such as emails, to exchange their copies of the document and get updated about the

© Springer International Publishing AG 2017
Y. Luo (Ed.): CDVE 2017, LNCS 10451, pp. 39–47, 2017.
DOI: 10.1007/978-3-319-66805-5_5

other people's work. Then, they can use some particular features of their editors, such as the "track changes" feature of Microsoft Word, or third-part tools, such as diff, to find out the particular updates made by the other people. They should also be coordinated, again with additional communication channels, for other tasks, such as who is responsible for integrating the concurrent updates in the following rounds. Without careful planning and coordination, they may risk unnecessarily duplicating their efforts on overlapping or conflicting work.

Another possible practice, which is more and more applied lately, is that people work simultaneously (online) on the shared document with a real-time collaborative editor, such as Google Drive[1]. People can see immediately what other people are doing with the document, so they can avoid duplicating their efforts. If several people are working simultaneously on the same area of the document, even if for non-overlapping or non-conflicting purposes, they can be easily distracted by concurrent updates of the other people. Furthermore, allowing concurrent partial updates to be integrated in local copies may cause other inconvenience such as compilation errors of software programs.

A middle ground is that people work on their own copies in isolation and are aware of other people's work at some specific time, such as at the time of saving the document or committing the updates to a shared repository.

We present yet another possibility: people can work collaboratively on the same document in such a way that they can limit the disturbance from other people's concurrent updates and at the same time have an overview of the concurrent work, all these in a controlled manner.

We have implemented support for collaborative editing in GNU Emacs, using CRDT (Commutative Replicated Data Types) and supporting selective undo [16]. In this paper, we present an experimental feature that lets the user handle the disturbance and awareness of concurrent updates.

This paper is organized as follows. Section 2 gives a short review on our CRDT approach to real-time collaborative editing [16]. Section 3 presents the new features for handling disturbance and awareness through an example. Section 4 describes briefly how we implemented the features in Emacs. Section 5 discusses related work. Finally, Sect. 6 concludes.

2   Document View and CRDT Model

With a collaborative editor, a document is concurrently updated from a number of peers at different sites. Every peer consists of a view of the document, a model, a log of operation history and several queues (Fig. 1).

A peer concurrently receives local operations generated by the local user and remote updates sent from other peers. Local user operations take immediate effect in the view. The peer stores executed view operations in Q_v and received remote updates in Q_{in}. During a synchronization cycle, it integrates the operations stored in Q_v and Q_{in} into the model and shows the effects of integrated

---

[1] https://drive.google.com.

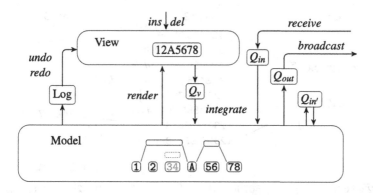

Fig. 1. View, model and operations

remote updates in the view. The peer stores the integrated local operations in Q_{out}. It also records the integrated local and remote operations in the log. Later, it broadcasts the operations in Q_{out} to other peers.

Every peer has a unique peer identifier *pid*. An operation originated at a peer has a peer update number *pun* that is incremented with every integrated local operation. Therefore, we can uniquely identify an operation with the pair (pid, pun). We use op_{pun}^{pid} to denote an operation *op* identified with (pid, pun).

A view is mainly a string of characters. A user can insert or delete sub-strings in the view, and undo earlier integrated local or remote operations selected from the log.

A model materializes editing operations and relations among them. It consists of layers of linked nodes that encapsulate characters. Conceptually, characters have unique *identifiers* that are totally ordered. For two characters c_l and c_r, if $c_l.id < c_r.id$, then c_l appears to the left of c_r.

Nodes at the lowest layer of a model represent insertions and contain inserted characters. Nodes at higher layers represent deletions. That is, a higher-layer node (outer node) deletes the corresponding characters in the lower-layer nodes (inner nodes).

A node contains the identifiers of its leftmost and rightmost characters. The identifiers of the other characters (i.e. not at the edges of the node) are not explicitly represented in the model. An insertion node also contains a string of characters.

New operations may split existing nodes. Nodes of the same operation share an *op* element as the operation's descriptor. A descriptor contains, among other things, information about undos, which influences the visibility of the characters.

There are three types of links among nodes: *l-r* links maintain the left-right character order; op_l-op_r links connect nodes of the same operations; *i-o* links maintain the inner-outer relations. The outermost nodes and the nodes inside the same outer node are linked with *l-r* links. When the view and the model are synchronized, the view equals to the concatenation of all visible characters of the outermost nodes through the *l-r* links.

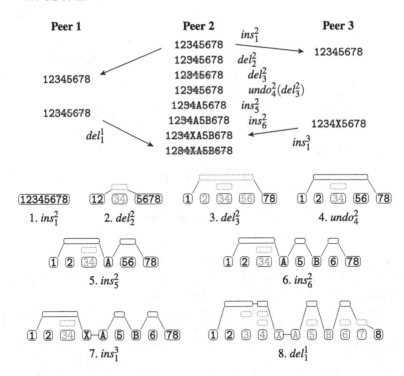

Fig. 2. Examples of model updates

Figure 2 shows an example with three peers. The upper part shows the operations generated at the peers. The lower part shows the model snapshots at Peer 2. Nodes of the same deletion are aligned horizontally. Nodes with dotted border are invisible. Characters in light gray are invisible in the view.

Different peers can update the model concurrently. The model data structure is a CRDT that has the following convergence property: when all peers have applied the same set of updates, the states of the model at all peers converge.

We refer the interested readers to [16] for more details on the data structure and algorithms on the model.

Materialization of editing operations in the model makes a number of tasks easier, including support for selective undo and handling of operation dependencies [16], as well as user friendliness features like display of operation history and selection of operations to undo or redo, and preview of concurrent remote operations as described in the following sections.

3   Handling Disturbance and Awareness of Concurrent Updates

Emacs has a feature called "narrowing" that allows the user to focus on a specific region of the document, making the rest temporarily inaccessible. We think it

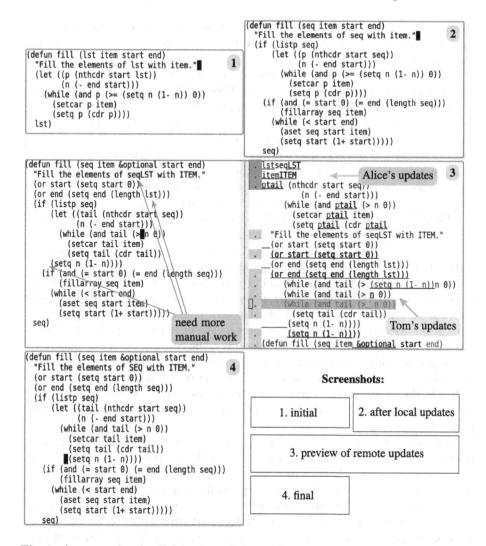

Fig. 3. An example of collaborative editing with awareness of concurrent updates (Color figure online)

is appropriate to augment the narrowing feature with non-disturbance control for collaborative editing, because when a user explicitly applies the narrowing, she signals the need to be focused and concentrated. No disturbance from the concurrent updates of the other users is clearly part of such concentration.

When a user narrows to a region while collaborating with other people, the editor starts a *focus region* and enters a non-disturbance mode. No concurrent updates in the region are immediately integrated.

While working in a focus region, the user may occasionally want to know what the other people are working on in this region. By knowing other people's work, she may be able to avoid duplicated work. She may even selectively integrate some concurrent updates to adapt early to compatible updates performed by other people.

Figure 3 illustrates with an example the steps involved in working with a focus region. Suppose three programmers, Bob, Alice and Tom, work concurrently on function `fill()` (in Emacs Lisp), which initially fills a segment of a list with a given item (Step 1). The lower right part of the figure shows the layout of the screenshots of the different steps performed by Bob.

Bob would like to generalize `fill()` to sequences (in Emacs Lisp, sequence is a general type that includes list, vector etc.). He first narrows down to the function as a focus region and works in the region without the disturbance of the concurrent updates generated by Alice and Tom.

When Bob is almost done (Step 2), he takes a preview of concurrent updates (Step 3). In the preview, every concurrent update is preceded with a leading dot. The color around the leading dots indicates who performed the updates. Notice that we support composite updates. For example, a text substitution consists of a deletion and an insertion; a global substitution consists of multiple deletions and insertions. The character strings of the updates are underlined. The insertion part of an update is displayed in blue and the deletion part is in pink. The surrounding text of the updates is also displayed. This helps the user recognize the context of the updates. Moreover, the editor keeps a mapping from the displayed updates to their positions in the document. The user can traverse up and down the updates in the preview. The current update is highlighted in yellow in the preview. The cursor in the main document, i.e. the `fill()` body in our example, moves accordingly. This helps the user further to localize the particular updates.

Bob noticed that Alice had capitalized two words in the doc-string and renamed variable `p` to `tail`. Meanwhile, Tom had refactored the code. He added two lines to deal with the default start and end positions in the list and moved the assignment of variable `n` from the loop condition to the end of the loop body.

Bob can traverse through the concurrent updates and selectively integrate some of them into the main document. In this particular example, he found that all updates performed by Alice and Tom were compatible with his work and opted to integrate all of them, which resulted in the `fill()` function as shown in Step 3. (Alternatively, Bob may reject some of the concurrent updates. For example, he may reject the renaming of variable `p`.)

Bob still had to do some manual work to get the final version as shown in Step 4.

4   Implementation

Emacs is a widely used open-source text editor. Emacs is also a run-time environment of Emacs Lisp. This make Emacs very suitable for customization and extension. We have earlier implemented the view and the CRDT model described in Sect. 2 in Emacs Lisp [16]. We have also implemented support for selective undo and selection of updates through a history view.

A focus region is marked with the identifiers (see Sect. 2) of the leftmost and the rightmost characters of the region. To show a preview of the concurrent remote updates, the peer integrates the updates stored in Q_{in} and displays those in the focus region in the history view. When the user accepts and rejects a number of selected updates, the peer marks the accepted ones and undoes the rejected ones.

When the user exits the preview, the peer handles the accepted and rejected (i.e. undone) updates in the same way as it normally handles remote updates. For the updates that are neither accepted nor rejected (i.e. the ones which the user wants to deal with when she exits the focus region), the peer undoes them and inserts them in a new queue $Q_{in'}$ (Fig. 1).

The next time the peer shows a preview of concurrent updates, it redoes the updates in $Q_{in'}$ and displays them, together with the new concurrent updates in Q_{in}.

When the user exits the focus region, she must accept or reject all updates in $Q_{in'}$.

5 Related Work

Most of the existing collaborative editing work is based on operational transformation (OT) [2,11,12]. A local operation is performed immediately on the local replica of a document; a remote operation is transformed and integrated in the local site based on the positions of the existing and concurrent operations. A critical issue with OT is that, it is hard to design correct operation transformation functions that is generally applicable to various integration algorithms [6]. One common way to relax certain required conditions for transformation functions is to enforce a global total order in which operations are transformed and integrated at all sites [14]. As a consequence, OT approaches practically require the involvement of central servers.

Lately, there appear a new family of approaches to collaborative editing based on commutative replication data types (CRDT) [1,7–9,13,15,16]. With CRDT, characters of concurrent insertions are ordered based on the underlying data structure. One benefit of CDRT is that different sites can integrate operations in different orders. Thus central servers are not necessary.

To achieve the same features as presented in this paper in OT is non-trivial. For example, for every remote operation, to detect whether it falls inside a focus region, we must first transform the operation. To preview an operation and keep a mapping to its position in the current document, we must also transform the operation. However, for these different purposes, we must transform the operations differently. With CRDT, the effect of an integration is materialized in the data structure, which can be used for different purposes, such as for selective undo [16] and for focus regions. To detect whether a remote update falls inside a focus region, we only need to compare the character identifiers of the operation and of the region.

Awareness during distributed collaboration has got wide attention for many years, such as in the context of collaborative software development [3,4,10]. A recent study suggests that "developers would appreciate having access to awareness information frequently but not in real time; they have, however, diverse preferences regarding the level of detail in which such information should be made available" [3]. Without the mechanisms for collaborative editing, tools typically provide information about concurrent updates with coarse granularity, such as at a per-file level [10]. On the other hand, they may take advantage of the capabilities of software development environments to detect conflicts that are specific to programming languages or platforms [10].

In our previous work, we were able to provide similar awareness features as presented in this paper [4,5]. Both [4,5] applied OT to localize concurrent remote updates in the context of local document states. In [4], we combined OT with a central version control repository. Because local and remote replicas share some common base version of the document, we need only to maintain operation histories after the base version. Thus the lengths of the operation histories are typically short and the OT algorithms do not have a significant run-time overhead. In [5], we focused on providing awareness without compromising privacy. For the awareness part, we modeled the document with a layered structure. The operation history of a document consisted of multiple shorter sub-histories. In that way, we were able to overcome the performance drawbacks of the OT algorithms. None of [4,5] supported disturbance avoidance, since the focus was on awareness, rather than integration of concurrent updates.

6   Conclusion

We have presented some features for handling disturbance and awareness of concurrent updates during collaborative editing. We implemented the features as part of our collaborative editing subsystem in GNU Emacs. Our implementation benefited from the CRDT model that materializes the operations and their relations. We plan to evaluate these features in real use scenarios and make improvements based on the evaluation.

References

1. André, L., Martin, S., Oster, G., Ignat, C.-L.: Supporting adaptable granularity of changes for massive-scale collaborative editing. In: CollaborateCom. IEEE (2013)
2. Ellis, C.A., Gibbs, S.J.: Concurrency control in groupware systems. In: SIGMOD, pp. 399–407. ACM (1989)
3. Estler, H., Nordio, M., Furia, C.A., Meyer, B.: Awareness and merge conflicts in distributed software development. In: ICGSE, pp. 26–35 (2014)
4. Ignat, C.-L., Oster, G.: Awareness of concurrent changes in distributed software development. In: Meersman, R., Tari, Z. (eds.) OTM 2008. LNCS, vol. 5331, pp. 456–464. Springer, Heidelberg (2008). doi:10.1007/978-3-540-88871-0_32
5. Ignat, C., Papadopoulou, S., Oster, G., Norrie, M.C.: Providing awareness in multi-synchronous collaboration without compromising privacy. In: CSCW, pp. 659–668 (2008)

6. Imine, A., Molli, P., Oster, G., Rusinowitch, M.: Proving correctness of transformation functions in real-time groupware. In: Kuutti, K., Karsten, E.H., Fitzpatrick, G., Dourish, P., Schmidt, K. (eds.) ECSCW 2003. Springer, Dordrecht (2003). doi:10.1007/978-94-010-0068-0_15
7. Oster, G., Urso, P., Molli, P., Imine, A.: Data consistency for P2P collaborative editing. In: CSCW, pp. 259–268. ACM (2006)
8. Preguiça, N.M., Marquès, J.M., Shapiro, M., Letia, M.: A commutative replicated data type for cooperative editing. In: ICDCS, pp. 395–403. IEEE Computer Society (2009)
9. Roh, H.-G., Jeon, M., Kim, J., Lee, J.: Replicated abstract data types: building blocks for collaborative applications. J. Parallel Distrib. Comput. **71**(3), 354–368 (2011)
10. Sarma, A., Redmiles, D.F., van der Hoek, A.: Palantír: early detection of development conflicts arising from parallel code changes. IEEE Trans. Softw. Eng. **38**(4), 889–908 (2012)
11. Sun, C., Jia, X., Zhang, Y., Yang, Y., Chen, D.: Achieving convergence, causality preservation, and intention preservation in real-time cooperative editing systems. ACM Trans. Comput.-Hum. Interact. **5**(1), 63–108 (1998)
12. Sun, D., Sun, C.: Context-based operational transformation in distributed collaborative editing systems. IEEE Trans. Parallel Distrib. Syst. **20**(10), 1454–1470 (2009)
13. Weiss, S., Urso, P., Molli, P.: Logoot-undo: distributed collaborative editing system on P2P networks. IEEE Trans. Parallel Distrib. Syst. **21**(8), 1162–1174 (2010)
14. Xu, Y., Sun, C.: Conditions and patterns for achieving convergence in OT-based co-editors. IEEE Trans. Parallel Distrib. Syst. **27**(3), 695–709 (2016)
15. Yu, W.: Supporting string-wise operations and selective undo for peer-to-peer group editing. In: GROUP, pp. 226–237. ACM (2014)
16. Yu, W., André, L., Ignat, C.-L.: A CRDT supporting selective undo for collaborative text editing. In: Bessani, A., Bouchenak, S. (eds.) DAIS 2015. LNCS, vol. 9038, pp. 193–206. Springer, Cham (2015). doi:10.1007/978-3-319-19129-4_16

Visual Design Using Case-Based Reasoning and Multi-agent Systems

Wojciech Palacz[✉], Grażyna Ślusarczyk, Barbara Strug, and Ewa Grabska

The Faculty of Physics, Astronomy and Applied Computer Science,
Jagiellonian University, ul. Lojasiewicza 11, 30-348 Kraków, Poland
{wojciech.palacz,grazyna.slusarczyk}@uj.edu.pl

Abstract. This paper deals with case-based reasoning (CBR) which
is adapted in the Computer Aided Design (CAD) system. The specialized CAD tools of the system allow the designer to visualize general
ideas about projects in the form of design drawings and automatically
transform them into graph data structures. The system's library provides source cases representing previously created solutions. Designer's
requirements are represented by graph patterns and the case library is
automatically searched for cases which fit these patterns. Target cases
result from the cooperation among the human designer and intelligent
software agents. The retrieved cases are evaluated on the basis of specific
design knowledge the agents are equipped with. The presented approach
is illustrated on the example of designing an indoor swimming pool.

Keywords: CAD · Graph data structures · Graph patterns · CBR

1 Introduction

Nowadays the designer often uses a visual language to create design drawings
(early solutions) on the monitor screen during the design process supported by
CAD tools. Using a visual language in the phase of conceptual design character-
izes so called *visual design*. On the other hand, the process of solving new design
problems is often based on *Case-Based Reasoning (CBR)*, i.e., on the solutions
of similar design problems created in the past.

The paper proposes combining these two methods useful in design. Thus, we
consider a CAD-like environment with the prototype visual design system, in
which the human designer and intelligent software agents [3] cooperate during
the conceptual phase of the design process and a methodology of CBR is used.
The described prototype system – Hypergraph System Supporting Design and
Reasoning (HSSDR) – dedicated to designing building layouts was presented in
[2]. The approach proposed in this paper enhances HSSDR by providing means
of exploring the library of previously created solutions.

HSSDR uses simple drawings to communicate with the designer, but internally each drawing is represented as a graph. A library of such graphs representing previously created solutions is a valuable resource, as it allows the designer

© Springer International Publishing AG 2017
Y. Luo (Ed.): CDVE 2017, LNCS 10451, pp. 48–56, 2017.
DOI: 10.1007/978-3-319-66805-5_6

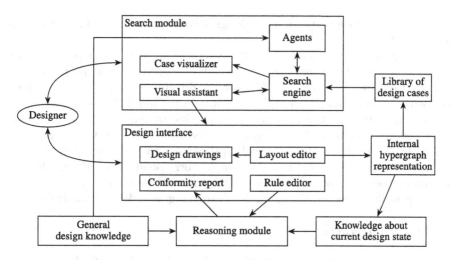

Fig. 1. HSSDR's internal architecture

to take advantage of previously created drawings. Since this library can be quite large, there is a need to provide the designer with a way of finding the most promising solutions. This paper proposes a new HSSDR module which uses graph pattern matching to find those drawings which most accurately match the designer's requirements. Then a multi-agent system is used to cooperatively evaluate retrieved drawings on the basis of specific design knowledge the agents are equipped with. The internal structure of the extended HSSDR is presented in Fig. 1.

The designer starts by invoking the search module and specifying his requirements. This is done by means of a set of dialog windows specific to the category of the design problem he is working on. These criteria are transformed into graph structures, and the case library is searched for graphs which match as many of these patterns as possible. The list of results is sorted by the number of matches, so that the solutions which fulfill the largest number of requirements appear first.

In the next step a system of agents, which are equipped with sets of requirements related to specific design knowledge, e.g. environmental context, architectural standards, legal norms, fire safety regulations, is used to perform further evaluation of retrieved design cases. The non-fulfilled requirements are reported by each agent to the distinguished manager agent, which – depending on the number of violated regulations – either removes the drawing from the set of admissible solutions or presents it to the designer.

The designer reviews presented cases, and either selects one of them as a basis for his new design, or refines his requirements and has the search module retrieve a new set of candidate solutions. A selected case is transferred to the HSSDR's editor, where it can be adjusted before being presented to the client. There is also the possibility that none of the existing cases are suitable as a basis for a new work. In such situation the designer can choose to start his new design from scratch.

The described new module allows the designer to specify design requirements related to a given design problem and then find solutions which are most compatible with these requirements. This search is directed by graph patterns, which represent requirements and should be present in the internal representations of existing solutions. The design requirements checked by agents of the search module, which are also in the form of graph patterns, are the ones which are to be fulfilled by designs in order to be legally realised in a given environment or country. The number of patterns found in graphs corresponding to existing designs determines the degree of requirements fulfillment by these designs. The presented approach is illustrated on the example of designing an indoor swimming pool.

2 Design Process

In our approach the system supporting building design (i.e., HSSDR) enables the designer to draw building layouts, which are automatically transformed into their internal representations in the form of special graphs called attributed hypergraphs [5]. In this way a database of hypergraphs representing all previously generated designs can be created. This database can be used for reasoning about the existence similar design tasks by means of CBR [1,7].

CBR methods are often combined with multi-agent systems. In [6] these two approaches are applied to comparative shopping, while using multi-agent systems to retrieve information from a set of heterogeneous case libraries in order to support sharing knowledge between coworkers is described in [8]. Our approach, where the designs retrieved using CBR are evaluated by intelligent agents, is oriented to support design in architecture.

At the outset of the case-based design process the designer specifies requirements and constraints which should be met by the proposed design. These criteria are automatically transformed into hypergraph structures. Then the library of hypergraphs representing existing solutions is searched for designs which satisfy the specified criteria. If one or more designs satisfying the designer requirements are found they are passed to the multi-agent system. Each agent checks if the indispensable requirements of the scope it is responsible for are fulfilled by these designs. There are four inspecting agents: one for fire safety regulations, second for architectural standards, third for legal norms and fourth one for environmental context. All these criteria are manually translated into corresponding hypergraph structures and constraints binding values of attributes assigned to them. The manager agent collects messages related to violated requirements from other four agents and makes an overall evaluation of designs. The admissible designs retrieved in such a way constitute an inspiration for the designer. It is rather rare that the user wants one of the "off-the-shelf" designs. Frequently, the designer wants something similar to one of the presented samples or a combination of several of them. If a modification is desired a description of a selected design is copied from the library and the required corrections are made in the layout editor.

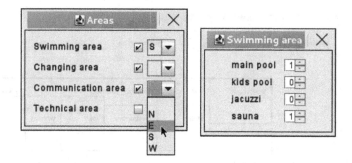

Fig. 2. Selection of functional areas and component parts of the swimming area

Example. Let us consider an example of designing a swimming pool. In the first step the designer chooses functional areas which should be present in the design. Each of the four areas (namely the communication area, swimming area, changing area and technical area) together with their orientation can be selected. For each of these areas, the designer can further select rooms which it should contain. The selection process of functional areas and elements of the swimming area is shown in Fig. 2. Rules checked by agents are related to the sizes of spaces and their distances from the exists.

3   Graph Data Structures

In this paper design structures are represented by means of attributed hypergraphs [9]. The considered hypergraphs are composed of object hyperedges corresponding to layout components and relational hyperedges which represent relations among fragments of components. Hyperedges are labelled by names of components or relations. The fragments of components that can be used as arguments of relations are represented by hypergraph nodes. To express design features being other type of semantic information concerning layout components, attributes representing properties (like shape, size, position, orientation) are used.

Example. The layout of a swimming pool is presented in Fig. 3. The continuous lines shared by polygons correspond to adjacency relations, the dashed lines represent visibility relations, while the lines with small rectangles on them correspond to accessibility relations. A hypergraph representing the layout of the designed swimming pool building is presented in Fig. 4. This hypergraph is composed of thirteen object hyperedges drawn as rectangles and thirty five relational hyperedges drawn as ovals, where fourteen of them represent the accessibility relation (denoted *acc*), fourteen represent the adjacency relation (denoted *adj*) and seven represent the visibility relation (denoted *vis*). Object hyperedges represent areas or rooms, while hypergraph nodes represent their walls. In this way walls are treated as objects (not as relations) and thus relations of one wall with several walls of other adjacent spaces can be expressed.

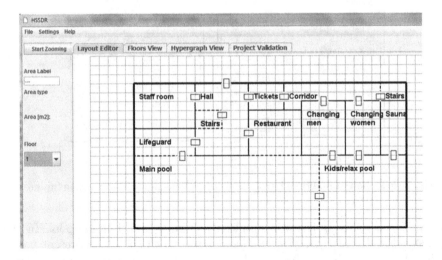

Fig. 3. The layout of the swimming pool

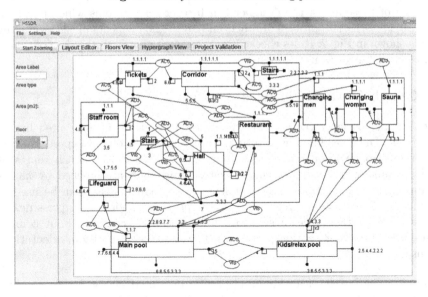

Fig. 4. The hypergraph representing the layout of the swimming pool

The hypergraph structure allows the system to store the knowledge about syntactic aspects of created drawings [4] and therefore makes it possible to efficiently reason about the conformity of designs with specified design criteria.

4   Searching for Potential Solutions

The conformity of the design solution with the specified design criteria is checked using semantic and syntactic information encoded in the graph patterns representing these criteria. When the designer selects functional areas and their orientations, these requirements are translated into hypergraphs. Design requirements referring to component parts of each area and to relations between rooms and areas can be mapped into the corresponding hypergraphs representing the relations between nodes representing these rooms and areas. For instance, the visibility relation between two rooms holds if there exist two hypergraph nodes representing walls and assigned to two different component hyperedges (representing rooms) and to the same relational hyperedge labelled *vis*. Moreover the attributes assigned to these nodes and specifying the wall material should have the value corresponding to the glass.

Example. Hypergraphs in Fig. 5 represent requirements which say that the swimming area should be placed in the south, the main pool should be visible from the restaurant, and the sauna should be accessible from the men and women changing rooms through doors in the same wall. The first two are subgraphs of (i.e., are equal to a part of) the graph presented in Fig. 4, while the third one isn't. Therefore, the design presented in Fig. 3 does not satisfy the last requirement.

The standard architectural norms for swimming pool designs related to required areas of spaces or their orientation are checked on the basis of the values of attributes assigned to nodes representing corresponding spaces. For example the agent inspecting architectural standards can test if in a given design system the area of the women changing room is not smaller than one seventh of the area of the main pool. Fire safety regulations and environment context conditions can be checked in a similar way.

The reasoning about compliance of generated design solutions with specified design criteria consists in testing whether the particular hypergraphs can be found in the graph-based representations of designs and if the attributes assigned to their elements have proper values. Then designs corresponding to the hypergraphs which fulfill the predefined number of conditions are sent by the manager agent to the case visualizer and shown to the designer as potential valid solutions of a given design task.

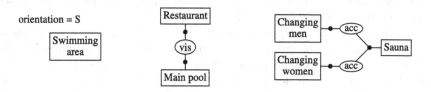

Fig. 5. Three hypergraph patterns representing different design requirements

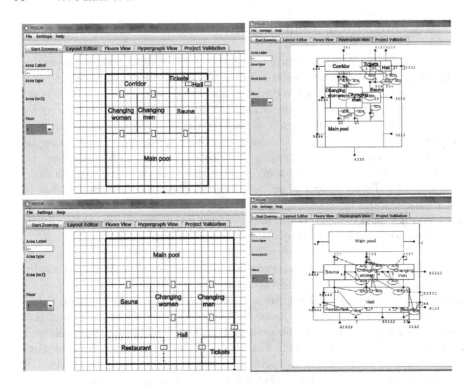

Fig. 6. Two swimming pool designs and their hypergraph representations

Example. Three example swimming pool designs existing in our data base together with their hypergraph representations are presented in Figs. 3, 4 and 6. The first hypergraph from Fig. 5 is found in representations of designs presented in Fig. 4 and in the top of Fig. 6, while the third hypergraph from Fig. 5 is not found in any of the shown designs.

Now the method of finding cases which satisfy specified requirements is described. Given the library of cases containing known solutions to the problem being solved, the function *FindSolutions* returns a set of all cases fulfilling some requirements (together with the requirement satisfaction rates) introduced by the designer via the visual assistant. The procedures used by inspecting agents for checking requirements are similar but their input is limited to the cases returned by the *FindSolutions* function.

The method $search(p, G)$ is responsible for actually finding a subgraph of G isomorphic with graph p representing a particular design requirement. As there may be more than one subgraph isomorphic with p only the first match is searched for unless the designer explicitly specified a number of times the pattern should be matched. Although in a general case searching for isomorphic subgraphs is a hard computational problem, in case of labelled graphs the solution can be found in practice in much shorter time. Moreover as there is a limited

Data: L – library of graphs representing cases, R – set of graphs representing requirements defined by the designer
Result: S – set of cases satisfying at least one requirement, fit – table of percentage satisfaction rates for these cases

```
function FindSolutions (L, R)
    S := ∅;
    for each G ∈ L do                    // G is a graph representing a case
        fit[G] := 0;          // counter: how many requirements does G fulfill?
        for each p ∈ R do         // p is a graph representing a requirement
            if search(p, G) = TRUE then
                fit[G] := fit[G] + 1;
                S := S ∪ {G};
    for each G ∈ L do
        fit[G] := fit[G] * 100 / |R|;           // convert count to percentage
    return S, fit;
```

Algorithm 1. Searching for matching cases

and well defined number of labels that can occur in a graph representing a design and each label can occur a limited number of times (for example there may be a limited number of swimming pools or restaurants in any sport complex) an index of graph nodes based on labels can be built to improve the search.

5 Conclusions

In this paper a new approach, in which case-based reasoning is adapted in graph-based CAD-like environment, is proposed. The human designer and the intelligent software agents cooperate during the conceptual phase of visual design. Moreover, the way of using graph patterns in supporting case-based reasoning is shown on the example of building design.

References

1. Aamodt, A., Plaza, E.: Case-based reasoning: foundational issues, methodological variations, and system approaches. AI Commun. **7**(1), 39–59 (1994)
2. Bhatt, M., Gajek, Sz., Grabska, E., Palacz, W.: Artefactual reasoning in a hypergraph-based CAD system. In: Burduk, R., Kurzyński, M., Woźniak, M., Żołnierek, A. (eds.) Computer Recognition Systems 4. AINSC, vol. 95, pp. 471–478. Springer, Heidelberg (2011)
3. Grabska, E., Grzesiak-Kopeć, K., Ślusarczyk, G.: Visual creative design with the assistance of curious agents. In: Barker-Plummer, D., Cox, R., Swoboda, N. (eds.) Diagrams 2006. LNCS, vol. 4045, pp. 218–220. Springer, Heidelberg (2006). doi:10.1007/11783183_29
4. Grabska, E., Ślusarczyk, G.: Knowledge and reasoning in design systems. Autom. Constr. **20**(7), 927–934 (2011)
5. Grabska, E., Ślusarczyk, G., Gajek, Sz.: Knowledge representation for human-computer interaction in a system supporting conceptual design. Fundam. Informaticae **124**(1–2), 91–110 (2013)

6. Kwon, O.B., Sadeh, N.: Applying case-based reasoning and multi-agent intelligent system to context-aware comparative shopping. DSS **37**(2), 199–213 (2004)
7. Leake, D.B., Plaza, E. (eds.): Case-Based Reasoning Research and Development. LNAI, vol. 1266. Springer, Heidelberg (1997). doi:10.1007/3-540-63233-6
8. Montazemi, A.R.: Case-based reasoning and multi-agent systems in support of tacit knowledge. In: AAAI Technical Report WS-99-10. AAAI Press (1999)
9. Palacz, W., Grabska, E., Gajek, Sz.: Conceptual designing supported by automated checking of design requirements and constraints. In: Frey, D.D., Fukuda, S., Rock, G. (eds.) Improving Complex Systems Today. ACENG, pp. 257–265. Springer, London (2011). doi:10.1007/978-0-85729-799-0_30

Cooperation of Agents in the Agent System Supporting Smart Home Control

Kamil Hawdziejuk[✉] and Ewa Grabska

Department of Physics, Astronomy and Applied Computer Science,
Jagiellonian University, Kraków, Poland
Kamil.Hawdziejuk@alumni.uj.edu.pl, ewa.grabska@uj.edu.pl

Abstract. This paper deals with smart home technologies which provide a flexible and comfortable home environment improving the quality of life for residents. The model of the Home Automation System proposed here integrates devices with one another under the control of an agent system. The research primarily focuses on the collaboration among agents which are responsible for the following problems: sensing the data, diagnosing states, running predefined rules and evaluating the system actions by gathering feedback from participants.

Keywords: Intelligent environment · Home Automation System · Agent system

1 Introduction

Nowadays society is interested in finding solution for intelligent buildings, monitoring of energy efficiency, data management and integration of other building infrastructure systems: utility metering, fire and security systems, etc. Therefore new software development solutions need to be provided.

The presented research is conducted in creating the extension for Home Automation System (HAS) with agents control. It focuses on modeling system framework that can be used in diagnosing the home and preventing its participants from uncommon situations. The concept of intelligence has been characterized by means of the following terms: reasoning, communication, learning, knowledge, creativity and problem solving. The paper presents a model of multi agent system that applies to smart home technology.

From the practical point of view this work deals with Lab of Things (LoT) [2] framework in case of realization of the presented model, i.e., additional devices can be simply integrated with existing drivers in the LoT framework which deals also with security issues. To fulfill the expectations, critical states in buildings and home environments are collected and prioritized. Solutions are defined and categorized to be used as agent system actions. Knowledge about the home is gathered and used automatically. Finally, the system decisions are confronted with user expectations and evaluated in terms of usefulness. The agent system model is taken into account and applied.

© Springer International Publishing AG 2017
Y. Luo (Ed.): CDVE 2017, LNCS 10451, pp. 57–64, 2017.
DOI: 10.1007/978-3-319-66805-5_7

2   Home Automation

In smart home technology a home environment is treated as a distributive system consisted of a group of devices that are components of a network related to distribution of middleware. From the point of view of the users the system which coordinates activities of devices and shares its resources is perceived as a single, integrated computing facility. A smart house provides services, such as multimedia and light control, energy efficiency control, security monitoring, etc. It contains a large number of distributed devices such as sensors and actuators that may be successfully configured with the use of editors. The system interface for defining and managing rules for household was presented in [8].

In this paper we focus on modeling intelligent systems with agents as main actors. To do this the real environment is described as a set of possible states of the world $W = \{w_0, w_1, \ldots\}$. The Home Automation System (HAS), denoted by S_{HAS}, is considered as discrete event dynamic system consisting of users U and the world environment E. It determines system's environment denoted by $E_{S_{HAS}}$ and is determined by the set $\Omega_{S_{HAS}}$ of states. The changes and actions are described within multi agent system terminology.

3   Multi Agent Systems

3.1   Related Work

Home systems have been successfully predicted [3] to develop in different prospective directions including their extension with many intelligent agents. Multi-agent systems are used for example in power management applications in smart buildings [1]. In the paper [14] there was a proposition for an agent system design framework to achieve smart house automation. The structure of the agent system which observes the environment by sensing devices through a network was described in [4] and equipped with a reasoning mechanism. Their different methods of collaboration were presented in [10]. Moreover, the solution proposed in [5] presents an approach for extracting the meaning of the situation using semantic agents in order to manage the interaction processes in the human environment. This paper focuses also on an agent architecture realization and application that deal with unexpected situations inside environments and interactions with users. Finally, applying well-established software engineering methodologies for delivering high quality and robust smart software applications were described in [11]. These methodologies were taken into account during the development process of the research presented.

3.2   A Formal Description

To fulfill contemporary expectations different models of intelligent systems were developed in last decades including Multi-Agent Systems (MAS) at the forefront. To present it formally, the following definitions are introduced.

An environment of system S_{HAS} consisting of users U and the world environment E, determines the system's environment denoted by $E_{S_{HAS}}$. A change of S_{HAS} occurs, i.e., an interaction between environment $E_{S_{HAS}}$ and system S_{HAS} occurs when users U influence an actuator or when external world E influences sensors. In other words, the interaction is determined by actions.

Let $C = \{c_1, c_2, \ldots, c_n\}$ where $n \in N$ denote a finite set of devices and At is a set of attributes for devices $c_i, i = 1, \ldots, n$ and D_a is the value range of an attribute $a \in At$.

Let $f_{At} \colon C \to 2^{At}$ be a function assigning a subset of attributes for each device of C. Denote by m_{c_i} the number of c_i attributes.

For instance, to a speaker (a piece of equipment) one attribute, loudness is assigned. Loudness is measured in decibels. In our notation we have $f_{At}(speaker) = \{loudnessValue\}$, where $D_{loudness} = [0, 80](dB)$.

Definition. A *state of device* c_i is a sequence $s(c_i) = (a_1(c_i), a_2(c_i), \ldots, a_{m_{c_i}}(c_i))$ such that $a_j(c_i) \in D_{a_j}$, where D_{a_j} is the value range of a_j, $a_j \in f_{At}(c_j)$ for $j = 1, \ldots, m_{c_i}$.

In other words the state of each device is determined by a sequence of individual values for all attributes assigned to the device.

Definition. A *state of system* S_{HAS} is defined by a sequence of states of all devices in C, i.e. $s(S_{HAS}) = (s(c_1), \ldots, s(c_n))$. Denote by $\Omega_{S_{HAS}}$ all possible states of the system.

States of the world W are detected in a discrete moments of time and interpreted by S_{HAS}. In this way a finite subset W of the set of possible states of W is determined. Every state of W is represented by a configuration of states of all devices determined by their attributes value.

There exists a need for defining an environment of S_{HAS}. Let us assume that the environment consists of users U and the external environment E and denote it by E_{HAS}. An interaction between the environment and the system occurs when users U influence actuators or when environment E influences sensors. In other words, the interaction is determined by events or actions.

The following definition is an extension of the definition of the interactive environment proposed in [7]:

Definition. An *Interactive Environment* of S_{HAS} is a structure $H = (E_{S_{HAS}}, A, Y, \Phi, \pi)$, where:

- $E_{S_{HAS}}$ is a system environment,
- A is a set of actions, and
- $Y = \{f | f \colon E_{S_{HAS}} \to A\}$ is a set of functions defining interactions with environment,
- $\Phi \colon W \to W'$ is a function that discretizes the worlds state (a way the system senses the environment), and
- $\pi \colon W' \to \Omega_{HAS}$ is perception process which is an interpretation of data obtained from sensors.

The above definition represents the structure S_{HAS} with it's participants, their actions and the ways the action can be applied. One of the goal is to extend S_{HAS} by reacting when unsteady situations occur. Their resolution in general can cause changing the priority of some actions, rolling back some of them or present other possibilities. Another aim is to add an extension that is responsible for controlling and evaluating the system flows. In the following definition actions related to interaction between the environment and system will be described in terms of a system-agent.

An agent is an autonomous application that can interact with other applications, following a specific predefined behavior. It can respond to states according to predefined individual behaviors [15,16]. An agent environment is determined by the set $\Omega_{S_{HAS}}$ of states. The behavior of an agent is described by an agent function, called action selection function, defined on the basis of the Interactive Environment.

Definition. A *Smart Home Agent* is a triple $A_g = (H, \Omega_{S_{HAS}}, g)$, where

- H is an Interactive Environment of S_{HAS},
- $\Omega_{S_{HAS}}$ is an agent environment, and
- $g: \Omega_{S_{HAS}} \to Y$ is a selection function that chooses interactions between environment and a system.

Definition. A *Smart Home Multi Agent System* (MAS) is a structure $AS = (H, \Omega_{S_{HAS}}, A_{g_1}, \ldots, A_{g_n})$, where

- H is an Interactive Environment of S_{HAS},
- $\Omega_{S_{HAS}}$ is an agent environment, and
- $A_{g_1}, \ldots, A_{g_n}$ are agents.

The result of work presented here is a model of Home Automation System with the use of the cooperative agents. The flow is realized by splitting the functionality to different actors which are: Sensing Agents, Validating Agents, Decision Agents, Acting Agents and Evaluation Agents (see: Fig. 1). The next sections will describe these layers more precisely.

3.3   Architectures

Software-based computer systems with properties such as autonomy, co-operativity, reactivity, mobility can by constructed in many ways. The system that is decomposed into agents is characterized by hierarchical relationship among different abstracts and concrete agents classes and identifies agents instances in the system. It also describes responsibilities of classes, associated interactions and control relationships between agents. Broadly speaking, MAS architectures are organized in one of the following ways [13]:

- *Hierarchical* where agents can only communicate subject to the hierarchical structure.

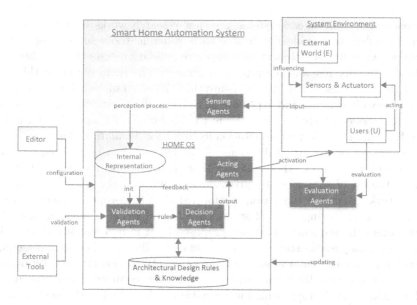

Fig. 1. The diagram of the Home Automation System and its components with multi-agent collaboration.

- *Flat organization* where each agent can directly contact any of the other agents. No fixed structure is applied on the system, however agents may dynamically form structures to perform a specific task. In addition, no control of one agent by another agent is assumed.
- *Subsumption* where some agents are components of other agents.
- *Modular organization* has a modular organization when it is comprised from several modules, where each of these modules can be perceived as a virtually stand-alone MAS.

Hybrids of above and dynamic changes from one organization style to another are possible as well. Various framework models can be compared in case of usability for home systems in general. Different models of decision making system can be considered and designed. To fulfill the expectations, critical states in home environments can be collected and prioritized. Solutions can be defined and categorized to be used as a system agents actions.

3.4 Validation

MAS systems operate in an open world, which requires context awareness. In particular, the character of software agents makes it difficult to apply existing software testing techniques to them [9], which includes: large amount of sensed data, non-deterministic behavior of agents (they can learn), cooperation with other agents (they can work differently in community), etc.

Concerning multi-agent systems very few research works have been undertaken in order to provide developers with valuable tools supporting testing activities. Actually formal methodologies give validation tests that are however applicable in very few and quite irrelevant cases. The main reason of this lack is that the activities, which should assure that the program performs satisfactorily, are very challenging and expensive since it is quite complicated to automate them. Authors conducted research [7] in the area of sensing and diagnosing the home by using Petri Net representation as input for *Validation Agents*.

The process of validating decisions of MAS system can be realized in many ways. We propose two methods. One of them is to perform integration tests by defining the set of scenarios of a given domain and rate the result of the agent system work, which are the actions performed after the proper sequences of the activities occur. Having a set of scenarios, the evaluation of agent is made by estimation of the sequence of actions proposed by it in different situations. The number of tests passed determines the system's intelligence. The second method consists on real-time interaction and allows agents to generate results online. The decisions, especially if contradictory occur, are confronted with the users. Such mediator agent responsible for evaluation is described in the next section.

3.5   Evaluation

According to MAS definition the agent's work is based on the selection function that delivers reactions to system state. Let $A := \{A_1, A_2, \ldots, A_n\}$ be the set of actions. System maintaining expectations can generate and apply above rules in the environment by delegating appropriate *Acting Agents*. The idea is to provide MAS system with the external evaluation tool running on-line that could evaluate system suggestions real-time.

The tests related to running software for the smart built environment need to be conducted to check which decisions of MAS system are beneficial. The intelligent software for a house should shift from problem-centered to user-centered, i.e., even more participants should be confronted with automated solutions.

The *Evaluation Agent* is a separate component apart from the reasoning mechanism of MAS system due to several reasons, which include:

- possibility to change the MAS system architecture considered in Sect. 3.3.
- performing the analysis in two moments: during commissioning of the system by installer or during its working in active household.
- using external libraries and tools supporting the HAS work (like for example different analyzers of Internal representation of MAS system).

MAS systems can be measured by evaluating the success of system agents. Making decisions can be rated. An agent that is measured is called *rational*.

Russell and Norvig [12] group agents into five classes based on their degree of perceived intelligence and capability: simple reflex agents, model-based reflex agents, goal-based agents, utility-based agents, learning agents.

There is a noticeable progression of agent-based system architectures starting from simple agents processing sensors data to self-sensing hybrid multi-agent systems [6]. Considering them the progression of their rationalism should be adequate to their complexity.

Let us introduce measures considered to evaluate level of advance in decision making.

Definition. Denote by $AG := \{A_{g_1}, \ldots, A_{g_n}\}$ a set of MAS agents. An *Feedback Measure* is a function $I : AG \times A \to \mathbb{R}$ that rates interactions between environment and a system.

Techniques of testing MAS system can be used to build confidence in using autonomous agents. The more user scenarios provided and verified the more accurate the system is. Let S be the set of user scenarios covering environmental cases represented as: '*If* user does something, *then* something happens'. The system knowledge is represented by rules in the State Chart XML format with associated *Feedback Measure* values. These ratings increase upon users feedback while the system runs in the background and learns their activities.

Evaluation Agents can for example measure the coverity of the situations in the system that can cause the system reaction. Agent system acts through the selection functions that provide results from the set of actions A. The judgment of the quality of system work is valuable if the tests are conducted on real environment with people. However this estimate can be as well evaluated. Let introduce some system properties that can be calculated upon evaluation:

- *Confidence* is the measure that evaluates the quality of the actions delivered - it is a measure that builds developers confidence in developing MAS systems as well.
- *Efficiency* is the measure that evaluates the time responsiveness of the MAS system.
- *Safety* is the measure of evaluating the damage that can be done by MAS system in case of performing actions leading to unstable system state.
- *Openness* is the measure that verifies how well the system accommodates to new requirements.

4   Conclusions and Other Research

Engineering home automation is a relatively new concept. Due to the large amount of sensed data, different expectations and often non-deterministic behavior the new models of representations and simulation with tools supporting decision making during commissioning are in much interests. Including the suggestions made by MAS system this approach helps in building smarter environments and infrastructures.

This work has presented the model of home automation system with the use of agents as actors. Each agent, responsible for different functionality, interacts with others to fulfill the requirements of the system and adopt its parameters for better execution.

References

1. Abras, S., Kieny, C., Ploix, S., Wurtz, F.: Mas architecture for energy management: developing smart networks with jade platform. In: 2013 IEEE International Conference on Smart Instrumentation, Measurement and Applications (ICSIMA), pp. 1–6 (2013)
2. Brush, A.J.B., Filippov, E., Huang, D., Jung, J., Mahajan, R., Martinez, F., Mazhar, K., Phanishayee, A., Samuel, A., Scott, J., Singh, R.: Lab of things: a platform for conducting studies with connected devices in multiple homes. In: Adjunct Proceedings, UbiComp 2013. ACM (2013)
3. Cook, D.J.: Multi-agent smart environments. J. Ambient Intell. Smart Environ. **1**, 51–55 (2009)
4. Dibley, M., Li, H., Miles, J., Rezgui, Y.: Towards intelligent agent based software for building related decision support. Adv. Eng. Inform. **25**, 311–329 (2011)
5. Dourlens, S., Ramdane-Cherif, A., Monacelli, E.: Tangible ambient intelligence with semantic agents in daily activities. J. Ambient Intell. Smart Environ. **5**, 351–368 (2013)
6. Fuhler, J.: Advances in Applied Artificial Intelligence. Calgary, Idea Group Inc. (IGI) (2006)
7. Hawdziejuk, K., Grabska, E.: Petri net-based management of smart environments supported by agent system. In: Proceedings of the 21st International Workshop on Intelligent Computing in Engineering , ISBN 978-0-9930807-0-8 (2014)
8. Hawdziejuk, K., Grabska, E.: An interface for the rule-based home automation system. In: Proceedings of the 16th International Conference on Computing in Civil and Building Engineering (ICCCBE 2016), 6–8 July 2016, Osaka, Japan, pp. 1373–1380. [S.l.] (2016)
9. Houhamdi, Z.: Multi-agent system testing: a survey. Int. J. Adv. Comput. Sci. Appl. **2**(6), 135–141 (2011)
10. Nguyen, V., Harmann, D., Konig, M.: A distributed agent-based approach for simulation-based optimization. Adv. Eng. Inform. **26**, 814–832 (2012)
11. Preuveneers, D., Novais, P.: A survey of software engineering best practices for the development of smart applications in ambient intelligence. J. Ambient Intell. Smart Environ. **4**, 149–162 (2012)
12. Russell, S.J., Norvig, P.: Artificial Intelligence: A Modern Approach. Prentice Hall, Upper Saddle River (2003). Chap. 2
13. Shehory, O.: Architectural properties of multi-agent systems. Technical report, The Robotics Institute, Carnegie Mellon University (1998)
14. Sun, Q., Yu, W., Kochurov, N., Hao, Q., Hu, F.: A multi-agent-based intelligent sensor and actuator network design for smart house and home automation. J. Sens. Actuator Netw. **2**, 557–588 (2013)
15. Wang, M., Wang, H.: Intelligent agent supported flexible workflow monitoring system. Adv. Inf. Syst. Eng. **2348**, 787–791 (2002)
16. Wang, M., Wang, H., Xu, D.: The design of intelligent workflow monitoring with agent technology. Knowl.-Based Syst. **18**, 257–266 (2006)

Cooperative Learning in Information Security Education: Teaching Secret Sharing Concepts

Yang-Wai Chow$^{(\boxtimes)}$, Willy Susilo, and Guomin Yang

Institute of Cybersecurity and Cryptology, School of Computing and Information Technology, University of Wollongong, Wollongong, Australia
{caseyc,wsusilo,gyang}@uow.edu.au

Abstract. Information security is an important yet challenging area of education. Much of the difficulty lies in the complexity of security schemes and the often perceived disjoint between theory and practice. This paper investigates the topic of adopting cooperative learning for teaching secret sharing concepts and schemes. The aim of this is to motivate and cultivate an interest in students to learn more about the topic. By designing hands-on cooperative learning activities, the goal is help students appreciate the connection between theory and practice, and to be able to help and encourage each other in their understanding of the area. In this paper, we analyze the suitability of this group-based learning approach in relation to addressing the five essential elements of cooperative learning.

Keywords: Cooperative learning · Cybersecurity · Education · Information security · Secret sharing

1 Introduction

Information security is an important area of education that is becoming increasingly essential to address the current cybersecurity landscape where the threat of cyber attacks is a common occurrence. As such, it is vital to educate and train individuals in ways of securing information and methods for protecting systems [3]. Educational institutions not only play an important role in researching technology that improve resiliency of systems, but are also responsible for growing a workforce that understands cybersecurity challenges [17]. However, security education is not an easy task as information security problems are growing more complex [12].

This paper investigates the use of cooperative learning in information security education. In particular, we examine the motivational and practical aspects of teaching secret sharing concepts via a group-based cooperative learning approach. Secret sharing is an information security technique that fundamentally involves a set of n parties to share a secret, and as such we believe that it is well suited for group-based learning. A secret sharing scheme refers to a method by which a dealer encodes a secret into a number of shares and distributes these

© Springer International Publishing AG 2017
Y. Luo (Ed.): CDVE 2017, LNCS 10451, pp. 65–72, 2017.
DOI: 10.1007/978-3-319-66805-5_8

shares to a group of participants. Individually, the shares reveal no information about the secret. The secret can only be reconstructed when information from an authorized number of shares is combined [1]. While the underlying notion is easy to understand, the mathematical details entailed in formal definitions of certain secret sharing schemes can be daunting and challenging for students to appreciate and grasp.

Cooperative learning has been defined as the instructional use of small groups in which students work together to maximize their own and each other's learning [9]. Many studies on cooperative learning exist, and it has been contended that cooperative learning has shown to evoke clear positive effects in terms of achievement and learning attitudes [7,11]. While cooperative learning is often use synonymously with collaborative learning, some practitioners make a distinction between the two. In particular, Johnson and Johnson [10] describe five elements that should be included in cooperative learning; namely, positive interdependence, individual accountability, face-to-face promotive interaction, social and interpersonal skills, and group processing.

In this paper, we examine the topic of teaching secret sharing concepts and schemes through a cooperative learning strategy. We describe the motivational and practical aspects of employing this approach to this area of information security education. In addition, we analyze the suitability of this group-based learning approach in relation to the five essential elements underpinning the successful adoption of cooperative learning in secret sharing learning activities. We believe that this strategy can also be applied to other areas of information security education.

2   Related Work

Innovative approaches to information security education have previously been proposed and examined by various researchers. These approaches typically motivate and encourage student learning through hands-on and collaborative methods. Researchers have found that by engaging students in learning activities outside the classroom, this not only increases the interests of students, but also effectively bridges the gap between theory and practice.

Among the work conducted in this area, Bhattacharya et al. [2] developed an approach to improve student learning through the development of a collection of labware using Android devices. Their purpose was to meet the need for mobile security education by exploiting the benefits of mobile devices and best practices in information security education. Their labware approach provided students with hands-on mobile-security experience to promote their interest and engagement in security.

To address the practical aspects of information security, a number of other researchers and educators have examined lab-based approaches facilitate the learning experience outside the formal classroom structure. Logan and Clarkson [13] present the challenges and explore the issues involved in designing an information security course with lab components that involve destructive actions.

Terry et al. [17] describe a hands-on computer lab, which they call a cyber battle lab, for teaching and research in cybersecurity. The purpose of the lab was to provide students with interactive learning experiences, to allowing them to solve practical, real-world problems to complement theoretical concepts discussed in classroom and textbooks [17].

Xu et al. [19] describe a collaborative hands-on approach for network security education using a collaborative model that encourages knowledge innovation and contribution through Web-based social platforms and virtualized resource sharing approaches. Others have also developed virtual laboratories for teaching information security, and have found that these hands-on approaches to teaching are effective in learning, especially when it comes to connecting theory with practice [8, 18].

3 Secret Sharing and Cooperative Learning

The concept of secret sharing was first introduced independently by Blakley [4] and Shamir [15]. Secret sharing schemes are important tools that have found many applications in cryptography and distributed computing [1]. In general, in a secret sharing scheme, a secret which is some data, D, is divided into n pieces, $D_1, D_2, ..., D_n$, where $n > 1$ [15]. These n pieces are commonly referred to as shares. The shares are split in a way where knowledge of any k, or more shares, makes D easy to determine, whereas knowledge of any $k - 1$ or fewer shares, leaves D impossible to determine. This is known as a k-out-of-n, or (k, n), threshold scheme.

3.1 Motivation

An example of a simple threshold scheme based on polynomial interpolation can be described as follows [15]: Given k points in the 2-dimensional plane $(x_1, y_1), ..., (x_k, y_k)$, there is one and only one polynomial $q(x)$ of degree $k-1$ such that $q(x_i) = y_i$ for all i. If D is a number, it can be divided into shares, D_i, by randomly selecting a $k-1$ degree polynomial $q(x) = a_0 + a_1x + ... + a_{k-1}x^{k-1}$, in which $a_0 = D$ and $D_1 = q(1), ..., D_i = q(i), ..., D_n = q(n)$. With knowledge of any subset of k or more of these D_i values, together with their indices, the coefficients of $q(x)$ can be determine by interpolation to find $D = q(0)$. However, with knowledge of any $k - 1$ or fewer values, there is insufficient information to determine the value of D.

Over the years, there have been a variety of different schemes that have been proposed, with varying levels of complexity. In some secret sharing schemes, complex numerical computation is involved in share generation and secret reconstruction, while in other schemes, little or no computation is required. A student learning the topic of secret sharing can quite easily be overwhelmed with the complexity in the formulation of some schemes. To address this problem, we propose an educational approach designed to motivate and cultivate student interest on the topic by adopting a cooperative learning strategy.

3.2 Activity Design and Practical Issues

To ease students into the topic, a visual approach to secret sharing can be used as an interesting and easy to understand starting point. For example, visual cryptography is a visual secret sharing approach that uses images to conceal information, and decryption requires no computation. Visual cryptography is a method of encoding and distributing a binary image, consisting of black and white pixels, into n shares, each to be printed on separate transparencies (the white pixels are transparent). When the qualified number of shares, k or more, are stacked together, the human visual system averages the black and white pixel contributions of the superimposed shares to recover the hidden information without the need for any computation.

By organizing students into groups, each student in the group can be given a visual cryptography share in the form of a physical transparency. Students will have to combine a certain number of their shares in order to determine the secret. This is meant to form the starting point for cooperation and face-to-face social interaction within the group. Once students are comfortable with this concept, they can be introduced to the formal construction of a general visual cryptography scheme [14]: The resulting shares can be described by two collections of $n \times m$ binary matrices, C_0 and C_1, where each row in these matrices represents the black and white subpixel configuration that are used to encrypt one share. To encrypt a white pixel in the secret image, one of the matrices in C_0 is randomly selected, whereas to encrypt a black pixel, one of the matrices in C_1 is randomly selected.

Stacking shares together has the effect of 'OR'ing the m subpixels of the respective matrix rows. The gray-level of the stacked shares is proportional to the Hamming weight $H(V)$ of the 'OR'ed binary vector V of length m. This gray-level is interpreted by the human visual system as black if $H(V) \geq d$ and as white if $H(V) < d - \alpha m$ for some fixed threshold $1 \leq d \leq m$ and relative difference $\alpha > 0$ [14].

Definition 1. *Let* k, n, m *and* d *be non-negative integers which satisfy* $2 \leq$ k $\leq$ n *and* $1 \leq$ d $\leq$ m. *Two collections of* n $\times$ m *binary matrices,* C_0 *and* C_1, *constitute a* (k, n)-VCS *if the following conditions are satisfied:*

1. *For any* S *in* C_0, *the 'OR' operation of any* k *of the* n *rows satisfies* H(V) $<$ d $- \alpha$m.
2. *For any* S *in* C_1, *the 'OR' operation of any* k *of the* n *rows satisfies* H(V) $\geq$ d.
3. *For any subset* $\{i_1, i_2, ..., i_q\}$ *of* $\{1, 2, ..., n\}$ *with* q $<$ k, *the two collections of* q $\times$ m *matrices* D_t *for* t $\in \{1, 0\}$ *obtained by restricting each* n $\times$ m *matrix in* C_t *(where* t $= 0, 1$) *to row* $i_1, i_2, ..., i_q$ *are indistinguishable in the sense that they contain the same matrices with the same frequencies.*

The first two conditions are known as the contrast and the third condition as the security [14]. For example, a (2, 2)-VCS can be represented by the following two collections of binary matrices, known as the basis matrices of a VCS:

$$C_0 = \{\text{all matrices obtained by permutating the columns of } \begin{bmatrix} 0 & 0 & 1 & 1 \\ 0 & 0 & 1 & 1 \end{bmatrix}\}$$

$$C_1 = \{\text{all matrices obtained by permutating the columns of } \begin{bmatrix} 0 & 0 & 1 & 1 \\ 1 & 1 & 0 & 0 \end{bmatrix}\}$$

Once the group understands the formal construction, they can then be given the task of discussing the limitations of such schemes. Traditional visual cryptography faces a number of issues such as the pixel expansion problem, the share alignment problem, along with visual quality and contrast issues [5]. Based on the group activity of combining the shares and by understanding the formal construction of the scheme, the problems that arise should be evident to the group. They can then be introduce to other related concepts, for example, visual cryptography shares consist of a random pattern of pixels. As such, it is easy for an adversary to identify visual cryptography shares. Extended visual cryptography on the other hand is a method of encoding shares using meaningful cover images to reduce the likelihood of attracting attention.

The next task that the students can be given is to cooperatively produce their own set of shares based a different secret sharing scheme. This will require them to work together to fully understand the scheme before they will be able to generate the shares. Each of the group members should individually produce different share configurations, e.g., one might work on a $(k = 2, n = 4)$, another $(k = 3, n = 4)$, etc. This way, they will all be working together on the same scheme, but the specific construction will be different. As such, they can then verify each other's implementation since they should all have an understanding of the scheme.

These activities will involve group members working together and participating in hands-on practical tasks of implementing secret sharing schemes. From a motivational standpoint, they can be given contemporary secret sharing schemes like using QR codes for secret sharing [6] or other visual secret sharing approaches like image secret sharing, as opposed to pure mathematical secret sharing schemes. The aim of this is for students to be able to clearly connect the theoretical concepts with practical implementations. Studies presented in the related work section of this paper have all asserted that the hands-on approach is what helps students appreciate the connection between theory and practice. Upon successful completion of the tasks, students can gradually be introduced to more and more complicated secret sharing schemes.

4 Analysis and Discussion

To evaluate the suitability of this group-based learning approach for teaching secret sharing concepts and schemes, in this section we analyze it in relation to the five essential elements underpinning cooperative learning. In particular, we discuss how each element is addressed in the hands-on secret sharing learning activities, as well as how the individual members of the group are important to the group's overall success.

Positive Interdependence. This has been described as the need for students to perceive that they are connected with other group members such that they cannot succeed unless others do [10,11]. In addition, it is important that group members need to cooperate to achieve the desired goal. This element of cooperative learning is one of the underlying principles of secret sharing, whereby it is essential for participants to work together in order to achieve the goal of obtaining the secret information from the different shares. Without working together, it will not be possible for group members to successfully recover the secret. As such, secret sharing inherently drives the importance that individuals are connected to other group members and that their goal necessitates the overall success of the group.

Individual Accountability. This is the property where each student must be an active member and are held individually accountable to do their part of the group work. Furthermore, the performance of individual members must be visible to others [10,11]. It has been stated that individual accountability can be created through task specialization in that each group member is responsible for a unique task [11,16]. This element of cooperative learning is clearly present in the group-based activity where students are given the task of constructing different configurations of the same secret sharing scheme. This is because all group members will be able to see the successful scheme implementations of other individual group members, while at the same time, any member who does not succeed will mean that there is a configuration of the scheme that is missing. In this way, individual accountability is present in the group activities.

Face-to-Face Promotive Interaction. This third element takes place when group members are able to give feedback to one another, which will in turn encourages other group members [10,11]. The secret sharing activities previously described must involve group members cooperating to reconstruct the secret information. Furthermore, but adopting a hands-on approach where individual members work on different configurations of the same scheme, each member should have an understanding of the general scheme before they can implement it in practice. Since they are all working on the same scheme, they can easily give each other feedback and help members who may not fully understand aspects of the scheme. This will help to strengthen the knowledge of individual group members and provide positive support for potentially weaker group members.

Social and Interpersonal Skills. This element refers to leadership, decision-making, trust building, communication and conflict-management skills [10,11]. This aspect is present in most group-based learning approaches as it relates to the dynamics of the group. For the group to succeed, many of these should be present in one form or another.

Group Processing. This occurs when group members regularly discuss and assess which actions were effective for achieving the goal [10,11]. Through practical hands-on activities of implementing different configurations of the same secret sharing scheme, group members must discuss and evaluate their efforts in achieving their common goal. In conjunction with other elements where group members give feedback and encourage other group members towards individual success, which in turn leads to the overall success of the group, group processing through regular discussions are necessary to achieve the common group goal.

Many researchers agree that for significant positive outcomes, two of the most important aspects of cooperative learning are individual accountability and group goals [10,11,16]. Both of these are very much present and take center stage in the described secret sharing group activities. Hence, it can be summarized that the group-based learning approach designed for teaching secret sharing addresses the five elements of cooperative learning.

5   Conclusion

This paper examines the topic of teaching secret sharing concepts and schemes through the use of a cooperative learning strategy. The aim of adopting cooperative learning through hands-on activities is to help facilitate student motivation and to generate their interest to learn more about the topic. Students will have to work together, and will typically only succeed when other do. At the same time, their individual performances in their specific tasks will be visible to all members of the group. Through their interactions and discussions, group members will be able to assist and encourage one another in these group-based activities. In this paper, we discuss how the described group-based learning approach addresses the five essential elements of cooperative learning. We believe that this strategy can also be applied to other areas of information security education.

Acknowledgments. The authors would like to acknowledge the support of the UOW UIC International Links Grant 2017 that was awarded for this study.

References

1. Beimel, A.: Secret-sharing schemes: a survey. In: Chee, Y.M., Guo, Z., Ling, S., Shao, F., Tang, Y., Wang, H., Xing, C. (eds.) IWCC 2011. LNCS, vol. 6639, pp. 11–46. Springer, Heidelberg (2011). doi:10.1007/978-3-642-20901-7_2
2. Bhattacharya, P., Yang, L., Guo, M., Qian, K., Yang, M.: Learning mobile security with labware. IEEE Secur. Priv. **12**(1), 69–72 (2014)
3. Bishop, M.: What is computer security? IEEE Secur. Priv. **99**(1), 67–69 (2003)
4. Blakley, G.: Safeguarding cryptographic keys. In: Proceedings of the 1979 AFIPS National Computer Conference, pp. 313–317 (1979)
5. Chow, Y.-W., Susilo, W., Wong, D.S.: Enhancing the perceived visual quality of a size invariant visual cryptography scheme. In: Chim, T.W., Yuen, T.H. (eds.) ICICS 2012. LNCS, vol. 7618, pp. 10–21. Springer, Heidelberg (2012). doi:10.1007/978-3-642-34129-8_2

6. Chow, Y.-W., Susilo, W., Yang, G., Phillips, J.G., Pranata, I., Barmawi, A.M.: Exploiting the error correction mechanism in QR codes for secret sharing. In: Liu, J.K.K., Steinfeld, R. (eds.) ACISP 2016. LNCS, vol. 9722, pp. 409–425. Springer, Cham (2016). doi:10.1007/978-3-319-40253-6_25

7. Decuyper, S., Dochy, F., Van den Bossche, P.: Grasping the dynamic complexity of team learning: an integrative model for effective team learning in organisations. Educ. Res. Rev. 5(2), 111–133 (2010)

8. Ernits, M., Kikkas, K.: A live virtual simulator for teaching cybersecurity to information technology students. In: Zaphiris, P., Ioannou, A. (eds.) LCT 2016. LNCS, vol. 9753, pp. 474–486. Springer, Cham (2016). doi:10.1007/978-3-319-39483-1_43

9. Johnson, D.W., Johnson, R.T.: Making cooperative learning work. Theory Pract. 38(2), 67–73 (1999)

10. Johnson, D.W., Johnson, R.T.: An educational psychology success story: social interdependence theory and cooperative learning. Educ. Res. 38(5), 365–379 (2009)

11. Kyndt, E., Raes, E., Lismont, B., Timmers, F., Cascallar, E., Dochy, F.: A meta-analysis of the effects of face-to-face cooperative learning. Do recent studies falsify or verify earlier findings? Educ. Res. Rev. 10, 133–149 (2013)

12. Locasto, M., Sinclair, S.: An experience report on undergraduate cyber-security education and outreach. In: Annual Conference on Education in Information Security (ACEIS) (2009)

13. Logan, P.Y., Clarkson, A.: Teaching students to hack: curriculum issues in information security. In: ACM SIGCSE Bulletin, vol. 37, pp. 157–161. ACM (2005)

14. Naor, M., Shamir, A.: Visual cryptography. In: Santis, A. (ed.) EUROCRYPT 1994. LNCS, vol. 950, pp. 1–12. Springer, Heidelberg (1995). doi:10.1007/BFb0053419

15. Shamir, A.: How to share a secret. Commun. ACM 22(11), 612–613 (1979)

16. Slavin, R.E.: When does cooperative learning increase student achievement? Psychol. Bull. 94(3), 429 (1983)

17. Terry, C., Castellano, A., Harrod, J., Luke, J., Reichherzer, T.: The UWF cyber battle lab: a hands-on computer lab for teaching and research in cyber security. In: Proceedings of the International Conference on Security and Management (SAM), p. 1. The Steering Committee of The World Congress in Computer Science, Computer Engineering and Applied Computing (WorldComp) (2014)

18. Wu, D., Fulmer, J., Johnson, S.: Teaching information security with virtual laboratories. In: Carroll, J.M. (ed.) Innovative Practices in Teaching Information Sciences and Technology, pp. 179–192. Springer, Cham (2014). doi:10.1007/978-3-319-03656-4_16

19. Xu, L., Huang, D., Tsai, W.-T.: Cloud-based virtual laboratory for network security education. IEEE Trans. Educ. 57(3), 145–150 (2014)

Gaming as a Gateway: Ensuring Quality Control for Crowdsourced Data

Shaban Shabani$^{(\boxtimes)}$ and Maria Sokhn$^{(\boxtimes)}$

Institute of Information Systems, HES-SO Valais-Wallis, Sierre, Switzerland
{shaban.shabani,maria.sokhn}@hevs.ch

Abstract. Crowdsourcing is a growing topic that has proved to be capable and cost effective solution for various tasks. Over the last decade it has been applied to numerous domains, both in research and enterprise contexts. Though there are several issues that remain open and challenging in crowdsourcing, here we address the issues of quality control and motivation. In this paper we present an ongoing work which explores the use of gamification in crowdsourcing settings, as means to: improve the task assignment and performance, incentivize people to participate and control the quality of their work. The developed crowdsourcing hybrid mobile application is applied to data within cultural heritage domain.

Keywords: Crowdsourcing · Gamification · Quality control

1 Introduction

As an emerging service platform on the Internet, crowdsourcing has shown to be an effective solution for problems which for computers are difficult to solve and that require human intelligence [1]. The rise of the Web, the popularity of online platforms and mobile crowdsourcing [2], has made it easy to reach crowds of workers that are available at any time to solve micro-tasks called HITs (Human Intelligent Tasks). However, there are significant issues that appear in crowdsourcing. In these online platforms, money is the main encouragement for crowds to participate. For some workers, this is a motivation plus to increase their profits and become lazy by providing random answers and not considering seriously the HITs [3] or malicious workers that try to sabotage the system by providing intentionally wrong answers [4]. In these scenarios, crowdsourcing may yield to relatively low-quality results, hence control mechanisms should be applied to maintain the quality of the work. On the other side, in a crowdsourcing environment with no monetary reward, a significant challenge it how to incentivize people to participate. As a result, main incentives used are services, entertainment or learning [5].

This paper demonstrates a crowdsourcing application within cultural heritage domain that addresses these two issues through the application of game based elements to increase the engagement of participants and to improve the quality of their work.

© Springer International Publishing AG 2017
Y. Luo (Ed.): CDVE 2017, LNCS 10451, pp. 73–76, 2017.
DOI: 10.1007/978-3-319-66805-5_9

2   Related Work

A widely applied preventive quality control mechanism is gold questions [6] which consists of a set of questions for which answers are known in advance. Its goal is to remove unethical workers from a task and educate incompetent workers to improve the accuracy of their answers. However, choosing the test questions without further considering worker's behavior and profile is challenging as that effects the worker's output. Reputation based systems [7] additionally rely on reputation score that is computed based on worker's feedback history to detect fraudulent workers.

Unpaid crowdsourcing systems additionally face the issue of participation as workers need extra incentives. A good example are Games with a Purpose (GWAPs) where users solve tasks while playing the game [8] or by learning [9]. Another method is stimulating contributors [10] by social achievements in form of scores, ranks and badges.

3   Crowdsourcing Application Design

In this work, we use data from two archival institutions for digital heritage: Mediatheque[1] and Digital Valais[2]. Datasets contain historical documents (audio, images, video and text) about the canton of Valais in Switzerland. The crowd-sourcing application enables users to participate through:

- Data sharing - allows users to insert new data to the multimedia repository and provide metadata by following a 5-step process in an interactive and self-descriptive user interface (illustrated in Fig. 2a). The application makes it relatively easy for the users to transfer their valuable documents such as photo and video albums, and share them through the application with other users.
- Data annotation - while integrating existing data and inserting new data into the repository, two different issues occur: *missing information* and *conflict-ual information*. For instance, some data miss particular information about the location, description, and sometimes two different dates for the same record appear. In this section participants are asked to annotate missing parts and/or solve conflicting data. These issues are designed and generated as small tasks/questions where users are asked to choose or provide an answer (Fig. 2c). As the data is specific and related to historical cultural heritage of the country, maintaining a high quality of users' annotations is crucial, there-fore we apply a quality control method through gamification described as follows.

To enable the requester assess the quality of posted contributions, and to make the crowdsourcing tasks more attractive and engaging, we apply a game

---

[1] http://www.mediatheque.ch/.

[2] http://www.valais-digital.ch/.

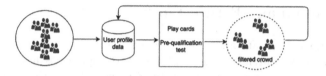

Fig. 1. Quality control process

(a)   Inserting   (b) Quality control process - Play cards game   (c)   Sample
new data   tasks

Fig. 2. Crowdsourcing application screenshots

based quality control mechanism that considers users' profiles and their interests. This process is illustrated in Fig. 1. The *play-cards* game adapts game-design elements in a non-gaming context. It acts as a pre-qualification test for users that are motivated to annotate data, similar to *gold questions* [6]. This test consists of 195 cards grouped in 13 categories and each one of these cards has a story behind. Initially, users provide information about their profile, especially information about their interests which fall within one or more of these 13 categories. Depending on this information, they are forwarded to read and answer questions/cards related to their predefined interests, hence avoiding unfair exclusion of workers due to non-relevant questions. For instance, a user that has chosen *sport* as his area of interest, he is asked to answer questions within that topic. He chooses to read the story of the cards and tries to guess the year which is related to the topic. To boost the motivation of users, two joker cards can be used. If the user successfully answers 70% of the cards, he is considered later as a potential worker for solving micro tasks related to that category. User's performance is visually displayed: on each category, the accuracy is shown in form of stars and a progress bar shows the completeness of the questions of that category (depicted in Fig. 2b).

To further motivate qualified users to participate in data annotation, we apply a reputation mechanism. Depending on their level of contribution, users gain reputation points and titles. Top contributors will have the chance to receive public recognition by the archival institutions.

4   Conclusion and Future Work

Game design elements are important to affect the human motivation and participation in crowdsourcing. In general, gamified approaches have reported an increase in engagement and output quality of workers [11]. In the near future, we plan to run an experiment by inviting users to use our application and collect data. To facilitate the challenge of participation, we have developed a hybrid mobile application, targeting stationary and mobile users. Further analysis will be employed to evaluate the quality of users work as well as their interaction and perception about the crowdsourcing application.

Acknowledgement. This work was partly funded by the Hasler Foundation in the context of the project City-Stories. We are grateful to "Médiathèque Valais", "Digital Valais Wallis" and "Archives de l'Etat du Valais" for providing the data.

References

1. Yuen, M.C., King, I., Leung, K.S.: A survey of crowdsourcing systems. In: IEEE Third International Conference on Social Computing (2011)
2. Ren, J., Zhang, Y., Zhang, K., Shen, X.: Exploiting mobile crowdsourcing for pervasive cloud services: challenges and solutions. IEEE Commun. Mag. (2015)
3. Ipeirotis, P.G., Provost, F., Wang, J.: Quality management on amazon mechanical turk. In: Proceedings of the ACM SIGKDD Workshop on Human Computation, HCOMP 2010. ACM (2010)
4. Li, H., Yu, B., Zhou, D.: Error rate bounds in crowdsourcing models. ArXiv e-prints arXiv:1307.2674 (2013)
5. Garcia-Molina, H., Joglekar, M., Marcus, A., Parameswaran, A., Verroios, V.: Challenges in data crowdsourcing. IEEE Trans. Knowl. Data Eng. (2016)
6. Oleson, D., Sorokin, A., Laughlin, G., Hester, V., Le, J., Biewald, L.: Programmatic gold: targeted and scalable quality assurance in crowdsourcing. In: Proceedings of the 11th AAAI Conference on Human Computation. AAAI Press (2011)
7. Daltayanni, M., de Alfaro, L., Papadimitriou, P.: Workerrank: using employer implicit judgements to infer worker reputation. In: Proceedings of the Eighth ACM International Conference on Web Search and Data Mining (2015)
8. von Ahn, L., Dabbish, L.: Designing games with a purpose. Commun. ACM **51**(8), 58–67 (2008)
9. von Ahn, L.: Duolingo: learn a language for free while helping to translate the web. In: Proceedings of the International Conference on Intelligent User Interfaces. ACM (2013)
10. Lee, T.Y., Dugan, C., Geyer, W., Ratchford, T., Rasmussen, J., Shami, N.S., Lupushor, S.: Experiments on motivational feedback for crowdsourced workers. In: International AAAI Conference on Web and Social Media (2013)
11. Morschheuser, B., Hamari, J., Koivisto, J.: Gamification in crowdsourcing: a review. In: 49th Hawaii International Conference on System Sciences (HICSS) (2016)

Context Similarity Measure
for Knowledge-Based Recommendation System

Case Study: Handicraft Domain

Maha Maalej[1]([⊠]), Achraf Mtibaa[2], and Faiez Gargouri[1]

[1] Higher Institute of Computer Science and Multimedia of Sfax, Sfax, Tunisia
maha.maalej@gmail.com, faiez.gargouri@gmail.com
[2] National School of Electronic and Telecommunications of Sfax, Sfax, Tunisia
achrafmtibaa@gmail.com

Abstract. Nowadays, there is an increasing development of intelligent systems like online social networks, personalized recommendation systems and knowledge-based systems which are especially based on ontologies. Personalized recommendation systems applied with online social networking assist delivering a personalized content to Web-based application users. Indeed, these systems offer services that can greatly improve the response to users' needs in their search for persons or for some products. In order to model these users, semantic web technologies such as ontologies are used to explicit the hidden knowledge through using rules. In this paper, we propose to measure the similarity between the user context and other users' contexts in our ontology. Then, we integrate this measure in recommendation model to infer recommendation items (raw material, production tool, supplier name, etc.) based on SWRL rules. The experiments and evaluations show the applicability of our approach.

Keywords: Context similarity measure · User context ontology · SWRL rules · Knowledge-based recommendation

1 Introduction

In the last decade, recommender systems have been introduced to facilitate the transition of the Web from the search to the discovery paradigm. Recommendation is a personalization service aiming at proposing elements of information which are likely to interest the user. With the increasing technological advances, personalized systems must adapt perfectly according to the users contexts and meet their expectations and needs. User Context plays an important role when measuring the similarity between two users, in order to decide recommended items in a recommendation system. Giving a clear and concise definition to the context is the object of several attempts. The most known definition is of Dey et al. [2], in which they defined context as a set of information that can characterize a situation to an entity (place, object or person). Context modeling using ontologies permits to the machine to understand the model and to reason about such information. Ontology-based reasoning is actually used in many domains due to its ability to infer new knowledge from explicitly described information

© Springer International Publishing AG 2017
Y. Luo (Ed.): CDVE 2017, LNCS 10451, pp. 77–84, 2017.
DOI: 10.1007/978-3-319-66805-5_10

such as medicine, e-commerce, etc. Many rules languages are used with ontology such as Jena rules, SWRL (Semantic Web Rule Language) rules, etc. In fact, they permit to reason on the instances defined in the ontology. This work is involved in the BWEC (Business for Women of Emerging Countries) project that treats handicraft women from emerging (Tunisian and Algerian) countries. In this context, in order to improve the socio-economic situation of these women, an interactive system will be built based on many works. In a previous work [7], we suggested some recommendations for training according to the context of handicraft woman without considering the context of other handicraft women. If we consider the other handicraft women contexts, we can recommend some raw materials, production tools, suppliers names, or other information that can help her in her business. Handicraft woman can use social networks to search for some useful information. In her searching, she admits an interaction context. This context is characterized by the fact that is changing every time she connects and searches. We need to detect this context in order to recommend her some valuable information. In this paper, we propose an approach for recommending items (raw materials, production tools, etc.) to handicraft woman. For that, we measure similarity between user (handicraft woman) context that connects to social network through our application and handicraft women contexts stored in the ontology. We infer user interest from his search query. We used SWRL rules for detecting the contexts and giving recommendation. After that, we give experiments and evaluation to show the applicability of our approach.

The rest of this paper is structured as follows. Section 2 presents some works related to context similarity measure and knowledge-based application. In Sect. 3, we present our context similarity approach for recommendation. Section 4 deals with experiments from our prototype SoNUMOnto (Social Network User Model Ontology) with evaluation using some known measures. We conclude and give further works in Sect. 5.

2   Related Works

We review, in this section, some works related to context similarity measure for recommendation models and some other works related to knowledge-based recommendation systems. Hannech et al. [3] proposed a generic model of user profiles based on their search histories. These profiles are using a contextual similarity measure between the user query and a target interest and between the interests. In the work of Liu et al. [6], authors consider semantic similarity in order to calculate similarity between context segments defined using ontology. For that, they proposed a method for providing context similarity measure within a recommendation approach. Concerning knowledge based recommendation, many works are proposed. Hudli and Arvind [4] presented their approach to build a knowledge-based system that encodes rules. In the work of Ameen et al. [1], authors proposed a rule based personalization system named SemRPer for Semantic Web which generates personalized recommendations using a generic rule reasoner. In literature, in order to perform recommendation, the comparison is done between user profiles or between user profile and product profile or between items from historical activities of the user. In this work, the main idea is to compare between two users' contexts through using contextual parameters, to perform recommendation. Contextual parameters represent what are the context elements that we must compare in order to obtain the correct comparison between two contexts. In this work, we propose to use three contextual parameters that are representative and can accurately give good results in comparing two contexts.

3   Context Similarity Measure Approach for Recommendation

In this section, we introduce our approach to recommend items to a user. Our approach is composed of three steps: first, we represent user context using contextual parameters. Second, we calculate similarity between contextual parameters. Finally, we recommend to user depending on his context.

3.1   Representing User Context

Context modeling is a quite important phase. We adopt in our work that the interaction context (i.e. the context when the user is interacting with the system) is composed of three dimensions as in [9]. These dimensions are User, Platform and Environment. User is described by its perceptual and cognitive abilities as well as its preferences and its interests. Platform is the set of hardware and software that intervene in the interaction. Environment refers to the physical environment supporting the interaction. It is described by a set of information dependent on the current activity like time, geographical location, etc.

Content personalization is intimately linked to the user model that is a representation of its characteristics, which is the ontology in our work. The main classes in our ontology are Context, Handicraft_woman, Production, Interest, Location, User_query and Recommended_links. We present, in Fig. 1, a fragment of our ontology to show different classes that we used to represent the user context (handicraft woman context in our case).

In order to compare two users, several difficulties appear: What is the context of the user when he is searching for information? Which features do we use to compare two

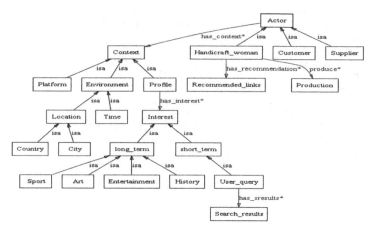

Fig. 1. A fragment of our ontology presenting user context modeling

contexts? We give example of two users having two different contexts. The first user context is composed of three instances which are "Bizerte", "Pottery" and "Pottery maker". In the second user context, we find the same location in "Bizerte" but different Interests and Activities such as "stitches" and "textile craft".

Hence, we proposed to use three parameters to compare between two users' contexts. In fact, we have noticed that the most important feature in detecting user context is his location. Secondly, we need to know the user's interests which represent the second parameter. In fact, the user's interests can be deduced from the search terms saved in his profile in the ontology. The last parameter or feature is the user activity which can give information about the exact user job in handicraft domain.

3.2   Calculating Similarity Between Contextual Parameters

Several similarity measures are proposed in the literature [5]. Authors in [3] exploit matching relying on two aspects: semantic aspect and contextual aspect. In our work, our hypothesis was that matching is based on three aspects: semantic aspect, structural aspect and lexical aspect. According to this hypothesis, we chose Wordnet as semantic-based similarity measure, Cosine as vector-based similarity measure (structural aspect) and Levenshtein as edit-based similarity measure (lexical aspect). In order to compare user (handicraft woman) context and other users' contexts in ontology, we created SWRL rules that takes two terms and compare between them using these similarity measures. To incorporate these measures in the ontology, we created a custom built-in that permits to calculate the similarity from a jar file that we created from the java project where we defined our SWRLBuiltInLibraryImpl java class. "actions:calculate_sim" is our custom built-in that calculates similarity between two terms using the three similarity measures. We present our algorithm for similarity measure contained in the java class related to the custom SWRL built-in actions:calculate_sim. In this algorithm, we chose the threshold 0.5 as it is revealed that it is the better value that can be employed in order to have suitable result. The three measures that we used are weighted equally because all of them are of great importance for the context detection.

Our Algorithm:

```
Input: 2 strings s1 and s2
Output: Boolean, true if similar strings else false
Begin
Read s1, s2
float sim1=0, sim2=0, sim3=0, sim_tot=0
sim1=levenshtein_sim_measure(s1,s2)
sim2=cosine_sim_measure(s1,s2)
sim3=Wordnet_based_sim_measure(s1,s2)
sim_tot:= (sim1+sim2+sim3)/3
If sim_tot <0.5 then s1 and s2 are different
Return false
Else
Return true
End if
End
```

Before calculating interest similarity measure, we proceed to detect them through a rule. In fact, when we extract user profile from his online social network account, it is implicitly extracted without bothering user time and effort. While activity and location are extracted from his profile, interests are inferred. We consider that user interests are really important factor in the detection of his context. Indeed, the interests express his attention to a specific subject. These interests are difficult to be known because they change with every query he writes when he uses our system. Thus, we noticed that the query terms that he enters are actually expressing his interests. The proposed rules for inferring the interest and for similarity measure are presented in Table 1.

Table 1. Interests' detection and similarity measure rules

Rule objective	Rule expression

Interests detection	`Handicraft_woman(?x) ∧ has_context(?x, ?y) ∧`
	`Interest(?y) ∧ Search_query(?q) ∧`
	`has_search_query(?x, ?q) ∧ query_terms(?q, ?qt)`
	`→ Interest_terms(?y, ?qt)`

Interests similarity measure	`interest(?x) ∧ interest_terms(?x, ?a) ∧ interest`
	`(?y) ∧ interest_terms(?y, ?b)`
	`→ actions:calculate_sim(?a, ?b)`

Activity similarity measure	`job(?c)∧job(?d) → actions:calculate_sim(?c,?d)`
Location similarity measure	`location(?l)∧location(?m)` `→ actions:calculate_sim(?l,?m)`

3.3   Recommending Items Depending on User's Context

We integrate these similarity measures in the system to recommend an item to the user after comparing contexts. In fact, the user can search in the social network through our application after logging into his account on the social network. Thus, the user (handicraft woman) profile and context are saved in our ontology. After he logs in his account via our application, we compare his context and other contexts of other users (handicraft women). If they have similar contexts, it will be probable that they need the same raw materials. Otherwise, we will not recommend items to him. This recommendation is mainly based on SWRL rules that we defined. These rules concerns Production tool and Raw material as items to be recommended. We chose these items as the domain is handicraft domain and the goal of our work is to help handicraft woman to improve her socio-economic status. These rules are presented in Table 2.

Table 2. Recommendation rules based on the proposed similarity measure

Rule objective	Rule expression
Production tool recommendation rule	`Handicraft_woman (?p1)∧ Handicraft_woman (?p2) ∧ has_context(?p1,?x) ∧ has_context(?p1,?y) ∧ has_context(?p1,?c) ∧ has_context(?p2,?d) ∧ has_context(?p1,?1) ∧ has_context(?p2,?m) ∧ interest (?x) ∧ interest_terms(?x,?a) ∧ interest(?y) ∧ interest_terms(?y,?b) ∧ actions:calculate_sim (?x,?y) ∧ job(?c) ∧ job(?d) ∧ actions:calculate_sim(?c,?d) ∧ location(?1) ∧ location(?m)∧ actions:calculate_sim(?1,?m) ∧ has_recommendation(?p1,?r) ∧ has_recommendation (?p1,?r) ∧ recommendation(?r) ∧ use_prod_tool (?p1,?prod) → recom(?r,?prod)`
Raw materials recommendation rule	`Handicraft_woman (?p1)∧ Handicraft_woman (?p2) ∧ has_context(?p1,?x) ∧ has_context(?p1,?y) ∧ has_context(?p1,?c) ∧ has_context(?p2,?d) ∧ has_context(?p1,?1) ∧ has_context(?p2,?m) ∧ interest (?x) ∧ interest_terms(?x,?a) ∧ interest(?y) ∧ interest_terms(?y,?b) ∧ actions:calculate_sim (?x,?y) ∧ job(?c) ∧ job(?d) ∧ actions:calculate_sim (?c,?d) ∧ location(?1) ∧ location(?m)∧ actions:calculate_sim(?1,?m) ∧ has_recommendation (?p1,?r) ∧ has_recommendation(?p1,?r) ∧ recommendation(?r) ∧ use_raw_material (?p1,?raw_m) → recom(?r,?raw_m)`

4   Experimentation and Evaluation

We perform our experiments on our prototype SoNUMOnto. We used different programming tools to achieve these experiments. For the extraction of user information we used Rest API. The query processing is realized through SPARQL language and Jena API. Protégé is the ontology editing tool that we used to create our ontology. Pellet is the reasoner that we used to execute SWRL rules. We used "WordNet Search for Java" (WS4 J) API for Wordnet based similarity measure. Our system is composed of four components which are User profile extraction, Interest detection, Comparison between user context and users' context in ontology and finally recommendation to user. We proceed to evaluate our system SoNUMOnto to calculate the error percentage that produces according to different experiments. We note that we evaluate the performance of the system to detect the user context not the performance of the system to recommend item to user. We concentrate on the context similarity measure and inference by SWRL rules. The scores generated by the similarity measures are of type "double" in similarity measures methods. We have defined a threshold (th = 0.5) under which we consider that two contexts are non similar. Greater than this threshold, we consider that two contexts are similar when executing SWRL rules as presented in Table 3.

Table 3. Prediction values generated after running SWRL rules

	Cosine measure	Levenshtein measure	Wordnet measure	Arithmetic mean	Midrange	Median	Prediction values	Actual values
Exp1	0.33	0.34	0.57	0.46	0.45	0.34	Different contexts	Similar contexts
Exp2	0.33	0.69	0.65	0.54	0.51	0.65	Similar contexts	Similar contexts
Exp3	0.33	0.56	0.79	0.56	0.56	0.56	Similar contexts	Similar contexts
Exp4	0	0.32	0.43	0.25	0.21	0.32	Different contexts	Different contexts
Exp5	0	0.17	0.23	0.13	0.11	0.17	Different contexts	Different contexts

After comparing three types of average functions, in Table 3, which are arithmetic average, midrange average and median average, we found that these three functions give the same results for the five experiments according to the threshold that we fixed which is 0.5. This justifies our choice to use arithmetic mean average. For experiments we have not a benchmark that we can test our system with it, related to context similarity measure and using the parameters that we proposed. Furthermore, Nielsen and Landauer have produced a formula which could be graphed and by which they have argued that five users is enough for evaluating small project [8]. Thus, we have tested our system for five users' contexts. The evaluation metrics that we used are calculated over these two measures Prediction and Actual values. Prediction value is obtained after running SWRL rules with the inference engine. Actual value is the value that we give to two contexts when comparing them manually. In Table 3, we give predicted and actual values of context similarity measures. We generate the confusion matrix for binary classifier related to our system. We use the TP, FP, TN and FN values in calculating the accuracy, precision, recall and F-measure measures.

- Accuracy = 1 − error_rate = 1 − [(FP + FN)/(TP + TN + FP + FN)] = 1 − 0.2 = 0.8
- Precision = TP/(TP + FP) = 2/2 = 1
- Recall = TP/(TP + FN) = 2/3 = 0.66
- F-measure = 2 * (Precision * Recall)/(Precision + Recall) = 2 * 0.66/1.66 = 0.79

After this evaluation, we can conclude that our approach can detect that two users have similar contexts through the comparison between three parameters which are interest, location and activity. This performance is greatly calculated structurally through Cosine and Levenshtein measures and semantically through Wordnet-based similarity measure. All these combinations have generated good results through our system.

5   Conclusion

In this paper, we gave a new method to calculate context similarity between the current user's context and users' contexts in ontology for recommendation purpose. The calculation method permits to combine different measures and is included in the custom SWRL built-in that we created. Our ontological model has helped to calculate similarity between contexts and to infer through SWRL rules the suitable recommendations. We opted for using three parameters to describe contextual information for the reason that much information about user context should be exploited but not exhaustively. In further works, we aim at exploring techniques from semantic web and social network analysis to improve recommendation in social network.

Acknowledgements. We are very thankful to the Algerian Tunisian Project dealing with the improvement of handicraft women business in emerging countries through affordable technologies and social networks.

References

1. Ameen, A., Khan, K.U.R., Rani, B.P.: SemRPer - a rule based personalization system for semantic web. Int. J. Web Appl. **7**(1), 23–38 (2015)
2. Dey, A.K., Abowd, G.D., Wood, A.: CyberDesk: a framework for providing self-integrating context-aware services. Knowl.-Syst. **11**(1), 3–13 (1998)
3. Hannech, A., Adda, M., Mcheick, H.: Recommendation model based on a contextual similarity measure. In: 15th IEEE International Conference on Machine Learning and Applications, 18–20 December, Anaheim, CA, USA, pp. 394–401 (2016)
4. Hudli, S., Arvind, H.: Learning in rule-based recommendation systems. In: The 27th Annual IEEE Software Technology Conference Long Beach, California, USA, 12–15 October 2015
5. Li, M., Chen, X., Li, X., Ma, B., Vitanyi, P.M.B.: The similarity metric. IEEE Trans. Inf. Theory **50**(12), 3250–3264 (2004)
6. Liu, L., Lécué, F., Mehandjiev, N., Xu, L.: Using context similarity for service recommendation. In: The Proceedings of the 4th IEEE International Conference on Semantic Computing, 22–24 September, USA, pp. 277–284 (2010)
7. Maalej, M., Mtibaa, A., Gargouri, F.: Ontology-based user modeling for handicraft woman recommendation. In: Ait Ameur, Y., Bellatreche, L., Papadopoulos, G.A. (eds.) MEDI 2014. LNCS, vol. 8748, pp. 138–145. Springer, Cham (2014). doi:10.1007/978-3-319-11587-0_14
8. Nielsen, J.: Why you only need to test with 5 users, 19 March 2000. http://www.useit.com/alertbox
9. Vanderdonckt, J., Grolaux, D., Van Roy, P., Limbourg, Q., Macq, B., Michel, B.: A design space for context-sensitive user interfaces. In: Proceedings of IASSE (2005)

Building Common Knowledge from Personal Historical Narratives

Paulo Carvalho and Thomas Tamisier[(⊠)]

Luxembourg Institute of Science and Technology (LIST), 41, Rue du Brill,
4422 Belvaux, Grand Duchy of Luxembourg
thomas.tamisier@list.lu

Abstract. Storytelling is a main source of information for cultural heritage. Many of our knowledge comes indeed from discussing events with other people. This paper addresses the benefits of storytelling for preserving cultural heritage. After introducing a policy for storing, harnessing and reusing personal and common narratives, it analyses the concrete impact of this storytelling policy for unleashing the information potential of the narratives.

Keywords: Storytelling · Common historical heritage · Narrative information

1 Introduction

Cultural heritage is the collection of past tangible and intangible facts or events that are of major importance to understand the present [1]. It is increasingly understood as digital memory [2]. One way to build historical information proceeds from the collection of narratives by people who lived or witnessed significant events and may enlighten their interpretation [3]. Such interactive collection of narratives is defined as storytelling. The traditional archetype of storytelling is the representation of an elderly person telling a captivating story to a group, where everybody is quiet and listens carefully to the orator [4]. This paper specifically the relationships between storytelling activity and the interpretation and exploitation of collected narratives. In particular, we investigate how the value of collected stories can be increased through a policy to store and foster the reuse of the information that may be extracted from them.

2 Extracting Information Through Narratives

Storytelling is used in several fields such as historical heritage [5], health monitoring [6, 7], general and specialised education [8], therapy [9]. While storytelling is an important source of information for cultural heritage, extracting this information is not a straightforward process and using it in various context poses a number of challenges [1]. In the scope of the Locale project we are building a storytelling platform to collect and interpret stories about facts and events that occurred in Luxembourg and the Greater Region within the period 1945–1960. In that purpose, we visited several retirement homes in Luxembourg to interview some residents who demonstrated

© Springer International Publishing AG 2017
Y. Luo (Ed.): CDVE 2017, LNCS 10451, pp. 85–89, 2017.
DOI: 10.1007/978-3-319-66805-5_11

particular interest in the period. In total, more than five hours of interviews were recorded, which allowed us to extract new and personal stories regarding this fast evolving period.

2.1   Context of Data Collection

Storytelling narratives are told by people. When dealing with people, we deal with different ages, various kinds of experiences, personalities and ways of thinking and coming from several social classes. People are emotional. The way how a story is narrated depends directly on the person who is telling it. Depending on the story being told, the person can turn it more affective and personal [10], which may lead to a different perception of the story when told by another person. The understanding of two different stories about the same subject coming from different sources opens the possibility of different interpretations. This leads to problems related with the level of trust given to the person who has told the story but also to the story itself. Criteria like reputation, easy understanding, error-free are well known in the field of data quality [11]. If these criteria are not met, the value of the narratives is compromised and may lead to their becoming useless. The challenge when obtaining stories from a narrator is to motivate the narrator to stay unbiased so the obtained information stays the most neutral possible. The interviews were about collecting stories from after World War II. This implied discussing about the times lived during and after the war. Obviously, it is difficult for some of the interviewed to stay completely neutral: they directly felt the impact of the war, whether by personally experienced events (among which a lot were important historical ones) or by events lived by people close to them. Sometimes, the narrator also discussed about events happened before the war to emphasize the differences between and after the war and how Luxembourgish population in general was impacted. The physical conditions of the narrator (which may include health and memory problems) had to be appropriately taken into account (e.g. breathing difficulty may turn the understanding of the conversation very difficult). When the conversation was interrupted because of the need to rest, it may be challenging to regain the flow of the narrative from the point where it had been stopped. Therefore, different causes related to the intrinsic content of the story as well as external features makes the collection of stories challenging. It becomes then even more complicated to extract valuable and reliable information from people when the subject turns around a sensible theme - like war memories. Therefore a lot of time in the interview and the immediate pre-processing of the records was invested to successfully get a significant repository of narratives about the period of interest.

2.2   Technical Processing of Data

After collecting the narratives of interviewed participants, we investigated and teste several technical solutions to translate the audio recorded into textual form.

1. **Fully-automatic audio to text transcription.** The idea is to automatically convert the narratives either live during the interviews or by post-processing the records.

Different up-to-date solutions are available: Transcribe [12], Google Speech API [13], Speechnotes Android application [14]. We encountered several issues when applying automatic audio to text transcription. With Transcribe, we have executed a python script in order to process the audio files of our interviews. The result is not what we have expected. Some words and small sentences are recognized. But others are completely wrong. We also tried Google Speech API but the result is similar. Finally, with Speechnotes, used to transcribe in real time a conversation, things went well when there is only one speaker, who speaks clearly and slowly. However, when another voice comes into the conversation, the application seems to have difficulties to continue its work and stops transcribing.

2. **Manual audio to text transcription.** This method consist of listening to the audio recordings and fully transcribing the content by hand. Initially, this was intended for only a small subset of the stories.
3. **Semi-automatic audio to text transcription.** This combines the 2 previous approaches in order to manually fill values not detected by the software used or correct the errors introduced, and allows to save time for processing manually the most critical records.

Based on the results obtained with these 3 approaches, the solution we have retained was to execute manually the transcription of all files recorded during the interviews. We took this decision because of the lack of quality from the results obtained by applying an automatic transcription but also because a mixed (automatic + manual) transcription would not be reliable enough. Indeed, automatic transcription introduced many errors and wrong transcription that we would not be able to detect without doing a manual transcription.

3   From Personal Narratives to Common Knowledge

We therefore arrived to obtain the content of audio conversations into text files. We are thus in possession of raw text, without any kind of processing. However, this is not enough to exploit the information collected. The content must be somehow interpreted for extracting useful stories. Furthermore, a dedicated format for the stories must be defined in order that the identified stories may be processed using dedicated applications, and through a web interface or a web service.

From the full text corresponding to an interview, the first task is to identify the stories it contains. Then we need to identify each sentence in order to extract the stories without ambiguity. Finally, for each sentence, we have to interpret its meaning and value within the narrative. For that, specific terms of the sentences must be recognized such as a person, a period, a local. Entity Recognition (ER) is a good candidate [15] to perform this task. Applying the correct ER technique gives the means to interpret each sentence and each story included on the extracted text. For instance, in the sentence "Before [Kirchberg] was nothing but fields. Afterwards, the [European Institutions] were installed and everything changed", the entity [Kirchberg] must be recognized as a location and the entity [European Institutions] must be recognized as an organisation.

So far, we processed 267 raw stories, and we still have some audio files waiting for transcription to extend the content of Locale storytelling platform.

The subsequent task is to store the stories into a data structure allowing to access and interpret them for building a common knowledge. The Locale platform is first dedicated to a centralized knowledge base that will be updated by the inclusion of new stories. Furthermore, Locale contributes to the reuse of the historical knowledge, in particular for unveiling the social and historical evolution of the country and its surroundings in the European context. In this regard, Locale relies on advanced text mining and multimedia visualisation for querying stories (e.g. by people, place, event...), navigating among them, exploring their relationships, as well as interpreting and representing their content from different points of view. Locale store the stories using the open JSON format, to prepare the reuse of the platform by the public at large and ease processing operations including visualisation relying on the D3js.org library [16].

4 Conclusion

Obtaining precise and reliable narratives from a given population is not straightforward. Difficulties may arise from different causes, such as weak health or lack of memory. This becomes even more challenging when the narration involves specific period or events that impacted life. The narratives may be impacted by feelings and opinions which may result in imprecise or even incorrect information. We have shown that if some solutions to extract audio into text files are available, they cannot be yet used massively and fully automatically. We therefore support that executing a manual audio-to-text transcription is nowadays the most efficient way. Furthermore, by analysing how stories can be extracted from raw text, we draw a first step toward the completion of automated tools. Entity Recognition is an adequate solution to identify topics involved in sentences in order to understand their meaning and pave the way to the automatic processing of stories. Last, some clues and indications have been presented to organise the repository of stories in order that they can be exploited and reused. Such an adequate strategy is indeed crucial to aggregate stories, increase the potential to reuse them, and finally enhance the value of collected information.

References

1. Vecco, M.: A definition of culturel heritage: from the tangible to the intangible. J. Cult. Herit. **11**(3), 321–324 (2010)
2. Kalay, Y., Kvan, T., Affleck, J.: New Heritage: New Media and Cultural Heritage. Routledge, Abingdon (2007)
3. Thomson, A.: The Oxford Handbook of Oral History. OUP, Oxford (2011)
4. Crawford, C.: On Interactive Storytelling. New Riders, Indianapolis (2012)
5. Lombardo, V., Damiano, R.: Storytelling on mobile devices for cultural heritage. New Rev. Hypermed. Multimed. **18**, 11–35 (2012)
6. Chelf, J.H., et al.: Storytelling: a strategy for living and coping with cancer. Cancer Nurs. **23**(1), 1–5 (2000)

7. Gubrium, A.: Digital storytelling: an emergent method for health promotion research and practice. Health Promot. Pract. **10**(2), 186–191 (2009)
8. Alterio, M.: Learning Through Storytelling. Higher Education Academy, York (2002)
9. Parker, T.S., Wampler, K.S.: Changing emotion: the use of therapeutic storytelling. J. Marital Fam. Ther. **32**(2), 155–166 (2006)
10. Papacharissi, Z., de Fatima Oliveira, M.: Affective news and networked publics: the rhytms of news storytelling on #Egypt. J. Commun. **62**(2), 266–282 (2012)
11. Pipino, L., Lee, Y., Wang, R.: Data quality assessment. Commun. ACM **45**(4), 211–218 (2002)
12. Really, W.: Transcribe (2017). https://transcribe.wreally.com
13. Google. Cloud speech API Beta (2017). https://cloud.google.com/speech
14. Ilan, R.: Speechnotes (2017). https://play.google.com/store/apps/details?id=co.speechnotes.speechnotes
15. Toral, A., Munoz, R.: A proposal to automatically build and maintain gazetteers for named entity recognition. In: Proceedings of EACL Conference (2006)
16. Bostock, M., Ogievetsky, V., Heer, J.: Data-driven documents. IEEE Trans. Vis. Comput. Graph. **17**(12), 2301–2309 (2011)

Collaborative Storytelling Using Gamification and Augmented Reality

Irene M. Gironacci, Rod Mc-Call, and Thomas Tamisier[✉]

Luxembourg Institute of Science and Technology (LIST), 41, rue du Brill,
4422 Belvaux, Grand Duchy of Luxembourg
thomas.tamisier@list.lu

Abstract. This paper describes a collaborative digital story telling environment which uses a tablet, an augmented reality visor and an advanced data mining back-end system. This paper primarily focuses on collaboration as a method of designing new stories (from new or existing contents), sharing the experiences and improving sense of presence, flow and place. It further enhances the experience through the use of gamification to encourage collaboration and interaction between users. It also examines issues relating to visualization of stories.

Keywords: Collaborative storytelling · Gamification · User involvement · Visual environment · Augmented reality

1 Introduction

Collaborative storytelling is a means to share and preserve historical knowledge and especially personal historical accounts that might not be included in standard historical literature. It relies on the quality of interactions between storytellers and authors and its main challenge lies in the contextual aspect and complexity of the information, in particular related to interpretations of words, emotional reactions and cultural background. The approach described here explores methods used to collect, create and work with location-based historical content that are implemented in the Locale platform for authoring and sharing multi-media historical heritage content about the period of 1945–1960 in Luxembourg and the surrounding Greater Region [1].

Locale's main features are as follows: first, advanced text and data mining functionalities provide useful knowledge for selective actions to be performed by the platform users; second, collaborative visualizations allow different users to share views of the same content with different focuses, and provide an intuitive way for navigating into complex information; last, different modalities of exploring and editing stories enhance the spatial dimension and feeling of flow and immersion by using a desktop, a mobile device, or an interactive augmented reality equipment.

This paper discusses the efficiency of collaboration and augmented reality in Locale to visualize the large amount of data while increasing the level of engagement by the end-user.

© Springer International Publishing AG 2017
Y. Luo (Ed.): CDVE 2017, LNCS 10451, pp. 90–93, 2017.
DOI: 10.1007/978-3-319-66805-5_12

2   State of the Art and Challenges

This section details the fundamental concepts addressed in Locale to support the navigation within a range of stories and increase the potential of interaction about location-based historical information through data visualization and augmented reality.

New Sense of Time, Space and Presence. Through enhancing the sense of place, Locale aims to make the user feel as present in the story as possible. There are many definitions of place [2] and presence [3], however, in general place is a product of physical properties and higher level emotional aspects, while presence is characterized by the feeling of being present within a location and sometimes with others. Early prior work found that users can feel as if they are present within digital story telling environments [4, 5] and that augmented reality games can also have an impact on sense of presence [6].

Augmented Reality. Locale seeks to create a new sense of place, where place is defined as the physical environment (space) plus augmented contents. For example, a route can be created which contains multiple stopping points, as the user walks along they can listen to stories about places, people and events at different locations. Furthermore, if there are many layers or stories at a specific location about a particular person or event this may give them a stronger sense of history and importance and ultimately shape their understanding of that place.

User Experience. Locale provides new ways of interaction through the use of an AR headset, a new type of non-command user interface able to track user movements and use them to create user interface elements the user can interact with. Additional visualizations provide: indications of the degree of agreement/disagreement between sources of information available and links between related information. The overall picture is of an interactive and immersive storytelling experience where the user can interact with the contents of the story (notably images and 3D models) in a simpler and natural way, for example using gestures or voice.

Gamification. Gamification [7] is the process of adding game-like elements to non-gaming environments. This research aims to use some attractive gamification features to encourage collaborative storytelling, such as: achievement, interpersonal relationship, and role-playing [8]. In fact, the users involved in the case study should achieve a set of goals (achievement), share different tools, experience and knowledge to reach the goals (interpersonal relationship), and cooperate to reach the goals within time limit (role-playing). For example, a goal could be to find an object related to the story in one of the locations and to read more detailed information about this object (such as ID or owner). This information can in turn be added to the Locale platform.

3   Case Study

Our previous work on location-based augmented reality games [5] illustrated the value of using collaboration (using two hand held PCs) to assist in collaborative problem solving and to improve user experience. The Locale platform builds on this idea in order to offer a concept aiming specifically at a digital story telling context. Locale enables thus the end-users to elaborate on their story from both an evolving base of content and a set of technical features constantly updated.

We considers two Locale users equipped with different tools, one with an AR headset (called *Uh*) and a smartwatch [9] and the other a tablet (called *Ut*) and they collaborate via voice chat. For example, *Ut* has already uploaded to the Locale system some contents (e.g. text, pictures, audio and locations) and created a story on the fly about the period shortly after WW2. The story is a real one, and is comprised of several locations which together act as a storyboard for the story. *Uh* should follow the path of locations included in the story and reach some goals in each location (e.g.: *Uh* should find in a location a 3D object similar to the one displayed in their AR headset). At each step, *Uh* communicates to *Ut* some additional data from the real world (e.g.: further information on objects, places, etc.) and *Ut* updates the story on the Locale system with more detailed data. The overall picture is of a system that is progressively populated with data obtained from an interactive and collaborative gamified experience (see Fig. 1).

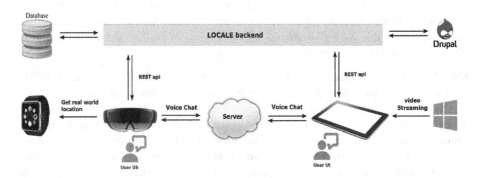

Fig. 1. Locale augmented reality architecture

Within the context of Locale, this new architecture defines a scenario-oriented *connectivist* learning framework, i.e. where tasks assigned to a user (*Uh*) are mediated by a tutor (*Ut*) responsible for organizing relevant information to perform them [10]. This framework serves as a complete test bench to assess the contribution of augmented-reality environments in the preservation of personal historical accounts, by improving awareness of ambient and spatial aspects of real-world location, facilitating the navigation within location-based information, and interacting with content through the data processing features provided by the application backend.

4 Conclusion

An interactive and collaborative storytelling system with advanced functionalities for exploring multidimensional data using various data mining strategies has been presented. The architecture was devised to increase the value of digital storytelling and to increase collaboration between users through the use of gamification and two devices. Through an in-depth integration of data processing techniques and an elaborated scenario-driven interface, this study also opens up new opportunities in collaborative visualization. In particular, it showcases the power of augmented reality environments in different fields relying on interaction between users and content through different learning paradigms such as connectivism.

References

1. Tamisier, T., McCall, R., Gheorghe, G., Pinheiro, P.: Visual analytics for interacting on cultural heritage. In: Luo, Y. (ed.) CDVE 2016. LNCS, vol. 9929, pp. 296–299. Springer, Cham (2016). doi:10.1007/978-3-319-46771-9_38
2. Gustavson, P.: Meanings of place: everyday experience and theoretical conceptualizations. Environ. Psychol. **21**, 5–16 (2001). Elsevier
3. Lombard, M., Ditton, T.: At the heart of it all: the concept of presence. J. Comput.-Mediat. Commun. **3**(2) (1997)
4. Wei, H., Bizzocchi, J., Calvert, T.: Time and space in digital game storytelling. Int. J. Comput. Games Technol. (2010)
5. McCall, R.: Mobile phones, sub-culture and presence. In: Proceedings of the Workshop on Mobile Spatial Interaction at ACM Conference on Human Factors in Computing Systems (CHI) (2007)
6. McCall, R.: The final timewarp: using form and content to support player experience and presence when designing location-ware mobile augmented reality games. In: Proceedings of the ACM International Conference on Designing Interactive Systems (2012)
7. Deterding, S., Sicart, M., Nacke, L., O'Hara, K., Dixon, D.: Gamification: using game-design elements in non-gaming contexts. In: Proceedings of ACM Conference on Human Factors in Computing Systems (CHI) (2011)
8. Hsu, S.H., Change, J., Lee, C.: Designing attractive gamification features for collaborative storytelling websites. Cyberpsychol. Behav. Soc. Netw. **16**(6), 428–435 (2013)
9. Gary, M.: Smartwatch-based activity recognition: a machine learning approach. In: IEEE-EMBS International Conference on Biomedical and Health Informatics (2016)
10. D'all Acqua, L., Santo, M.: Orientism, the basic pedagogical approach of PENTHA ID model vs. 2, to manage decisions in unpredictability conditions. In: Proceedings of World Congress of Engineering and Computer Science (2014)

A Multiplayer Game with Virtual Interfaces

C. Marin, J. Cloquell, Y. Luo, and B. Estrany$^{(\boxtimes)}$

Universitat de les Illes Balears, Cra. de Valldemossa, km 7.5,
07122 Palma, Illes Balears, Spain
{y.luo,tomeu.estrany}@uib.es

Abstract. This article discusses the development of a simple webapp, based on the famous pong game, using our Internet of Interfaces (I-o-I) architecture, the application uses virtual interfaces for its interaction. The game allows the interaction of a variable number of users and different forms of interaction.

Keywords: Virtual interface · Pong game · I-o-I · Internet of interfaces · Web application · Gyroscope · Accelerometer

1 Introduction

Pong (or Tele-pong) was a video game of the first generation video consoles published by Atari, created by Nolan Bushnell and released on the 29th November in 1972. The aforesaid game is based on the sport of table tennis (or ping pong) [1].

Our example application, pong4, is based on the original idea of this popular and simple game, our aim is to show the ease with which it is possible to develop virtual interfaces that are able to control client applications and web pages by means of our I-o-I infrastructure (Internet of Interfaces), using in turn web pages acting as interaction devices.

Moreover, we show the possibility to develop applications in a collaborative interaction environment as different players interacting on the same client application or web pages can intervene in the game. It is important to observe that, in our view, a client web page and a client application are practically the same thing.

The fact of choosing a simple interaction game, it is not accidental, we choose this game for the simplicity of the players' interaction. These can only move the paddle upwards or downwards and this allows as to focus on our goals without the need of generating a complex code for the interaction. This means, we focus on the necessary components for the interaction among the different system elements and their proper operation.

The extension to a more complex interaction is just a matter of code complexity in order to control a wide range of interaction events, but the process of managing these components and the information exchange among them will follow exactly the process followed by this simple game.

© Springer International Publishing AG 2017
Y. Luo (Ed.): CDVE 2017, LNCS 10451, pp. 94–102, 2017.
DOI: 10.1007/978-3-319-66805-5_13

2 The I-o-I Architecture

The pong4 is an example of an application integrated in our I-o-I architecture based on WebSockets. For a better understanding on how this game works, it is important to describe some components of the I-o-I system. In this case three elements are distinguished: the client application, the virtual interface server module and the virtual interface. We describe these components hereunder.

The Virtual Interface Server Module: This is a special module that allows multiple virtual interaction devices to be connected to it and offer these elements through a single WebSocket. In general, web pages designed as virtual interaction devices will be connected to this module and for the purpose of connecting to the client web pages through this module. In principle, a single virtual interface module is used for all interface clients and virtual interface pages. Although it would be possible to use several if necessary (Fig. 1).

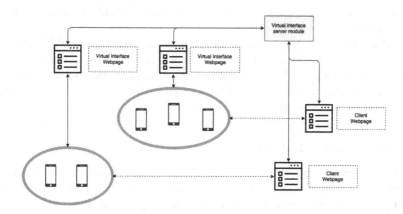

Fig. 1. Diagram on the connection of the different components integrating the system.

Client Applications: Client applications or client webpages are those that incorporate a small piece of code, which allows them to connect to the appropriate WebSockets server, in our case it is connected to a virtual interface server. Once the connection is made, they obviously interpret this information to give it an appropriate use.

In general, they will be web pages that want to use the interaction devices but they can also be applications installed in a specific system. They can also handle virtual mice and keyboards on a conventional computer with some added software.

A special case is those web pages acting as virtual interfaces and that, in essence, are the interaction servers. But in our architecture, they are treated in the same way except that when being connected to the WebSockets server, they will indicate their own function and the client page to which they would send their interaction data. The virtual interface server module will perform the data sending action.

Virtual Interface Webpage: This component, which must be adapted to the device executing it, acts as interaction device on either client application or web page. It is important to mention that for the fact of being a simple web page it admits numerous designs of interaction interfaces.

3   The Pong4 Game: System Description

It is described both the general view of the system and a detailed description of each of the different elements in the aforesaid infrastructure, such as the Virtual Interface Server (VIS), the client application (pong4) and the virtual interface web page. In this case, the virtual interface requires a kind of smartphone device with acceleration sensors and gyroscope. These requirements are given by the design of the virtual interface which make use of them. The web page, which acts as the virtual interface, registers the movements of the x and y components of the device, being these used as the interaction parameters. It is crucial to observe that other interfaces permitting the interaction with the game without using these sensors could be designed, as for example, a slide button on a web page.

The different components are connected among them through the web technology of WebSockets. For its part, the VIS acts as the router, since it knows where to redirect all the messages it receives. That is to say, the messages sent from the virtual interface web page aiming the client state updating will be sent to the VIS so that it can redirect it to the corresponding client (Fig. 2).

3.1   Virtual Interface Server (VIS)

The VIS is a server developed with the NodeJs [3] technology whose main function is to act as router of WebSockets connections, as well as to store the clients and servers structure, as can be seen hereunder, and to generate a log file for each connected client, with the aim of being able to analyze the interactions between users and clients.

```
let VISStructure = [
        {
                id: 1023,
                maxUser: 3,
                servers: [ 12, 14 ]
        }
]
```

As it can be seen in Fig. 3, the actions of the router's functions are:

1. To accept or reject new users or clients' requests:
   (a) The clients are rejected when an existing client has that same identifier, otherwise a client structure is created, with its identifier, the maximum number of users it accepts and the identifiers of current servers.
   (b) However, the servers can be rejected for several reasons, the client it wants to connect either doesn't exist or doesn't have space to accept other servers. If the connection to the server is accepted, it is added to the structure of the client requested.

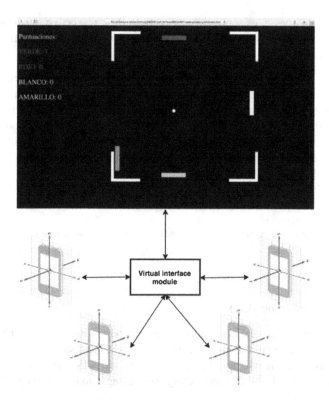

Fig. 2. This diagram shows the connection between the virtual interfaces web pages and the client application by means of the Virtual interface module.

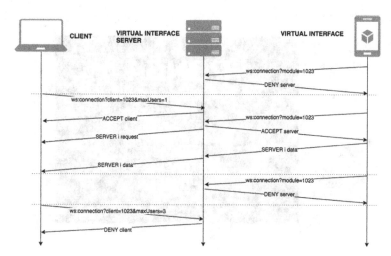

Fig. 3. General diagram on the Virtual Interface Infrastructure where the three characteristic elements of it are distinguished. The client is the one receiving the information from the different server devices and updating its state according to this information. The Virtual Interface Server is the main node of the infrastructure as it acts as router redirecting the messages to their receivers. Finally, the virtual interface provides the client with the interaction information to update its own.

2. To redirect the messages sent by the servers to their respective clients solely with the server's identifier, since the VIS has the routes that the messages must follow at its disposal.

Finally, by generating the log of the messages received by the VIS, the patterns of the players can be analyzed since both the identification of the own server and the type of movement it has done are available. In the case of pong4, the type of movement or the extra information it receives, is the normalized value of the beta coordinate and gamma the mobile, as it is explained at the point *Virtual Interface* with which the movements of all the devices can be reproduced throughout time. The log file format is the one that follows:

```
00:25:119 (Current TIMESTAMP)
Connection established with WebSocket
00:25:743
{id: 1, data: {beta: 678, gamma: 189}} (Server action)
00:25:782
{id: 1, data: {beta: 690, gamma: 190}}
```

3.2   Client Application (CA)

On the other side we have the client application, the pong4 itself. As it can be observed in the Fig. 4, the game start menu appears on the right hand side of the screen. When the application starts, it will try the connection to the VIS server, described in the previous point, as this is the one redirecting the messages to the clients and vice versa.

Fig. 4. After the connection between VIC and VIS, the latter sends the client the information to generate a QR code which the server devices will connect with. The URL which the QR connects with, is also indicated. For each accepted connection, a new player with an identifier, a nick name and a color will be generated.

In case it achieves the connection to the server, this client application will wait for the first server to connect to start the game.

By default, the game is based on a match to eliminate the rest of players and each time the amount of scored goals reaches the prearranged maximum, this player is eliminated as it can be observed in the Fig. 5. Another difficulty added to the game is the growth in the number of balls if the players fail to score the opponents.

Fig. 5. Depending on the amount of active players that have not been eliminated, the game map will be adapted, eliminating the players and closing the goals. In addition, in order to offer more competitiveness and playability, the option of increasing the number of balls every certain time interval has been added.

The way the paddles move on the screen depends on the messages received from the server. There are different types of messages, for instance *new connected server* or *game start* but in our case the message expected is the paddle movement. This message will be described whit detail in the next point. It should be said that the client receives normalized values between 0 and 1 which depend on the orientation of the virtual interface device.

3.3   Virtual Interface (VI)

The device that hosts the virtual interface can be any smartphone or tablet of the current market, no matter the operating system or the brand. The only requirement for it to work is to have a web browser HTML5 compatible, internet connection and, in our case, both a gyroscope and an accelerometer in order to detect the device orientation.

As it can be seen in Fig. 3, there are three types of messages between the virtual interface and the VIS:

- **ws:connection?module=1023&name=Carlos:** When creating the WebSocket, a request is generated to the VIS, which handles it according to its internal logic, already described previously. There are two answers to this request:
  - **ACCEPT SERVER:** This generates a unique id for the device and sends it to the virtual interface. In addition to indicating if it is the administrator of the requested client (1023 in our case).
  - **DENY SERVER:** The request is not accepted if there is no client or if the client doesn't accept more connected users.
- **SERVER and data:** Any information sent from the server to the client has the following format: *{id:idUser, data:object }*, where the field *data* can be the virtual interface data that must interact on the client state or the actions of the administrator server (for example start game) (Fig. 6).

Fig. 6. Screenshots of the virtual interface that sends the data to the client application. In the screen on the left, we show an insertion of credentials to access a specific client. On the right, we show the screen where the axes are calculated and the information send.

In the particular case of the *pong4*, which is the main topic in this article, the field *data* can be:

- Administrator actions: When the virtual interface has the administrator privileges, it can both start the game at any time it wants and indicate the maximum amount of points that a player can let in against before being eliminated.
- Status data: To move the paddles, we have opted to use HTML5 API to detect the device orientation [2] and sent it to the client application. In particular, the players on the left and on the right (green, yellow), use the Y axis while the other players use the X axis (red, lilac). The axes orientation in relation to the physical device, it is shown in Fig. 7.

A JavaScript library, called Gyro.js [4], which combines both the gyroscope and the accelerometer information has been used to obtain the movement data of the device and its orientation. With this information a normalization process is performed, so that a relative value is returned, despite the changes of degrees in the axes of the coordinates.

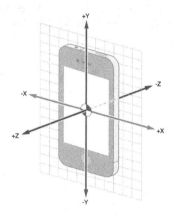

Fig. 7. This figure shows the axes orientation in relation to the physical device. (Color figure online)

4   Results

We have developed an example webapp, pong4, which allows the interaction of a variable number of users with a set of virtual interfaces using our I-o-I (Internet of Interfaces) architecture. The application can run on any device that supports web browsers compatible with HTML5 and webGL. Interaction devices can be diverse and are independent of the client application. It is necessary that the device running the client application and the devices running the virtual web page interface are connected to a local network or the internet.

5   Conclusions

The use of our I-o-I architecture, simplifies the development of applications with the need/possibility of interaction of multiple simultaneous users. It is also possible to use different virtual interfaces for this purpose so a multimodal interaction is possible. In addition, since the virtual interfaces are web pages, these interfaces can be adapted to different devices and to different methods of interaction, it is only necessary to adapt these virtual interfaces to the devices or to the preferences of the users.

References

1. Pong. Wikipedia. https://es.wikipedia.org/wiki/Pong. Accessed 01 July 2017
2. Detecting device orientation. Mozilla Developer Network. https://developer.mozilla.org/es/docs/Web/API/Detecting_device_orientation. Accessed 01 July 2017
3. Node.js is a JavaScript runtime. https://nodejs.org/en/. Accessed 01 July 2017
4. Gyro and Accelerometer information. Tom Gallacher. http://tomg.co/gyrojs. Accessed 01 July 2017

Enhancing Accuracy of Dynamic Collaborative Labeling and Matching Through Semantic Augmentation Method (SAM)

Saman Kamran[1,2]([✉]), Zaikun Xu[1], and Mehdi Jazayeri[1]

[1] Università della Svizzera italiana, 6900 Lugano, Switzerland
{saman.kamran,zaikun.xu,mehdi.jazayeri}@usi.ch, saman@COD.OOO
[2] COD Technologies Sagl, 6900 Lugano, Switzerland

Abstract. Social media are using several automatic, semi-automatic or even manual labeling approaches in order to match the shared contents with their users' interests. The low degree of Click Through Rate (CTR) on the social media platform, however, suggests that labeling of shared contents and users' active interests contain inaccuracies, leading to unsuccessful matching. One of the main reasons of unsuccessful matching is the heterogeneity of the labels assigned to the contents and users' interest. In our previous work, we have proposed the Interactive and Dynamic Collaborative Labeling (IDCOLAB) framework in order to collect homogeneous and commonly agreed opinion of a group of users who are knowledgeable about the assigned labels dynamically. An essential step of IDCOLAB is Semantic Augmentation Method (SAM) which enables collaborative labeling of shared contents by dynamically augmenting semantically related labels to labels assigned initially to the contents and users' interests. A goal of the augmentation process is to avoid irrelevant and noisy labels. We have applied SAM on COD which is a collaborative labeling platform based on IDCOLAB framework and evaluated SAM with two separate focus groups in the domains of Artificial Intelligence and Entrepreneurship.

Keywords: Emergent semantics · Collaborative labeling · Semantic labeling · Dynamic community formation · Knowledge sharing · Information retrieval · Recommender systems · Social semantic tagging systems

1 Introduction

The main purpose of many businesses and individuals who publish contents about their products, services or professions on the Web is to communicate them with relevant audiences. Reaching audiences who are interested in, passionate about, or even expert in, the content of the shared resources increases the chance of enlisting their engagement with those contents. Appearance of social networking platforms made on-line publishers optimistic about reaching and engaging more relevant users to their contents on the Web. Although social

© Springer International Publishing AG 2017
Y. Luo (Ed.): CDVE 2017, LNCS 10451, pp. 103–113, 2017.
DOI: 10.1007/978-3-319-66805-5_14

networking platforms have provided the opportunity of reaching larger number of audiences in a shorter time, they cannot yet guarantee the relevance of shared contents to users' current active interests and in consequence they have not been successful in increasing users' engagement. Most of the current popular social networking platforms have very low degree of Click Through Rate (CTR). CTR metric can show what percentage of the users who have visited a content (e.g. an advertisement) clicked on it for doing any type of further engaging activities with that content (i.e., reading, signing up, buying, etc.). Relevance of the content of the recommended resources to the current users' interest plays an important role for maximizing users' engagement. Statistics show much higher CTR on the specialized websites and weblogs that are providing very specific contents to their audience rather than general-purpose websites and weblogs. Even the most popular social networking platforms usually have less than one percent CTR which makes contents publishers skeptical about the effectiveness of their marketing campaigns on such platforms. The main reason of not being able to target relevant users is that such platforms have little information about their users general interests and even less on their current active interests. Most recommendations by social networking platforms are based on their users demographic information or history of their activities which cannot necessarily give useful information about their current active interests. In our previous work we have demonstrated the importance of dynamic and collaborative labeling over static and heterogeneous labeling [1]. Our proposed framework, called IDCO-LAB, addresses the shortcomings of the current social platforms for interactive and dynamic collaborative labeling and matching of the most relevant contents with the active users' current interests. In Sect. 2.1, We describe in detail the main issues in the design and architecture of current static platforms that are problematic for dissemination of "knowledge contents"[1]. In Sect. 2.2, we describe in brief the main steps of IDCOLAB framework which are described in detail in our previous paper [1]. The main contribution of IDCOLAB is in addressing the sparsity problem by introducing Semantic Augmentation Method (SAM).

A key contribution of SAM is in decreasing the heterogeneity among assigned labels that is one of the main existing challenges in most labeling and matching systems. This paper describes the mechanism and accuracy of SAM in decreasing heterogeneity and its empirical evaluation. In Sect. 3 we describe SAM in detail. We have applied SAM on COD which is a collaborative labeling platform based on the IDCOLAB framework and evaluated it in a challenging environment in the domains of Entrepreneurship and Artificial Intelligence.

2   Background and Motivation

This section covers the background and context of our work in the area of collaborative labeling platforms and recommendation systems for knowledge-sharing.

---

[1] By "knowledge content" here we mean those contents that are conveying some piece of knowledge for the relevant users. Such contents are usually specific and specialized. The other characteristic of knowledge contents is that they can be retrieved and used at any time by relevant users and they do not usually expire over time.

2.1   Problems of Static Social Platforms

The design and architecture of most current popular social networking platforms are aimed at "trendy contents"[2]. These platforms are not suitable for dissemination of "knowledge contents".

1. Users of such networks usually have to be directly connected to the profile page of the publishers to be able to have access to their shared contents. "Friendship connections" on Facebook[3], "following" users or "hashtags" on Twitter[4] or users' "connections" to the companies or users profiles on LinkedIn[5] or Xing[6] are not necessarily even representing the current active interests of their users.
2. Experience shows how fast trends can be spread on the current platforms mainly because of the density of users' connections and matching of temporal interest of the majority of users with trendy contents in the short period of time in which they are visible for the users. Professional knowledge contents, however, usually do not get much visibility because they have a very short time span to be visible for relevant professional users who have to be directly connected to the account of content publisher. Therefore, knowledge contents usually do not receive enough engagement and the results disappear fast because of the chronological ordering of most social networking platforms.
3. The feedback mechanisms of current social networking platforms are not suitable for collecting professional feedback on knowledge contents. Users' feedback mostly represent relevance or quality of the content publisher with its audience rather than the relevance or quality of the shared content itself. For instance, Facebook users are mostly showing their "thumbs up"(or "like") on the contents that are shared by their favorite connections. Therefore, those feedback cannot be used for evaluation of users' interests or relevance of the contents to their interests.
4. Although users' perception and interests might change over time, most current approaches assign fixed labels to them because they postulate a fixed source of knowledge. The new social systems need mechanisms which enable them to accurately recognize and label the shared contents and users' current interests dynamically.

In the design of IDCOLAB framework we have taken into consideration all the above mentioned problems of static social platforms for knowledge-sharing.

---

[2] By "trendy content" here we mean those contents that are usually very general and can be relevant to the majority of users. The relevance of such contents, however, usually diminishes rapidly because they typically represent some events. Therefore, the interest of people in those contents decreases drastically over time.
[3] https://www.facebook.com/.
[4] https://twitter.com/.
[5] https://www.linkedin.com/.
[6] https://www.xing.com/.

2.2 Interactive and Dynamic Collaborative Labeling (IDCOLAB) Framework

In order to match relevant knowledge contents with users' interests, we need to first identify both the contents and interests accurately. A variety of automatic and semi-automatic methods exist for extracting characteristics of the Web contents and users' tastes and assigning representative labels to them in order to match relevant entities to each other. In our initial experiments we tried to use the already existing systems to add dynamic contents' and users' labeling features. We could simulate our proposed approach by using the available labels on such systems but we could not evaluate the quality of our dynamic labeling and matching since we could not update the source of knowledge and improve the recommendations based on the new defined labels on such systems. In order to improve contents' and users' representation with relevant labels and in consequence increasing the accuracy of recommendations of relevant contents to the users' current active interests, we have designed the IDCOLAB framework. This framework enables dynamic labeling and matching of the users' current interests and shared contents on the Web in four main recursive steps described below. We have also developed COD[7] a new model based on IDCOLAB that has all the resources, elements and procedures that we designed for such an interactive and dynamic system.

(I) In the initial step, we create a knowledge-base which includes almost all the main concepts in a specific domain of knowledge and also semantic similarity measures between them through a source of knowledge like Wikipedia[8]. We use the initial extracted knowledge for semantic labeling of the shared contents and users' interests in the next step. We need to map plain keywords to the meaningful concepts that are defined in our knowledge-base in order to prevent ambiguous labeling.

(II) In the second step, IDCOLAB automatically recognizes Name Entities[9] from the content of the shared resources and also from the customized interest list of the users and assigns appropriate labels to them. We use Wikipedia articles (i.e. DBpedia concepts) as the reference of the semantic labels assigned to the shared contents and users' interests.

(III) In the third step, IDCOLAB automatically forms communities of relevant users around each of the shared contents based on the similarity of the initial assigned labels to the content of the shared resources and users' interests. Forming relevant communities of interested users around each of the shared contents, however, is a challenging task for the system considering the heterogeneity of the initial labels assigned to the users' interests and contents. In order to address this problem which can cause a low degree

---

[7] https://www.COD.OOO/.

[8] https://www.wikipedia.org/.

[9] Name Entity Recognizers (NER) like Alchemy API, DBpedia Spotlight, Extractive, OpenClalais and Zamanta could be used for mapping extracted keywords to meaningful concepts or semantic labels. In this experiment we used DBpedia Spotlight.

of similarity even between relevant entities, IDCOLAB uses Semantic Augmentation Method (SAM) which is described in Sect. 3.

(IV) In the fourth step, IDCOLAB gathers the collective opinion of the evolving communities of most relevant users based on their interactions with the assigned labels and improves the accuracy of labels' relevance to the contents and as a consequence the accuracy of recommendations dynamically.

As a proof of concept we have developed a model based on IDCOLAB called COD (Collaborative Ontology Development), which is an interactive and dynamic collaborative semantic labeling platform to facilitate exchange of knowledge contents. COD has been used as a model to evaluate our proposed framework in practice. The main contributions of the proposed framework is in the third and fourth steps. Fortunately, the results of the third and fourth steps also have beneficial effects on the preceding steps. Collaborative labeling activities of the relevant users formed around each of the shared contents can influence the weight of the assigned labels and as a result influence SAM in the formation of communities of more relevant users around each of the shared contents.

2.3   Related Work

COD falls in the category of social semantic tagging systems that allow for the annotation of resources with tags extended by semantic definitions and descriptions that also evolve collaboratively within the same system [2]. A few social semantic tagging systems exist, namely Bibsonomy [3], Faviki[10], GroupMe [4], Twine[11], Annotea[12] [5], Fuzzzy[13] [6] and SOBOLEO [7] with different features and purposes. To the best of our knowledge, only COD enables interactive and dynamic collaborative labeling while addressing the mentioned problems in Sect. 2.1. The IDCOLAB framework enables COD to form dynamic communities of most relevant users around each of the shared contents through augmenting semantically relevant labels to the initial heterogeneous labels that are assigned to the objects. Heterogeneity and sparsity of the labels assigned to the contents and users is one of the most common problems of the matching algorithms, referred to as the *"Cold Start"* problem in collaborative tagging and recommender systems [8]. Different solutions exist for addressing the sparsity problem. Many use *Principle Component Analysis (PCA)* or *Eigen Value Decomposition (EVD)* in *Latent Semantic Analysis (LSA)* in order to reduce dimensions or features [9]. Using such approaches removes less significant labels from the collection to achieve higher degree performance and similarity between objects. These approaches are not promising solutions for labeling systems, however, removing a label only because it is not used frequently in the whole collection (i.e., which is mostly the case in labeling systems), doesn't guarantee their low importance and representativeness for an object. Semantic Augmentation

---

[10] http://www.faviki.com.
[11] http://www.twine.com.
[12] http://www.annotea.org.
[13] http://www.fuzzzy.com.

Method (SAM) uses all the available labels and even augments more relevant labels in order to bring the similarity measure between each pair of objects to a higher or a lower degree with a reasonable performance.

3   Semantic Augmentation Method (SAM)

The IDCOLAB framework enables interactive and dynamic collaborative labeling and matching of the shared contents and users' interests based on the opinion of the formed communities of most relevant users around each of the shared contents. IDCOLAB uses SAM in order to address the initial sparsity problem known as *"Cold Start"* problem by augmenting semantically relevant labels to the heterogeneous but possibly relevant labels that are assigned to the users' interests and contents. In the design of SAM's algorithm we had to take into consideration the following challenges:

(1) **Heterogeneity of the Labels:** In most labeling systems, more than 90% of labels are used less than 10 times for the contents or users. Frequency of the labels assigned to the objects in both automatic and manual labeling systems always follows the *Power Law* pattern. Approaches that measure semantic similarities between concepts in most knowledge domains are reliable. SAM uses some of the most reliable semantic similarity metrics for choosing relevant labels to the assigned labels to each object. For instance, if label i is assigned to object j (i.e., by the system or by relevant users' collaboration), in addition to having frequency of assigning label i for object j with value X for the cell with index $[i, j]$ in the Label-Object (LO) matrix, we also increase the value of the cell $[k, j]$ of LO matrix with values "M times X". M is a value between zero and one that represents measured semantic similarity between label i and label k.

(2) **General vs. Specific Labels:** SAM's algorithm has to automatically decide on the labels that should be augmented to the used labels of an object and how much they should have influence on the similarities between objects. SAM cannot treat all the labels the same. In every domain of knowledge there exist some general and some specific concepts. Labels that are referring to the general concepts are relevant to many labels rather than labels that are referring to specific concepts. If many of the assigned labels to an object are specific, SAM considers more semantically relevant labels to the assigned labels to be augmented to the LO matrix. On the contrary, if the used label is referring to a general concept, few other very relevant labels will be augmented to the LO matrix. SAM automatically sets the threshold on the number of the labels that are going to be augmented for each label based on a) *Inverse Document Frequency (IDF)* or b) *Quantile*[14] metrics. If *IDF* of a concept in the whole collections of collected concepts

---

[14] In our experiments we considered quantile of distribution of each concept (or label) similarities with all the other concepts (labels) in the collection as one of the metrics for setting threshold on the number of labels going to be augmented.

(or labels) is higher, it usually means the labels that are referring to those concepts are more specific. In Entrepreneurship domain which *IDF* measures (i.e., or specificity of the labels) were more diverse, *IDF* was a good metric for choosing the threshold on the number of labels that should be augmented relevant to a used label. On the other hand, most of the labels in A.I. domain were referring to very specific concepts with very high and close measure of *IDF*s to each other. Therefore, we have decided to use quantile metric for choosing the threshold for number of relevant labels that SAM augments for each of the used labels.

(3) **Preventing Augmentation of Noisy Labels:** If SAM augments every related label to the used labels, after some time every object becomes relevant to every other object. Because every label is somehow relevant to the others, after several SAM iterations the LO matrix will be saturated. Therefore, SAM has to be selective in choosing augmented labels. Furthermore, By augmenting each of the semantically relevant labels to the used labels of an object we are adding a new feature for measuring similarities between objects. The new feature might bring two objects closer to, or further from, each other. If the augmented label is not relevant enough to the assigned labels, however, it will add a noisy feature which does not have the right effect on similarity measures between objects. Choosing the right source of knowledge for similarity measurements among the concepts in a domain of knowledge and also the right threshold for number of relevant labels that are going to be augmented for each label guarantee preventing augmentation of noisy labels.

(4) **Performance of Dynamic Semantic Augmentations:** We model the main entities of our collaborative labeling system with three disjoint sets of U (representing Users), L (representing Labels) and O (representing labeled contents or Objects) that are vertices of a hypergraph. We represent three facets of this hypergraph including its entities and interactions between them with three matrices LU, LO and OU. Values of the cells in these matrices represent the frequency of their co-occurrences. Having a proper data structure enables SAM to guarantee high performance dynamic retrieval and updates. We have optimized the mechanism of SAM algorithmically and mathematically in order to update correspondent cells of the large matrices in a reasonable time (e.g. in this experiment in less than a second we could choose and update correspondent labels of each object with more than 17'000 features) as soon as any interaction (i.e., new labeling or voting on the assigned labels by relevant users) occur on the COD platform.

4   Evaluation: SAM in Action

We had originally run an experiment on the "Entrepreneurship" domain which is still running on the COD platform. In that experiment we could show how IDCOLAB could enable "CODer Entrepreneurs" (or COD users who were interested in Entrepreneurship domain) to benefit from such a dynamic labeling and matching system [10]. We are still testing and improving the COD platform continuously in different aspects based on opinion of a focus group of entrepreneurs who are using it. However, in order to also examine the performance of the semantic recommender engine of the platform in utilizing Semantic Augmentation Method (SAM) and evaluate its accuracy in labeling and matching tasks we have designed a new challenging experiment. We have decided to run SAM this time on a completely different kind of domain. Unlike the broader domain of Entrepreneurship which includes very diverse concepts (or labels), we wanted to run this new experiment on a more specific domain which includes very specific concepts. We have done this new experiment on the focused domain of "Artificial Intelligence (A.I.)" to examine SAM on a more challenging labeling and matching task and observe the effect of domain breadth on its accuracy. If SAM could still (a) recognize relevant interests that are labeled with heterogeneous but semantically similar concepts or (b) distinguish interests that are labeled with some common concepts but with some diverse concepts that are not semantically relevant, in such a specific domain, we could have more confidence in its mechanism and accuracy. To do so, as subjects, we asked for volunteers among researchers of three institutes[15] whose domain of research were relevant to A.I. to participate in this experiment. After registering on the COD-AI platform that was the customized version of COD for this experiment, each of those A.I. researchers could search among Wikipedia concepts for those labels that could represent their current active interests. They could also bring some knowledge contents that were interesting for them and wanted to share with other interested researchers without knowing who might currently have similar interests. During this experiment, 92 knowledge contents were matched with the interest lists of 25 researchers based on semantic similarities between their labels. One of the main differences between this experiment and our previous experiment was users' behavior in labeling tasks. In Entrepreneurship domain we have a variety of startups, investors, business angels, venture capitalists with different backgrounds from "ICT", "Clean-Tech", "Bio-Tech" and so on who are using very diverse labels from different disciplines for the knowledge contents they share and also specifying their interests. In A.I. domain, however, although we had researchers with different backgrounds like "Statistics", "Robotics", "Computational Science", "Biology", "Computer Vision" and so on, all were labeling contents and their interests mostly with specific concepts that were often semantically relevant to each other. We have generated initial Label-Object (LO) and Label-User (LU) matrices based on the initially assigned labels to the shared contents or users' interests. As we expected, similar to any other labeling system, we had very high sparsity of 98% on the LO matrix and 96% on the LU matrix with 373 unique labels initially assigned to the contents and users' interests. After applying SAM on LO and LU matrices with 95%, 90% and 80% quantile thresholds, the number of unique labels increased to 4'709, 9'095 and

---

[15] (1) The Swiss A.I. Lab IDSIA (Istituto Dalle Molle di Studi sull'Intelligenza Artificiale), (2) Faculty of Informatics of University of Lugano, (3) Institute of Computational Science of the University of Lugano.

17'242 respectively. Although we could reduce sparsity of LO and LU matrices in Entrepreneurship domain by 18 to 20%, on the specific domain of A.I. sparsity of the matrices remained almost the same even though it has meaningful effects on semantic similarity measures. In Entrepreneurship domain we used *IDF* and in A.I. domain we used *Quantile* as the threshold for choosing the number of most relevant labels to the used labels to be augmented to an object. SAM could bring two labeled objects closer or farther by adding relevant similarity features (or labels). We have done a qualitative evaluation of the differences that SAM made on the measured semantic similarities of the objects based on labels assigned to the object before and after augmentations.

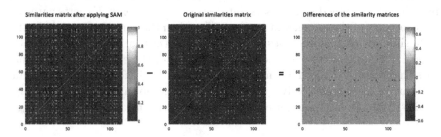

Fig. 1. The left matrix shows semantic similarity measures between objects (including both labeled users' interests and knowledge contents) after applying SAM in comparison with semantic similarities between objects before applying SAM in the middle matrix. The right matrix shows the effect of applying SAM by subtracting similarity matrices before and after semantic augmentation by SAM by subtracting the middle matrix from left matrix.

We picked the top 20 maximum and minimum values of the right matrix in Fig. 1 for qualitative evaluation of the SAM's accuracy. We showed the results to the experts in A.I. domain and asked their opinion on (a) the correctness of augmented labels to the users' interests and knowledge contents; and (b) on the correctness of their effect on objects similarity considering the augmentations.

For instance, one of the researchers has chosen "Python (programming language)", "Deep Learning" and "Artificial Neural Network" and the second researcher has chosen "Recurrent Neural Network" as the labels representing their current active interests on the COD platform. Considering only the initially assigned labels to the researchers' interests, the measured semantic similarity between these two researchers' was zero but after augmentation of semantically relevant labels to the initially assigned labels, the semantic similarity of researchers' interests has increased by 40%. Because there has been many relevant common labels between "Deep Learning" and "Recurrent Neural Network" (e.x, like "Convolutional Neural Network", "Types of Artificial Neural Networks", "Feedforward Neural Network" and so on) after semantic augmentations.

In the contrary example, "Information Retrieval" has been the only common label between two researchers' interests lists. However this common label could cause initial semantic similarities between these two researchers as high as 50% without considering their other diverse interests in this specific domain. But after applying SAM, the semantic similarity between these two researchers decreased to 15% considering low semantic similarity of their other used labels. Although both of the researchers were interested in "Information Retrieval" domain, considering their other interest labels, for example one of them is more interested in "Blogs" and the other one in "Sentiment Analysis" or "Topic Model" that are different specialties in "Information Retrieval" research domain. Therefore SAM correctly lowers the similarity measure in this specific domain.

These two examples show how well SAM can influence increasing or decreasing semantic similarity between objects by considering the combination of all the labels that are assigned to the users' interests or the contents. Experts agreed on the correctness of the augmentations by 97% and on the correctness of their effect on the similarities' changes considering the correctness of the augmented labels by 100%. This high degree of accuracy in opinion of the experts in A.I. domain shows that the SAM mechanism is behaving reasonably for (a) automatic augmentation of the semantically relevant labels to the initial heterogeneous labels and also (b) in having the right effect on the similarity measures between object.

5   Conclusions and Future Work

The goal of businesses and individuals who use social media is to generate and share contents that will help them reach and engage relevant audiences. In response, social media platforms use recommendation engines to match users with contents relevant to their interests. We propose IDCOLAB as a framework for dynamically updating of the users and Web contents identified characteristics based on the latest collective interactions and opinion of the evolving communities of most relevant users.

We have evaluated IDCOLAB with an implemented model of it called COD in the "Entrepreneurship" and "Artificial Intelligence" domains to see if we can improve accuracy of the recommender engine and as consequence reach and engagement opportunity of the relevant audiences to the shared contents in that domain.

IDCOLAB enables COD to form dynamic communities of interests around each of the shared contents by utilizing SAM which is augmenting semantically relevant labels to the heterogeneous labels that are assigned to the users' interests and knowledge contents manually or automatically.

In this paper we have presented the mechanism of SAM and the results of its evaluation in a more specific domain of Artificial Intelligence in contrast to our previous evaluation on a more general domain of Entrepreneurship. In our future work, we plan to also evaluate users' satisfaction on the recommendations based on SAM in these two domains directly on the COD platform.

Three general takeaways from our experiment with the two domains are:

- Choosing the right threshold for augmentation of semantically relevant labels to the initial labels should depend on the broadness of the domain. According to our experiments, IDF is a good metric if the domain is broad and we have both general and specific concepts. $Quantile$, on the other hand, is a better metric for setting the threshold when the domain is more specific.

- Although done commonly, removing dimensions (labels) by using PCA is not a good approach for labeling systems because it removes labels just because they are used rarely in the collection. While it is true that the frequency of labels in most labeling systems is low, mere frequency does not indicate a labels' lack of importance or representativeness of the object. SAM could address the heterogeneity problem among the assigned labels by augmenting semantically relevant labels to the initial labels while preventing noisy augmentation.
- SAM is capable of increasing or decreasing the initial similarity among objects automatically based on the examination of other labels. Our experiment indicates that the increase and decrease were successful according to expert evaluation in Entrepreneurship and Artificial Intelligence domains.

References

1. Kamran, S., Jazayeri, M.: Dynamic content and user identification in social semantic tagging systems. In: Luo, Y. (ed.) CDVE 2015. LNCS, vol. 9320, pp. 36–47. Springer, Cham (2015). doi:10.1007/978-3-319-24132-6_5
2. Braun, S., Schora, C., Zacharias, V.: Semantics to the bookmarks: a review of social semantic bookmarking systems. In: Proceedings of I-KNOW (2009)
3. Hotho, A., Jaschke, R., Schmitz, C., Stumme, G.: Bibsonomy: a social bookmark and publication sharing system. In: CS-TIW06. Aalborg University Press, Aalborg (2006)
4. Abel, F., Henza, F., Krause, D., Plappert, D., Siehndel, P.: GroupMe! where semantic web meets web 2.0. In: Proceeding of the 6th International Semantic Web Conference (2007)
5. Koivunen, M.: Semantic authoring by tagging with annotea social bookmarks and topics. In: Proceedings of the Semantic Authoring and Annotation Workshop at the International Semantic Web Conference, ISWC (2006)
6. Lachica, R., Karabeg, D.: Quality, relevance and importance in information retrieval with fuzzy semantic networks. In: Proceeding of TMRA 2008, University of Leipzig LIV (2008)
7. Zacharias, V., Braun, S.: SOBOLEO: social bookmarking and lightweight ontology engineering. In: Proceedings of the Workshop on Social and Collaborative Construction of Structured Knowledge at WWW 2007, vol. 273. CEUR Workshop Proceedings (2007)
8. Bollen, D., Halpin, H.: An experimental analysis of suggestions in collaborative tagging. In: IEEE/WICI/ACM International Joint Conference on Web Intelligence and Intelligent Agents Technology, Milan, Italy, pp. 108–115 (2009)
9. Yang, Y.H., Bogdanov, D., Herrera, P., Sordo, M.: Music retagging using label propagation and robust principal component analysis. In: Proceeding of the 21st International Conference on World Wide Web. ACM, New York (2012)
10. Kamran, S., Jazayeri, M., Ettefagh, T.: CODer entrepreneurs: how entrepreneurs can benefit from a dynamic social semantic tagging system. In: Proceedings of the 19th ACM Conference on Computer Supported Cooperative Work and Social Computing Companion, San Francisco, California, USA, pp. 305–308 (2016)

mSIREMAP: Cooperative Design
for Monitoring Teacher's Classes
in K-12 Schools

Manuel J. Ibarra[1], Angel F. Navarro[2], Vladimiro Ibañez[3],
Wilfredo Soto[1], and Waldo Ibarra[4(✉)]

[1] School of Informatics and Systems Engineering,
Micaela Bastidas National University of Apurímac, Abancay, Peru
manuelibarra@gmail.com, wilsotopal@gmail.com
[2] School of System Engineering, Jose Maria Arguedas National
University of Apurímac, Andahuaylas, Peru
angelnr22@gmail.com
[3] Faculty of Informatics and Statistic, National University
of Altiplano Puno, Puno, Peru
viqibanezquispe@gmail.com
[4] School of Informatics and Systems Engineering, San Antonio
Abad National University of Cusco, Cusco, Peru
ibarrazambrano@yahoo.es

Abstract. Nowadays, mobile-based data collection can advantageously replace paper-and-pencil questionnaires. The data rate production is very high and the to collect and store them are increasing as fast as the strategies for analysing and processing reducing the time for data processing. This paper describes how to improve traditional paper based methodologies with a mobile-based question-naires approach. The mSIREMAP system was tested by monitors, persons who supervise the teacher's classes, and teachers from Apurimac Peru. The monitors used the mobile based questionnaires to gather the information from the classes. To validate this proposal, we used focus groups and daily meetings methodology. The proposed strategy was tested with 10865 mobile-based questionnaires in 1453 schools during the years 2015 and 2016. A mobile device based questionnaire was developed using a cooperative design where the users are involved during all the phases of the Software Development Life Cycle, SDLC, providing immediate feedback to the development team to correct designs and performance specially in the user interface. The test result shows that monitors are satisfied with this new approach of filling the questionnaires out using mobile devices due to the ease of use, quick report generation, and decision making for teacher's classes improvement.

Keywords: Monitoring · Cooperative design · Data visualisation · Mobile devices · Questionnaire · Teacher · Class session · Tablet

© Springer International Publishing AG 2017
Y. Luo (Ed.): CDVE 2017, LNCS 10451, pp. 114–122, 2017.
DOI: 10.1007/978-3-319-66805-5_15

1 Introduction

Teacher's Pedagogical Practice Monitoring. To meet the fourth commitment: *"Accompaniment and monitoring of the pedagogical practice in Schools"*, one of the Eight School Management Commitments given by the government of Peru [1], the Director (the Principal in a School) promotes pedagogical practices monitoring to improve the teacher's performance in their schools. How can a teacher improve the pedagogical practices in K-12 schools (K-12 comprises the sum of primary and secondary education in Peru)?, through the accompaniment and monitoring promoted by the school principal. There are three important aspects to conduct adequately the monitoring task: *pedagogical use of time, use of pedagogical tools* and *use of educational materials*. These three axes imply respectively: (a) prioritizing the development of high cognitive demand activities, reducing those that do not necessarily contribute to the achievement of learning; (b) use of pedagogical tools provided by the Ministry of Education, called "learning routes", guidelines for curriculum planning, learning sessions or others, with the aim of guaranteeing learning achievements; (c) use of educational materials and resources distributed by the Ministry of Education.

According to González et al. [2], an evaluative culture can be defined as the set of values, agreements, traditions, beliefs and thoughts that an educational community attaches to the action of evaluation. Bolseguí and Fuguet [3], point out that the evaluative culture is an evolving concept that refers to evaluate on an ongoing basis. The evaluation processes and functions require multi-dimensional variables and has a high reliance on effective information communication among DRE (from Spanish Dirección Regional de Educación), UGEL (from Spanish Unidad de Gestión Educativa), School (in Spanish Institución Educativa or IE), Director and Teachers [4].

After the monitoring process, it is necessary to analyse and interpret the results and it is important that data be properly displayed; this topic has been widely discussed by the authors around data visualization [5]. Most frequently, a key feature of such an approach is to show relationships between different data groups of a given statistical selection to compare relative proportions between several indicators [6].

Interactive Data Visualization. Interactive data visualisation is a basic concept on how a reader or writer (person that inputs data to the system or person that sees the report results in different representations) can interact with the information. The readers want to customise the variables of the report, use dashboards panels and interact with queries for data interpretation in multiples devices including personal computers, mobile devices like cell phones or tablets [7]. The writers prefer enter data using digital questionnaires similar to inputting data in paper written questionnaires. However, it's necessary to define clearly the dataset and data definition, intuitive user interfaces, because data visualisation by itself can't automatically reveal the meaning and story behind it, this means that data visualisation is more than simply display raw data with visual representations [8]. Displaying numeric results is more attractive for people's attention. Showing the information using shapes, statistical graphs, with different colours, enabling sense-making in different layers [9] is better than simple tables or plain text values.

Collecting Data with Questionnaires. During the past years, collecting data using paper based questionnaires was a good traditional method; nevertheless, it has some problems described as follows: (a) difficulty to process huge amount of questionnaires (b) expensive cost of paper base questionnaires (c) time delay in the systematization of data for subsequent queries and reports (d) expensive cost in translating paper based questionnaires to centralised databases, (e) in case of error, it is difficult to modify the marked response.

Online data collection could advantageously replace paper based questionnaires in some cases, because, it can reduce the logistic burden, the cost and the duration of data processing [10]. Also, in cases of mistakes, it is possible to change immediately the marked response.

This article presents a strategy for monitoring teacher's classes in Apurimac-Peru; for this purpose, a mobile and web based system was implemented to collect data using tablet-based questionnaire. After collecting data using the mobile-based questionnaire, the system processes the data and shows the obtained results using statistical charts sharing achievement results for each teacher. This information is useful for the Monitor and Principal who can then use improvement strategies to help underperforming teachers. In addition, the tool also allows you to display statistical graphs of the results by teacher, by school, by province and other options. This also allows the Directors of DRE, UGEL and School to make decisions to improve teacher's class session.

Section 2 of this article presents and discusses the work related to data visualisation, web based and paper based questionnaires and cooperative design outcomes; Sect. 3 explains the design and implementation of the proposed strategy; Sect. 4 explains the evaluation methodology used to validate the proposed strategy; finally, Sect. 5 describes the conclusions and future work of this research.

2   Related Works

Data visualisation is a general term that describes any effort to help people understand the significance of data by placing it in a visual context. Patterns, trends and correlations that might go undetected in text-based data can be exposed and be recognized easily with data visualization software. There are techniques for facilitating data selection in the data transformation process [11], techniques for selecting chart type and visual components (e.g., line style, point face, axis range) automatically in the visual mapping process [12]; and techniques for changing visual effects to clarify the user's viewpoint and assertion easily in the view transformation process.

Hardre et al. [13] conducted a research titled "Testing differential effects of computer-based, web-based and paper-based administration of questionnaire research instruments". They investigated the conversion of questionnaire instruments for digital administration systems, both self-contained and web-based, is widespread and increasing daily. In this study, two university student samples were administered 16 questionnaires across three separate administration conditions: paper-based, computer-based and web-based. Overall, few differences in data quality were observed between administration conditions despite some evidence in favour of paper-based administration (PBA) over the other two. Effective responses of participants favoured the PBA over web and computer-based administrations. Implications for research use of digital systems for data collection are discussed.

Touvier et al. [10] conducted a research titled "Comparison between web-based and paper versions of a self-administered anthropometric questionnaire", it was applied to the medicine field; they argue that online data collection could advantageously replace paper-and-pencil questionnaires in epidemiological studies by reducing the logistic burden, the cost and the duration of data processing. The results show that he web-based version was preferred by 92.2% by users. In conclusion, the quality of information provided by the web-based anthropometric questionnaire used in the NutriNet-Santé Study was equal to, or better than, that of the paper version, with substantial logistic and cost advantages.

Sánchez-Figueroa et al. [14] conducted a research titled "Designing Cooperative Social Applications in Healthcare by Means of SocialBPM" they argue that the appearance of the so-called first-generation of social tools such as blogs, wikis or content management systems CMS made possible for the Web to be used as an interaction, especially for healthcare purposes. The business world, not to be left behind, is rapidly catching up with this change in interpersonal communications, allowing third parties (clients, patients, colleagues, providers, etc.) to participate in the process execution by performing social operations such as voting, commenting, ranking, sharing, following, inviting, etc., this integration must be participative with understandable notations to include social interactions in Business Process Modelling (BPM). The study denotes the combination of social technologies and BPM. Social BPM eases both, the cooperative design of social processes, and their cooperative execution.

3   mSIREMAP: Design and Implementation

To acquire requirements for a Pedagogical Monitoring and Accompaniment Regional System - mSIREMAP (in Spanish: Sistema Regional de Monitoreo y Acompañamiento Pedagógico para dispositivos móviles), we gathered information from interviews of the DRE's workers. The goal of these interviews was to define system requirements and test the software functionality; each user used the software and gave us feedback for possible improvements of the tool. Such activity was done in meetings during the design and implementation. The analysis highlights that the most relevant information to collect data into the questionnaire is described as follows: the monitored teacher, the monitoring date, the topic to be developed in class, pedagogical use of time in the learning sessions, use of pedagogical tools by teachers during sessions class, use of materials and educational resources during the class session, and so forth.

Educational Business Process Management for mSIREMAP. The process starts when DRE proposes a schedule for monitoring and defines the items for the questionnaire and then UGEL proposes the Specialists to develop the monitoring process (previous task). Each Monitor has one or more schools assigned to perform monitoring task, to accomplish this purpose they must define a route to visit each school, and then the Monitor starts with the teacher's monitoring session. The Monitor evaluates the teacher's development in classroom and uses a tablet (or personal computer) to fill out the questionnaire with sixteen questions oriented to measure three aspects: pedagogical use of time, use of pedagogical tools and use of educational materials, Finally, the Monitor returns to his/her UGEL and when the internet connexion is available the filled out questionnaires in the tablet are downloaded to the database server, then the System processes the data and generates reports that are available for all users. The entire process is shown in Fig. 1.

System Architecture

In Apurimac, more than 60% are rural schools without internet connexion, so for this reason mSIREMAP was designed to fill out questionnaires in tablets without internet connexion (off-line mode). Once the internet connexion is available, all the filled out questionnaires are downloaded from the tablet to database server. This is the context of the developed information system.

The system architecture is composed of three tiers: the data tier, the business tier and the presentation tier. In the *Data Tier* the DRE's server stores the operational data in a Mysql Database, this data is related to each monitoring, a teacher's attributes, answers given by the Monitor for each question. In the *Business Tier,* a Web server stores *php* pages and procedures to optimize queries. The *Presentation Tier* shows the questionnaire based on HTML (Hyper Text Mark-up Language), CSS (Cascade Style Sheets) and JavaScript files to decorate and validate webpages of the client side personal computer and mobile devices like tablets. Figure 2 shows the logical architecture of the proposed tool.

Questionnaire Design. The questionnaire is designed with CSS, HTML and php files, with two types of interfaces: one for mobile devices like a tablet and the other one for personal computers. The questionnaire has three important sections: The first section contains general information like: monitoring school, teacher monitored name, name of monitoring specialist, monitoring date, questionnaire name, and so forth. The second section contains sixteen questions divided in three sub sections: Pedagogical use of time (four questions), use of pedagogical tools (eight questions) and use of pedagogical materials (four questions). The third section contains the punctuation summary of each item defined in the second section.

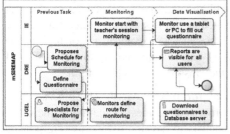

Fig. 1. BPM for mSIREMAP.

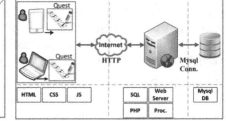

Fig. 2. System architecture

Assigning Reached Level. Each questionnaire has 16 questions divided in three sub-sections. To determine the teacher's evaluation reached level, specialists use a distribution, as shown in Table 1. For example, if the teacher gets a score of 16, then, the acquired level is "Initiation"; if the teacher gets a score of 30, then, the acquired level is "In Process"; and if the teacher gets a score of 40, then, the acquired level is "Achieved".

Table 1. Distribution of reached level according to punctuation and colour assigned.

Item	Reached level	Punctuation	Colour
0	Initiation	0–16	Red
1	In process	17–32	Orange
2	Achieved	33–48	Green

Questionnaire Cooperative Design. It is important to remark that the second section of the questionnaire interface was designed with the perspective of *how it will be understood and used by the user* (Monitor in this case). The user interface was based upon an explicit understanding of users, tasks, and environments; it was driven and refined iteratively by user centred evaluation. Fill out the questionnaire as close as possible to fill it out in a paper based questionnaire was an important user requirement. The first version of the software used a list-box to select the score (one two or three), then the second version was using a radio button to select the score, but none of the previous options were accepted by end user; finally, in the third version we used the "finger-touch" strategy to mark the punctuation with "X" over the number (or a click on non-tactile screens), this option was the best one and seemed natural to the end-user. The "finger-touch" and "mouse-click" icons used to mark the punctuation (Fig. 3).

Other important user requirement was the automatic and instantaneous calculation of the summary punctuation for each item in the third section.

4   Evaluation of the Proposed Strategy

Focus Group. The validation of the tool was conducted with Education Specialist (workers) of the DRE-Apurímac through focus groups. The events took place on May 22, September 21 and October 22, 2015, in a meeting room of the Pedagogical Management Area of DRE. The participants were four evaluation specialists. All participants had significant years of experience in monitoring and supervising educational schools.

Before starting the activity in each iteration, the developed system was briefly explained and shown to each Monitor. Then, each Monitor login into the mSIREMAP system giving the username and password assigned previously and then access to the *teacher class session questionnaire*.

Some questions were asked to the Monitors: the first question was: *"will the use of the designed software help you to make it easier to fill out questionnaires for monitoring teacher's class session?"*, they all answered that in their opinion that assumption

http://siremap.nybblebots.com			
Monitoring School: Las Mercedes			
Name of Monitored Teacher: Juan Quispe			
Name of Monitoring specialist: Manuel Ibarra			
Monitoring Date: 27/03/2017			
I)Pedagogical use of time			
	Description		Punctuation
1	The teacher uses more time in pedagogical activities than non-pedagogical activities	X	2	3
...	...	...	...	...
4	The teacher plans the pedagogical activities measuring the time in the learning session	1	X	3
II)Use of pedagogical tools			
5	The teacher problematizes or generates cognitive conflict according to the learning paths	X	2	3
...	...	...	...	...
12	The teacher adapts, if it is necessary, strategies according to learning paths	1	2	X
III) Use of educational materials			
13	The teacher uses educational materials opportunely	1		3
...	...	...	...	...
16	The teacher presents the session plan	X	2	3
Summary			
	I)Pedagogical use of time	1	4	3
	II)Use of pedagogical tools	2	6	12
	III) Use of educational resources	0	4	4
	total	3	14	19

Fig. 3. Questionnaire filled by the monitor (education specialist).

was valid; then they were asked: "*does the use of tablets to fill out questionnaires reduce the time to process data compared with paper-pencil based one?*", they all replied that a positive answer would be valid. After this simulated process, the Monitors provided us feedback, suggestions and opinions, and finally agreed that the system can help and improve questionnaires time process, cost to process it and decision making.

Daily Meeting in Cooperative Design

A daily team-meeting methodology was used by the software developers to synchronise the technical problems, the requirement status, in some of these meetings the customer (Principal) and user (Monitor) were involved frequently; it means that they were part of our software development team. The participation of the customers in every meeting was important, because we could ask directly about the change in the software requirements, the ambiguous software requirements and they also had the opportunity to test the look and feel of the mobile-based questionnaire.

5 Conclusions and Future Work

The mobile devices have captivated the interest of the educational society, and are being inserted in the daily tasks of the people. This has generated many possibilities to create software-based solutions in many scenarios, for example in education field. This paper describes a cooperative design and the strategy to collect data using tablet-based questionnaires to monitor teacher's session learning. The Monitor uses the tablet to fill out the questionnaire in schools without internet connection (more than 60% of schools), then when internet connection is available, the Monitor download all questionnaires from the tablet to a database server, finally the system process data and the reports are available for all users. The tool was tested with 10865 mobile-based questionnaires in 1453 schools in 2015 and 2016. According to the opinion of the Monitors, the proposed strategy allows them to reduce time collect and process data, they feel that the system is easy to use because the interface is similar as to paper–based questionnaires; also, the Principal could have accurate information when making decisions based on the questionnaire indicators.

For the future, we are improving the tool by giving the Monitor the option to get the coordinates (latitude, longitude) of each visited school; then these coordinates will be marked and shown as Point of Interest in Google maps when internet connection is available. On the other hand, two new functionalities will be added to the application: Monitoring Schools and UGEL mobile-based new questionnaires.

Acknowledgments. Thanks to the Education Specialist Edith Montalvo and the Principal Walter Altamirano of Regional Education Apurimac in Peru.

References

1. http://www.minedu.gob.pe/campanias/pdf/gestion/manual-compromisos-gestion-escolar.pdf. Accessed 5 Feb 2017
2. González, J.R., Soledad, M., Montoya, R., Rivera, J.A.: Cultura de evaluación en instituciones educativas. Perfiles Educativos **33**(131), 42–63 (2011)
3. Bolseguí, M., Fuguet, A.: Cultura de evaluación: una aproximación conceptual. Investigación y Postgrado **21**(1), 77–98 (2006)
4. Ibarra, M.J., Serrano, C., Navarro, A.F.: SIERA: visual analytics for multi-dimensional data for learning assessment in educational organisations. In: Luo, Y. (ed.) CDVE 2016. LNCS, vol. 9929, pp. 283–287. Springer, Cham (2016). doi:10.1007/978-3-319-46771-9_36
5. Guchev, V., Massimo, M., Giuseppe S.: Design guidelines for correlated quantitative data visualizations. In: Proceedings of the International Working Conference on Advanced Visual Interfaces. ACM (2012)
6. Spence, R.: Information Visualization: Design for Interaction. Pearson Educational Limited, London (2007)
7. Segel, E., Heer, J.: Narrative visualization: Telling stories with data. IEEE Trans. Vis. Comput. Graph. **16**(6), 1139–1148 (2010)
8. Few, S.: Now you See It: Simple Visualization Techniques for Quantitative Analysis. Analytics Press, Berkeley (2009)

9. Schoffelen, J., Claes, S., Huybrechts, L., Martens, S., Chua, A., Moere, A.V.: Visualising things. Perspectives on how to make things public through visualisation. CoDesign **11**(3–4), 179–192 (2015)
10. Touvier, M., Méjean, C., Kesse-Guyot, E., Pollet, C., Malon, A., Castetbon, K., Hercberg, S.: Comparison between web-based and paper versions of a self-administered anthropometric questionnaire. Eur. J. Epidemiol. **25**(5), 287–296 (2010)
11. Derthick, M., Harrison, J., Moore, A., Roth, S.F.: Efficient multi-object dynamic query histograms. In: IEEE Symposium on Information Visualization Proceedings, pp. 84–91 (1999)
12. Mackinlay, J.D.: Automating the design of graphical presentations of relational information. In: Readings in Intelligent User Interfaces (1998)
13. Hardre, P.L., Crowson, H.M., Xie, K., Ly, C.: Testing differential effects of computer-based, web-based and paper-based administration of questionnaire research instruments. Br. J. Educ. Technol. **38**(1), 5–22 (2007)
14. Sánchez-Figueroa, F., Preciado, J.C., Conejero, J.M., Rodríguez-Echeverría, R.: Designing cooperative social applications in healthcare by means of socialBPM. In: Luo, Y. (ed.) CDVE 2014. LNCS, vol. 8683, pp. 118–125. Springer, Cham (2014). doi:10.1007/978-3-319-10831-5_17

Supporting Collaborative Ideation Through Freehand Sketching of 3D-Shapes in 2D Using Colour

Frode Eika Sandnes[1,2(✉)], Yuriy Lianguzov[2],
Osmar Vicente Rodrigues[3], Henrik Lieng[1], Fausto Orsi Medola[3],
and Nenad Pavel[1]

[1] Oslo and Akershus University College of Applied Sciences, Oslo, Norway
{frodes,Henrik.Lieng,nenad.pavel}@hioa.no
[2] Westerdals Oslo School of Art, Communication and Technology,
Oslo, Norway
yuriylianguzov@gmail.com
[3] School of Architecture, Arts, and Communication,
Sao Paulo State University (UNESP), Bauru, Brazil
{osmar,fausto.medola}@faac.unesp.br

Abstract. The modelling of 3D shapes is a challenging problem. Many innovative approaches have been proposed, however most 3D software require advanced skills that hinders collaboration and spontaneous ideation. This paper proposes a novel framework that allows designers to express their ideas in 3D space without extensive training such that they can reuse their 2D sketching skills collaboratively in teams.

Keywords: Collaborative design · Sketching · 3D-modelling · Color-map

1 Introduction

Sketching is a technique used by designers to rapidly represent and communicate ideas. Sketches are often freehand paper drawings allowing ideas to be quickly captured as ideas may leave ones head as quickly as they emerge [1]. Operating computer for making sketches is often too cumbersome and time-consuming and are often thus hindrance to the creative process [2] and collaborative design teams. Sketches may take many forms, including 3D objects. For example, product designers may create 3D sketches using flat perspective drawings.

Sometimes, one wants a more immersive representation than a simple one-view rendering. It may for instance be a panoramic image or sketch of some three-dimensional space that allows viewers to observe a scene in all directions [3–5] using spherical coordinates [6], or it may be some artefact to be explored through virtual reality. To create such experiences designers have to use some modelling tool. This process is often time-consuming, require special software operation experience and the resulting models may look like the finished products when rendered photo-realistically.

Y. Luo (Ed.): CDVE 2017, LNCS 10451, pp. 123–134, 2017.
DOI: 10.1007/978-3-319-66805-5_16

During the last two decades, courses related to the practice of drawing both 2D and 3D, including 3D modeling, has vanished from fundamental and high school curricula. This becomes a huge shortcoming in the development of students' abilities and tools needed in any creative process. Moreover, this is a challenge for society, in particular for educational boards and teachers worldwide that need new tools, methods and new approaches in the development of their course contents.

Thus, students who become the future professionals, is less able to visualize and physically interpret 3D space, such as the reading of 2D representations including drawings, sketches and renderings, and the right visualization of any 3D representation including physical objects, sculptures and products.

The novel contribution of this paper is a sketching framework that allows designers to quickly represent imperfect three-dimensional shapes. The sketch is drawn as two images. The first image represents the origin of the shape in a two-dimensional flat plane with its texture. The second image provides the shape information as height.

2   Background

A study of physical 3D modeling [7] involving three groups of participants with different levels of knowledge and experience in such area (professionals with over five years of experience, design students and those without any such knowledge), evaluated the capacity of the participants to translate and interpret 2D drawings in 3D physical models. The results were compared to results from a similar study conducted 21 years earlier. The results showed that all the participants had difficulties in translating the 2D information into 3D physical models. The students came first followed by the experienced professionals and those without knowledge. This phenomenon was especially noticeable during the start of the sculpturing phase where one searches for the basic shapes of the models. The results are quite different from those observed in the 1989 study, where the participants without any knowledge came first following by the students in second. The overall level of difficulty was lower compared to the results of the 2010 study. Therefore, the results suggest that offering students a narrower contact with courses focusing on 2D and 3D representation has contributed to reinforcement of this problem in Brazil, in particular, where this study took place.

In a study of the design studio application of visual media in the design collaborative groups [8] the researchers concluded that the design workflow including both CAD and sketching have advantages over isolated digital and manual workflows. Accordingly, the seamless transition between sketch and digital media seems to be beneficial especially for design novices because of the translation from tacit knowledge to explicit actionable knowledge. Furthermore, the communication in design studios benefit from a mixed method design process, such as initiating a quick conceptual sketch followed by detailed conceptual analyses. The current CAD solutions offer sharp transition between sketching, digital conceptualization and analyses.

The literature on sketching in 3D is vast and several innovative techniques have been proposed. Most of the techniques are based on modelling directly in 3D [9, 10] by somehow creating and shaping objects from simple primitives and placing these in a scene. Other approaches allow 3D shapes to be constructed from curves [11]. There are also domain specific tools that limit some of the choice provided by the general purpose modelling tools, and may thus be easier to use. For example, Ijiri et al. [12] proposed a 3D sketching tool for flower construction where the user first create a crude initial sketch and then the sketch is gradually refined where components are reused. Such tools are easier to use and can be used to generate very complex models, but the range of possible models are very limited.

Since the operation of 3D modelling tools often is difficult and require training several researchers have attempted to turn original line drawings on paper into 3D models. Most of these methods document concept implementations that can convert very simple sketches [13] and acknowledge that this is a difficult problem. Varley et al. [14] concludes that the success of such systems depends on the number of lines in the original sketch and whether the sketches represent certain basic shapes, as there are many shapes that it is easy for humans to recognize but very hard for machines.

Another approach is to sketch on top of 3D-dimensional views, being it real images, virtual reality or augmented reality, and then infer the three dimensional models from the 2D projective sketch and information about the scene geometry [15]. Example applications include annotation and sketching in archeological sites [14] and sketching and modelling of cartoon like scenes for animation [17]. Ambiguities in where points in the 2D sketches are in the 3D model can be resolved fixing the points using multiple views of the scene [16].

Simplifications can be made such as in the Harold system [18] where the goal is not to make photorealistic models, but rather understandable 3D environments that can be navigated. They introduced three drawing modes, namely billboard, terrain and floor. The billboard mode allow the user to edit planar sketches in the environment, or billboards. These billboards remain flat in the scene but are affected by the perspective projection as the user moves around the scene. They represent recognizable flat representations of objects in the scene, although the objects themselves are not three-dimensional. The terrain mode allows the ground to be modelled with hills and valleys, and the floor mode is used to model the floor.

Common for animation and sketching is that it is not necessary to make accurate and complete models, but rather sufficient scenery to create an experience. In addition to flat or billboards, curved canvases has also been proposed as objects that are easily drawable by 2D means to create scenery suitable for animation and "film-sets" and then these canvases can be placed anywhere in the scene [19]. Another approach for sketching 3D experiences is to sketch projective scenes from various angles and then combine these into panoramic images that can be viewed with panoramic viewers [20, 21]. Such 3D experiences are though only observable from one point and no actual 3D information is captured.

More interactive methods has also been proposed such as the Napkin sketch [22] where a napkin is placed on a table and the world is viewed through a tablet computer with a camera. The tablet tracks the napkin to gain information about the observation point of the tablet. The designer then draw on top of the touch screen showing the view. The stroke information can then be combined with the scene information to build the model. Moreover, the user can immediately move around the model.

A totally different approach is the use of database systems containing existing models [23, 24] where a sketch is made of a scene, and then through manual intervention the scene is broken into objects. Relevant objects are found in a model database. Finally, the computer helps place these objects back in the original world according to the sketch.

Some of the 3D modelling methods that are focused on 2D input include those that uses planar cross sections of the scene or objects. Then multiple planar sections can be combined in various placement of the 3D scene to obtain the 3D model [25, 26]. Various perspective views of an object can also be used to build a 3D model of an object. This for instance has been used for generating 3D models of cartoon characters based an artist's renderings from different angles [27].

Reliefs has also been mapped onto three dimensional objects using line drawings [28] where the 2D dimensional line drawing controls minor surface offsets on the three-dimensional object.

The relief approach can be considered a special case of shading based modelling where a shade is used to control the height of an object's surface [29]. Another approach is to use a shade of gray to indicate height of a surface where white means no offset, medium gray some offset and black max offset. One practical approach employing this scheme took simple line sketches as input, the system would come with a first suggestion to a height map based on shading which then the designer could adjust and edit through paining operations before the final model is rendered into the 3D model [30]. Another attractive prospect of shading based modelling method is to create models from photographs [31].

One problem with shading based approaches is that humans are unable to objectively asses the absolute intensity of a tone as neighboring colors affect each other. Simultaneous contrast occur as the effect that the same level of gray is perceived differently if it is surrounded by darker gray than when it is surrounded by a lighter gray. For this reason this study instead attempts to use fixed colors instead of shades of gray based on the assumption that it is easier to distinguish the main color classes than shades of gray.

3   The Proposed Method

3.1   Assumptions and Motivation

The motivation of this work is to allow people without 3D perspective drawing experience to make 3D illustrations. The framework is not intended to be as accurate and general as state of the art modelling software.

This work leans on the observations that modelling software require training and are generally hard to use. The proposed framework was designed to be used independently of specific software packages, hence allowing users to rely on skills they are already familiar with, namely drawing and sketching on flat two-dimensional surfaces. A rationale for 2D sketches is that they can be produced fast and thereby facilitate rapid and spontaneous ideation processes.

User indicate heights directly in the sketch. Unlike previous approaches that use gray-levels, the current approach uses a palette of distinct color hues. This is because it is hard for humans to determine the absolute intensity of a color [32–34]. Colors, on the other, hand are easier to recognize. These colors represent discrete height levels.

To allow for smooth shapes represented by the values between height-levels, a visual gradient semantic is proposed. This semantic allows smooth height transitions between the various levels for arbitrary shapes, where the level of smoothness can be controlled. The gradients are made automatically as it is challenging to manually make gradients for arbitrary shapes. Moreover, it is very hard to control the nature of the gradient to achieve the desired 3D shape. This is because it is very difficult to visualize the mapping between a gradient and the corresponding shape in 3D space. Another advantage is that it is easy and quick to alter the shape sketch.

3.2 Sketching Language

A shape can comprise a texture image, a shape image or both. The texture image is simply a direct representation of what will be painted onto the object. In our implementation, the color white is used to code transparency in the texture.

The shape image defines the height variations in the z-dimension by default. The user simply uses colors and shades of gray to define the height contour. In the current implementation the 12 hues on the color wheel defined by the projection of the color cube was used to define the various heights. The colors of the color wheel were representing equally spaced heights along the z-dimension. Yellow was defined as base height at 90° on the color wheel. Warm colors defined positive heights relative to the base, and cold colors defined negative heights.

It is difficult to manually create gradients between the hues that correspond to desired smooth transitions. Instead, shades of gray were used to define areas of gradients. That is, a gray area between two different colors are defined as an area of gradual transition from one color to the other. To avoid a transition being affected by certain color regions, black is used to define no transition and is instead replaced by the nearest color.

The level of gray controls the smoothness of the gradient. Dark gray signals linear interpolation and light gray signals smooth interpolation, where the degree of brightness is related to the degree of smoothness.

The texture image and height image are dependent on each other, and each of these can be used as basis for overlay tracing with respect to each other. Overlay tracing will ensure that the content of both the texture image and shape image are aligned.

3.3 Preprocessing Height Maps

The height maps are preprocessed [35, 36] before the 3D model is generated. First, checks are made to ensure that the texture image and the height map images have the same dimensions. If they are different, the height map image is resized to match that of the texture map using an off-the-shelf resampling algorithm.

Second, the image is quantized into discrete hues and shades of gray to emphasize the discrete steps and eliminate inaccuracies incurred by drawing applications. The saturation of each pixel is used to determine if it is color or grayscale.

3.4 Gradients Algorithm

The gradient algorithm is similar to the classic Gouraud shading algorithm, but considers arbitrary shapes. The algorithm for detecting the gradients first scan all the pixels to find all color pixels that is the neighbor of a gray or gradient pixels. These border points represent the color pixels around a given gradient area. These points are organized according to color.

A list of color pixels neighboring black areas are also extracted, and these points are the surrounding pixels of a black area. The border pixels between black and grey areas are not recorded, that is the boundary between the gradient area and blocking areas.

Next, the gradient pixels are filled as follows. For each pixel x, y the closest edge pixel for each color category is detected, and then two largest edge pixels are selected, namely pixel x_1, y_1 with color c_1 and pixel x_2, y_2 with color c_2. The color c of the gradient pixel at x, y is thus computed by interpolating between color c_1 and c_2 according to the distance between the gradient pixel and the two border pixels. More exactly, the linearly interpolated color was

$$c = \frac{c_1 d_2 + c_2 d_1}{d_1 + d_2} \tag{1}$$

where d_1 and d_2 where computed using

$$d_i = \sqrt{(x_i - x)^2 + (y_i - y)^2} \tag{2}$$

Linear interpolation was used for grays centered at value 192. For a softer interpolation the smoothstep function, Ken Perlin's 6 h order step function and a 7th order polynomial step functions were used.

Hues are represented on the color wheel from 0 to 360°. Since the height origin is located at 90° the following H(x) transformation was used before the interpolation of the color values and again used to convert back to the color wheel representation:

$$H(x) = \begin{cases} 90 - x, x < 270 \\ 450 - x, x \geq 270 \end{cases} \tag{3}$$

Finally, black pixels are filled with the color of the closest edge pixel.

3.5 Model Building

Finally, the model is built as follows. For each pixel $i.j$ on the texture and height maps, the corresponding color point $[x, y, z, c]$ in space is generated, where $x = i \cdot \delta$, $y = j \cdot \delta$,

$z = H(height(i,j) \frac{thickness}{360}$ and $c = hexture(i.j)$. Here, δ is the unit distance between consecutive points in the model space. If the width of the object in physical space id with, then $\delta = width/x_{pixels}$, where x_{pixels} is the number of pixels in the texture along the horizontal direction.

Next, *thichness* is the maximum height bound of the object, $height(x, y)$ is the pixel value of x, y in the height map and $\underline{texture}(x, y)$ is the pixel value at x, y in the texture map. Note that white pixels in the texture maps are considered transparent and not included in the final set of points. Sets of four neighboring points make up polygons, namely $p_{i,j}$, $p_{i+1,j}$, $p_{i+1,j+1}$ and $p_{i,j+1}$ with the color of $p_{i,j}$.

4 Case Studies

A height map interpreter and model synthesizer was implemented in java. The PLY format was used to represent the 3D models as polygon meshes. The models were rendered using CloudCompare.

Figure 1 shows a simple example of the modelling technique where the height map comprises a red background with yellow handwritten text, the yellow and red are both on the warm side of the color wheel and relatively close. The resulting image shows this text as a highened relief on top of the flat plane. A wood texture was also used in this example giving this example the impression of a carved wooden plate.

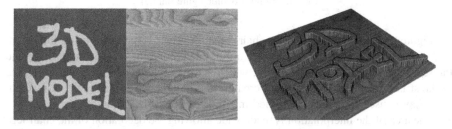

Fig. 1. Text engraving (Color figure online)

Figure 2 (top) shows an example of constructing a set of stairs. The ground is modelled with the blue and each consecutive step is modelled using a color up on the color wheel from light blue, via cyan to two shades of green. The bottom example illustrate the use of interpolation where there soft ramps are created on each side of the stairs. The soft ramp is indicated using a medium gray color. To ensure that it only interpolates between the top stair marked in green and the floor the two black lines are used to separate against the sides and the other stairs.

Figure 3 shows how to modelling a bathtub. First, the top edge of the bathtub is modelled using magenta and the tub bottom is modelled using blue. A rounded rectangle is used to get the roundedness of a bathtub. Then, a lighter gray is used to indicate a smooth interpolation between these two levels. Next, a uniform light brown is used for texture and white is used to cut out the top of the tub and the drain. Therefore, only the brown pixels in the texture map are included in the model.

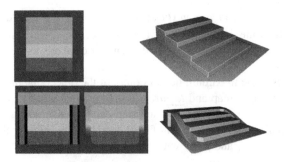

Fig. 2. Stairs (Color figure online)

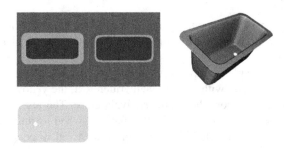

Fig. 3. Bathtub (Color figure online)

Figure 4 shows how to model a chair. First, the chair is modelled using the height map. Blue is used to model the floor as a thin line around the edges of the image and the seat itself is modelled using green, which is in the middle of the height scale. The backrest is modelled using magenta creating the highest top of the chair. A medium dark gray is used to specify smoothed interpolation from the ground to the seat.

The area of the interpolation is made wide allowing the decoration of the chair legs to be modelled more accurately. The first chair is decorated with a uniform red texture. The middle chair has four distinct legs cut out using white and the final chair is decorated with a more elaborate pattern and brown legs.

5   Experimental Evaluation

An experiment was carried out to test the hypothesis that the proposed framework simplifies 3D modelling. Eight male participants working as web-developers were recruited. None of the participants works with 3D. The experiment comprised ten tasks presented in increasing order of complexity involving designing a cube, open box, staircase, Mexican pyramid, cylinder, skyscraper, ramp, pyramid, cone and ramp with stops. A complete and interactive JavaScript version of the framework running in a browser was used for the testing. No texture mapping and only linear interpolation was included in the tasks. The participants were tested individually. They were given instructions and time to familiarize themselves with the tool.

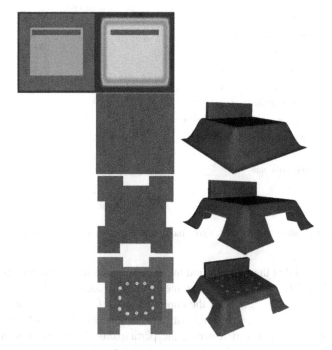

Fig. 4. Chair (Color figure online)

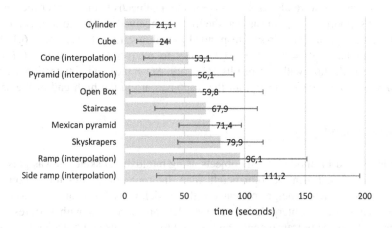

Fig. 5. Time to complete 3D modelling tasks (seconds). Error bars show SD.

All the participants managed to perform all the tasks and Fig. 6 shows that all participants managed to design the skyscraper, cylinder and Mexican pyramid on the first attempt. The most difficult task was the ramp with stops. Here, five of the participants made a total of 12 reattempts before successfully completing the task.

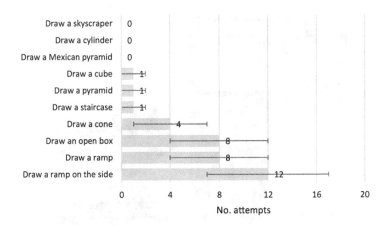

Fig. 6. Number of attempts per task. Error bars shows number of participants with reattempts.

Figure 5 shows that the cylinder and the cube were the fastest models to create both taking less than 30 s on average. The mean time to complete the remaining tasks increased gradually from 53.1 s for the cone to 111.2 s for the side ramp. Clearly, the time to complete the tasks correspond with the complexity of the task. Note also that the task completion times varied across the participants. However, a within-subjects repeated measures anova reveals the time to complete the ten tasks were statistically different ($F(9, 63) = 3.49$, $p < .001$).

The participants were also asked to complete a subjective survey after the session. The results support the hypothesis that the tool is perceived as easy to use. On a seven point Likert scale, the participants responded as follows: Easy to use ($M = 6.1$, $SD = 0.6$), easy to learn ($M = 6.4$, $SD = 1.1$), easy to recover from mistakes ($M = 6.4$, $SD = 1.1$), satisfaction with the results ($M = 5.9$, $SD = 0.6$) and satisfaction with the tool ($M = 6.1$, $SD = 0.6$). Clearly, all the responses are in the high end of the scale.

6 Conclusions

A simple method for modelling 3D objects using intuitive 2D sketches was presented. Shapes are specified using a color height map. Interpolation allows for smooth transitions between different height-plateaus of the model. Gray levels are used to control the smoothness of the interpolation. The models are decorated with textures where white is used to specify transparency and is used to make cuts and holes in the objects. The models can be generated with any drawing program and does not rely on any particular 3D modelling software. Closed objects such as spheres cannot be modelled.

The proposed method combined with digital stylus has a potential to be integrated into a design process and workflow as an initial quick conceptual sketch tool, whose outputs can be later used in more advanced computer software for analyses. The results of the conducted experiment show that users are able to get grasp of declarative command knowledge [37]. By introducing the pre-learned hot-cold color metaphor and gradients, a novice may have a better chance of effective adoption of specific procedural knowledge. Further testing is necessary to study acquisition of strategic knowledge of this CAD software and its adoption in a design workflow.

Acknowledgement. This work is supported by and SIU UTFORSK grant UTF-2016-long-term/10053.

References

1. Sandnes, F.E., Jian, H.-L.: Sketching with Chinese calligraphy. Interactions **19**, 62–66 (2012)
2. Black, A.: Visible planning on paper and on screen: the impact of working medium on decision-making by novice graphic designers. Behav. Inf. Technol. **9**, 283–296 (1990)
3. Sandnes, F.E.: Communicating panoramic 360 degree immersed experiences: a simple technique for sketching in 3D. In: Antona, M., Stephanidis, C. (eds.) UAHCI 2016. LNCS, vol. 9738, pp. 338–346. Springer, Cham (2016). doi:10.1007/978-3-319-40244-4_33
4. Sandnes, F.E.: PanoramaGrid: a graph paper tracing framework for sketching 360-degree immersed experiences. In: Proceedings of the International Working Conference on Advanced Visual Interfaces, pp. 342–343. ACM (2016)
5. Sandnes, F.E., Huang, Y.P.: Translating the viewing position in single equirectangular panoramic images. In: Proceedings of the 2016 IEEE International Conference on Systems, Man, and Cybernetics (SMC), pp. 389–394. IEEE (2016)
6. Sandnes, F.E.: Determining the geographical location of image scenes based on object shadow lengths. J. Sig. Process. Syst. **65**, 35–47 (2011)
7. Rodrigues, O.V.: Modelagem de veículos utilizando espuma rígida de poliuretano expandido. In: Ensaios em Design – Ensino e Produção de Conhecimento, pp. 128–157. Canal 6 (2011)
8. Ibrahim, R., Rahimian, F.P.: Comparison of CAD and manual sketching tools for teaching architectural design. Autom. Constr. **19**, 978–987 (2010)
9. Olsen, L., Samavati, F.F., Sousa, M.C., Jorge, J.A.: Sketch-based modeling: a survey. Comput. Graph. **33**, 85–103 (2009)
10. Kondo, K.: Interactive geometric modeling using freehand sketches. J. Geom. Graph. **13**, 195–207 (2009)
11. Das, K., Diaz-Gutierrez, P., Gopi. M.: Sketching free-form surfaces using network of curves. In: EUROGRAPHICS Workshop on Sketch-Based Interfaces and Modeling (2005)
12. Ijiri, T., Owada, S., Igarashi, T.: Seamless integration of initial sketching and subsequent detail editing in flower modeling. In: Computer Graphics Forum, vol. 25. Blackwell Publishing, Inc. (2006)
13. Cruz, L.M.V., Velho, L.: A sketch on sketch-based interfaces and modeling. In: 2010 23rd SIBGRAPI Conference on Graphics, Patterns and Images Tutorials (SIBGRAPI-T). IEEE (2010)
14. Varley, P.A.C., Martin, R.R., Suzuki, H.: Can machines interpret line drawings. In: EUROGRAPHICS Workshop on Sketch-Based Interfaces and Modeling, vol. 1 (2004)
15. Turner, A., Chapman, D., Penn, A.: Sketching space. Comput. Graph. **24**, 869–879 (2000)
16. Chen, X., et al.: An integrated image and sketching environment for archaeological sites. In: 2010 IEEE Computer Society Conference on Computer Vision and Pattern Recognition Workshops (CVPRW). IEEE (2010)

17. Bourguignon, D., Cani, M.P., Drettakis, G.: Drawing for illustration and annotation in 3D. In: Computer Graphics Forum, vol. 20. Blackwell Publishers Ltd. (2001)
18. Cohen, J.M., Hughes, J.F., Zeleznik, R.C.: Harold: a world made of drawings. In: Proceedings of the 1st International Symposium on Non-photorealistic Animation and Rendering. ACM (2000)
19. Fei, G., et al.: 3D animation creation using space canvases for free-hand drawing. In: Proceedings of the 7th ACM SIGGRAPH International Conference on Virtual-Reality Continuum and Its Applications in Industry. ACM (2008)
20. Tolba, O., Dorsey, J., McMillan, L.: Sketching with projective 2D strokes. In: Proceedings of the 12th Annual ACM Symposium on User Interface Software and Technology, pp. 149–157. ACM (1999)
21. Tolba, O., Dorsey, J., McMillan, L.: A projective drawing system. In: Proceedings of the 2001 Symposium on Interactive 3D graphics. ACM (2001)
22. Xin, M., Sharlin, E., Sousa, M.C.: Napkin sketch: handheld mixed reality 3D sketching. In: Proceedings of the 2008 ACM Symposium on Virtual Reality Software and Technology. ACM (2008)
23. Shin, H., Igarashi, T.: Magic canvas: interactive design of a 3-D scene prototype from freehand sketches. In: Proceedings of Graphics Interface 2007. ACM (2007)
24. Xu, K., et al.: Sketch2Scene: sketch-based co-retrieval and co-placement of 3D models. ACM Trans. Graph. 32, 123 (2013)
25. Dorsey, J., et al.: The mental canvas: a tool for conceptual architectural design and analysis. In: 15th Pacific Conference on Computer Graphics and Applications, PG 2007. IEEE (2007)
26. Sandnes, F.E.: Sketching 3D immersed experiences rapidly by hand through 2D cross sections. In: Proceedings of REV 2017. LNCS (in press)
27. Triki, O., Zaharia, T.B., Preteux, F.J.: 3D virtual character reconstruction from projections: a NURBS-based approach. In: Electronic Imaging 2004. International Society for Optics and Photonics (2004)
28. Kolomenkin, M., et al.: Reconstruction of relief objects from line drawings. In: 2011 IEEE Conference on Computer Vision and Pattern Recognition (CVPR). IEEE (2011)
29. Gingold, Y., Zorin, D.: Shading-based surface editing. ACM Trans. Graph. 27(3), 9 p. (2008). Article no. 95. https://doi.org/10.1145/1360612.1360694
30. Feng, X., Shi, M.: Shading-based surface modeling and editing. In: 2012 International Conference on Computer Science and Electronics Engineering (ICCSEE), vol. 2. IEEE (2012)
31. Zhang, R., et al.: Shape-from-shading: a survey. IEEE Trans. Pattern Anal. Mach. Intell. 21, 690–706 (1999)
32. Sandnes, F.E.: Understanding WCAG2.0 color contrast requirements through 3D color space visualization. Stud. Health Technol. Inform. 229, 366–375 (2016)
33. Sandnes, F.E., Zhao, A.: A contrast colour selection scheme for WCAG2.0-compliant web designs based on HSV-half-planes. In: Proceedings of SMC 2015, pp. 1233–1237. IEEE (2015)
34. Sandnes, F.E., Zhao, A.: An interactive color picker that ensures WCAG2.0 compliant color contrast levels. Procedia-Comput. Sci. 67, 87–94 (2015)
35. Huang, Y.-P., Chang, T.-W., Chen, J.-R., Sandnes, F.E.: A back propagation based real-time license plate recognition system. Int. J. Pattern Recognit. Artif. Intell. 22, 233–251 (2008)
36. Huang, Y.P., Hsu, L.W., Sandnes, F.E.: An intelligent subtitle detection model for locating television commercials. IEEE Trans. Syst. Man Cybern. Part B 37, 485–492 (2007)
37. Chester, I.: Teaching for CAD expertise. Int. J. Technol. Des. Educ. 17, 23–35 (2007)

BIM-Agile Practices Experiments in Architectural Design

Elicitation of Architectural Intentions and Refinement of Design Tasks

Henri-Jean Gless$^{(\boxtimes)}$ ⓘ, Damien Hanser, and Gilles Halin

MAP-CRAI, 2 rue Bastien Lepage, 54000 Nancy, France
gless@crai.archi.fr

Abstract. The digital transition is changing the way architectural firms are making design. The BIM technology, which tends to become mandatory for legal and competitive reasons is both convincing because of its parametric and global modeling sides and frightening because of changes caused by the arrival of new digital tools. Indeed, our basic postulate is that the emergence of new digital tools must necessarily be followed by the emergence of new practices and new project management in design stage.

This research focuses on innovative project management methods and collaborative practices allowing to facilitate the integration of new digital tools in order to create innovative practices and methods adapted to computer-assisted and collaborative architectural design. We take inspiration from agile methods and practices born in the software engineering world in the 1990s. Agile methods are innovative project management methods that focus mainly on a better reactivity. We have thus identified that a better reactivity is corroborated to a better collaboration around the understanding and repartition of design tasks.

Thus, we focus in particular in this paper on elicitation of architectural intentions and refinement of design tasks in collaborative groups of students working on a BIM project. For this purpose, we have set up a collaborative matrix that students fill up by explaining together their architectural wills and intentions for this project exercise. Naturally follows a defining "tasks to be done" process, which we will detail in this paper.

Keywords: BIM · Agile methods · Agile practices · Collaboration · Architectural design · Project management · Collaborative and digital uses · Collaborative and digital practices

1 Introduction

Our research takes place in the French architectural design field where the digital transition still has not succeeded to implement BIM technology. Nowadays, on the field, we notice that this transition is only seen through a technological approach. We

© Springer International Publishing AG 2017
Y. Luo (Ed.): CDVE 2017, LNCS 10451, pp. 135–142, 2017.
DOI: 10.1007/978-3-319-66805-5_17

make the assumption that this could be a major reason explaining why the transition is still at an early stage of the BIM evolution.

We propose in this article to adopt a more human-centered approach in order to make evolve project management methods relying on BIM technology. Current methods need to be improved to complete the digital transition, and in this research, we seek to evaluate if methods used in software engineering, like so-called agile project management methods can be applied to the architectural field. These methods have been created to meet the needs of a greater responsiveness and customer involvement, and for being applied on a non-linear and iterative design process, as such architectural design [1]. Links between BIM technology and agility are numerous: such as adaptability to change, the will to reduce information redundancies, or to improve communication between actors [2, 3].

The experiments we are conducting propose to apply agile design practices in architectural school study projects, in order to help them correctly identify design tasks, their perimeters as also their complexity. This experiment protocol consists of three steps: the students translate collaboratively their architectural intentions, then identify the tasks that they should do, and finally estimate their complexity and duration. These steps are done using agile practices based on a tool for design assistance called "Conceptual matrix" and an agile practice called "Planning Poker". Expected results are improvements in adaptability, reduction wastes and communication.

2 Context of AEC in France

The world of architecture, engineering and construction (AEC) in France, more particularly in the field of architectural design, is currently going through an important period of changes; digital field as well as collaborative practices are in a phase of transition and adaptation while the BIM technology becomes a regulatory demand in public construction. However, there is some inertia from architects towards Building Information Modeling. This trend is based on the French architecture firms' size. Most of them are small (90% of it have 9 or fewer employees, and 75% have 4 or fewer employees) [4], but also in the current socio-economic context which encourages low investment in the medium and long term.

In the construction context, proven working methods, such as LEAN Management for production activities or agile methods developed in the software engineering field, tend to apply to the construction field. We can mention LEAN Construction [5], which particularly targets the management of working site, or methods which bet on humans and lead to a reduction of waste and accidents [6]. It aims to make the actors responsible and to ensure that they take care of each other, while trying to anticipate everyone's needs. BIM technology and these innovative project management methods, and especially agile methods [2, 3] share common values such as the application of better communication and a significant reduction in the "work to be redone" [3].

The experiments we propose are part of a research focusing on agile practices identification, their implementation in BIM oriented experiments for measuring their benefits within architectural student's projects on the one hand, and on the other in architectural firms.

Our analysis is that BIM implementation issue cannot be resumed by a simple technological problem, it is crucial to study the situation in the light of a global digital transition of the architecture firms through a collaborative practices approach.

Indeed, architecture students and architectural firms we meet are becoming more and more informed and aware of the concept of BIM, but we noticed that the task definition remains a difficult activity to perform in the design process because it often depends on other tasks performed by other actors, or simply difficult to quantify.

3   Agile Practices Experiments in Architectural Design

3.1   Toward an Agile Architectural Conception

Agile methods are innovative project management methods that have emerged in the software engineering field in the 1990s. Wanting to be more pragmatic than traditional methods, they involve more the customer in the production chain by realizing numerous feedbacks and demonstrations in order to correctly identify his needs. They also follow three other fundamental values which are: collaborating team, working production, and responding to change. In addition to these four values, we found twelve agile principles which are by example a frequent work delivery, encourage face-to-face conversations, or making emerge self-organizing teams.

We can also add that these methods are based on an iterative, incremental and evolutionary productive cycle. On regular cycles, we develop a functional model improved by incremental functions. This model regularly evolves with the customer feedbacks. We then can see the links which are forged between the BIM technology and agile methods. The true nature of BIM technology is to evolve by design cycles, and its parametric side allows it to be responsive to change.

We have thus oriented our work towards methods allowing the different actors of a project to better identify the definition of a task in its whole complexity. We were inspired by the Suh's matrices [7] and created a table called "Conceptual Matrix" adapted to an agile architectural design.

Conceptual matrix is a tool that allows to "write down" the designers' architectural intentions. This matrix makes it possible to collaboratively express the needs or intentions of a project in order to prepare the realization of BIM tasks. These tasks will be first "refined" by the use of another agile practice: the "planning poker".

3.2   Elicitation Process: Writing Down Architectural Intentions

Elicitation is the act of formalizing an idea, a concept or an intention to be understood by its interlocutors. Or, in a collaborative context, the main goal is to be on the same page as its coworkers.

For this purpose, we have designed a conceptual matrix that project actors fill up together to confront their ideas and their understandings of architectural subjects.

As we seen in Fig. 1, conceptual matrix is an online spreadsheet where we find in rows the inputs (the intrants): the programmatic elements of a project, the needs of the

		Extrants (visual representation, words)				
		Ground plane		Functional diagram		Keywords
Intrants (programming, needs, constraints)	Boat center			Boats size Boats stockage Dimensions depends capacity High selling		visibility
	Seminar center		- facilitated visibility and access for external people		links with intership	panorama
	Intership	- cohesion between project buildings - private access for delivery	- calm and privacy - private exterior spaces	- spaces versality ex: same kitchen for club house and intership	- keep night and day spaces distinct - closer spaces for kids	centered
	Club house		- lake access - panoramic terrace - facilitated visibilité and access for external people		- restaurant in links with panoramic terrace - office near the dock	introspection

Fig. 1. Example of a conceptual matrix filled up by one student group

project manager or his constraints; and in columns the outputs (the extrants): the geometric or semantic translation of the inputs.

The conceptual matrix allows the different actors of a project to formalize conceptual elements by keywords and sentences to compare each other ideas. The main goal is not to fill all the spreadsheet cases, but to give actors a way to collaboratively determinate concepts and expectations by dialogue and debate. The matrix is a tool which valid intentions explorations.

Once achieved, this conceptual matrix makes it possible to realize a list of tasks to be executed, which we will define and specify with a planning poker.

3.3 Refinement Process: Perimeter Identification and Duration Estimation of Tasks

We have formalized the definition of a task according to the following characteristics:

- Title: how we name a task
- Complexity: allows a debate to define what constitutes the task
- Duration: in minutes or hour with a deadline
- Attribution: who will be in charge of this task

While title is defined after realization of the conceptual matrix, the other characteristics are defined during a planning poker. The planning poker is set of 13 cards with facial values from 1 to 100 and following an exponential distribution (1, 2, 3, 5, 8, 13, 20, 40 and 100).

Each turn corresponds to the definition of a task n. Thus, for the definition of the complexity of the task n, each player chooses a card of his game, poses face down in front of him, then return them at the same time. The objectives are to encourage negotiation between participants, avoid biased opinions following the first speaker, and allow all actors to speak (the "I do not know" card does not exist). When the discussion is over, participants choose a compromise value before doing the same process for the duration estimation, then move with the next task.

In Fig. 2, time estimations of each group 1 student for each task have been reported under the "Student x" label. "Estimation" bar is the final result of the group estimation after debating. "Real time" is the time measured at the end of the task. These last two values are reported in the Fig. 3.

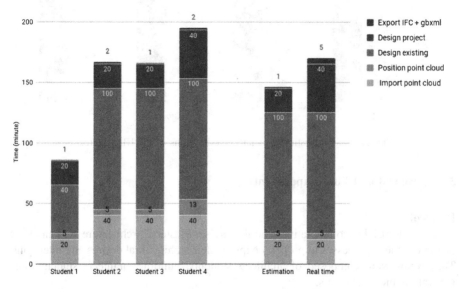

Fig. 2. Students estimations for a BIM exercise with planning poker

Even if their estimates of time or complexity are mistaken, they allow the actors of a project to start the negotiations, to find who does what, who has the best skills to carry out the task, and bring them closer to the optimal effective duration. Indeed, necessary exchanges and debates permitted to highlighting the different skills and expectations of each actor. We then notice that high or low estimations of time for realize a task show either a lack of knowledge about the subject complexity, or on the contrary a high appreciation due to an expert view. Ensuing exchanges permit all the actors to understand the overall scope of the task to be accomplished.

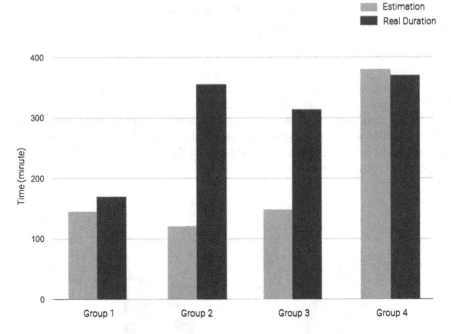

Fig. 3. Students estimations and real durations of the BIM exercise

3.4   Protocol and First Experiments

Protocol

During a short BIM collaborative school exercise, Master 2 architecture students have had to use these processes to properly express their architectural desires and intentions. The groups were composed of architects students, building engineers students, and general engineers students.

We followed this protocol:

- Theoretical phase: introductive course on agility, followed by a planning poker explanation.
- Practical phase: conceptual matrix presentation, filled collaboratively.
- Practical phase: matrix translation in tasks (titles), followed by a planning poker.
- Practical phase: project modeling, where durations are measured by students and reported in a table for analysis.
- Data gathering: students make a report of their matrices, results of planning poker and real tasks durations, with a comment on the practices.
- Data analysis: bias sort and practices improvement.

The theoretical phase allows the students to understand the challenge involved in making the project management evolve in parallel with the digital tools, and to adopt simple and effective agile methods. The practical phases enable students to apply the presented collaborative practices as exercises. Finally, data phases allow students to debrief their work and their matrices in order to adopt a task reference estimation for their future project; they also allow us to have students' feedbacks on the experiments, in order to improve the elicitation of intentions and the refinement of tasks process for the next school year.

Since spreadsheets matrices are online, we can collect data after the experiment. We then compare estimations in these spreadsheets with the real duration work, and sort concluding bias like bad subject comprehension, computer failure, or any unexpected event (keeping in mind that adaptability to change is nature of agile).

Experiments

The next figure shows estimations and measurements of duration tasks. Students have converted the conceptual matrix in a task table with planning poker corresponding the practical phases. Their goal was to import a point cloud from another course they followed before, position it in a BIM software, design the existing building thanks to this point cloud, design their architectural project with the help of the conceptual matrix and export the result for another course. The class was divided into four groups of four students, mixed academic origins and skills.

As we see in Fig. 3, some total estimations and real durations can be really different. Three groups estimate total work for 120–150 min, the last one 380. Final durations are between 310 and 370 min. The gap is due to hard tasks (import point cloud and position it) that only Group4 has planned. The Group1 has not accounted in its estimation this task, and has just got the work of another group. Sort this two tasks, each group correctly estimate their design tasks with the help of the conceptual matrix and dialogues and debate resulting from.

4   Conclusion and Perspectives

The experiments propose a defined process for students to make collaborative projects. The exchanges allow to collaboratively filling up spreadsheets in a rational and objective way to compare and measure wills and architectural intentions. Following by a planning poker, they can estimate the duration of their work in a BIM environment by an efficient manner thanks to their own skills and experiences.

The perspectives opening to us are now twofold. First, a work on field to implement our agile-BIM practices with an architectural firm wanting to realize a BIM transition. After the translation of agile methods to architectural field, we must then confront and transmit them to professionals. Indeed, we will commit ourselves to testing these innovative practices for the agencies, having no R&D department. Second, another pedagogical experiment during a semester duration project studio. We will be then able to confront our work with long architectural projects. Moreover, this paper shows the first two agile practices that we have experienced, which are more team-oriented. The next ones will be more customer-oriented, like a scrum-like method translated for our needs, a stand-up meeting, and a management dashboard which will be supported and fed with our matrix, providing an overall project view for the designers.

References

1. Halin, G., Hanser, D., Bignon, J.-C.: User adaptive visualization of cooperative architectural design. Int. J. Archit. Comput. **2**(1), 89–107 (2004). doi:10.1260/1478077041220188
2. Succar, B.: Building information modelling framework: a research and delivery foundation for industry stakeholders. Autom. Constr. **18**(2009), 357–375 (2009). doi:10.1016/j.autcon.2008.10.003
3. Beck, K., et al.: Manifesto for agile software development (2001). http://agilemanifesto.org
4. Numbers and maps of the architectural profession, a professional environment composed mainly of small structures, p. 48 (2015). http://www.architectes.org/sites/default/files/atoms/files/archigraphie-light_1.pdf
5. Dupin, P.: LEAN applied to construction: how to optimize project management and reduce costs and delays in building? Eyrolles (2014). ISBN 978-2212138320
6. Womack, J., Jones, D.: Lean Thinking: Banish Waste and Create Wealth in Your Corporation, 2nd edn. Revised and Updated. Free Press (2003). ISBN 978-0743249270
7. Suh, N.: Axiomatic Design: Advances and Applications. Oxford University Press, Oxford (2001). ISBN 978-0195134667

The Interactive Projection Mapping as a Spatial Augmented Reality to Help Collaborative Design: Case Study in Architectural Design

Xaviéra Calixte[✉] and Pierre Leclercq

LUCID - Lab for User Cognition and Innovative Design,
University of Liège, Liège, Belgium
{xaviera.calixte,pierre.leclercq}@ulg.ac.be

Abstract. This article describes the first implementation of a new SAR, spatial augmented reality, equipped here with a IPM, interactive projection mapping. It presents and analyses it as a new configuration of CSCW, Computer-Supported Cooperative Work. It reveals its success (support encouraging the collective understanding of complex shapes) but also the precautions and limits of this system of graphic interactive projection on a 3D model (delicate calibration, cognitive overload of utilization). It gives details of the adjustments to the status of co-participants (more passive), the status of work space (becoming an extended we-space) and the status of the common artifact (unmovable but polymorphic).

Keywords: Human computer interface for cooperative working · User interfaces for concurrent visualization · Spatial augmented reality (SAR) · Interactive projection mapping (IPM) · Case studies of cooperative design in architecture and engineering

1 Introduction

1.1 The Stakes in Collaborative Design

The technical and economic stakes in big construction projects, forces one today to begin the preliminary design work in a multi-disciplinary fashion: architects, engineers, technicians, builders, and managers. Therefore users find themselves involved in dynamic participation already in the "competition" phase [1]: together, they have more or less fifteen weeks of work to imagine, develop and pre-design a large scale architectural object with many functional, structural, formal and economic dimensions. Today, in addition to their technical expertise, the designers must imperatively consider the idea of collaborative design [2]. But how to master the complexity of such a human enterprise?

Modern-day communication and information technologies provide innovative means to achieve this but most of them (BIM systems, building information modeling

© Springer International Publishing AG 2017
Y. Luo (Ed.): CDVE 2017, LNCS 10451, pp. 143–152, 2017.
DOI: 10.1007/978-3-319-66805-5_18

and PLM (product live management) concern the sharing of detailed but asynchronous information.

Our work focuses rather on the linkage of competence, in real time, for meetings of experts and project reviews [3]. We try to equip co-designer meetings, during which the participants find themselves around the same table and interact, often graphically, on shared documents.

1.2 Spatial Augmented Reality

We have designed and set up different tools to encourage multi-disciplinary collaboration in the design process, all based on the idea of SAR, spatial augmented reality.

This is defined as a real space onto which virtual information is projected, perceived and, above all, manipulated at the same time by different participants [4]. Our co-design environments allow them to visualize and vote, by a show of hands, to annotate documents shared in real time. Specifically, the co-design environments are composed of a surface for graphic work, real and flat (wall, desk or table) on which all the documents that are useful for the design work (drawing, plans, sketches, texts, photos, perspectives, etc.) are projected. Software, named SketSha (for sketch sharing, Fig. 1) enables the synchronous manipulation and annotation of the documents with the help of a digital pen. It also enables one to invite another post, with the same characteristics, to join the session and integrate in the same way on the shared documents, in co-presence or remotely (in this case, with the support of a video-conference system [5].

Fig. 1. SketSha, real time sketch sharing software.

1.3 Support to the Collaborative Design Configurations

We have developed and set up several configurations of augmented collaborative space (SAR), in order to respond to the precise collaborative situation conditions. As explained earlier [3, 7], they concern:

- Remote Consulting (RC), to consult remote experts peer to peer (with graphic console and video-conference).

- Collaborative Remote Meeting (CRM), for team work of geographically distant designers (with interactive desk and video conference).
- Group Co-located Review (GCR), to review the collective project in a big group in co-presence (with desk and interactive wall).
- Group Co-located and Remote Evaluation (GCRE), to review the collective project with the co-participants in co-presence and others at a distance (with interactive desk, video-conference and interactive wall).

Each SAR configuration has been validated by being set up in an advanced training project for Architectural Engineers Masters Degree at the University of Liège. The observation and practice of their uses have shown real contributions to the quality of the collaboration, especially by reconsidering several statuses such as the status of the participants, the status of artifacts and the status of work spaces [7, 8].

We have shown that the SAR facilitates sharing of view points, construction of common referential operations and cognitive synchronization; in this way, they participate in the construction of a mutual conscientiousness of the activity and make the participants' status converge, developing the exchanges between them instead of competition.

Likewise, by their capacity to share graphic interaction in real time, the different SAR, assure the immediate "action/perception" coupling. Each co-author can maintain the causality link between the statements and the perception of the line on the shared artifact, giving it an operational status of boundary object shared interactively between the collaborators [9].

Finally the implementation of these SAR led to the revision of the "co-presence/remote" dichotomy in synchronous collaboration proposed by Johansen in 1998 and reused by Ellis et al. [10] revealing the emergence of a "distance in co-presence" situation when an interaction that is based on both a direct modality (conversation in the same physical space) and an indirect modality (the annotation of a virtually shared artifact on differentiated physical supports but situated in the same place) is established.

2 The Research Question

Therefore, the SAR configurations implemented provide new means enabling collaborative practices around design artifacts. However, until now, the discussions and interactions were only possible for projected 2D documents (plans, cross-sections, schema, photos, views, etc.) while, in all design works, the use of physical objects is frequently observed to support the reflection process (reduced technical model, industrial prototype, architectural scale-model, etc.). When the shape becomes more complex (for example, organic or non-structured architecture), classical projected 2D presentations are indeed not enough to easily communicate the necessary information. The use of three-dimension artifacts remains in fact an effective means to assure this kind of communication. The first solution that comes to mind in these digital environments would be to simulate the physical object by a 3D digital model. But to use this type of virtual model for the purposes of presentation/creation, it is necessary that the co-designers have at their disposal a CAD software permitting synchronous collaborative work. However, this type of interaction in real time is not obvious on complex digital models because it is subject to numerous technical constraints: very heavy software interface, high-speed 3D information, management of users' interaction contradictions, etc.

Therefore, our research proposes to study the use of a real physical model in augmented design. The principle is to put the model in the Group Co-located Review (GCR) and to project the information on this model, in particular to be able to interact on the 3D surface for annotation in real time.

To encourage exchanges and understanding between designers working on complex volumetric or technical projects, it is necessary to mobilize two ideas that have been little articulated in collaborative design until now: (1) the technology of "projection mapping" with (2) the capacity to integrate synchronous graphic interaction, both in support of the idea of "interactive projection mapping" (IPM) described below.

3   Current Uses of "Projection Mapping"

The projection of images and animations on physical surfaces is a technology that has been available for several years. Without going into a technical description of this kind of augmented reality [8], let us identify 3 principle elements of which it is composed: (1) 3D support, which is the physical element on which the projection is made; (2) the projection system and the video sequences or the images, which are the graphic elements calibrated and adjusted to the object on which they are projected; (3) finally the manual or automatic command system that manages the projection sequence.

Projection on physical objects of different scales (natural elements, water surface, buildings, urban models, furniture, etc.) are broadcast more and more in public spaces. Depending on their use, two categories can be distinguished.

- Projections of shows, which concern "sound and light" exhibitions showed to a large public during special events. This projection shows predefined and synchronized animations, often on existing urban elements, augmented by the projection to represent new visions of space. Arousing artistic emotion, this augmented reality is foremost meant to entertain the spectators but not to interact with it. (see the examples given in the Figs. 2a, b and 3a here below).
- Interactive projection which, beyond the projection of preliminary synchronized images, stand out by the stakes of complementary interaction with the augmented object. The physical element serves therefore as the support for information that can be adapted on command (custom made scenarios). The interaction with the object is then carried through the bias of the command system, in the form of a game of buttons causing this or that projected episode on demand (see the examples given in the Fig. 3b below).

Certainly, both scenarios described here augment the object through projection. However, even if this is announced as interactive, it follows one or another previously defined scenario: it is not possible to get away from scripts that are planned and pre-recorded. They are not useful to collaborative design work.

Fig. 2. (a) Audio-visual show at festival of lights in lyon (www.fetedeslumieres.lyon.fr), (b) Immersive art experience in the Carrière de lumière (http://carrieres-lumieres.com/en),

Fig. 3. (a) Dining experiences with "Le Petit Chef" (www.ilovebelgium.be/dinner-and-show-le-petit-chef), (b) Historical interactive mockup of Nantes city (http://devocite.com/?page_id=1202).

4   Towards a "Interactive Projection Mapping" (IPM)

To enable collaborative interaction around an object in a synchronous way, a new configuration of SAR is proposed. Called "interactive projection mapping" (IPM), it is set up in the university context mentioned above (point 1.3) and is composed of:

- an architectural model, a white-colored reduced model of a building, which makes up the physical support on which interactive information is project, and which is placed on a table in the core of a group of collaborators;
- a series of still images, chosen and organised beforehand to contain the initial digital information, augmenting the model (presentation scenario);
- a high resolution beamer, located above the reduced model, projecting the digital data sent by SketSha software;
- a digital tablet, an Apple iPad® or a Wacom Companion®, on which SketSha works and whose interface permits an actor to interact, with an electronic stylus in real time (collaborative situation).

Together they enable the projection of the initial presentation scenario, composed of the preliminary still images on the physical model and to interact on the information projected at any time with the pen from the tablet.

5   Context of the Implementation

This new configuration of IPM-SAR was implemented in 2016 in the context of an architecture workshop at the 1 Master architecture civil engineers level at the University of Liège in which one of the developed projects presented strong formal particularities: conceived to accommodate two auditoriums in the heart of the city of Nîmes (France), this ambitious architectural project was characterized by a complex exterior shape (organic architecture) to accommodate cultural functions such as complex organizational limits on interior spaces linked to the spectacle (Fig. 4).

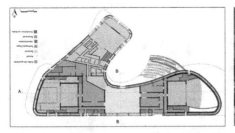 

Fig. 4. Architectural plan (ground floor) and perspective drawing.

A group of two student-designers tried at first to master this double complexity, by means of a parametric digital 3D model developed by Rhino® and Grasshoppers® [11] but the realization of this sophisticated virtual model ran up against the limits of manipulation of the model, which was very complicated to permit efficient evolution of its multi-constraint shape. So they chose to work on their real model with a 1.5 meter-long physical model made in clay. This malleable matter permitted the development of their concept and to adapt it in a fluid and rapid manner throughout the three months of their design work.

However, we observed, during different reviews of the intermediary projects, all carried out on the configurations presented in point 1.3, a clear difficulty to communicate their complex project based on the traditional 2D elements.

This case study answers the hypotheses raised in the problem (point 1.2): in fact, the physical model was at the heart of the design considerations, but lacked a means to communicate the under-lying intentions of the complex formal renderings. Therefore the new IPM-SAR configuration was adopted to support the trial of the final presentation of this architectural product. To meet the pedagogical demands, two concerns needed to be mastered: (1) present the result of the design from still images calibrated on the white model and (2) assure the defense by permitting a graphic interaction in real time on the augmented model in answer to the questions and remarks of the jury. The scaling and the rotation/translation of the images on the white model were supported through the basic functions of Sketsha, the mapping between the images and the model was realized with some landmarks common to both supports (as it is necessary to guarantee the matching of the model to the projected images).

6   Observations and Discussion

The implementation of the situation was held in December 2016 (Fig. 5). It concerned the 2 student-designers, who sat at either end of the 1,80 m × 1,20 m projection table, and several evaluating experts who sat on a 3rd side of the table (E). One of the students (S1) assured the presentation by drawing with SketSha on a tablet (T). The clay model, painted white (M), was augmented by different images and by his interactively projected drawings. The other student (S2) commented on the interaction by hand (Fig. 6). A camera recorded (C) the whole presentation sequence to enable the analysis which follows.

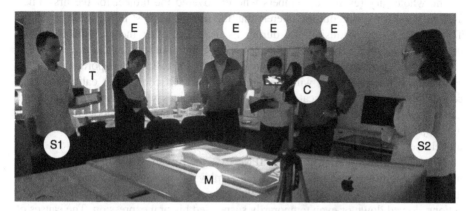

Fig. 5. Interactive Projection Mapping implementation.

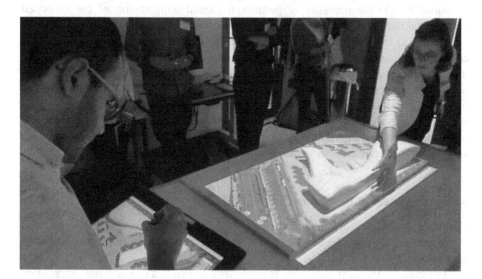

Fig. 6. Interactive Projection Mapping in action: the first student is drawing lines on the mobile tablet, whereas the second student is commenting on the augmented white model while these lines are appearing simultaneously for the whole jury.

6.1   Qualitative Observations

First, let us emphasize the success of the experiment: and the jury declared that it was filled with enthusiasm by the formula and assured us that they had well understood the speech and the complexity of the presented model. The trainers confirmed that the understanding of the project proved to be better than that noticed during earlier reviews which had only used projected 2D documents.

Indeed, several members of the jury attended intermediate presentations of the same project without the IPM and they were able to compare both types of the presentation. Specific project information (like users' access, pluvial flow, structure principles, etc. - notions difficult to develop and to argue in complex architecture), were all understood by the whole jury (even the members who discovered the project for the first time). This fact comforts us about the interest that the use of the IPM in the SAR can have. This first test was promising, so, during its next use, other means will be used to develop validation criteria around this notion of communication efficiency.

The implementation of this configuration led us to realize the importance of good calibration of the projection with the physical object. Of course, this calibration concerns the position and the scale of the projected images whose characteristic points must correspond to those of the model, but also the position of the model in relation to the projector, in order to reduce the inevitable impact of self-caused shadows on the model itself.

The experimentation of the new IPM-SAR then enabled us to observe that an important cognitive load had to be put into play by the drawing participant. Even though he knew perfectly well his presentation speech, the video shows that the drawn actions slowed down or even temporarily suspended his oral expression. The causes of this difficulty, noticed more in this configuration than in the other SAR, can be explained by (1) the necessity of permanent mental reorientation of the annotated drawing, taking into account that the tablet is mobile compared to the model which is stable and (2) the necessity to assure that the drawing, shown in 2D on the tablet, is correctly reflected on the 3D surface of the model. Drawing while looking only at the model proved to be impractical because of the relief of the object and the lateral position of the participant. Finally the project presentation by its augmented 3D model was not sufficient: if it proved to be a powerful means of communication to explain complex shapes, it had to be be completed by a presentation of classic projected views (plans, intersections, interior views of the model, etc.) that were put into play here in another SAR, in this case on the interactive whiteboard (GCRE SAR).

6.2   Adjustment of the Statuses in the IPM-SAR

How does the status characterizing the earlier SAR evolve? Referring to those recalled in point 1.3, we can notice that the new IPM-SAR configuration brings the following adjustments.

The status of the participants has temporarily returned to a classical one: the posture has remained that of students and evaluators. This is due to the conditions of the first experiment that gave the means of interaction to one lone participant (the student drawer), the others could only remain passive in relation to the augmented object.

The work space has kept its status of we-space, bringing together all the participants in co-presence in the same collaborative space. However, this could be qualified as "extended we-space" because it integrates all the persons in the projection space (concept of "collaborative bubble") around the augmented artifact that is the catalyst.

The status of the artifact is very special in the IPM-SAR. Due to its size and weight (1.5 m one side and 30 kg.), it is evidently unique and unmovable during the interaction, in contrast to other documents put into play in the earlier SAR, whose projection enabled the alternation in the work space. However, this uniqueness is enriched by the polymorphic quality of the physical support: the object can include interactive projections of multiple subjects, as do the flat surfaces of the other SAR. Here, the model of the building is augmented, for example, by the 3D graphic representations of the supporting structures, by the flux of internal circulation, by the position of vertical circulation (elevators) or even by the sides of the roof to collect rainwater. Let us also notice that, in any case, the flat surface of the table remains accessible around the 3D model and enables annotations and interactive drawings like the other SAR (the idea of second drawings [12].

7 Conclusions and Perspectives

This article describes the first implementation of a new SAR, spatial augmented reality, equipped with a IPM, interactive projection mapping. It presents it and analyses it as a complementary configuration to the 4 configurations already known in the heart of CSCW, Computer-Supported Cooperative Work. It points out its success (support encouraging the understanding of complex shapes) but also the precautions and limits of this system of graphic interactive projection on a 3D model (delicate calibration, cognitive overload of utilization). It gives details of the adjustments to the status of co-participants (more passive), the work space (becoming here an extended we-space) and the common artifact (unmovable but polymorphic). To go beyond the observed limits in this first experiment we plan two main actions:

- to make the participants active by putting at their disposal a personal tablet that will enable them to take control in their turn of the interaction with the shared 3D artifact;
- to complete the interface of the SketSha software which establishes the graphic link between the collaborators and the artifact, by an auto-orientation function of the 2D drawing shown as graphic support on individual iPads, in relation to the fixed orientation of the augmented model.

This last action will enable us to reduce the cognitive load that is necessary for the graphic interaction on the tablet: no matter what position and orientation of each participant, he can draw an image that corresponds to his point of view on the shared model.

Acknowledgments. The LUCID-Ulg team thanks C. Vergnaud and E. Stylianidis, first-master students in architectural engineering 2016–17 of the ULg, for their investment in this experiment and for the risk-taking that they consented to in their final jury.

References

1. Skair, L.: The transnational capitalist class and contemporary architecture in globalizing cities. Int. J. Urban Regional Res. **29**(3), 485–500 (2005)
2. Visser, W.: Co-élaboration de solutions en conception architecturale et rôle du graphico-gestuel: point de vue de la psychologie ergonomique. In: Détiennes, F., Traverso, V. (eds.) Méthodologies d'analyse de situations coopératives de conception: Corpus MOSAIC. Presses Universitaires de Nancy, Nancy, pp. 129–167 (2009)
3. Ben Rajeb, S., Leclercq, P.: Using spatial augmented reality in synchronous collaborative design. In: Luo, Y. (ed.) CDVE 2013. LNCS, vol. 8091, pp. 1–10. Springer, Heidelberg (2013). doi:10.1007/978-3-642-40840-3_1
4. Furth, B.: Handbook of Augmented Reality. Springer, New York (2011). doi:10.1007/978-1-4614-0064-6
5. Safin, S., Leclercq, P.: User studies of a sketch-based collaborative distant design solution in industrial context. In: Luo, Y. (ed.) CDVE 2009. LNCS, vol. 5738, pp. 117–124. Springer, Heidelberg (2009). doi:10.1007/978-3-642-04265-2_16
6. Safin, S., Juchmes, R., Leclercq, P.: Use of graphical modality in a collaborative design distant setting. In: Dugdale, J., Masclet, C., Grasso, M.A., Boujut, J.F., Hassanaly, P. (eds.) COOP 2012. Springer, London (2012). doi:10.1007/978-1-4471-4093-1_17
7. Ben Rajeb, S., Leclercq, P.: Apports des configurations spatiales augmentées aux activités de formation par projet. In: van de Leemput, C., Chauvin, C., Hellemans, C. (eds.) Activités humaines, technologies et bien être, pp. 171–178. Sciences Publishing, Paris (2013)
8. Ben Rajeb, S., Leclercq, P.: Spatial augmented reality in collaborative design training: articulation between i-space, we-space and space-between. In: Shumaker, R., Lackey, S. (eds.) VAMR 2014. LNCS, vol. 8526, pp. 343–353. Springer, Cham (2014). doi:10.1007/978-3-319-07464-1_32
9. Star, S.L.: The structure of ill-structured solutions: heterogenous problem solving, boundary objects and distributed artificial intelligence. In: Distributed Artificial Intelligence, vol. 2, pp. 37–54. Morgan Kaufmann Publishers Inc., San Fransisco, (1990)
10. Ellis, C.A., Gibbs, S.J., Rein, G.: Groupware: some issues and experiences. Commun. ACM **34**(1), 39–58 (1991)
11. Tedeschi, A.: Parametric Architecture with Grasshopper: Primer. Le Penseur (2011). ISBN 8895315103
12. Leclercq, P., Elsen, C.: Le croquis synthé-numérique. In: Leclercq, P., Martin, G., Deshayes, C., Guena, F. (eds.) Actes de la conférence SCAN, Séminaire de Conception Architecturale Numérique: Apports de l'image numérique en conception. Université de Liège, Belgium (2007)

Extension-Evaluation-Based Alternative Resource Selection for Cloud Manufacturing

Li-Nan Zhu[1(✉)], Wan-Liang Wang[1], Yan-Wei Zhao[2], Xin Xu[3], and Jing-Hui Hu[1]

[1] School of Computer Science and Technology, Zhejiang University of Technology, Hangzhou 310023, People's Republic of China
{zln,wwl}@zjut.edu.cn, hzbellahu@l63.com
[2] Key Laboratory of Special Purpose Equipment and Advanced Processing Technology, Ministry of Education, Zhejiang University of Technology, Hangzhou 310023, People's Republic of China
zyw@zjut.edu.cn
[3] Engineering Design Group Co., Ltd., Zhejiang University of Technology, Hangzhou 310023, People's Republic of China
xuxin@zjut.edu.cn

Abstract. As one of the networked collaborative manufacturing modes, cloud manufacturing was put forward in the early 2000s and has gained more and more attention by governments and research institutions in recent years. Because of the diversity and uncertainty of cloud resource, the cloud manufacturing platform should have the ability of manufacturing risk evaluation to search a suitable alternative resource when a certain cloud resource fails suddenly during the manufacturing process, with the aim of making the probability of the alternative resource failing again come down to the lowest and enabling the manufacturing process implemented well. In this article, a new risk evaluation method based on the extension theory is proposed. The details and a theoretical example study are introduced, and the result shows that the proposed method reflected accurately the manufacturing risk and could effectively support alternative resource selection for cloud manufacturing.

Keywords: Alternative resource selection · Manufacturing risk evaluation · Extension theory · Cloud manufacturing

1 Introduction

Attributed to cloud computing theory and application, cloud manufacturing (CMfg), as the extension and development of networked manufacturing, was put forward in the early 2000s, and has gradually risen and become the main direction of manufacturing industry. CMfg reflects the idea of "distributed resources being integrated for one task" and "integrated resources being distributed for services". It achieves the many-to-many service mode, which provides multiple users with services at the same time by aggregating and centralized managing distributed resources and services [1]. CMfg is a stable, robust and flexible manufacturing system with strong self-repair ability. When a certain manufacturing node fails due to a sudden reason such as blackout or natural

© Springer International Publishing AG 2017
Y. Luo (Ed.): CDVE 2017, LNCS 10451, pp. 153–159, 2017.
DOI: 10.1007/978-3-319-66805-5_19

disaster during the manufacturing process, the system can search an alternative resource to finish the manufacturing task. In this condition, the manufacturing risk evaluation of alternative resources is very important. Because the sudden failure of the original manufacturing node has damaged the stability of the whole manufacturing process in a certain extent, this puts forward higher requirement on the manufacturing reliability of alternative resources, and system needs to choose an alternative manufacturing resource in lower manufacturing risk, so that the probability of the entire production process destroyed again comes down to the lowest. In this paper, we will propose a manufacturing **R**isk **E**valuation method based on **E**xtension **E**valuation (REEE) for alternative resource selection in CMfg.

The remainder of this paper is organized as follows. Section 2 briefly describes the problem on alternative resource selection. The extension evaluation model is introduced in Sect. 3. Section 4 presents a theoretical example study. Finally, Sect. 5 gives the conclusion.

2 Problem Description

2.1 Structure of Cloud Manufacturing

In the research result from our previous work [2], cloud manufacturing is a kind of new manufacturing mode, which connects different manufacturing resources with modern information technology such as Internet, RFID, and so on. There are three kinds of roles: (1) The Resource Demander (RD), who is the demander of products, manufacturing resource or service; (2) The Resource Provider (RP), who is the provider of products, manufacturing resource or service; (3) The Manager, who designs, develop and maintain the cloud manufacturing equipment and related software. So, the cloud manufacturing system is composed of cloud manufacturing platform (CMP) and cloud end (CE), and CE contains cloud demander (CD) and cloud provider (CP) which are corresponding to RD and RP respectively.

2.2 Scenario Description

In CMfg, manufacturing resources located in different areas are diversity and complexity, so they always hold uncertainty for completing the manufacturing task. Due to emergence situation such as equipment failure, enterprise management failure, natural disaster and breach of contract, a manufacturing resource (a manufacturing node in the manufacturing lifecycle) may not finish the manufacturing task such as product design, processing and test analysis in accordance with the original plan. This sudden failure requires that the CMP should have the abilities of manufacturing risk evaluation, manufacturing task re-planning, and dynamic adjustment for manufacturing plan, in order to rapidly search an alternative resource to make the whole manufacturing process not be destroyed and the probability of the alternative resource failing again come down to the lowest. Just showed as the Fig. 1, when the manufacturing node CS_i failures, there are many alternative manufacturing scheme consist of one or more manufacturing resources, which have three categories of relationship: (1) Serial

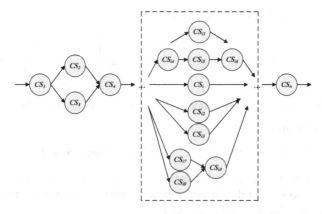

Fig. 1. Alternative resource selection in cloud manufacturing

Manufacturing Chain (SMC); (2) Same Product Parallel Manufacturing Chain (SPPMC); (3) Different Product Parallel Manufacturing Chain (DPPMC). In the final analysis, the core question is to evaluate the risk of every manufacturing unit.

3 Manufacturing Risk Evaluation Model Based on Extension

In this section, we will detail the calculation procedure of the new manufacturing risk evaluation algorithm REEE.

Step 1: Define the classical field and the limited field.
    Assume,

$$R_0 = \begin{bmatrix} N & N_1 & N_2 & \cdots & N_m \\ C & V_1 & V_2 & \cdots & V_m \end{bmatrix} = \begin{bmatrix} N & N_1 & N_2 & \cdots & N_m \\ C_1 & \langle a_{11}, b_{11} \rangle & \langle a_{12}, b_{12} \rangle & \cdots & \langle a_{1m}, b_{1m} \rangle \\ C_2 & \langle a_{21}, b_{21} \rangle & \langle a_{22}, b_{22} \rangle & \cdots & \langle a_{2m}, b_{2m} \rangle \\ \vdots & \vdots & \vdots & \ddots & \vdots \\ C_n & \langle a_{n1}, b_{n1} \rangle & \langle a_{n2}, b_{n2} \rangle & \cdots & \langle a_{nm}, b_{nm} \rangle \end{bmatrix},$$

where R_0 is the matter element with the same characteristics, and means the set of the same kind of manufacturing resource; N_j is the risk evaluation level, and $j = 1, 2, \cdots, m$; C_i is the risk evaluation index, and $i = 1, 2, \cdots, n$; $V_{ij} = \langle a_{ij}, b_{ij} \rangle$ named the classical field is the value range of risk index C_i on the level of risk grade N_j, and $\langle \rangle$ can be open interval (), or closed interval [], or half open interval [) and (].

Assume, $R_p = (P, C, V_p) = \begin{bmatrix} P, & C_1, & V_{1p} \\ & C_2, & V_{2p} \\ & \vdots & \vdots \\ & C_n, & V_{np} \end{bmatrix} = \begin{bmatrix} P, & C_1, & \langle a_{1p}, b_{1p} \rangle \\ & C_2, & \langle a_{2p}, b_{2p} \rangle \\ & \vdots & \vdots \\ & C_n, & \langle a_{np}, b_{np} \rangle \end{bmatrix}$, where

P is the set of all alternative resource; $V_{ip} = \langle a_{ip}, b_{ip} \rangle$ named the limited field is the value range in risk index C_i of all the alternative resource. So, $V_{ij} \subset V_{ip}$ $(i = 1, 2, \cdots, n$ and $j = 1, 2, \cdots, m)$ must be hold.

Step 2: Describe the matter element to be evaluated.

The matter element to be evaluated is described as $\begin{bmatrix} q, & C_1, & v_1 \\ & C_2, & v_2 \\ & \vdots & \vdots \\ & C_n, & v_n \end{bmatrix}$. Here, q is the

certain alternative resource to be evaluated; v_i is q's value in risk index C_i.

Step 3: Define the weight.

Define the weight ζ_i of risk index C_i, so $\sum_{i=1}^{n} \zeta_i = 1$ must be hold.

Step 4: Define correlation degree between C_i of q and every risk grade N_j.

Establish extension correlation function as formula (1) to calculate the correlation degree between C_i of q and every risk level N_j.

$$K_j(v_i) = \begin{cases} \dfrac{\rho(v_i, V_{ij})}{\rho(v_i, V_{ip}) - \rho(v_i, V_{ij})}, & \rho(v_i, V_{ip}) - \rho(v_i, V_{ij}) \neq 0, \\ -\rho(v_i, V_{ij}) - 1, & \rho(v_i, V_{ip}) - \rho(v_i, V_{ij}) = 0. \end{cases} \tag{1}$$

Here, $\rho(x, \langle a, b \rangle) = \left| x - \dfrac{a+b}{2} \right| - \dfrac{1}{2}(b - a)$.

Step 5: Calculate the correlation degree between q and every risk level N_j with the formula (2).

$$K_j(q) = \sum_{i=1}^{n} \zeta_i K_j(v_i) \tag{2}$$

Step 6: Calculate the evaluation result.

Set $K_{j_0}(q) = \max_{j \in \{1,2,\cdots,m\}} K_j(q)$, the evaluation result of q is level j_0. Set

$$\overline{K_j(q)} = \frac{K_j(q) - \min_j K_j(q)}{\max_j K_j(q) - \min_j K_j(q)} \tag{3}$$

$$j^* = \frac{\sum_{j=1}^{m} j \bullet \overline{K_j(q)}}{\sum_{j=1}^{m} \overline{K_j(q)}} \tag{4}$$

Thus, j^* is the level variable characteristic value of q.

This model can be used where there is standard evaluation index and level. But if not, the classical field can be defined by user's requirement, and the limited field is the union of classical field and the value range of resource to be evaluated.

4 Theoretical Example

4.1 Experiment Introduction

Take the car tire as an example, and the experiment result will be analyzed and compared with the method of fuzzy pattern recognition (FPR) [3] and fuzzy evaluation (FE) [4].

Experimental hardware environment: Lenovo Notebook Computer (ThinkPak T61), CPU is Inter® Core™ 2, 1.80 GHz, and memory is 3 GB.

Experimental software environment: The operating system is Windows XP Professional (32 bit), and programming software is Microsoft Visual C++ 6.0.

4.2 Example Data

According to the characteristics of car tire production, we adopt the following four evaluation indexes: (1) index C_1, total manufacturing task; (2) index C_2, capacity load. Set the total manufacturing capacity is MC_t, the manufacturing capacity needed by the task on-load is MC_h, and the new task C_1 is MC_n, thus C_2 is $(MC_n)/(MC_t - MC_h) \times 100\%$; (3) index C_3, historical completion rate, here we set the time range is the recent three years; (4) index C_4, equipment depreciation rate. There are 8 candidate resources, every index value of which is showed in Table 1, and the weight of every risk index given by the technicians of enterprises is as Table 2.

Table 1. The values in every risk index of the 8 enterprises

ID	1	2	3	4	5	6	7	8
C_1	2500	2500	2500	2500	2500	2500	2500	2500
C_2	0.8860	0.5630	0.8882	0.8829	0.6942	0.8201	0.5568	0.8830
C_3	0.9675	0.8769	0.8845	0.9566	0.8689	0.9062	0.8269	0.8175
C_4	0.1091	0.2727	0.3818	0.1818	0.6545	0.2727	0.8182	0.1818

Table 2. The weight of every risk index

Risk index	C_1	C_2	C_3	C_4
Weight ζ	0.1437	0.3311	0.1683	0.3269

There are five risk levels from the lowest to the highest: N_1, N_2, N_3, N_4 and N_5, and the classical field and the limited field of every level in every index given by domain experts are showed in Table 3.

Table 3. The classical field and limited field in every risk index

Risk index		C_1	C_2	C_3	C_4
Classical field	N_1	[0,1000]	[0,0.65]	[0.99,1]	[0,0.1818]
	N_2	[1000,2000]	[0.65,0.8]	[0.95,0.99]	[0.1818,0.5091]
	N_3	[2000,3000]	[0.8,0.9]	[0.87,0.95]	[0.5091,0.6545]
	N_4	[3000,6000]	[0.9,0.97]	[0.7,0.87]	[0.6545,0.8182]
	N_5	[6000,10000]	[0.97,1]	[0,0.7]	[0.8182,1]
Limited field		[0,10000]	[0,1]	[0,1]	[0,1]

4.3   Result and Analysis

Showed in the experimental result as Table 4, the enterprise No. 1 is the best one, and its risk level is 1 with strong trend to level 2, so the accurate risk level is 1.941. The result comprehensively and accurately reflects the manufacturing risk.

Table 4. The result of experiment

ID	1	2	3	4	5	6	7	8
N_1	0.2946	−0.1483	−0.4863	−0.3604	−0.3798	−0.3901	−0.3162	−0.3707
N_2	−0.0656	0.0106	−0.0782	−0.1256	−0.1406	0.0431	−0.3698	−0.2478
N_3	−0.2440	−0.2205	0.0217	−0.1438	−0.0508	0.0504	−0.2758	−0.1622
N_4	−0.4813	−0.3693	−0.2139	−0.4343	−0.1555	−0.3717	−0.1027	−0.2219
N_5	−0.6844	−0.5784	−0.5200	−0.6489	−0.4576	−0.5886	−0.3275	−0.5570
max	0.2991	0.0106	0.0217	−0.1256	−0.0508	0.0504	−0.1027	−0.1622
j_0	**1**	2	3	2	3	3	4	3
j^*	**1.941***	2.218	2.846	2.422	2.846	3.519	3.535	2.715
FPR	2	**1***	2	2	3	2	5	2
FE	0.8080	**0.9357***	0.5056	0.7693	0.1783	0.7509	0.1926	0.7832

Comparatively speaking, the risk level of each resource can only be explained simply by FPR, and the deviation can't be shown. In addition, through the method of FE, the best and the worst vector is gotten by values in each index of candidate resources, then calculate the membership degree of candidate resource relative to the best vector, and the biggest one would be chosen. This method is influenced deeply by the amount of candidate resources, so the much the candidate resource is, the more accurate the result will be, or vice versa.

5   Conclusion

With the increasingly fierce competition in the global market and increasingly serious energy and environmental issues, the integration and sharing of manufacturing resource has been becoming more and more important during the design, production, usage and reproduction of the product and related services. As a kind of "Cloud Theory", CMfg has been gradually accepted and paid more attention by research institutions and enterprises all over the world. However, because of the diversity and uncertainty of resource, it is a need that the CMP can evaluate the manufacturing risk of resource, and rapidly search an alternative resource when a certain manufacturing node fails suddenly during the manufacturing process. In this paper, we proposed a manufacturing risk evaluation method based on extension. Extension evaluation model can show not only the risk level, but also the membership degree to risk level with the level variable characteristic value, so that we can get more accurate risk value.

Acknowledgement. This work was partly supported by the National Natural Science Foundation of China Grant No. 61379123, 61572438 and 61701443 and the Natural Science Foundation of Zhejiang Province, China (Grant No. LQ15E050006).

References

1. Zhu, L.-N., Zhao, Y.-W., Shen, G.-J.: Performance-matching-based resource selection for cloud manufacturing. In: Proceedings of the 13th International Conference on Cooperative Design, Visualization and Engineering, Sydney (2016)
2. Zhao, Y.-W., Zhu, L.-N.: Service-evaluation-based resource selection for cloud manufacturing. Concur. Eng. Res. Appl. **24**(4), 307–317 (2016)
3. Lu, Z.Z., Wang, J., Lu, Y.P.: Direct method of fuzzy pattern recognition and its application to stability classification of surrounding rocks. J. Hohai Univ. **19**(6), 97–101 (1991)
4. Zhang, B.X., Li, L.Z., Du, Z.C.: The evaluation system and fuzzy evaluation method for dynamic supply chain. J. Tianjin Normal Univ. (Nat. Sci. Ed.) **21**(3), 19–23 (2001)

The Cognitive Visualization of Space in City Walking: Spacescape Experimentation in Italy

Dario Esposito, Giulia Mastrodonato, and Domenico Camarda[✉]

DICATECh, Polytechnic University of Bari, Bari, Italy
{dario.esposito,d.camarda}@poliba.it,
julie.mastrodonato@gmail.com

Abstract. Spacescapes are often shaped by spatial behaviour. However, their dynamic complexity makes it difficult for them to be simulated in AI-based environments. As a result, degrees of uncertainty often arise when one describes spaces, trying to give shared importance to structural, fundamental, peculiar spacescape qualities.

This paper explores space ontologies built by human agents. With the use of app features of personal smartphones, students of the Technical University of Bari have explored an urban commercial street. The results they obtained in the context of spatial cognition have been analysed and discussed for environment planning and management.

Keywords: Spatial behaviour · Spacescape · Urban planning

1 Introduction

Over time many scholars [3, 5, 6] have studied spacescapes, as knowledge-intensive entities that humans adapt for their life. It is difficult to simulate spatial behaviours in virtual environments due to their dynamic complexity. Hence, agents who use them in their daily life, often wonder about the basic features, or 'fundamentals', of spacescapes. Questions arise by agents living and moving in these spaces. On the one hand, it is recognized that humans understand well designed space architecture more easily than amorphous spaces. Yet, the overload of landmarks and symbols in cities often gives rise to social marginality and negatives effect on some people. Goodman claims that when people try to give a common meaning to spacescape structural, fundamental, peculiar qualities, there is often an amount of uncertainty [4]. In artificial intelligence there is a need for this kind of fine-tuning characterization of space. In fact, when planning automatic navigation it is essential for robotics to have a sort of ontological representation of space. Cognitive science and AI need each other. As a result, an increase in the knowledge on human behaviour in space emerges. In strategic spatial planning space imaging can be of great interest. In fact, it can be seen that it results in a stronger representation of the structural, invariant, resilient characters of the environment. This is essential for the development and management of human spaces. This paper aims to look at human agents shaping space ontology, with a spatial cognition approach in an urban layout. Students of the Spatial Planning course in the Polytechnic University of Bari (Italy) have explored a commercial street in the centre of Bari.

© Springer International Publishing AG 2017
Y. Luo (Ed.): CDVE 2017, LNCS 10451, pp. 160–167, 2017.
DOI: 10.1007/978-3-319-66805-5_20

In order to develop this task, they were asked to take photos of significant places of their choice and take notes on their sensations and perceptions along the street. They were also asked to record their path and collect data using automatic app features of personal smartphones. Chapter two deals with research background and aims. Chapter three describes the experimentation layout and the fourth chapter carries out data analysis and discusses relevant results achieved in the context of spatial cognition. The conclusion extends the outcome with particular reference to broader perspectives of complex environment planning and management.

2   Research Background

Pedestrians spontaneously use all their senses to immerse themselves in the urban space experience. It implies the perception and recognition of some particular elements available in the surrounding environment. The study of spatial cognition using a camera aims to explore and possibly understand what are the fundamental elements of urban space, in terms of people's relation to them. In fact, the visual experience often imprints in people the first impression of space [8]. This is even more interesting in the particular case of historic urban spaces, which are rich with architectural details. The experimentation is mainly aimed at assessing:

1. whether, when and why pedestrians' attention is captured by significant features of the urban environment. Features are intended as significant when useful to accomplish a navigation task and/or when able of capturing the pedestrians' attentions due to their own characteristics. Knowing what scenes and elements are significant helps us understand people's spatial experience;
2. if favourite spacescapes emerge from analysing photos taken on location points.

The on-site experiment aims to collect measurable data in order to extract qualitative information about the urban context. In fact, we assume that features frequently taken may represent significant elements. The next step could be the analysis of both collected pictures and preferred photo-taking locations in order to understand if and how the elements of the urban space could influence pedestrians explorative behaviour, i.e. their idea about space and their feelings during the experimentation.

3   Description of the Experimentation

Almost 200 individuals, aging 20 to 26, took part in the experiment. They were recruited among the students of the Technical University of Bari. The experiment was carried out individually. The study area is located in the city centre of Bari (Italy). The central area offers many services, offices and shops and it is usual to bump into public performances and recreational events. The experimental pathway runs between the station square, through the main square of Piazza Umberto, to the last block of Via Argiro - a pedestrian street where it is possible to stroll around comfortably (Fig. 1).

All the participants had to start from a given starting point: the rail station square. Then they were allowed to walk freely, exploring the urban environment to reach a

Fig. 1. The experimentation layout.

designated destination located in the last street block of Via Argiro. The total length of the pathway is approx 1 km. Participants were not allowed to use navigation supports, so increasing the possibility that the trail was influenced more significantly by the real surrounding environment [2]. Further, start and end points of the trail were predetermined to minimize the dispersion of gathered data, so as to better manage ex-post statistical analysis. Participants were asked to use MyTrack smartphone app (not in use anymore) to record the path and take photos. The app automatically registered information such as photo-taking time and geographic coordinates of locations. They were also asked to make comments on electronic sheets, when they felt that the features of the context deserved it. Amounts of photos and statements were not limited. Moving through the urban environment, participants came across various scenes and cityscapes. They freely recorded what they considered interesting and relevant. At the end of the experiment, written comments and photos were filed and categorized for subsequent analysis. In general, the navigating agent was to perform a sequence of navigation tasks. At the starting point, the agent looks at the neighbouring spaces trying to relate herself to the spatial environment, in order to work out what is the most suitable direction for her navigation activity. In this location, she receives feedback from the surrounding space and may decide to take photos and write comments to fix signs and impressions. As photos and notes are geotagged, the location of snapshots and comments is determined. Then the agent activates MyTrack path recorder (time starts running) and starts walking along her decided path. During this walking activity, she is supposed to be unable to write comments or take photos: yet path length and elapsed time are recorded for subsequent analyses. If the agent decides to stop somewhere along her navigation, than she can take photos and/or written comments, that will be

Table 1. Record sheet of agent #67 navigating activity (excerpt).

AGENT #67	Activity	Time	Coordinates (length)	photo snapshot	photo comment	note comment
Start point	start walking, and path recording	0:00	41.120108, 16.869763		I like this statue	Calm place to reflect
Path	Cross square	5:46	(77m)			
Intermediate location #1	Stop on sidewalk	5:46	41.121700, 16.870599		-	Not sure about where to go
......	......	....	...	.....	......	.....
Path	Cross sidewalk	...	....			
End point	Stop on sidewalk	37:32	41.125985, 16.870240		I knew door was here	It was a really exciting experience

recorded by GPS coordinates and times. Each agent's records are summarized in a synthesized framework sheet, for final analysis aims, as reported in the following example (Table 1).

Basing on such database, within the above general research framework, the present paper deals with preliminary findings of a more extensive analysis still ongoing.

3.1   Some Discussion Notes on the Experimental Outputs

The experimentation leads to several interpretations of data. Below we present a focus on the cognitive visualization of space made by agents and conveyed by the collected urban space snapshots. The pathway as shown in Fig. 2 runs through a uniform grid of city blocks. To schematize the path in the aftermath, we subdivided it into eleven elements of the same length, corresponding to the blocks and taken the length of the block as base unit. Moreover, the very length of the block fits the maximum distance that is possible to take with a camera smartphones devices are equipped with in a bi-dimensional urban environment. For this sequence of blocks, the shape of space, made by architectural elements and their composition, is similar to each other, so that moving through it urban formal and aesthetic patterns are easily recognizable. This fact, together with the linear development of the path, makes the agent experience of the experimentation somehow monotonous. This situation is fundamental for us, because we want to investigate how small detail and changes in a uniform urban environment, perceived just around the agent personal area, may attracts the pedestrian's attention modifying his understanding of space. For that reason, it is also

Fig. 2. Pathway subdivision.

plausible to speculate that it is the agent's position along the path, in relation to the level of accomplishment of the task of reaching a fixed end, which affects decisively the agent's level of attention through the surrounding environment. From another point of view, the sharp alternation between green and built up areas and between multi-purpose and targeted space, as for car and pedestrian streets, also as an effect on participants' perception (Fig. 2).

Then, we identified the most frequently reported elements in the photos, trying to infer qualitative information. To this purpose, the elements in the photos were classified into typological categories such as (a) Landmarks (distinctive, symbolic and well-known urban elements) [7]; (b) Long perspectives street views; (c) Small urban elements (natural such as plants and artificial such as street furniture); (d) Outstanding elements (sharply interrupting the continuity of the spatial structure); (e) Historical and modern facades; (f) Street signals and advertisements; (g) Other (Tables 2 and 3).

Table 2. Shows the total number of photos taken for each category (a–g).

Category	(a)	(b)	(c)	(d)	(e)	(f)	(g)
Nr. of photos	86	178	219	79	134	52	45

Table 3. Shows the total number of photos taken for each street block (1–11).

Street block	(1)	(2)	(3)	(4)	(5)	(6)	(7)	(8)	(9)	(10)	(11)
Nr. of photos	122	39	129	78	91	65	90	53	60	40	19

The next figure (Fig. 3) shows the percentage of each typological categories according to the photo-taking location, i.e. considering each street block.

The aim of the previous considerations was to depict an organizational layout on which to investigate the reasons why they took certain pictures, i.e.: because they are

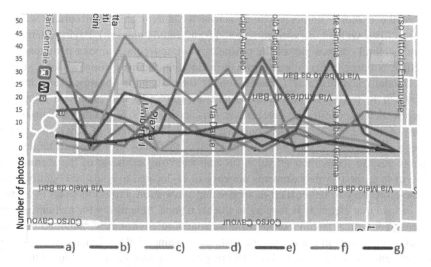

Fig. 3. Snapshots distribution.

interesting to participants *per se*; because they support/hamper the progress of the movement task; because they enhance the understanding of space environments.

We did not get any direct information from participants to answer this question: yet, we tried to investigate on possible correlations with previously identified categories and at the late day the place where the photos were taken. We recognized that some of these categories are strongly linked with more than one of the three suggested hypothesis. However, this assumption needs to be fully validated. Some elements in the cityscape, i.e. benches, asphalt pattern, ornamental flower pots etc. identically repeat along the path, so appearing as hardly useful for spatial orientation. It could be more plausible that they were captured because of their peculiar appearance as small urban elements.

Conversely, other elements are unique along the path. Even if they may not look either significant in terms of their shape or from an esthetic point of view, they can be useful to accomplish the movement task, as in the case of road signs and advertisements. Moreover, they attract the pedestrian attention because of the written information they convey. Finally, other elements such as historical and architectural facades could perform both functions at the same time. Furthermore, we recognize that participants often interpret urban space at the scale of long perspective views. It allows them to catch macro elements such as facades, views of buildings and long streets, without capturing a specific detail. In fact, several photos capture sets of big elements structuring the surrounding cityscape: their approximate prospective field measuring 20 mt. to 100 mt. We hypothesize that these photos reveal the moment when the exploring agent tries to allocate herself into her mental path.

On the other hand, the attention is often captured by micro-urban elements, such as the type of pavements, the specific furniture, the zebra crossing, or the species of plants. In this case, the depth of the photo field shortens and it varies from 2 mt. to 5 mt. Interestingly, there is a photo subject repeated many times, which represents the scaffolding between two buildings. We speculate that it is a surprising occurrence, because the explorer suddenly comes across a vacuum along the curtain walls of buildings filled with an unexpected solution (outstanding element). Paying attention to the architectural composition of the prospects is quite frequent among participants. In particular, building fronts different from the monotonous constructions scheme, such as glass, modern and historical facades, attract their attention (historical and modern facades). It is worthy to note that participants take very few photos of temporary elements, such as pedestrians, street artists, cars and animals, in fact they are almost not present in any of the above mentioned categories. Photos refer mostly to permanent elements. We speculate that it is due to the fact that, moving towards a target, participants tend to focus their attention on characterizing elements of the surrounding space. In fact, the reported elements are easy to be located in a spatial cognitive map and therefore easy to be recalled in succeeding navigation. From this point of view it must be said that elements belonging to the set named "interesting for participants *per se*" represent typical features of the local surrounding environment, although they did not help participants in the orientation task, as explained before. Finally, we observed the preference toward certain photo taking points. In fact there is a high density of photos taken at crossroads and street corners. According to some literature [1], it can be related to the circumstance that they represent decision points along the path.

4   Conclusion and Outlooks

This target-orientated study of cityscape exploration tries to analyze some relations between walking agents and urban spaces. The study aims to show up either implicit or explicit features of the interacting nexus between human agents and the spatial environment of a city center, driven by the search for a specific location target. The possibility of using ITC-based equipment to record the route was oriented to improve the precision of outcomes. As a matter of facts, this made it possible to draw out each agent's path with the best accuracy granted by the used device. The particular analysis carried out here, even if qualitative, was oriented to find out the classes of photo subjects and to connect them with the most probable causes of capturing the agent's attention. Indeed, it is assumed here either that the photographed elements could support the spatial orientation of navigating agents, or that they hit agents' attention because of their embodied characteristic aesthetical features, or both aspects. In all cases, the present analysis may be helpful to understand the extent to which some elements of city spatial environments are able to influence the orientation task in walking agents, even indirectly or unconsciously. Furthermore, image protocols of this experimentation seem to show that agents preferred almost totally to disregard transitory elements, i.e., items that were not permanent but moving along the urban space scene, such as other people, cycles, cars, buses and the like. That occurrence may be related to the fact that during their process of inherently building up the spatial cognitive map of the navigated environment, agents could not consider mobile items as stable reference points. As a final remark, a further aspects can be reported, apparently in line with the outcomes of some evolving literature [9]. In particular, photo snapshot locations seem to largely correspond to major decision-making points for walking agents. In general, the present research gives rise to a number of intriguing issues in the field of spatial cognition of city environments. As it was possible to store the locations of photo snapshots and of walking notes with embedded GPS coordinates, an articulate investigation on results is possible for deeper research perspectives. In particular, deeper analyses will be carried out (i) on the text notes in relation to their exact place and time and (ii) on the time of displacement for each block. A final correlation of the previous analysed aspects will aim at referring it to the precise point and time where path notes and photos were taken. This might possibly explain if there is a drop in attention from the start point to the end, which, in fact, results in a reduction of the number of photos and notes taken at different stages of the path. Their right combination may lead to a more comprehensive representation of the space ontologies built by human agents.

Being a preliminary study, such questions can be addressed only partially and require more detailed analysis that is currently being organized on collected datasets. Also new experimentations are planned in order to complement issues resulted so far, possibly based on more articulated and heterogeneous samples of agents, in terms of different age, field of work/activity, residence and so on. Such initiatives represent an interesting perspective for future research investigations.

References

1. Conroy, R.: Spatial navigation in immersive virtual environments. Ph.D. thesis, Bartlett School of Graduate Studies, London (2001)
2. Duckham, M., Kulik, L.: "Simplest" paths: automated route selection for navigation. In: Kuhn, W., Worboys, M.F., Timpf, S. (eds.) COSIT 2003. LNCS, vol. 2825, pp. 169–185. Springer, Heidelberg (2003). doi:10.1007/978-3-540-39923-0_12
3. Golledge, R.G.: Wayfinding: Cognitive Mapping and Other Spatial Processes. Johns Hopkins, Baltimore (1998)
4. Goodman, N.: The Structure of Appearance. Harvard UP, Cambridge (1951)
5. Lloyd, R.: Spatial Cognition: Geographic Environments. Springer-Verlag, Amsterdam (2009). doi:10.1007/978-94-017-3044-0
6. Lynch, K.: The Image of the City. The MIT Press, Cambridge (1960)
7. Gillner, S., Mallot, H.A.: These maps are made for walking - task hierarchy of spatial cognition. In: Jefferies, M.E., Yeap, W.K. (eds.) Robotics and Cognitive Approaches to Spatial Mapping. Springer Tracts in Advanced Robotics, vol. 38, pp. 181–201. Springer, Heidelberg (2008). doi:10.1007/978-3-540-75388-9_11
8. Rashid, M.: On space syntax as a configurational theory of architecture from a situated observer's viewpoint. Environ. Plan. B: Plan. Des. 39(4), 732–754 (2012)
9. Zhang, H., Lin, S.H.: Affective appraisal of residents and visual elements in the neighborhood: a case study in an established suburban community. Landsc. Urban Plan. 101(1), 11–21 (2011)

Digital Synchronous Collaboration Workspace and 3D Interactions for an AEC Project. Decision-Making Scenario Evaluation

Veronika Bolshakova[1,2(✉)], Gilles Halin[1,3], Pascal Humbert[1,4], and Conrad Boton[5]

[1] MAP-CRAI - Centre de Recherche en Architecture et Ingénierie, UMR n°3495 Modèles et simulations pour l'Architecture et le Patrimoine, Nancy, France
{bolshakova,halin,humbert}@crai.archi.fr
[2] CNRS - Centre National de la recherche scientifique, Paris, France
[3] Université de Lorraine, Nancy, France
[4] ENSAN - Ecole Nationale Supérieure d'Architecture de Nancy, Nancy, France
[5] École de Technologie Supérieure, Montréal, Canada
Conrad.boton@etsmtl.ca

Abstract. The success of a digitally developed architecture project requires a new vision of collaboration and design practices and the adaptation of the current ones. The recent innovative tools and media extend the design capabilities, and foster the proposal of complex architectural solutions.

This paper aims to evaluate the existing interactive synchronous collaboration technologies and solutions. The evaluation must reveal their potential advantages and future uses for professionals and education in the architecture, engineering, and construction (AEC) industry are assessed. Furthermore, suggestions are made on how to improve the current synchronous collaboration practices in decision-making sessions. Such suggestions consider the complexity of 3D-based project and the multidisciplinary of a project team.

The paper introduces a summary of the current digital AEC practices and identifies digital synchronous collaboration requirements for an efficient decision-making session through observation and evaluation of several collaborative session experiments.

Keywords: Computer-supported collaborative work · Architecture · Engineering and construction · Multi-user interface · Natural interaction · Decision-making session · Building Information Modeling · 3D model

1 Introduction

AEC project development practices have centuries of history, but recent decades have brought a digital-age challenge into the field. Since the project development was transferred not only to a digital sheet but also, to a virtual 3D model of the building, the classic practices of the field had to evolve [1]. Thus, the new tools must resolve the old tasks, and the new aims cannot be achieved from the usual approach angles.

© Springer International Publishing AG 2017
Y. Luo (Ed.): CDVE 2017, LNCS 10451, pp. 168–176, 2017.
DOI: 10.1007/978-3-319-66805-5_21

This paper is based on an evaluation of AEC collaborative practices and on experiment observations. It provides the basis for further development of digital synchronous collaboration tools and methods for the Building Information Modeling (BIM) projects (at the international research project 4D Collab). Identifying the efficiency factors is essential for a proposal of collaborative work optimization, and is also a key for the digital collaboration protocol definition. The solution must foster natural interface usages and the use of a BIM project model as main support for a decision-making collaborative session (CS).

2   Synchronous Collaborative at AEC

2.1   Digital Age and BIM in AEC

A transformation of conception process will bring a change to the work habits, as well as an adaptation of work methodology to a modernized toolkit. The generation of pioneers in digital architecture has prepared some theoretical and practical basis through many experiments [1]. However, the current generation suffers from a lack of digital tool practices methodology. Yet, the extended 3D models and BIM practices have been integrated into the project development by certain AEC professionals.

Nowadays, many of the AEC professionals develop their projects with the help of the digital tools and practices. But not all of them have yet fully integrated, into their project development and design, the work with 3D semantic enriched models, which is fundamental for the BIM project management and development methods [1, 2]—«*The building information model is a three-dimensional geometric model that is data rich*» [3]. Though, the AEC projects developed with the innovative digital practices of 3D modeling reveal the advantages of the improved communication, coordination, and production on a project due to the possibility of interacting with the 3D model content [4]. Such an approach adds a supplementary model components and information annotations to the geometry visualization [5].

The complexity of project model development engages intense collaboration of all AEC professionals; they should find their own new efficient ways of cooperation on a project. Such a modernization of the current practices aims to simplify the work methods and to improve the quality of the project. But as with any innovation, this takes time before complete integration into professional practices, due to the appropriation period. So, the next important step towards BIM-oriented work methods and progressive project management requires us to question the collaborative practices of the AEC project design [6]. The projects conducted with the integration of these practices benefit from improvement in the development coordination inside the project as well as in the communication around the project. These new aspects increase the project complexity. Such a complexity leads to efficient method development for collaboration and exchanges, for a better representation and visualization, for an intense discussion and for more participative decision making.

2.2   Collaborative Development of an AEC Project Basis

Every collaboration approach values the specific features, which correspond to the needs of the work process. For an AEC decision-making a synchronous collaboration has traditionally been the most relevant approach of the interactions on a project [7].

The AEC project collaboration hinges on project content. The project scale (a small residential, a large public building, or an urban project) and the development phase (concept, design development, technical design, construction) will together define the development strategy [3]. And such a connection was summarized as a BIM sociotechnical system [8] (Fig. 1), where a project technical core (3D CAD, Intelligent Models, Information Management) prepares a project data and work tools for the collaborative manipulations. So, the project progress relies on this system, where the synchronous collaboration plays the role of the first social base to operate the project and creates a work field for further larger scale interactions.

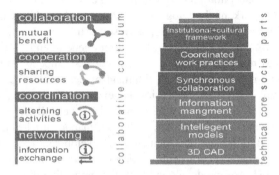

Fig. 1.   (Left) collaborative continuum concept according to A. Himmelmann [7] (right) a BIM sociotechnical system.

The social part of the AEC sociotechnical system coordinates with the top of the collaborative continuum concept [9] (Fig. 1), because the representation is based on a level system, where the evolution and the complexity grow with the levels along the continuum, as the complexity increases in a sociotechnical system. There are greater levels of trust, time and committed effort in the relationship progressing through the collaborative continuum, which means that every core must fulfill its purpose.

2.3   Collaborative Workspace Experiments

Collaboration engages all the users to share the same environment, to bring the same vocabulary to a work process and to unite project information [7, 10]. Many research works have been dedicated to developing Computer-Supported Collaborative Work (CSCW) scenarios and environments for AEC and design, therefore various collaborative solutions experiments were performed to reveal potential usage: a 3D virtual workspace environment, a holodesk with direct 3D interactions on a see-through display, life-size 2D sketch representations and hybrid ideation space with an even more immersive environment [11–14]. The CSCW session analysis reveals an importance of a quality interaction (gesturing, navigation, annotation, viewing [15]).

3 Collaborative Experiment Summary

A synchronous collaborative workspace must ensure the physical workspace comfort, along with the uniformity and usability of the virtual workspace [1, 14, 15], which provides ergonomic interactions with the session workflow.

3.1 Protocol

An efficient collaboration relies on the pertinence and the quality of the equipment set, of the interactions and of the collaborative approach choice. A specific protocol organizes the CS. Beforehand the equipment set puts the physical space in order: room measurements and insulation, distances between the equipment and collaborator spaces, as well as, accesses and circulation. Afterwards the equipment setup creates a virtual workspace environment by virtue of the hardware and software installation.

The protocol also includes a collaborative scenario, determined by the CS main objective and interaction requirements. Every CS has an established checklist (equipment, data, users) and corresponding scenarios for a preparation phase (data gathering, scheduling), for the collaboration phase and for the session feedback phase, since every session passes through these phases. Every preparation phase starts from a CS objective, project data, and participants' definition, and then launches a scenario choice (equipment, interactions, roles, etc.). Nevertheless, a protocol leaves a space for an improvisation during the CS. Through the collaboration phase users work with the project data: visualize, manipulate, and annotate. Annotations create a new data and a feedback on the project development.

3.2 Objective

The performed experimental sessions have primarily targeted an identification of possible uses for the digital synchronous collaboration protocols on an AEC project. And at the same time, they also have quest for the digital collaborative method advantages and limits, for uses in the AEC industry. The final objective is the specification for efficient new equipment and better protocols.

3.3 Equipment Description

The decision-making scenario was experimented at the Digital Synchronous Collaboration Workspace (DSCW) of the research center MAP-CRAI (Fig. 2). The DSCW associates two digital touch screens, a horizontal one called "The table" (98 in), and a vertical one "The wall" (46 in). Both displays are plugged to computers and use a collaborative software "Shariiing" (by Immersion) for the CS experiment.

Fig. 2. Design development decision-making session at DSCW of MAP-CRAI, 2016

The Shariiing software creates a unified digital environment for the project work-flow (images, textured 3D models, web pages, pdf files, txt files, etc.) and for homogeneous interactions (upload, visualization, manipulation, annotation, browsing and sharing). The annotation tool functions as a digital pen, so the annotations are mainly sketches or notes. The annotated document is always saved as a new 2D image, so there is no modification made to the original digital 3D model; however, this means that it cannot operate enriched BIM models.

3.4   Content for a Decision-Making Session

A design development scenario was investigated at the AEC project decision-making session, with a renovation of residential tower as CS subject (Kennedy tower, Nancy, France). The AEC project at a design development stage [3] is typical for a creative development activities. The goal of the session was to design renovation solutions of an exterior facade and an interior entrance hall.

All the participants work in the AEC field, and DSCW experiments gathered them around the subject as users-interactors at the DSCW with a role on a project (architect, client, BIM manager, engineers). The following 2D documents, typical for an AEC project workflow, were uploaded to Shariiing: urban master plan image; facades photos; entrance hall interior photos; the tower master plan, ground floor plan; typical floor plan; local urban development plan text document. In addition, and as a main subject of the study, the 3D digital model of the building with its neighborhood context (BIM NV3 [16]) was suggested by the experiment as a main collaborative interactions base, due to the fact that such a model contains all the information to ensure the creative design development without additional sources.

CS proceeded in a following way: informal part; aim and contents by a collaboration manager for the participants; then a problem-solving part - problem visualization, annotation of the existing documents through creative sketching, interprofessional discussion, solution visualization and evaluation; followed by a summary and further definition of development tasks, with an informal farewell at the end. After the first task, users achieve the next one with a higher level of confidence.

A value engineering scenario was also surveyed at the CS, with the ongoing project of an architecture agency Mil Lieux, in Nancy, France. The decision-making was on a design development project stage with a client, a BIM manager, engineers, and an architect at CS. The goal of the CS was to find a solution for the heating equipment repositioning and for the building borders on unit (Fig. 3).

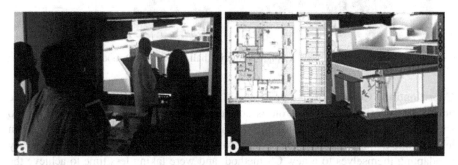

Fig. 3. (a) Value engineering session, ongoing AEC project of Mil Lieux agency; (b) annotations on a 3D model and a floor plan, Mil Lieux agency.

3.5   Interaction Observation

The interaction during the CS was observed from four main perspectives: visualization, manipulation, annotation, and coordination.

Visualization. The first step was always the overview of the CS content. The document quality and the manipulation ergonomics defined the choice of a visualized document as a work base, and not the relevance or complexity of the represented information about the project on a document. After a while simultaneous visualization of the same document in a separate window for every user was replaced by a solo document visualization on a larger support surface with an only one person in charge.

Manipulation. Operation, control and management manipulation types were performed. The choice of a document depends directly on the architect's (or other session-leading professional) habits and working methods. A scale change and detail zoom manipulation appeared as a strong argumentation support. The comparison of document versions was another major kind of manipulation. Even with an annotation as the main activity result, users tended still to focus on a verbal discussion to prove their point rather than to explain an idea by sketching or annotation.

Annotation. The annotations are an outcome from the creation or decision-making interactions (Fig. 4). Users were often focused only on a 2D annotation of one document, mostly on a 3D virtual model. A creative sketching type of manipulation was most commonly used on the pictures of the project, and on the 3D model fixed views. Meanwhile, an independent sketch drawings and text notes have been used only once. AEC typical procedure was the most efficient: two types of documents were annotated simultaneously - the 3D model fixed point of view and a floor plan. The annotations appear mostly to complete the sketched idea rather than to define a task or a problem.

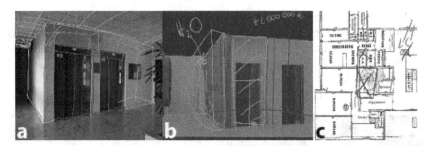

Fig. 4. Design development session: a. interior hall photo, b. 3D model, c. floor plan.

Coordination. Contrary to the professional fixed roles distribution, the CS roles are not fixed. The guiding session role is not permanent, and it passes from one user to another through the development of ideas and interventions, which indicates a certain level of interaction fluency. Experienced professionals from the field had no difficulty in adapting themselves to a new CS method, and were taking less time to achieve the task than their less experienced colleagues.

3.6   Interpretation and Discussion

The study highlights some notable advantages of the DSCW, but also some challenges to overcome in order to fully benefit from its potential.

Advantages. Efficient decision-making CS are possible with the existing setups of the DSCW. On the equipment level: the most prominent advantages are the quality of the document display, simultaneous visualization, and multi-user interactions. On a decision-making support level: the possibility of 3D digital model interaction enables a very complex level of project management. And on a coordination level: an additional value is the unification of all the document types within the same work environment which follow the same logic.

Limitations. On the equipment aspects: a certain technical improvement and tool development should be undertaken to achieve the addition of new values for the digital synchronous collaboration. The main criticisms are related to the annotation toolkit's lack of instruments, navigation, and ergonomics, and to the CS report creation. The most important problem is the navigation comfort level, users would not interact with the document if it is hard to manipulate. On a decision-making support aspects: A pencil-case, line type choice and the layers have been traditionally a part of the AEC practices and their analog presence is crucial for the DSCW. And the current 3D model use is not yet well adapted for interactions on it. Also, a clear and structured feedback of the CS should be developed. And on a coordination level: Digital synchronous collaboration is relatively new for AEC professionals. DCSW Equipment manipulation and appropriation effort are required for task completion, therefore it takes time to find an efficient mean of expression.

4 Conclusions

The digital collaborative workspace technology implementation and current tests by some professionals will raise the future standards, and certainly arouse a wider implementation into the collaborative practices at AEC industry. The DSCW use is simple enough to make the users feel confident in their tool manipulation skills, so the lack of a DSCW use experience has no influence on the collaboration process.

The future work should focus on a technical improvement research: ergonomics, simplicity navigation, additional equipment and instrument development. And also must consider a development of the AEC BIM project collaborative protocols and uses according to the project phase of development (conception, technical design, construction) and the project contents, with a full integration of the BIM methods and on a large scale long-term collaborative AEC projects.

Acknowledgments. This study was developed under the patronage of the Agence Nationale de la Recherche No. ANR-16-CE10-0006-02 (FR) and Fonds National de la Recherche (LU), as a part of the international research project 4D Collab. We are grateful to the architecture agency Mil Lieux and to all the participants of experiments.

References

1. Oxman, R.: Digital architecture as a challenge for design pedagogy: theory, knowledge, models and medium. Des. Stud. **29**(2), 99–120 (2008). Elsevier
2. Delcambre, B.: Rapport de la Mission numérique bâtiment, Ministère du. Logement, de l'Égalité des territoires et de la Ruralité, France (2014)
3. Kensek, K.: Building Information Modeling, 1st edn. Routledge, Abingdon (2014)
4. Succar, B.: Building Information Modelling: conceptual constructs and performance improvement tools. Ph.D. thesis, School of Architecture and Built Environment Faculty of Engineering and Built Environment University of Newcastle, Australia (2013)
5. Mazza, R.: Introduction to Information Visualization. Springer, London (2009)
6. Boton, C., Kubicki, S., Halin, G.: Method to design coordinated multiple views adapted to user's business requirements in 4D collaborative tools. In: AEC, 15th International Conference on Information Visualisation, pp. 96–101, London, United Kingdom (2011)
7. Wilkinson, P.: Construction Collaboration Technologies: The Extranet Evolution. Taylor & Francis, London (2005)
8. Kennerley, B.: BIM is a Sociotechnical System. WSP Group plc., 20 February 2017. http://www.wspgroup.com/en/wsp-group-bim/BIM-home-wsp/what-is-bim/
9. Himmelman, A.: Collaboration For A Change: Definitions, Decision-Making Models, Roles, and Collaboration Process Guide. Himmelman Consulting, Minneapolis (2004)
10. Achten, H.H.: Requirements for collaborative design in architecture. In: Timmermans, H.J.P, Vries, B. (eds.) Sixth Design and Decision Support Systems in Architecture and Urban Planning, Part One: Architecture Proceedings Avegoor, pp. 1–13. Technische Universitet Endhoven, Eindhoven, The Netherlands (2002)
11. Achten, H.: Futures scenario for a collaborative design session and feature list. In: Stellingwerff, M., Verbeke, J. (eds.) Accolade – Architecture, Collaboration, Design., pp. 163–167. Delft University Press, Delft, The Netherlands (2001)

12. Hilliges, O., Kim, D., Izadi, S., Weiss, M., Wilson, A.D.: HoloDesk: direct 3D interactions with a situated see-through display. In: SIGCHI Conference on Human Factors in Computing Systems, CHI 2012, pp. 2421–2430. ACM, New York (2012)
13. Dorta, T., Kalay, Y.: Comparing immersion in collaborative ideation through design conversations, workload and experience. In: Integration Through Computation. Presented at the ACADIA, pp. 216–225. Bnaff, Canada (2011)
14. Dorta, T., Kinayoglu, G.: Towards a new representational ecosystem for the design studio. In: Rethinking Comprehensive Design: Speculative Counterculture, The 19th International Conference on Computer-Aided Architectural Design Research in Asia, pp. 699–708. Kyoto Institute of Technology, Kyoto (2014)
15. Tory, M., Staub-French, S.: Physical and digital artifact-mediated coordination in building design. Comput. Support. Coop. Work 4(17), 311–351 (2008). Springer
16. "Le Moniteur – Cahier pratique", Cahier détaché n2, no. 5763, pp. 44 (2014)

Collaboration and Creativity Support for Interdisciplinary Engineering Teams Using Component Based Systems and Cognitive Services

Matthias Merk(✉), Gabriela Tullius, and Peter Hertkorn

Reutlingen University, Alteburgstrasse 150, 72762 Reutlingen, Germany
{matthias.merk,gabriela.tullius,peter.hertkorn}@reutlingen-university.de

Abstract. In this paper we suggest an ubiquitous system with an implicit HCI. A basic concept of a middleware as well as design recommendations for future creativity and collaboration environments in an engineering context are presented in this paper.

Keywords: Collaboration · Creativity · Implicit HCI · Augmentation · Ubiquitous systems · Cognitive services

1 Introduction

This paper is structured in four section to show our design method. The following section gives a summary of findings from interviews with engineers and from an eye tracking study done to reveal known creativity techniques and their use. Based on our findings we propose in sections two to four the basic concept and three recommendations for designing such MBSE/CSCW systems to overcome the gap stated before, namely (1) transformation of artifacts, (2) component based architecture and (3) domain specific augmentation. In Sect. 5 we describe the usage of cognitive services to enhance creativity support systems using sketch recognition as an example.

2 Creativity and Collaboration in Engineering

New methods in engineering will be more and more characterized by collaboration and interdisciplinarity throughout the engineering design phases and product lifecycle. New trends in engineering like model-based systems engineering (MBSE) are demanding appropriate software systems to meet the changing requirements in the engineering process [1]. MBSE is defined as a formalized usage of modeling to support the definition of requirements, development, verification and validation of a system beginning with the concept and development phase as well as all the subsequent phases in the product lifecycle [2].

© Springer International Publishing AG 2017
Y. Luo (Ed.): CDVE 2017, LNCS 10451, pp. 177–184, 2017.
DOI: 10.1007/978-3-319-66805-5_22

Working in distributed and/or co-located engineering teams, using all kind of software apps and tools people are accustomed to from private life, leads to altered expectations of users and their user experiences and consequently to the need of new methods [3]. With an MBSE approach, methods known from the field of computer science are combined with engineering methods with respect to the criteria listed above.

In the research project "Digitaler Produktlebenszyklus(DiP)[1]", engineers are confronted with MBSE using a graph based design language for modeling. From this model all other engineering artifacts like CAD drawings or simulations can be generated. One of the main challenge for the engineers in this project is, that the workload moves towards early ideation phases where creativity of the engineers is the key element. This early ideation phase in the creativity process is characterized by generating, developing, and communicating new ideas. Traditional engineering workflows like in mechanical engineering are therefore more and more adapted to workflows known from creative and software engineering teams [4].

The transition to this kind of model-based engineering is challenging. Analyzing the traditional engineering process reveals a gap of support in the ideation phase with respect to process and thus tool support. Setting up and using computer supported collaborative work (CSCW) is not common either. The main focus of our research is to overcome that gap by using methods from CSCW and by enhancing the ideation phase in MBSE. Within the research Project DiP we propose such an approach. The goal of the project is to show that it is possible to digitize the complete product lifecycle by applying model driven systems engineering using design grammars and creating a single central model containing all the information for every domain involved in the product lifecycle. For the analysis of the requirements we used a two-folded approach: a field study with interviews for gaining qualitative insight on the engineering working environment and an eye tracking study in a controlled environment for quantitative feedback.

2.1   Collaboration in an Interdisciplinary Research Project Using Model-Based Systems Engineering

We conducted semi-structured interviews with engineers who have a traditional engineering background to gain insight on collaborative work within engineering groups. The engineers we interviewed are research associates in the research project. In our first round of interviews, we asked about collaboration in the domains the different engineers are working in. One unexpected result was, that computer supported collaborative work, i.e. engineers working on the same model, does not happen. Right now engineers are only using repositories to store, share and work remotely on the models. In follow-up interviews we will discuss the outcome of working with such repositories as a next step of our research.

---

[1] dip.reutlingen-university.de.

Because of the interdisciplinary nature of big engineering projects it seems to be common to meet using highly specialized infrastructure to support collaboration with teams all over the world. However our findings showed that these rooms are rarely used nowadays. Nearly all of the engineers we interviewed are aware of such a room, but hardly used it for various reasons, e.g. the room is too far away from the workspace or there are organizational drawbacks like reservation and the like.

These obstacles hinder spontaneous creative collaboration sessions within interdisciplinary engineering teams. After working together with the engineers for about 18 months, they started to communicate via synchronous and asynchronous team chat systems. We analyzed the usage and found, that only 16% of the communication consisting of 10500 messages, was written with a collaborative aspect in mind. The remaining 84% are simple direct private messages. These findings show that CSCW and working with such systems is strongly affected by personal communication patterns and the underlying need for relations. To enhance task focused communication and thus collaboration advanced approaches in terms of User Experience are necessary.

2.2 Creativity Support in CSCW Systems

Computer-aided innovation (CAI) systems are used to support the actual design process of a product. In an engineering context, these systems are often based on the theory of inventive problem solving developed by Genrich Altschuller. (See [5] for a state-of-the-art overview on those systems).

At Reutlingen University, an interactive system called "Accelerator"[2] is currently being developed to support web-based learning. Our goal is to extent this CSCW system to be able to support creativity techniques. As part of a study on Accelerator, we asked a group of 35 participants consisting of 24 computer science students, 2 chemistry students, 2 engineering students, one professor (Informatics) and 6 participants from the faculty staff with an engineering background about creativity techniques they know and use. We presented a selection of well known techniques which were evaluated beforehand in terms of the possibility to implement and use them in a web based CSCW system (see Table 1 for the results and [6] for further reading on creativity techniques).

We conducted this study using an eye tracker. A visualization of the different creativity techniques as well as a short textual description o the techniques were shown to the participants. The techniques were shown in groups of three techniques at a time, followed by the question which ones they already knew and which ones they have already used. We had only two participants who did not know any of the techniques or have used them before.

---

[2] accelerator.reutlingen-university.de.

Table 1. Known (left) and used (right) creativity techniques

Rank	Technique	Known
1	Inspirational Wall	83%
2	Brainstorming	74%
3	Image Boards	66%
4	Collaborative Writing	66%
5	Brainwriting	49%
6	Collaborative Sketching	46%
7	Affinity Diagram	26%
8	SCAMPER Questions	17%
9	Perspective Diagram	17%
10	Method 635	11%
11	Empathy Map	9%
12	Idea Blueprint	6%

Rank	Technique	Used
1	Brainstorming	69%
2	Collaborative Writing	51%
3	Image Boards	41%
4	Inspirational Wall	37%
5	Brainwriting	34%
6	Collaborative Sketching	23%
7	SCAMPER Questions	14%
8	Affinity Diagram	11%
9	Method 635	6%
10	Perspective Diagram	6%
11	Empathy Map	3%
12	Idea Blueprint	3%

3   Design Recommendations for Future Collaboration and Creativity Support Systems

There are multiple resources and best practices for designing collaborative systems (see [5] for our findings and basic requirements). We can therefore give the following three recommendations for future collaboration and creativity support systems in the field of model-based systems engineering:

1. **Allow the transformation of artifacts to make data reusable.**
   We need to find solutions to support the transformation of different engineering artifacts throughout all stages of the product lifecycle. As an example, we use a scenario about hosting collaborative sketching sessions using tablet PCs with pencil support. A number of engineers would sketch out the idea of how to solve the problem (in this example we assume the engineers are sketching UML class diagrams). The sketches are then discussed together. Using cognitive services like sketch and text recognition, we are able to transform the digital hand written sketches into a machine readable digital representation. This representation is then imported into a software tool to further detail the model of the design language intended to solve the engineering problem (see Sect. 5 for more information about the usage of cognitive services). Working within the software tool, it should be possible to access a repository containing already solved problems. This allows the engineers to reuse parts of other projects for the current project in progress.
2. **Centralize the data and knowledge to allow fast exchange of information and data.**
   The analysis of the team communication showed that discussions about a model, the engineers are currently working on, is not only tied to the actual model. Instead of working and discussing directly using the actual representation of the model, screenshots are used in real-time communication. This poses the problem, that it is not possible to work together on a model in an

interactive way having a direct feedback. By centralizing all data, communication and visualization, we are enabling designs that support communication and visualization systems with direct manipulation and feedback.

Currently we are working on a modular chat based system which is able to provide different visualization and interaction modules at any time (see Sect. 4), allowing engineers to adaptively use different combinations of CAx modules in various discussions happening in the chat system at the same time. Within the system a feedback to the user can be enabled for different types of engineering models.

3. **Allow domain specific augmentation and visualization of data.**
Working together with different engineering disciplines, we found that every discipline uses their own languages, metaphors and tools to communicate and solve problems. In our research project every discipline is working on the same central model. However our intention is not to have the user to adapt to a certain way of interaction or visualization that seems to be suitable for everyone. Our vision is, to generate visualizations and interaction paradigms not only tailored to the domain or the current project state but also to the working environment including other people, devices, location and so on by using a multi sensory approach for situation detection combined with information derived from a central model, thus having a setting for an implicit HCI.

4   Basic Concept

Figure 1 shows the basic design of our system. In an approach using a representation, data and analysis layer, we augment the power of the human intellect with data generated by analysis of all available data in the ongoing engineering project. To do this, we transform the product model into a separate but synchronized working model. This approach enables us to augment the model without taking care of how the base model was created. We focus on creating a system for the user group that adapts to the user in contrast to an approach that require the user to adapt to the system. Therefore we need to provide data structures that allow fast, easy and unrestricted editing, manipulation and augmentation of the project data or its visualization. Because of the adaptive design of the system, different representations and visualizations of the data can coexist in different versions.

In [5] a deeper insight into the requirements for our system as well as a conceptual base and an example scenario is presented. The high grade of adaptability of our system requires a highly modular system architecture. In the example of a modular chat system used for both team and personal communication within an interdisciplinary engineering team we will explain our modular approach further. The chat system is a component in the representation layer shown in Fig. 1. Figure 2 shows the component based modular approach to the chat system.

The chat system, introduced in Sect. 3, is a structured accumulation of different components. The benefit of this approach is, the possibility to exchange the components to make the chat system suitable for different needs. For example

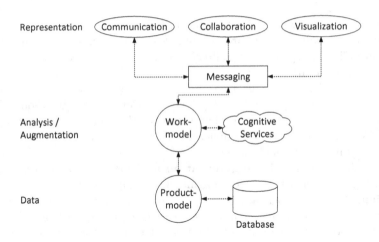

Fig. 1. The basic concept of the system

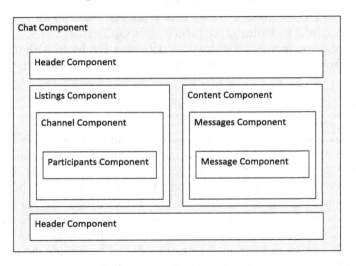

Fig. 2. The component based architecture of a modular chat system

one could replace or extend the message component by the functionality to view CAx models without the need to make changes to the chat system itself. Just like the message component we could replace the whole massages component, to quickly allow the usage of one of the creativity techniques discussed in Sect. 2.2 in a virtual team scenario. We are currently developing multiple prototypes of this chat system to choose the the most appropriate technology for our modular concept.

5   Augmenting Engineering Artifacts Using Cognitive Services

Combining new emerging technologies, methods and algorithms are key components in our vision. There are multiple providers of cognitive services like Microsoft Cognitive Services[3], IBM Watson[4] or more specialized providers like MyScript[5] focusing on special problems like sketch or text recognition. Using these services we are able to enhance our system by the possibilities of machine learning and artificial intelligence in a simply and efficient manner.

For augmentation of artifacts, especially with creativity support in mind, we are able to use services providing search and discovery, agents, classification, retrieving and ranking, visual recognition, auditory recognition, knowledge exploration and recommendation functionality. Currently we are working on sketch recognition and automated classification of engineering sketches and diagrams as one example of an implicit HCI. The sketch recognition is the first step, from which numerous actions could be automatically triggered (e.g. generating events like calendar inputs and the like). For this purpose we are using MyScript as a provider for sketch recognition.

At the moment our goal is to detect a subset of the UML class diagram. This will allow engineers to sketch out their solutions using a pen and paper like natural form of interaction. While sketching, our system identifies the classes and generates a machine-readable version of the sketch, that can be imported into the working environment to allow for further multi-modal forms of interaction. See Fig. 3 for a basic approach of sketch recognition using MyScript as a cognitive service for sketch recognition.

Fig. 3. The process of sketch recognition for UML-classdiagramms

6   Summary and Further Work

We described our vision of future collaboration support in MBSE and showed the importance of supporting engineering creativity. By giving recommendations for the design of such systems and providing examples of how we think these recommendations can be implemented, we showed how an adaptive approach, enriched by cognitive services can be a solution for future collaboration in engineering.

We need to focus our work on implementing prototypes to further validate our findings and show the advantages of implicit HCI for CSCW and creativity

---

[3] https://www.microsoft.com/cognitive-services.

[4] https://www.ibm.com/watson.

[5] http://www.myscript.com/.

support systems. A first approach will be to use interconnected input and output devices like pico projectors to augment the workspace and engineering artifacts.

Acknowledgments. The project "Digitaler Produktlebenszyklus" (dip.reutlingen-university.de) is funded by the European Fund for Regional Development (EFRD - or EFRE in German) and the Ministry of Science, Research and the Arts of Baden-Wuerttemberg, Germany.

References

1. Eigner, M., Roubanov, D., Zafirov, R.: Modellbasierte Virtuelle Produktentwicklung. Springer, Berlin (2014)
2. International Council on Systems Engineering: Systems engineering vision 2020 (2007)
3. Sproll, S., Peissner, M., Sturm, C.: From product concept to user experience: exploring UX potentials at early product stages. In: Proceedings of the 6th Nordic Conference on Human-Computer Interaction: Extending Boundaries, pp. 473–482. ACM (2010)
4. Sommer, A.F., Slavensky, A., Nguyen, V.T., Steger-Jensen, K., Dukovska-Popovska, I.: Scrum integration in stage-gate models for collaborative product development a case study of three industrial manufacturers. In: 2013 IEEE International Conference on Industrial Engineering and Engineering Management (IEEM), pp. 1278–1282. IEEE (2013)
5. Merk, M., Tullius, G., Hertkorn, P.: Towards a collaborative working environment to support model-based systems engineering. In: Hertweck, D. (ed.) Digital Enterprise Computing (DEC 2016), 14–15 June 2016, Böblingen, Germany. Gesellschaft für Informatik, Bonn (2016)
6. Hanington, B., Martin, B.: Universal Methods of Design - 100 Ways to Research Complex Problems, Develop Innovative Ideas, and Design Effective Solutions. Rockport Publishers, Rockport (2012)

Research Issues in Attempting to Support an Architecture Firm Transition from Fragmented CAD to BIM Collaborative Design

Daniel Forgues and James Lapalme[✉]

École de technologie superieure, Montreal, QC, Canada
{daniel.forgue,james.lapalme}@etsmtl.ca

Abstract. Research emphasizes the importance of BIM use to be collaborative in order to reap its benefits. However, little research has been conducted regarding the impact at the organizational level of breaking boundaries between specialties for a more collaborative approach to design using BIM. The originality of this longitudinal research is to present not only the challenges of an architecture firm in adopting a multidisciplinary collaborative design, but also the challenges of a Construction Engineering approach to research. Various research strategies derived from activity theory and cognitive sciences were used more or less successfully to accelerate the transition from fragmented to integrated design practices.

Keywords: Collaboration · BIM · CEM research · Organizational development

1 Introduction

This paper is a critical review of a recently completed longitudinal study that was undertaken in order to study the dynamic transformation of a specific actor within the construction industry: an architecture firm. Initially, the firm requested help from the research team in order to increase collaboration between its various departments and specialties. Later, the architecture firm demanded help on implementing Building Information Modeling. For the research team, these request for help were an opportunity to pursue research on two concepts: the cogeneration of knowledge and the radical transformation of practices through the introduction of BIM as a disruptive technology. For the remainder of this paper, we will refer to the architecture firm as the partner.

BIM proposes to address the issues of collaboration and innovation as well as to increase performance by promoting the stakeholders use of a single shared work platform. However, little research has been done to understand the implications of adopting such a platform in a fragmented environment constituted of multiple disciplines. An environment where each discipline may be understood as a unique social world, with its own culture, organization of work and artefacts.

The research perspective guiding the longitudinal study was Construction Engineering and Management (CEM). CEM is a response to the critics made about how

© Springer International Publishing AG 2017
Y. Luo (Ed.): CDVE 2017, LNCS 10451, pp. 185–192, 2017.
DOI: 10.1007/978-3-319-66805-5_23

research has been done traditionally in the field of construction Traditional research has been criticized as being overly focused on theoretical and conceptual issues at the expense of the needs expressed by industry, particularly by applied disciplines [1]. Many of the problems researched in CEM are related to the organizational, the managerial and the social dimensions of construction. Consequently, innovations emerging from CEM frequently involve modifications to practices and procedures grounded in the social sciences. Consequently, the idea that "knowledge emerges as aspect of practice – or 'praxis' p. 95" [2] is also relevant to CEM. Accordingly, to the studies' concern for praxis, it shares many of the characteristics of an Action Research or Participative Action Research study. Hence, it also shares many of the risks of such studies with regards to achieving change and being helpful.

As stated previously, this paper aims at providing critical view of the CEM research strategies explored in the longitudinal study. Consequently, the paper will present a retrospective critique of the issues and challenges experienced by the research team while conducting the three-year study to help the partner. The critical review will focus on the management of the researcher-client relationship and will be grounded in concepts from the field of organizational development (OD) field. OD has a history of investigating the researcher-client relationship in the context of organizational change [3]. Consequently, we believe that the CEM field can learn from the OD field in order to guide interventionist research practices. Moreover, we believe that concepts from OD can help explain some of the challenges met by CEM researchers when trying to research and instigate change within organizations. It is within this context that this critical analysis, or meta-study, is situated. This meta-study is a first step in trying to create bridges across the CEM and OD research fields in order to advance the research practices of the CEM field. The contribution of this paper are two-fold. Firstly, from a knowledge generation perspective, a number of gaps within current CEM practices are identified and possible solutions are discussed. Secondly, from an engage scholarly perspective, this paper strives to contribute to the tearing down of walls across disciplinary silos.

2 The Longitudinal Study: A Summary

The research team, which we will refer to as the team for the remainder of this article, concerned by the study primarily investigates the reconfiguration of practices through transformational technologies, such as BIM, or practices such as Lean construction. To achieve this goal, the team actively seeks industrial partners that are interested in contributing to the production of new practical knowledge: praxis. The team's research perspective is inspired by the concept of knowledge coproduction [4]. This concept is grounded in the belief that researchers must acquire transdisciplinary skills and engage in the co-generation of knowledge with industry.

The partner, notwithstanding its multidisciplinary nature, defined itself as an architecture firm. The partner employs architects, engineers and other specialties. A key goal that motived the partner to contact the team was its desire to transform its siloed working environment. The partner's intention for desiring such as transformation was to foster a more collaborative and synergistic approach to construction design.

This was perceived as a great opportunity for the team to study the impact of the introduction of new technologies on work patterns. The study was done across two separate both interdependent projects. It first started with a small research project focused on a very specific problem to demonstrate the value that the partner could achieve by working with the research team. The second project was far more ambitious; its objective was to transform CAD oriented practices to BIM oriented ones.

The theoretical framework guiding the first research project was Activity Theory (AT) [5]. Two reasons motivated the research team to adopt this theory. Firstly, according to the team, it is well suited to explore the realm of professional practices, which are built around specific artefacts. Secondly, in accordance to AT, an intervention method called Change Laboratory (CL) is provided by the literature for fostering work design related change. During the first project, two Change Laboratories [6] were conducted and they were greatly appreciated by the partner because they exposed issues and contradictions in their organization of work that were hindering collaboration. The results were convincing enough for the partner to engage in a three-year research relationship with the research team for a second project.

For the second project, in conjunction with a theoretical grounding in AT, a Share Lab Workshop (SLW) intervention was used. The reason for using this second intervention will be explained in a subsequent section. The intervention was used in order to guide the implementation of BIM across the organization.

2.1   Challenges in the Research Process

The core principal team member for the first project was a student, a PhD candidate, whose thesis was directly related to the project. The student prepared for the project by receiving training from an international research ground that is recognized for its expertise in AT as well as the planning and execution of the CL. Given that the partner appreciate the results of the first project and given that the intention of the second project was similar but at a larger scale, it was the intention of the research team to use AT and the CL intervention for the second project. Moreover, it was expected by the partner that the research team, as experts, would plan and execute once again the intervention. However, the team was faced with the challenge that the student that had received the training was no longer part of the team. Moreover, the team did not have any other members with the necessary knowledge and experience that would be capable of meeting the expectations of the client. In order not to lose face as well as to secure the partner as a field for research the team decided to develop a new intervention, a SLW, with another international research team. The creation of the new intervention was perceived by the research team as a desired solution because it solved the problem of providing the partner with an intervention and it allowed the research team to establish a new research collaboration.

The partner was content with the results of the SLW. Accordingly, the partner requested that the project go further and wanted BIM to be implemented across the organization. Moreover, it was the partner's expectation that the team design and orchestrate the necessary process for the implementation. The team faced two key challenges with this new request. Firstly, the principal member of the team responsible for the project, a research associate, had to take a one-year leave of absence. This left the team once again in a vulnerable situation from an expertise perspective. Still wanting to please the partner as well as to secure the research field, the research team accepted. For the research team, this was a great opportunity to develop further the research team's skills and knowledge on how to foster changes in industry practices.

From the execution of the BIM implementation process surfaced multiple challenges that the team had to cope with. Firstly, the partner was not committing adequate resources to the project because of its concerns for billable hours and cost control. Secondly, the implementation process that was selected by the team fostered a bottom-up approach but the process was experiencing friction with the top-down decision-making culture of the organization. Quickly, the research team was "stuck" acting as mediators between employees and upper-management with regards to expectations, decision-making, resource allocation, etc.

The researcher realized that multiple organizational dimensions (culture, power, finances, etc.) were influencing the BIM implementation process, the subject of the research project, and were not taken in account. It was not the intention of the team nor a lack of willingness on their part, but the organizational dimensions are not generally considered in CEM research. Typically, the underlying concern of CEM is to sufficiently please industrial partners in order to achieve research goals, which are often about testing theories and tools with the aim of developing artefacts and methods for future research projects.

3   The Role of a Researcher: Expert or Helper?

The question of what is the nature and the contours of a researcher's role in the context of a working relationship with an industry partner is an important one. Underlying this question are sub-questions such as: "what should the researcher be expect to do and contribute?" and "what should the partner be expect to do and contribute?"

The first question is particularly important and basically can be restated has: "Is the researcher acting like an expert (or not) and what should he (or shouldn't he) do?" Moreover, we would content that this question is just as critical as the question on how CEM research should be conducted because these two questions are inseparable. What follows is both a reflection on what we have learned as well as a framing of our learnings with literature that provides appropriate language that we wish to share with the CEM community.

Unknowingly, the research team was trying to reach two objectives: do research and be helpful. However, the objective of being helpful was only identified in retrospective. One might be surprised how such an objective could be overlooked but in the context of research, we would content that all researchers believe that their work is useful and helpful. Nobody wishes to do useless activities. However, given that researchers strive for the discovery of new knowledge, the objective of being useful was easily overlooked, especially with the team's methodological concerns. The consequence of not actively reflecting on this second objective meant that the research team never reflected on the question: what does it mean to be useful and helpful in the context of working with the partner. In the context of the case study, the research team tried to help the firm with multiple objectives (as well as reach their own objectives). What is important to account for is that the research team, by trying to help a human system (the partner), exposed itself to the important issues of designing helpful interventions as well as defining what is not helpful. Moreover, with respect to being helpful, the researcher must actively manage the fine line between his responsibilities and those of the human system.

How the researcher frames and manages the previous aspects will determine the methodological foundation of a research project but also the potential risks of the project, because of the underlying assumptions of the methodology. It is also this relationship between defining what is helpful and choosing a research methodology that links both concerns: the role of the research about being helpful and how to conduct research.

A research project may have a number of intentions. The intention of a project will determine the type of knowledge that it contributes. Given a desired research intention, a researcher must select amongst a number of research methodologies and data analysis techniques. When the desired outcome is concerned with the adoption of some technology by an organization, depending on the researcher's assumptions about the nature of technology, the nature and existence of organizations and the nature of the technology-organization relationship, the researcher will implicitly or explicit select a particular research intention. In the case of this article, BIM related technologies as well as the interventions are considered technologies. If the researcher assumes that technologies may be designed and understood separately from organizational or social concerns, then the researcher will probably initiate a project with the intention of pursuing knowledge about solving the problem that is adopting technologies. If the researcher selects a research methodology that is congruent with his intention, he will probably select Design Science Research (DSR) [7]. If the researcher assumes that it is necessary to consider technology within a specific organizational or social context, but is still concerned with solving a technology problem, then the researcher will probably select Action Design Research (ADR). However, if the researcher believes that the desired outcome is mostly about changing human systems, then the researcher will adopt an interventionist methodology such as Action Research (AR), Clinical Inquiry Research (CIR), etc. Given length restrictions, it is not possible in this article to systematically explore the risks associated with different research methodological choices. Instead, we will contrast intervention oriented methodologies because of the nature of the study under critic: Action Research (AR) [8], Participative Action Research (PAR) [9] and Clinical Inquiry Research (CIR) [10]. Before going further, we acknowledge the fact that multiple research methodologies are associated with PAR and that PAR is not a homogenous body of practices, but for space restrictions, it is not reasonable to explore the particularities of each methodology. However, many of the methodologies share some common ground that will be the focus for the discussion.

AR and PAR, as research methodologies, are similar in that they both acknowledge the situated and contextual nature of organizational and social change. Hence, they both avoid risks caused by pursuing universal truths that do not exist. However, AR and PAR are very different in another respect. AR projects are initiated and guided by the concerns of the researcher. Hence, the researcher is ultimately responsible and accountable for the project's outcome. At the opposite, PAR projects are typically initiated by clients. However, since it promotes an equal share of responsibility and accountability between the client and the researcher, such projects are not just guided by the concerns of the client, the needs and biases of the researcher are at play. As such, AR projects expose themselves to risks that they will try to create change that is unwanted by the client and/or is biased by the researcher. PAR projects are exposed to the risk that the research project will fail because of the incompatibility between the needs of the client on one hand and the needs of the research on the other.

In the context of this case study, the research team did not explicitly select a research methodology in order to guide the projects. The choice was implicitly made by the fact that they made interventions and by the guidelines of the intervention methods they used: CL and SLW. Few articles have made an explicit link between a CL and a research methodology. Some have argued that there is a difference between a CL and AR [11]. We would argue that a CL is a particular type of AR intervention because it is focused on creating change and that method for achieving that change is controlled by the researcher. We would make a similar argument for the SWL intervention. Consequently, the project was exposed to the risks that project would try to create a change that was not desirable for the client or was biased by the researchers. In simpler terms, the research project was exposed to the risk that the research team would pursue goals and behavior in ways that were not helpful for the client. In the challenges perceived by the research team, we can clearly see instances of this when the team did the necessary to "save" the research field and choose intervention methods that "they" deemed adequate without necessary taking in consideration holistically the partner's context.

Edgar Schein defined that three general stances were possible when striving to be helpful [3]. Each stance is rooted in different assumptions about the meaning of what is helpful and how one should act: doctor, expert, process consultant. In the doctor stance, the helper is useful by unilateral make a diagnostic and defining an appropriate solution for the client. Hence, the helper assumes that only he has relevant knowledge. In the expert stance, the helper accepts the problem as defined unilaterally by the client and unilaterally defines an appropriate solution. Hence, the helper assumes that the client identified the proper problem and assumes that only he as relevant knowledge for defining the solution. In the process consultation stance, both the client and the help participate in the diagnosis as well as design of the solution. Hence, the process consultation stance assumes that both parties have relevant knowledge to contribute. However, this stance has another important assumption, which is that the helper must not solve the client's problems but must transfer the necessary knowledge, through the collaboration, so that the client way, learn how to solve his current and future problems. The other stances are not concerned with transferring knowledge.

The collaborative nature of the process consultation stance for investigating problems and helping a client is very similar to PAR approaches. However, this is one fundamental different that can make a big difference, and we believe made a big difference in this case study. Process consultation as a means to learn about human systems change was coined by Edgar Schein as Clinical Inquiry Research [10]. As mentioned previously, it is similar to PAR insofar that is it concerned with creating organizational change that is initiated by the client systems. However, it is different than PAR because is subjugates the research concerns of the researchers to the needs of the client and believes that responsibility of the outcome of the project cannot be shared; it must stay with the client. CIR, because of its clinical heritage, is grounded in the notion of always being helpful from the perspective of the client systems needs and problems because anything else would be considered harmful from a clinical perspective. CIR also believes that everything a researcher does is an intervention... nothing is neutral. In other words, both the decisions to gather data and the means of data gathering are interventions. In addition, other subtler behaviors of the researcher are also considered interventions such as how the researcher enters and maintains the working relationship with the client. Typically, PAR practitioners are not concerned by what is considered an intervention and what it not. Given the fact that a CIR practitioner will subjugate his needs and concerns in order to stay focused on those of his client, if he deems it necessary, he will not shy away from a confrontational intervention that could end the working relationship. By definition, a CIR practitioner must not collude with organizational dynamics that are problematic, especially those that directly concern what the client is trying to achieve. Consequently, the CIR practitioners will necessarily at times need to confront the client with regards to such dynamics at the risk of generating sufficient cognitive dissonance and anxiety to put an end to the working relationship. A PAR practitioner will not necessarily be concerned by the notion of colluding hence will not necessarily confront the client on such issues. Ultimately, a CIR practitioner will put an end to a partnership is what is most helpful.

In the longitudinal study, the research team had a deep concern for establishing a working relationship with the firm in order to gain the opportunity to investigate certain phenomena. Consequently, in retrospective, it became clear that the team never questioned if the interventions they were doing were congruent with what they were trying to achieve nor if how they were managing the working relationship with the client was appropriate. For example, implicitly, the research team wanted to help the organization adopt BIM as well as make the necessary adjustment to the organization. However, the team used an expert stance for their intervention, hence not transferring the necessary knowledge to the organization. Moreover, when the client demonstrated on multiple occasion that it did not have sufficient time to allocate to the project, which wasn't behavior that was congruent with the changes that the organization desired, the research team didn't confront the client in fear of losing the opportunity to do research. From a clinical stance, it would have been necessary to constantly keep the client responsible for the project and the desired outcome and walk away from the project is the client was not willing to help itself. From an organizational development perspective, CIR uses a strategy for change based on the reeducation. Such a strategy is only possible if the client willingly and actively invests time and energy in the reeducation process.

4 Discussion and Conclusion

CEM Researchers are confronted with the requirement to generate new knowledge while helping the industry to move forward with better, more collaborative practices. To achieve this, new research approaches have been adopted in recent years to conduct these field researches. However, from a socioconstructivist perspective, they cannot ignore the bias that could result from the researcher's desire to demonstrate empirically the value of a theory or the changes required to adopt a new technology. Moreover, as explored in this paper, when working with a human system, it is necessary to go beyond strict research methodological concerns if one wishes to be helpful. The critical analysis of the study, which we believe is not atypical from the studies pursed by other research teams in the CEM field, revealed that the research team might not have been helpful in the end. The partner might be happy with the outcome of the activities but that does not mean that the necessary change took place. This is similar to when patient get relief from taking medication that relieves symptoms but do not make the necessary change to solve the underlying problem.

The goal of this paper was not to propose solutions but to expose issues related to not questioning the nature of the relationship and the role of the researcher within a partnership. With the acceleration of changes, cogeneration of knowledge was proposed by social science as a means to cope with the need for generating praxis. However, consideration of the needs and expectations of industrial partners as well as a clarification of the researcher's role are required to provide the appropriate conditions to instantiate knowledge cogeneration processes.

References

1. Azhar, S., Ahmad, I., Sein, M.K.: Action research as a proactive research method for construction engineering and management. J. Constr. Eng. Manag. **136**(1), 87–98 (2009)
2. Somekh, B., Nissen, M.: Cultural-historical activity theory and action research. Mind, Cult. Act. **18**, 93–97 (2011)
3. Schein, E.H.: Process Consultation Revisited: Building the Helping Relationship. FT Press, Upper Saddle River (1998)
4. Van de Ven, A.H.: Engaged Scholarship: A Guide for Organizational and Social Research. Oxford University Press, Oxford (2007)
5. Engestrom, Y.: Activity theory as a framework for analyzing and redesigning work. Ergonomics **43**(7), 960–974 (2000)
6. Virkkunen, J.: The Change Laboratory: A Tool for Collaborative Development of Work and Education. Springer Science & Business Media, Heidelberg (2013)
7. Hevner, A.R., March, S.T., Park, J., Ram, S.: Design Science in Information Systems Research. MIS Q. **28**(1), 75–105 (2004)
8. Stringer, E.T.: Action research. Sage Publications, Thousand Oaks (1999)
9. Chevalier, J.M., Buckles, D.J.: Participatory Action Research: Theory and Methods for Engaged Inquiry (2013)
10. Schein, E.H.: Process consultation, action research and clinical inquiry: are they the same. J. Manag. Psychol. **10**(6), 14–19 (1995)
11. Thorgeirsdottir, H.: Investigating the use of Action Research and Activity Theory to Promote the Professional Development of Teachers in Iceland, Ph.D. Thesis, University of Exeter and University of Iceland (2015)

Aesthetics Evaluation of Architecture in Context

Agnieszka Mars[(✉)] and Ewa Grabska

Jagiellonian University, Kraków, Poland
{agnieszka.mars,ewa.grabska}@uj.edu.pl

Abstract. This paper deals with evaluation of architecture designed by multiple users. Presented approach concentrates on comparison of two languages – a language of an assessed building and a language of its context. The proposed method requires a CAD-like system to be equipped with an agent capable of some cognition and creative thinking that will allow to assess the project on the basis of its structure and given surroundings. Therefore, the system must contain a knowledge base about the context language and be able to extend it on the basis of designer's actions. The internal structure of the design requires conceptualization, which is performed on the basis of a visual perception model. Also, some sense of aesthetics should be present. Methods of graph representation of a design, defining the context language by automatic preparation of its graph grammar, and evaluating aesthetic fitness are presented.

Keywords: Computer aided design · Collaborative design · Aesthetic measure

1 Introduction

Every city consists of a mix of different approaches to architecture design. Human concepts, goals, creativity and opportunism interwave to constitute inseparable whole. A task performed by an architect when designing a new building to fit in existing context is complex and requires wide knowledge about culture, history and present expectations of the place. It is not about imitation – a real dialogue does not simply consist of repetition of other side's words, it is constant questioning and contribution combined with deep respect.

However, everyday life shows that the dialogue is often broken by inconsiderate interlocutors. Some of them want to overshadow the rest, other simply do not care. It is a matter of stormy discussions whether (and to what degree) aesthetics of architectonic objects should be subject to inspection [3]. Of course, everyone would prefer to live in an environment full of harmony and beauty, but what exactly do those concepts mean? Who has a right to decide? And what are the costs of prioritizing aesthetic values over others? Although aesthetics is strongly dependent on individual preferences and architecture very often refers to subtle cultural allusions understandable only for experienced recipients, we believe that a tool which enables automatic assessment of everyday designs in order to give an idea about their relation to the context could improve the process of environmental planning. In result multiple designers would be able to confront their ideas with unified aesthetic measure able to detect some basic

© Springer International Publishing AG 2017
Y. Luo (Ed.): CDVE 2017, LNCS 10451, pp. 193–201, 2017.
DOI: 10.1007/978-3-319-66805-5_24

defects of a conception. This paper deals with a problem of defining a method of such measurement. It is not our goal to question individualism of great masterpieces. Instead, we would like to prepare a tool based on human visual perception process that can alarm a designer of "everyday" architecture – like a private house or a block of flats – when there is something controversial in a way their work responses to the context. This can lead to a greater coherence of public spaces formed by multiple contributors.

There have already been some attempts to define, verify or provide coherence in computer-aided design. Soddu [2] has created generative software called Argenia, capable to produce designs of complex cities with consistent identity. Our approach concentrates on comparison of two languages – a language of an assessed building and a language of its context. In response to designer's action of adding a component to the project's drawing an internal graph representation is created. On the basis of the current internal structure a graph grammar containing production rules that enable generation of the given graph is determined. Finally, a graph grammar of the resultant building and a graph grammar of its context are compared and level of both harmony and novelty of a new building can be assessed. Methods of graph representation of a design, defining the context language by automatic preparation of its graph grammar, and evaluating aesthetic fitness are presented. The first section describes application of a visual perception model in graph representation of an object, while the next one presents implementation of composite graphs adjusted for the purpose of aesthetic measure. Further sections contain a description of graph grammars used to define architectonic context and a method of aesthetic evaluation. Finally, some conclusion is made.

2   CAD-Like Environment for Aesthetics

Although Computer Aided Design (CAD) belongs to well-established research areas, aesthetic evaluation of architecture in context is very rarely supported by a computer. To change this situation CAD-like systems should be equipped with an agent capable of some cognition and creative reasoning. This involves many internal mechanisms and processes, including background knowledge, ability to learn, ability to conceptualize and sense of aesthetics [1]. Aesthetic evaluation can be performed on a CAD-like system's internal structure, which represents objects in the form of an architectural drawings created through the user interface and is used for wide variety of operations, like e.g. verification of building standards. Knowledge-based systems or knowledge-based agents are committed explicitly or implicitly to some conceptualization.

2.1   Conceptualization

A conceptualization is an abstract view of the world that we wish to represent for some purpose. It is based on objects and concepts that are assumed to exist in some area of interest, and relationships that hold between them. Computational ontologies are the means to formally model the structure of a system, i.e., the entities and relations that emerge from its observation [6]. In this paper our view of the world is based on the Biederman's Recognition-by-Components perception model (RBC), which assumes

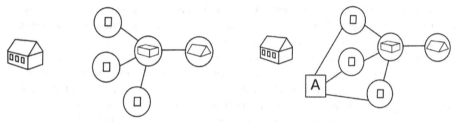

Fig. 1. Building graph

Fig. 2. Hyperedge in building graph

that human brain recognizes objects by identifying shape and relations of its components [4]. Their extraction requires to find edges and sharp concavities. Resultant component lacks sharp concavities and its edges mark it out from the surroundings, even when they are partially covered by something else. The idea to use a visual perception model in assessment of aesthetics is not accidental. Human evaluation of aesthetics is a complex cognitive process, heavily bound to perception. Figure 1 presents a building divided into components according to RBC theory and its graph representation that is machine readable. Each graph node represents one component, while each edge represents a relation of attachment. Human brain is very sensitive to any kind of order. Identifying order in complex structures is crucial for comprehension. Aesthetic value of an object is associated with the amount of information it provides to satisfy one's curiosity and the level of order it represents to enable understanding. Therefore, it seems necessary to regard some relations of order in computational assessment of aesthetics. Windows of the building from Fig. 1 are arranged in a deliberate way – all aligned to the same line. This can be represented in graph by a hyperedge, capable of connecting more than two nodes. Figure 2 shows a hyperedge of alignment relation (the square with label A) added to the building graph added to the building graph. In an object there may be many different lines and planes that components are aligned to. Representing each alignment relation by a separate hyperedge (Fig. 3) enables to assess the level of order more accurately.

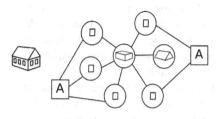

Fig. 3. Hyperedges in building graph

As it has been considered, architectonic objects are defined as sets of related components. Investigation of a structure they constitute and its reference to the context enables to find some information about aesthetic impression that may be given to a viewer. There are many requirements for a building to harmonize with its surroundings, especially other buildings that are designed often by a lot of different architects. A large part of these requirements responds to a very subtle (and hard to define in a formal way) dialog between culture and individualism. However, many others reflect a basic need of order and can be used quite easily in computational measurement of aesthetics. It is possible to verify whether a new building corresponds to its neighbours' style by investigating shapes and relations.

According to RBC theory, each component of an object's structure may be characterized by two sets of properties, non-accidental or metric ones. Non-accidental properties, like cross section shape, its symmetry and size change, as well as axis shape describe features of a solid that are easily recognized independently from the point of view. Another group, metric properties, involves parameters of a solid that can be easily mistaken and their perception may vary depending on the point of view, for example length, width or exact location. All these properties can be used as attributes of a graph node in order to fully define components of an architectonic object.

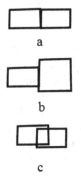

a

b

c

Fig. 4. RBC Relations

Components of an object can be related to each other in many different ways. Again, RBC theory provides a list of such relations. It is presented in Fig. 4, enriched by an overlap relation for the purpose of architecture design. These relations are represented by edges in a graph structure and can be attributed by some metric values. For instance, an end-to-side relation in which a basis of the first component is attached to a side of the second one may be described by geometric data informing where exactly the connection occurs. Analogically, a hyperedge used to represent a relation of alignment may be attributed by a definition of a plane.

It seems necessary to notice that mentioned relations take place between component's sides rather than between whole solids. It is a chimney's bottom basis that is attached to a roof side and windows' bottom bases that are aligned to a common line. In order to keep such information, composite graphs are used [5]. Figure 5 presents a composite graph of the building from Fig. 1. For clarity, only one window is presented. Each node consists of bonds representing component's surfaces. Their num-

shape: straight
symmetry: vertical & rotational
size: constant
axis type: constant

end-to-end

shape: straight
symmetry: vertical
size: constant
axis type: constant

end-to-side

shape: straight
symmetry: vertical & rotational

Fig. 5. Composite graph

ber may vary depending on the solid's cross section shape. The first bond (in black) represents a top basis, the second one (in grey) – a bottom basis, while the rest of bonds (in white) represent other surface types (it is enough to specify whether it is a large or a small side of a solid in case of size difference). Planar components are treated like a solid of height equal to 0 and lack non-accidental attributes describing size and axis as well as bonds other than a top basis bond.

Except from an ordinary edge, the bonds can be joined by a hyperedge representing a relation of alignment. According to Birkhoff's remarks about aesthetic measure [4], complexity of an object is increased by lines and planes that are not perpendicular or parallel to the ground. Therefore, we have decided to attribute the relation of alignment by values "straight" and "skew" not to lose information about complexity.

Summing up, internal structure of a designed architectonic object may have a form of a composite hypergraph. Its nodes represent building's components, its bonds – component's surfaces, its edges – spacial relations between components, and its hyperedges represent relations of components alignment. Graph edges connect surfaces bonds instead of components nodes which enables to store more detailed information about the whole object.

2.2 Knowledge Base and Learning

A sole structure of an evaluated building is of course not sufficient to assess its fit for surroundings. It is necessary to provide some architectonic context in which the new object is intended to be placed. It will be then possible to compare properties of the new building with general style of the context in order to assess coherence and novelty. Although context style can be very difficult to define fully, for the purpose of initial aesthetic evaluation it seems sufficient to compare some basic properties, like size, components' shapes and relations between them.

In the proposed aesthetics evaluation method, each building added to the project constitutes context for further designs. Multiple designers may compare their propositions with surroundings defined by others. Assessment on the basis of RBC theory does not require very detailed and accurate models, because mostly non-accidental properties are taken into account. It means that components' shapes are important, but their exact geometric parameters are disregarded by the aesthetic measure. Therefore, the user interface of a design system may consist of a set of basic shapes and some simple modification tools. This approach makes it relatively quick and easy to insert already existing context, so the project of collaborative design may start with some predefined surroundings. Let us consider an example when a new housing estate is built. In the beginning the building plot is empty, but there may be some objects fast beside and style of the estate ought to be consistent with them as well. The project should then start with predefined context, reflected in the internal representation as any other buildings, and with an empty area for new objects. Every new building added to the housing estate project is then verified on the basis of the internal structure and may be saved to constitute the context for a new design, or deleted. Evaluation can regard houses designed by different architects and in different time.

A dialog with architecture context is too sophisticated to be assessed by computational measure. However, especially in everyday architecture design for private investors, it may be very useful to have a tool alarming when a project is too eccentric or imitates another building.

It is easy to notice that the project's internal graph grows during design. In case of large projects it will soon become inefficient to perform operations of pattern search on a complex structure. The solution is to make use of the coherence of designed objects. Every settlement has its own language – buildings' styles correspond with each other, some patterns repeat. Having a formal structure of each building in the form graph, one can define a grammar of the settlement language. Graph grammars consist of production rules used to transform one graph into another. Figure 7 shows a grammar able to generate buildings presented in Fig. 6. This is a simple grammar that can be

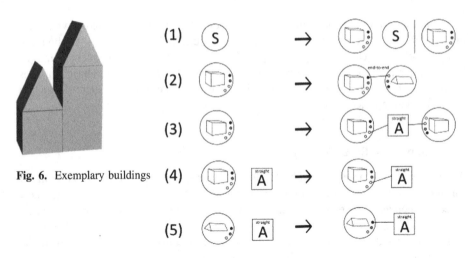

Fig. 6. Exemplary buildings

Fig. 7. Graph grammar of the buildings from Fig. 6

automatically created on the basis of the building graph. Every relation between components is represented by a production rule. The left side of the production contains a subgraph that is to be transformed, while the right side – the same subgraph after transformation. Only non-accidental attributes of nodes that define shape are set. This reduces number of rules – attachment of a roof to a prism is defined only once, although such relation occurs twice in the buildings from Fig. 6. For clarity, non-accidental attributes' values have been presented as a sketch of the shape they describe.

Every building added to the project may extend existing grammar or use its rules. During the design process, every relation between components is remembered as a number of applied production rules. In result frequency of each production of the whole architectonic context can be computed. Figure 8 presents a new building added to the one in Fig. 6, while Fig. 9 shows grammar consisting of two production rules used to generate the new object. Once it is accepted and added to the context, the graph grammar of the context is extended by these additional rules.

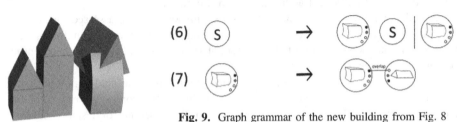

Fig. 9. Graph grammar of the new building from Fig. 8

Fig. 8. New building

3 Aesthetic Measure

A system capable of evaluation of architecture in context ought to be equipped in some sense of aesthetics. It should be able to find both analogy and novelty and decide whether their ratio is appropriate. In order to solve this problem we propose to compare an internal structure of the assessed building with an internal structure of the context. In case of the presented idea both of them are graph structures which can be generated by a graph grammar. The previous sections contain description of graph representation of the project's drawing and a method of determining graph grammars. In this section we are going to present aesthetic measure based on graph grammar comparison. This will allow to assess to what degree a language of context is used by a designer and how it can be enriched by a new building.

Figure 10 contains mapping of grammar rules of architectonic context from Fig. 7 into the new building grammar from Fig. 9. For each rule of the grammar of the context, the most similar rule from the building grammar has been found. The similarity level is assessed only between isomorphic subgraphs from right sides of productions by verification of their attributes. In the presented example the rule 1 has been mapped into the rule 6, and the rule 2 into the rule 7. There are no rules from the building grammar that can be mapped into the production rules 3, 4 and 5. Attribute values' differences have been presented in the column "Diff". Production rules are divided into two categories – those which contain a relation of alignment (order rules) and those which do not (structure rules). For each rule ratio is computed by dividing a number of occurrences ("Occ") of the given production in generated objects (context or a new building) by a total number of production rules of the given category. If there are no rules belonging to a category, the ratio value is 0. Let ratio1 and ratio2 denote ratios of the grammar of the context and the building grammar, respectively, and d is a number of attribute values' differences between subgraphs. For each production its grade g is computed according to the formula:

	Rule		Occ	Ratio	Rule		Occ	Ratio	Diff	Grade
STRUCTURE	(1)	⬚ S	2	0.5	(6)	⬚ S	1	0.5	axis type	-0.1
	(2)	⬚ ⬚	2	0.5	(7)	⬚ ⬚	1	0.5	axis type relation	-0.2
ORDER	(3)	⬚ A ⬚	1	0.33				0		-0.33
	(4)	⬚ A	1	0.33				0		-0.33
	(5)	⬚ A	1	0.33				0		-0.33
									TOTAL GRADE:	-1.3

Fig. 10. Computation of similarity level

$$g = -|\text{ratio1} - \text{ratio2}| - 0.1 * d$$

The final grade consists of a sum of rule grades and represents similarity between a language of the new building and the language of its context. It is easy to notice that this value is always smaller than or equal to 0. A low value describes an object very different from the surroundings, while a value equal to 0 indicates a building of a very low level of novelty.

Fig. 11. Małopolski Ogród Sztuki - example of architecture in context

In order to test the presented method of evaluation let us consider a piece of architecture that is appreciated for its regard to the surroundings – Małopolski Ogród Sztuki by Ingarden & Ewý (Fig. 11, from www.iea.com. pl). The language used by the building resembles the language of a context to a large degree except from the fact that the windows are aligned to non-parallel lines. In the graph structure it is represented by an alignment relation attributed by "skew" value. The total grade of similarity to the context has been computed as −1.49.

4   Conclusion

The presented concept of aesthetic evaluation of architecture in context may be a step to achieve a tool to combine ideas of multiple designers. In result, some feedback about the designed object will be given to its creator, regarding human visual perception process and consequential aesthetic preferences. Further work will concentrate on extending the concept of context, which is not only limited to surrounding buildings, but also consists of historical buildings and cultural references. Ideally, the obtained system will be able to substitute a city planner in case of everyday architecture acceptance/rejection issues.

References

1. Besold, T.R., et al.: Computational Creativity Research: Towards Creative Machines. Atlantic Press, Paris (2015)
2. Soddu, C.: The discovering of persistent deep memory in generative design. study case: duets. In: Proceedings of XIX Generative Art Conference, pp. 15–35. Domus Argenia Publisher, Milan (2016)
3. Turner, T.: Landscape Planning and Environmental Impact Design EID (2007). Electronic edn. Gardenvisit.com
4. Mars, A., Grabska, E.: Generation of 3D architectural objects with the use of an aesthetic oriented multi-agent system. In: Luo, Y. (ed.) CDVE 2016. LNCS, vol. 9929, pp. 340–347. Springer, Cham (2016). doi:10.1007/978-3-319-46771-9_44

5. Grabska, E., Borkowski, A.: Assisting Creativity by Composite Representation. In: Gero, J.S., Sudweeks, F. (eds.) Artificial Intelligence in Design 1996, pp. 743–759. Kluwer Academic Publishers, Dordrecht (1996)
6. Guarino, N., Oberle, D., Staab, S.: What is an ontology? In: Staab, S., Studer, R. (eds.) Handbook on Ontologies. IHIS, pp. 1–17. Springer, Heidelberg (2009). doi:10.1007/978-3-540-92673-3_0

A Case Study of Cooperative Design on Integrated Smart-Car Systems: Assessing Drivers' Experience

Jaume R. Perelló[(⊠)] and Alexandre García

University of the Balearic Islands, Mallorca, Spain
jaume.r.perello@gmail.com, alex.garcia@uib.es

Abstract. Multimodal operating systems such as Apple or Android are being integrated into several platforms and devices, increasing users' connectivity experience. Recently, both operating systems (OS) had been integrated into modern vehicles, extending connectivity possibilities to road transport, providing them with new driving experiences for the user. In the present study we attempt to evaluate, under a holistic scope, the users' experience with these systems while driving. We have developed a new scale based on a user-centered and cooperative design approach which will be tested for the first time in a two-case study. With this scale, we will assess the main variables that influence the user's experience when interacting with in-vehicle smartphone integration systems while driving. We hypothesized that the scale will be capable of discriminating between both systems, their tested functions and between users. Despite results seeming to support this hypothesis, further research with wider samples and systems is needed.

Keywords: Cooperative user experience design · In-vehicle integrated · Operative systems · Multimodal human machine interfaces

1 Introduction

In this paper we focus on the development of a tool for system user experience assessment. This tool is based on a cooperative design approach including several frameworks from human factors literature: affective design (Khalid and Helander [1]; Norman [2, 3]), Technology Acceptance Model (Davis et al. [4]; Davis [5]), Attentional Model (Kahneman [6]) and Multiple Resources Theory (Wickens [7]). Using an already existing set of tools [8–10] and our new tool; we assess two in-vehicle systems that provide an interface for using smartphone applications while driving. Applications run inside the user smartphone and then a middleware (which is permanently installed in the vehicle) is used enabling communication between the mobile device and the instrument panel. The panel does not only project application data through a customised user interface, but it can also be controlled by the user. Thus, the smartphone data is accessible through the instrument panel to run applications using, for instance, voice commands (among other communication channels). Integrating the smartphone represents remarkable advantages: first, it enables the driver to automatically customise the services offered by the car related to the applications that s/he has installed on the

Y. Luo (Ed.): CDVE 2017, LNCS 10451, pp. 202–206, 2017.
DOI: 10.1007/978-3-319-66805-5_25

phone. Furthermore, it avoids having to install a Wi-Fi generating system in the car, since the device can perform the anchoring function. Finally, it is much easier to update apps from the smartphone than from the vehicle. This solution is also preferred by manufacturers, as it allows the development of applications following the guidelines for a specific platform, without the need to take into account the characteristics of the instrument panel that will display this information.

2   Method

As a case study, an Android user - owning a Samsung Galaxy S6 Edge running Android Lollipop 6.0.1 OS - and an iPhone user - owning an iPhone 5S running iOS 10.2.1 - were recruited. Both participants completed three trials testing Navigation (N), Multimedia (M) and Phone call (P) functions while driving. After each trial, participants had to fill out a set of scales composed by the Driving Activity Load Index [9], the System Usability Scale [8], the Acceptance Scale [10] and the Global User Experience System Assessment, our new scale.

3   Results

3.1   System Usability Scale

Figure 1 shows the usability results for each three experimental conditions. As can be seen, the Android system (AOS) gets a score of 92.5/100 in N conditions, while iOS gets a score of 85/100. In M condition, this pattern is reversed; as the score of the AOS is 50/100 whereas the iOS score is 87.5/100. In the third condition, P, both systems obtained similar high scores: 95/100 the AOS and 100/100 the iOS. These results suggest that for both OS, the P function is the easiest to use, followed by N and, lastly, M.

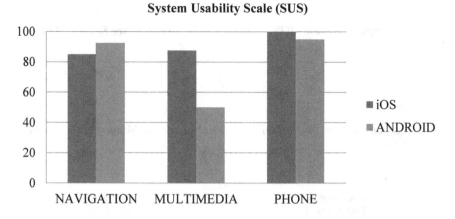

Fig. 1. System Usability Scale

Driving Activity Load Index (DALI)

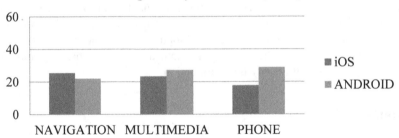

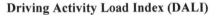

Fig. 2. Driving Activity Load Index

3.2 Driving Activity Load Index

Figure 2 presents the workload scores for the different experimental conditions with their respective OS. The scores in general terms, are relatively low, given that the maximum is 60. Both OS obtain similar workload scores. N function proves to be the most demanding condition for the driver using iOS, with a score of 25.3, while for the driver using AOS it proves to be the least demanding (21.9). In the condition interacting with M function, this pattern is reversed, the iOS system being less demanding to use (23.3) than AOS (27.1). Finally, in the P condition is where the most notable differences between the two OS have been observed, with AOS being especially demanding (28.8) when compared to iOS (17.7).

3.3 Van der Laan Acceptance Scale

According to this scale, system acceptability has been evaluated in two different subscales: usefulness and satisfaction. Results for AOS are presented in Fig. 4. These results suggest that M is the most useful (M = −.2; SD = .46) and satisfying (M = 1.5; SD = .86) function in this system. On the other hand, iOS acceptance results are

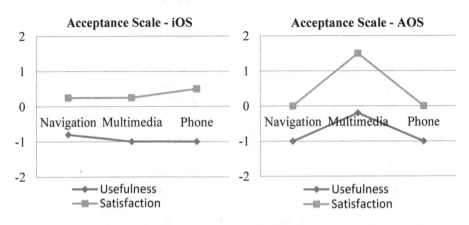

Fig. 3. Acceptance Scale iOS

Fig. 4. Acceptance Scale AOS

presented in Fig. 3 and suggest that while N is the most useful (M = −0.8; SD = .15) function, P is the most satisfying (M = 0.5; SD = .14). Overall results do not allow clear identification of the most acceptable OS.

3.4   Global User Experience System Assessment

We have used this case study to carry out a first exploratory analysis of the tool, and the descriptive statistics showed a high standard deviation from the mean (>1) except for items 9 (SD = 0.518) and 14 (SD = 0.408). The overall scores for each OS in the three experimental modalities are presented in Fig. 5. These results show that for the iOS user, the greatest experience was provided by the P function, while for the AOS user it was the M. Global results suggest that AOS provides a better user experience in all its tested applications. However, as may be apparent, there are no big differences between the same system's functions in both cases, showing a homogenous global pattern of the OS user experience clearly differentiated in both participants.

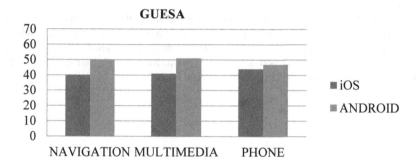

Fig. 5. Global User Experience System Assessment

4   Conclusion

This study opens the gate to the development of new user experience assessment tools based on a cooperative design framework. We attempt to assess usability, acceptance, workload and affective design features in a simple and efficient manner. As a case study, results do not allow us to determine the validity of this scale, but provide some interesting first data about its acceptance and application. The GUESA scores followed a similar pattern to that observed in the set of comparable questionnaires, which may suggest that we are on the right path. Therefore, further research with wider samples and different systems is needed in order to carry out a factorial exploratory analysis to determine the factors underpinning the scale.

References

1. Khalid, H.M., Helander, M.G.: A framework for affective customer needs in product design. Theoret. Issues Ergon. Sci. **5**, 27–42 (2004). doi:10.1080/1463922031000086744
2. Norman, D.: Interactions. Emot. Des.: Attractive Things Work Better **9**(4), 36–42 (2002). doi:10.1145/543434.543435
3. Norman, D.: Interaction design for automobile interiors (2004). http://www.jnd.org/dn.mss/interaction_des.html. Accessed 21 Nov 2016
4. Davis, F., Bagozzi, R., Warshaw, P.: User acceptance of computer technology: a comparison of two theoretical models. Manag. Sci. (1989). http://pubsonline.informs.org/doi/abs/10.1287/mnsc.35.8.982
5. Davis, F.D.: Perceived usefulness, perceived ease of use, and user acceptance of information technology. MIS Q. **13**(3), 319 (1989). doi:10.2307/249008
6. Kahneman, D.: Attention and effort. Am. J. Psychol. **88** (1973). doi:10.2307/1421603
7. Wickens, C.D.: Multiple resources and mental workload. Hum. Factors **50**(3), 449–455 (2008). doi:10.1518/001872008X288394
8. Lewis, J.R., Sauro, J.: The factor structure of the system usability scale. In: Kurosu, M. (ed.) HCD 2009. LNCS, vol. 5619, pp. 94–103. Springer, Heidelberg (2009). doi:10.1007/978-3-642-02806-9_12
9. Pauzié, A.: A method to assess the driver mental workload: the driving activity load index (DALI). IET Intell. Transport Syst. **2**(4), 315–322 (2008). doi:10.1049/iet-its:20080023
10. Van Der Laan, J.D., Heino, A., De Waard, D.: A simple procedure for the assessment of acceptance of advanced transport telematics. Transp. Res. Part C: Emerg. Technol. **5**(1), 1–10 (1997). doi:10.1016/S0968-090X(96)00025-3

Mobile Application for Collaborative Scheduling and Monitoring of Construction Works According to Lean Construction Methods

Julia Ratajczak[1,2](✉) ⓘ, Christoph Paul Schimanski[1],
Carmen Marcher[1], Michael Riedl[1], and Dominik T. Matt[1,2]

[1] Fraunhofer Italia Research, via Macello 57, Bolzano, Italy
julia.ratajczak@fraunhofer.it
[2] Free University of Bozen-Bolzano, Piazza Università 1, Bolzano, Italy
Julia.Ratajczak@natec.unibz.it

Abstract. In the construction industry, an efficient management of information flow as well as enhanced communication and collaboration among stakeholders are crucial to improve construction process management. Construction processes are still managed by means of paper-based documents, e.g. scheduling. To ensure on-time delivery of projects and automate construction management, especially scheduling and monitoring process, a mobile application based on Lean Construction methods is being developed within the ACCPET project. This application aims to improve productivity, collaboration between project participants as well to provide tailored information to the user. To reach this goal the following methods and technologies have been adopted: Location-based Management System, Last Planner System, Tiered Structure methodology and Building Information Modelling. This paper describes concept, framework and functionalities of this mobile application.

Keywords: Lean Construction · Mobile application · Construction processes · BIM

1 Introduction

1.1 Research Background

The construction industry (CI) is a project-based industry characterized by heterogeneity, extreme complexity and fragmented supply chain. Its complexity is increased by mutual relationships between different stakeholders involved in the construction process [1] as well as by necessity for effective cooperation, communication and collaboration on construction site [2]. Over the years, the CI has been struggled by a difficulty in sharing information between construction project participants, which is a primary cause of its poor performance [2]. Moreover, the productivity and reliability of construction processes are highly affected by the accurate and timely information availability on site [3]. Therefore, an efficient management of information flow as well

© Springer International Publishing AG 2017
Y. Luo (Ed.): CDVE 2017, LNCS 10451, pp. 207–214, 2017.
DOI: 10.1007/978-3-319-66805-5_26

as better communication and collaboration among project participants are crucial to improve construction processes.

In major construction sites, information is still managed by means of paper-based documents, including construction drawings, construction log and scheduling. This situation leads often to misunderstanding between stakeholders, construction errors and low ability to make rapid and right decisions. Construction scheduling is an essential part of construction projects. The main reason for still manual generation of scheduling is caused by not sufficient software support [4].

In recent years, the adoption of Information and Communication Technologies (ICT) in the CI has had a significant impact on both productivity and economic growth of construction companies [5]. Many improvements have been already done, especially in monitoring of building quality, where wireless sensor networks have been adopted to control building systems or to detect the degeneration of building materials [6, 7]. However, the monitoring of construction processes need still IT support combined with Lean Construction (LC) methods to provide automatically real-time information on construction progress, to streamline flow of work and to decrease cost and project delivery.

This paper describes a concept, framework and functionalities of a mobile application to support the construction management system based on LC methods. The mobile application, so-called SiMaApp, is currently being developed within the ACCEPT project. More information on the ACCEPT project can be found on web page: www.accept-project.com.

2   Construction Management According to Lean Principles

2.1   Location-Based Management System (LBMS)

The LBMS consists of planning and scheduling of construction works. It considers that the project is broken down to physical location, to which different activities can be assigned [8]. Each activity is defined according to location hierarchy level, so-called Location Breakdown Structure (LBS). Construction activities and their controlling should refer always to those locations. Organizing activities by locations allows user to get more comprehensive information, avoid interruption between different trades, and enhance constancy of the workflow [8]. In recent case studies, a successful implementation of LBSM in software and tools have been observed [9–11]. However, they are still lagging in supporting real-time monitoring of construction works.

2.2   Last Planner System (LPS)

LPS is complementary to LBMS and it focuses more on the collaboration processes of planning and task commitment, which engage all project participants to ensure the achievement of agreed goals. It aims at increasing schedule reliability, streamlining flow of work and reducing cost and project delivery. The authors in [12] claim that every construction task can be technically gathered into four groups during its execution phase: SHOULD-task, CAN-task, WILL-task and DID-task. According to [13, 14], the SHOULD-CAN-WILL-DID (SCWD) process is supposed to be applied in five consecutive steps, which are characterized by corresponding plan phases with increasing level of detail: (1) *Master Scheduling*, which sets up milestones and durations; (2) *Phase Scheduling*, which defines construction plan involving project participants, identifies handoffs and operational conflicts; (3) *Make Ready Planning*, which considers 4–6 week look-ahead planning to ensure that work is made ready for installation; (4) *Weekly Work Planning*, which defines daily commitments to perform during the following week; and (5) *Learning and Improvement Planning*, which monitors progress of scheduled activities and evaluates successes and failures of the previous week's plan. LPS uses a percent planned complete value (PPC) to establish how well the planning system is working, and Reason for non-completion (RNC) parameter to prevent the recurrence of errors in successive work plan [12].

3   Construction Management System in SiMaApp

3.1   Tiered Structure Methodology

A Tiered Structure (TS) methodology has been created for the ACCEPT system to improve its communication and information flow as well as to structure its architecture and develop its modules in a simple and understandable way. This allows users to have direct access to information relevant for their requirements. The TS methodology is comprised of four tiers (Tier 0–3) and establishes the breakdown structure of a construction project in SiMaApp, responsibilities of project participants (owner) and construction process controlling though KPIs as shown in Fig. 1.

Tier 0 represents high-level of project information - building level and construction phase (e.g. building A, superstructure respectively), where tailored information are delivered to a client and general contractor by means of a Gantt chart. The Gantt chart visualizes graphically status of construction works, highlighting with different

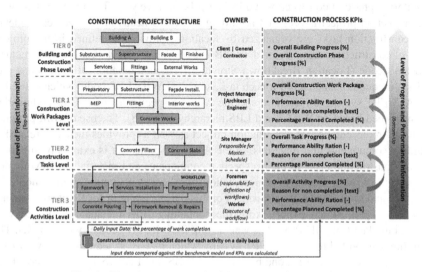

Fig. 1. Tiered structure methodology (Color figure online)

colors – works on schedule (green), behind schedule (orange), ahead schedule (blue). Users are also informed about accumulated delays in terms of days as well as about the overall building progress.

Tier 1 refers to Construction work package level (e.g. concrete works). Relevant information are provided to the owner (e.g. Project Manager), who can control through graphical representation the overall task progress, performance ability ration (PAR), reason for non-completion (RNC) and percentage planned completed (PPC). The owner of this tier has access to Gantt chart of construction works, which can be filtered by location, construction phase and status of construction works. The status of construction works on Gantt chart are represented graphically as in Tier 0.

Tier 2 is related to Construction task level (e.g. concrete slab) with its responsible figure – site manager. Site manager can manage information at task level using Gantt chart in an analogous manner to the previous tiers.

Tier 3 represents the lowest level of project information – Construction activities level, which defines a sequence of construction works that should be performed by a crew to complete a task on Tier 2. These activities define a workflow (e.g. concrete slab workflow), which is created by a foreman. Tier 3 is the most important level, since it manages and controls construction works at detailed level. It creates a basis for the monitoring of the entire construction process. Each scheduled activity is monitored though a daily checklist, which collects data from field (percentage of work completion) to calculate progress and performance KPIs. These KPIs (Tier 3) are used to derive KPIs to upper levels.

3.2   Integration of Lean Construction to BIM and Ms Project

The SiMaApp application takes advantage of both lean construction methods and Building Information Modelling (BIM) to improve the reliability of scheduling and monitoring phase of construction works in a collaborative way. The master schedule of a construction project is prepared according to LBMS needs in Ms Project. It means that construction tasks are organized by locations, previously defined in the project. Each of construction task is defined by WBS code (WBS – Work breakdown Structure) and LBS code (Location Breakdown Structure). The combination of both codes provides a unique nomenclature for each task, so-called WBS/LBS code, which is used in the ACCEPT system to identify a specific task in a specific location. This codification is established based on WBS's and LBS hierarchy levels [8]. The use of BIM provides better 3D representation of construction project as well as provides metadata related to building components and materials. In the ACCEPT project, it is extremely important to link construction tasks to their respective components and materials in BIM model, because it allows a graphical representation of where construction works should be executed and how they are progressing. For this reason, a plugin for Revit software has been developed, which exports xml. file containing BIM metadata combined with scheduling data from Ms Project as well as obj. file with 3D geometry of a model. The xml. file is imported to the ACCEPT system, which merges scheduling data with BIM metadata. This operation is done by means of WBS and LBS codes, which have been inserted in BIM model and Ms Project beforehand. It allows the visualization of location-based scheduling Gantt chart in SiMaApp (Fig. 2).

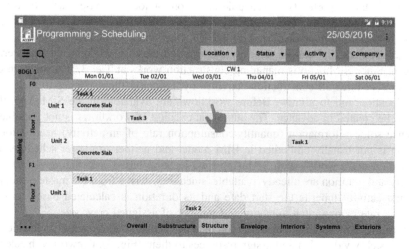

Fig. 2. Location-based Gantt chart in SiMaApp

3.3   SiMaApp Functionalities

SiMaApp is a process engineering tool for field created according to Lean Construction (LC) methods. It is designed to provide users with intuitively working functionalities that enable the implementation of both LPS and LBMS. The application is available for Android mobile devices such as smartphones and tablets. According to TS methodology, SiMaApp provides users with tailored information such as: (a) project scheduling and work commitments for crews; (b) project data: project drawings, construction details, component and material inventory, obtained from BIM model; (c) up-to-dates reports of construction progress; (d) alerts and notification (user-user and system-user) to inform about any occurred problem on site or about deviations in construction progress. Moreover, this application allows users (foremen) to manage resources such as workers, crews and shared equipment, materials and digital assets (e.g. instructions, videos, 3D models, technical documents, etc.).

In this paper, authors focus on SiMaApp functionalities, which are related to the project scheduling and construction process monitoring according to Tier 3. In this context, SiMaApp allows site managers/foremen to automate the following phases using data from both Ms Project and BIM model of the construction project:

- Planning of construction activities (workflows);
- Detailed schedule of construction activities on a weekly basis;
- Daily controlling of activities by worker and site manager or foreman;
- Monitoring of activity progress and performance for scheduled week;
- Weekly reports, notifications and alerts.

3.4   Workflow Scheduling

The concept of "pitching" described in [15] is used to apply LBMS to SiMaApp and thus entails the opportunity to schedule and monitor location-based tasks on a daily basis. Consequently, this concept offers wide possibilities for real-time measuring of the entire construction process according to TS. One "Pitch" is defined as the maximum daily job content that can be done by a composed crew of workers within a certain location. Since SiMaApp is managing construction works at Tier 3, it is foreseen that the user schedules all construction activities by assigning those pitches to their dedicated location and to a crew. Before workflows are available in the SiMaApp, they have to be created in advance. The automatic creation of workflows is not possible so far since some information (quantity/consumption rate of an activity) needed for its creation is not usually embodied in BIM model and neither in master schedule. The foreman creates a workflow in SiMaApp for a location-based task. Start/end date, task quantity and duration are already available, since they derive from the master schedule. The first activity inherits the start date and its duration is calculated based on consumption rate or one pitch, quantity and number of assigned crew size.

Once the workflow is created, the foreman can schedule these activities in calendar using a weekly work plan and assign resources to them (Fig. 3). Crew(s) with selected workers can be chosen from the Crew Database and assigned to each activity. A shared equipment (e.g. crane), construction components/materials and digital assets can be assigned to an activity as well. Construction components and materials can be selected from BIM inventory. Since they are linked to a specific location-based task, BIM elements of this task are only displayed. Finally, based on scheduled workflow, SiMaApp automatically generates a list with work commitments and sends it to involved workers by means of To Do List functionality in SiMaApp.

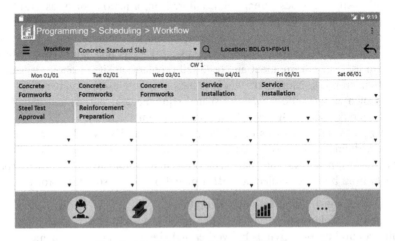

Fig. 3. Workflow scheduling in SiMaApp

3.5   Construction Process Monitoring

A daily construction progress monitoring is performed at workflow level (Tier 3) and it controls progress and performance of scheduled location-based activities. The monitoring process is done by means of checklists available in SiMaApp. The checklist displays all location-based activities scheduled on that particular day, providing information about the programmed daily work content (Daily work goal). It is the crew's duty to fills out the checklist at the end of working day and indicates the percentage of completion for each activity as well as the reason for non-completion, if the daily goal has not been achieved. At the end of each working day foreman has to countercheck to verify worker's input data. Final foremen's input data will be used for calculations of construction process KPIs. If a crew has not met the activity daily goal on one day, the remained work content will be considered during the following days. With this, an updated daily work content will be calculated automatically, indicating a Dynamic daily goal, whose total fulfilment would still lead to an accurately timed completion of the entire activity. In SiMaApp, there will be integrated an alert system, which controls continuously values of KPIs and triggers notifications to site managers and foremen, when values for monitored KPIs are out of range. For instance, a possible alert's condition is when a dynamic daily goal exceeds the initial daily goal by more than 10%. This threshold can be set up based on how much backlog of work a crew can catch up with per day or how many extra working hours per day are allowed. Moreover, workers have a possibility to send manually a feedback to foremen if the workload is too high.

The KPIs that are going to be monitored at each tier are represented in Fig. 1. Regarding PPC, fully completed tasks will be considered to provide information regarding scheduling reliability and smoothness of the workflow. Daily PPCs and the overall PPC can be used during regular LPS meetings. Special emphasis is given on the recording of RNC, which need to be discussed regularly during the meetings in order to truly disclose root causes for completion failures. Moreover, SiMaApp provides a usable framework for the implementation of LPS. Last but not least, daily so-called PAR-Values [8] for each task and their comprising activities can be calculated.

4   Conclusions

This paper describes a framework of SiMaApp mobile application for scheduling and controlling of the construction process according to Location-based Management System and Last Planner System. The Tiered Structure methodology has been created for this application to improve its communication and information flow as well as to provide users with tailored information. SiMaApp functionalities allow user to manage and control scheduling data as well as construction process KPIs. It can analyze data and visualize them more effectively using Gantt chart, graphs and activity/task status. This application empowers users involved in LPS to reduce waste and cost, smoothen processes, improve productivity as well enhance collaboration among different stakeholders. The first prototype of SiMaApp functionalities has been developed using Excel sheet. In the meantime, the SiMaApp application is being developed and its functionalities are going to be implemented by the end of 2017. Considering the current development phase, it has not been possible to evaluate benefits of this application and to test user acceptance and feedback. It is planned that fully working Excel sheet and SiMaApp will be validated in three European construction sites this summer.

Acknowledgments. The authors would like to thank the European Commission for their funding of the ACCEPT project within the Horizon 2020 Framework Program (Grant Agreement: 636895). The authors gratefully acknowledge the contributions of other partners from the consortium, especially of Nicolas Mayer form Ascora GmbH responsible for SiMaApp development; Peter Leo Merz from TIE Germany responsible for the implementation of lean construction methods in Profile Nexus; Jason Page and Edward Gooden from Ingleton Wood for the co-development of Tiered Structure.

References

1. Clough, R.H., Sears, G.A., Sears, S.K.: Construction Project Management: A Practical Guide to Field Construction Management. Wiley, Hoboken (2008)
2. Dainty, A., Moore, D., Murray, M.: Communication in Construction. Taylor & Francis, New York (2006)
3. Dave, B., Boddy, S.C., Koskela, L.J.: Improving information flow within the production management system with web services. In: 18th Annual Conference of the International Group for Lean Construction, pp. 445–455, Haifa, Israel (2010)
4. Tauscher, E., Mikulakova, K., Beucke, K., König, M.: Automated generation of construction schedules based on the IFC object model. In: ASCE, Computing in Civil Engineering, Austin, TX (2009)
5. Li, H., Irani, Z., Love, P.: The IT performance evaluation in the construction industry. In: 33rd Hawaii International Conference on System Sciences, Maui, Hawaii (2000)
6. Garcia, M., Bri, D., Sendra, S., Lloret, J.: Practical deployment of wireless sensors networks: a survey. Int. J. Adv. Netw. Serv. 3(1&2), 170–185 (2010)
7. Sendra, S., Lloret, A.T., Lloret, J., Rodrigues, J.J.P.C.: A wireless sensor networks deployment to detect the degeneration of cement used in construction. Int. J. Ad Hoc Ubiquitous Comput. 15(1–3), 147–160 (2014)
8. Kenley, R., Seppänen, O.: Location-Based Management for Construction: Planning, Scheduling and Control. Spon Press, New York (2010)
9. Kala, T., Mouflard, C., Seppänen, O.: Production control using location- based management system on a hospital construction project. In: 20th Annual Conference of the International Group for Lean Construction, San Diego, California, USA (2012)
10. Seppänen, O., Ballard, G., Pesonen, S.: The combination of last planner system and location-based management system. Lean Constr. J. 6, 43–54 (2010)
11. Dallasega, P., Rauch, E., Matt, D.T.: Increasing productivity in ETO construction projects through a lean methodology for demand predictability. In: 5th International Conference on Industrial Engineering and Operations Management, Proceeding, Dubai, United Arab Emirates (2015)
12. Ballard, G.: The last planner system of production control. Ph.D. dissertation, School of Civil Engineering, The University of Birmingham, UK (2000)
13. Howell, G.: A guide to the last planner for construction foremen and supervisors. Lean Construction Institute, California, USA (2000)
14. Ballard, G., Tommelein, I.: Current process benchmark for the last planner system (2016). p2sl.berkeley.edu
15. Dallasega, P., Matt, D.T., Krause, D.: Design of the building execution process in SME construction networks. In: Thompson K. (ed.) Proceedings of 2nd International Workshop on Design in Civil and Environmental Engineering, Worcester, UK, pp. 7–15 (2013)

Industrial Data Sharing with Data Access Policy

Felix W. Baumann[1](✉), Uwe Breitenbücher[2], Michael Falkenthal[2],
Gerd Grünert[1], and Sebastian Hudert[1]

[1] TWT GmbH Science & Innovation, Industriestr. 6, 70565 Stuttgart, Germany
{felix.baumann,gerd.gruenert,sebastian.hudert}@twt-gmbh.de
[2] Institute of Architecture of Application Systems,
University of Stuttgart, 70569 Stuttgart, Germany
{uwe.breitenbuecher,falkenthal}@iaas.uni-stuttgart.de

Abstract. In current industrial settings, data is dispersed on numerous
devices, systems and locations without integration and sharing capabilities. With this work, we present a framework for the integration of
various data sources within an industrial setting, based on a mediating
data hub. Within the data hub, data sources and sinks for this industrial application are equipped with data usage policies to restrict and
enable usage and consumption of data for shared analytics. We identify
such policies, their requirements and rationale. This work addresses an
industrial setting, with manufacturing data being the primary use-case.
Requirements for these policies are identified from existing use-cases and
expert domain knowledge. The requirements are identified as reasonable
via examples and exemplary implementation.

Keywords: Industrial data · Data aggregation · Policies · Data hub

1 Introduction

Industrial data utilisation and usage is currently influenced by a number of
domains such as Cloud Computing, the Internet of Things (IoT), smart services and smart data analytics [2], artificial intelligence, machine learning, and
data mining. The previous concepts and technologies are all part of the fourth
industrial revolution, called Industry 4.0 [6]. One commonality of these concepts
is the increased reliance and foundation in data. Industrial settings and especially manufacturing enterprises create and consume large amounts of data from
numerous data sources and sinks.

While endeavours in the field of Industry 4.0 are promising approaches to
provide new insights into and to create opportunities from the analysed data and
the underlying processes, many problems arise. Formerly isolated data sources
are integrated which can cause compliance issues, privacy, security or even legal
violations. Moreover, often business critical data and details about processing
steps and whole production processes are to be analysed by data scientists, which
are often externals to the data-owning companies and, furthermore, are currently
rare. This is due to the fact that the knowledge and expertise about analytics

© Springer International Publishing AG 2017
Y. Luo (Ed.): CDVE 2017, LNCS 10451, pp. 215–219, 2017.
DOI: 10.1007/978-3-319-66805-5_27

algorithms, techniques and platforms is typically not part of the core business of manufacturing companies. Further problems arise from the heterogeneity of data sources that must be unified and adapted for efficient and shared usage.

On the one hand, this trend is mainly driven by developments in IoT, allowing devices of reduced size and price. This miniaturization facilitates bringing out many sensors in manufacturing environments to collect data about production processes, processing steps of machinery, and surrounding parameters. Environmental parameters include humidity, light irradiation, and temperature in production environments [3,10] and many more. On the other hand, cloud technologies and evolution of new analytical approaches and platforms enable the rapid processing of the acquired large datasets, even on-line via streaming analytics frameworks. Analytics platforms, such as Apache Flink [11], are developed under the constraint to be highly optimized to provide application programming interfaces and libraries specifically for developing analytics algorithms among runtimes and integration middleware. Flink allows data to be either processed via batch jobs or continuous data streams. Such analytics platforms and algorithms often profit from processing data in parallel, distributed among dynamically allocated compute nodes. Thus, they can leverage the scaling capabilities of cloud infrastructures, platforms and services, be it in public, hybrid or private clouds.

With this work, we propose a data integration and sharing framework that is constrained by a set of policies to enable the secure and efficient usage of distributed data sources within industrial environments. New optimization opportunities in manufacturing processes are leveraged by integrating data from a manifold of different data sources to overcome their isolation and enable holistic analysis approaches.

2   Related Works

Yu et al. [12] provided a rationale for the sharing of information amongst business partners, especially within a supply chain to minimise risks and uncertainties. In the context of clinical data, Malin et al. [8] discussed requirements, such as privacy, for data sharing to achieve beneficial results. These authors identified regulatory and legal constructs as restrictive functions. Gardner et al. [7] also researched the academic and medical domain of data sharing with mandatory requirements for specific cases and distinguished forms and methods of sharing, such as direct, i.e. two party, and public sharing. The work by Zhao et al. [13] on the secure data sharing over untrusted cloud storage providers also influenced our work, since issues of transitivity of rights are discussed therein. Breitenbücher et al. [4,5] showed how policies can influence the deployment of applications, e.g., to enforce secure passwords or deployment in specific regions. Current work on the issue of data sharing is mainly focused on scientific data sharing, thus, only partially applicable for our industrial setting and, furthermore, does not explicitly combine the multitude of problems encountered, such as privacy and compliance awareness, security and heterogeneity of data.

3 Secure Data Integration and Sharing Framework

To enable the collaborative usage of data among partially competing entities, trust is required in safekeeping of information and enforcement of rules or policies. With this work, we propose such a trusted instance in form of policy enforcement directly at the logical location of the data source or sink. We present a secure data integration and sharing framework, that enables that every such source or sink is equipped with a filtering and access software component. This component is under the direct control of the respective data owner.

Finally, sharing data for enabling analytics approaches among many data sources can ultimately be extended to scenarios where formerly classified data is shared with external companies in an aggregated and obfuscated form. Thus, business secrets remain protected while new analytics opportunities are generated. Each of these issues demand that data security and privacy have to be assured to protect the data from illegitimate and undefined uses.

See Fig. 1 for a depiction of the implementation schematics. In this figure, the data hub is shown as the central rectangle that allows access to the four depicted data-sources and sinks (S1–S4), which can be of diverse type such as databases, machine and sensor data or file data, for authorised parties. The access is mediated through the triangular software adapters on premise of the data owner. The policies (indicated as P1–P4) are directly attached to the adapters and under the control of the data owner. These policies, of which there can be multiple for each source, are propagated from the source to the consumer or user, as data hubs can function as data sources and sinks for further data hubs, thus, allowing for propagated access. In the figure, Party A and Party B, both make use of the data hub. Both parties can be distinct and from different entities, with different properties of ownership of the data sources. The proposed framework is comprised of the data hub, the corresponding adapters and the policy enforcement

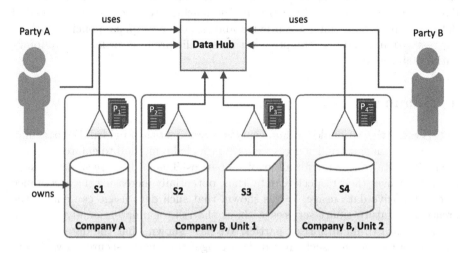

Fig. 1. Framework architecture overview

component. The geometrical shapes in the figure indicate the variety of different data source types.

We implement adapters for various data sources and sinks that transform data to be uniformly accessed through the data hub. The data from the data hub is exposed through the OData protocol (OASIS Open Data Protocol [9]). This protocol enables third party software to interact with the data hub and its exposed data in an uniform and standardised method. The data hub integrates the varying schemas of the data sources so that unified querying and application of policies is enabled. Constraint and policy application is enforced at each point equipped with a policy.

We present in this work findings from the project SePiA.Pro [1], which investigates these issues in the above described context. Furthermore, we illustrate the elaborated requirements for protecting industrial data in the context of Industry 4.0 endeavours via data policies. Such data policies are means to specify constraints, restrictions, or instructions that apply to the data, taking into account aspects such as data accessibility, utilisation, processing, obfuscation, storage or generation. The policies extend common access control rules and restrictions to incorporate concepts such as temporal, logical, and organisational triggers. The policy definition is flexible and extensible to allow individual and specific policies to be defined by implementing parties. It is further discussed, how and through which means, i.e. systems and parties, such policies are enforced at several points in time of the lifecycle of smart services—specifically at modelling time, deployment time, and runtime—to overcome the above mentioned obstacles. Specific scenarios for enabling trust and enforcing implementation are analysed within this work. We also discuss the concept of attaching data policies to relevant data sources. The rationale for such an attachment of policies is to secure and protect data from manufacturing environments in standards-based deployment models such as cloud computing. These models are used to provision smart services and wiring them with arbitrary data sources, such as databases, data aggregation services, industry specific machine to machine or IoT related data streaming endpoints. We provide and discuss exemplary policies, such as the restriction of data consumption within specific premises or logical groupings within enterprises.

4   Summary

In this work, the rationale for data sharing components is provided. By attaching policies to data sinks and sources we have provided a method to enforce requirements for data processing for all involved parties. The parties are shown to keep sovereignty over their respective data, thus, potentially increasing the acceptance of collaborative data usage. It was shown, that such data usage can enable the creation of future smart services without the risk of unintentionally exposing sensitive data to unauthorised parties. We have shown, that the data hub as a central component for such shared data usage, can enable secure, privacy and compliance aware collaboration on data.

Acknowledgments. This work is partially funded by the project SePiA.Pro (01MD16013F) of the BMWi program Smart Service World.

References

1. Service Plattform für die intelligente Anlagenoptimierung in der Produktion. http://projekt-sepiapro.de. Accessed 12 May 2017
2. Allmendinger, G., Lombreglia, R.: Four strategies for the age of smart services. Harv. Bus. Rev. **83**(10), 131 (2005)
3. Atzori, L., Iera, A., Morabito, G.: The internet of things: a survey. Comput. Netw. **54**(15), 2787–2805 (2010)
4. Breitenbücher, U., Binz, T., Fehling, C., Kopp, O., Leymann, F., Wieland, M.: Policy-aware provisioning and management of cloud applications. Int. J. Adv. Secur. **7**(1&2), 15–36 (2014). http://www.iaas.uni-stuttgart.de/RUS-data/ART-2014-08%20-%20Policy-Aware%20Provisioning%20and%20Management%20of%20Cloud%20Applications.pdf
5. Breitenbücher, U., Binz, T., Kopp, O., Leymann, F., Wieland, M.: Policy-aware provisioning of cloud applications. In: Proceedings of 7th International Conference on Emerging Security Information, Systems and Technologies (SECURWARE 2013), pp. 86–95. Xpert Publishing Services (2013)
6. Dais, S.: Industrie 4.0 - Anstoß, Vision, Vorgehen, pp. 261–277. Springer, Heidelberg (2017)
7. Gardner, D., Toga, A.W., et al.: Towards effective and rewarding data sharing. Neuroinformatics **1**(3), 289–295 (2003)
8. Malin, B., Karp, D., Scheuermann, R.H.: Technical and policy approaches to balancing patient privacy and data sharing in clinical and translational research. J. Invest. Med. **58**(1), 11–18 (2015). http://jim.bmj.com/content/58/1/11
9. OASIS: Oasis open data protocol (odata). Technical report, OASIS (2014). http://docs.oasis-open.org/odata/odata/v4.0/os/part1-protocol/odata-v4.0-os-part1-protocol.html
10. Sundmaeker, H., Guillemin, P., Friess, P., Woelffle, S.: Vision and challenges for realising the internet of things. In: European Commission Information Society and Media (2010)
11. The Apache Software Foundation: Apache Flink: Scalable Stream and Batch Data Processing. https://flink.apache.org. Accessed 12 May 2017
12. Yu, Z., Yan, H., Cheng, T.E.: Benefits of information sharing with supply chain partnerships. Ind. Manag. Data Syst. **101**(3), 114–121 (2001)
13. Zhao, G., Rong, C., Li, J., Zhang, F., Tang, Y.: Trusted data sharing over untrusted cloud storage providers. In: 2010 IEEE 2nd International Conference on Cloud Computing Technology and Science, pp. 97–103, November 2010

Surface Tension Fluid Simulation
with Adaptiving Time Steps

Xu Liu, Pengfei Ye[✉], Xiaojuan Ban[✉], and Xiaokun Wang

University of Science and Technology Beijing, Beijing, China
xuliu213@163.com, 1434497449@qq.com,
{banxj,wangxiaokun}@ustb.edu.cn

Abstract. In this article, a surface tension fluid simulation algorithm based on IISPH is proposed. Based on the SPH algorithm, the surface tension and the adhesion model are constructed to solve the problem about particle clustering, fluid surface area minimization and interaction between different particles. The method can make the simulation effect of fluid be more in line with the actual physical scene. Furthermore, an adaptive time-stepping method is added in the algorithm. The efficiency of the simulation is significantly improved compared to the constant time-stepping.

Keywords: Surface tension · Cooperative visualization · Adaptiving time steps · Implicit Incompressible SPH

1   Introduction

Fluid phenomenon exists widely in our daily life, such as rain, oil and so on. As a visualization technique, the fluid simulation has important applications in the field of collaborative visualization, and also has been a great challenge at the same time. Fluid simulation methods can be broadly divided into two categories: Eulerian method and Lagrangian method. In the Lagrangian method, the Smoothed Particle Hydrodynamics (SPH) [1, 2] method is a very popular algorithm because of its simplicity. The early SPH used the EOS equation to directly calculate the pressure of the particles, which is called standard SPH (SSPH) [3, 4]. The SSPH has a good effect on the simulation of compressible fluids, but it will lead to a strong sense of compression in the visual. Later, Becker et al. used the Tait equation to replace the ideal gaseous equation and use a high hardness control coefficient, which is called Weakly Compressible SPH (WCSPH) [5]. The WCSPH significantly increases the authenticity of the simulation by limiting the time step, but reduces the efficiency of the algorithm. In order to improve the efficiency of the algorithm, Solenthaler and Pajarola proposed Predictive-Corrective Iteration SPH (PCISPH) [6]. PCISPH can set the global maximum density fluctuations, and use Predictive-Corrective Iteration to achieve fluid incompressibility, and the algorithm eliminates the limitation of time step in WCSPH, which improves the overall efficiency of the algorithm by 10–50 times [7]. There are other similar algorithms, such as the Local Poisson SPH [8] and the Position Based method [9]. The above methods are based on the state equation to calculate the pressure, there is another way to achieve fluid incompressibility by projection method, which is called Incompressible SPH

© Springer International Publishing AG 2017
Y. Luo (Ed.): CDVE 2017, LNCS 10451, pp. 220–227, 2017.
DOI: 10.1007/978-3-319-66805-5_28

(ISPH) [10–12]. The main idea of this method is to use the force outside the pressure to predict the middle speed of the particle, and then solves the pressure Poisson equation, and finally calculates the other properties according to the pressure, but this will make the calculation cost significantly improved. To solve this problem, Ihmsen et al. proposed the Implicit Incompressible SPH (IISPH) [13]. IISPH constructs a similar iterative algorithm by carefully constructing the pressure Poisson equation and solving the linear system by using the Relaxed Jacobi method. IISPH is better than PCISPH in algorithm stability, convergence speed. Cornelis et al. demonstrated the excellent properties of IISPH once again by combining IISPH and FLIP methods [14].

Surface tension is an important physical property of fluid phenomena, and its simulation research has been an important part of the fluid simulation. The surface tension is generated by the cohesion between adjacent fluid particles. Using SPH method to simulate the surface tension of the fluid is a very challenging problem. The density of the fluid particles at the fluid and air junctions is too small because of the lack of neighbors, and this causes a problem of particles clustering. In addition, there are many other problems, such as surface curvature minimization and momentum conservation. In 2005, Tartakovsky and Meakin [15] proposed a method by using molecular cohesion to produce fluid surface tension, which uses cosine functions to control the gravitational and repulsive forces between particles. Becker and Teschner [16] used the kernel function of the SPH method to replace the cosine function to control the computational range of the gravitational force. However, both of these methods can not effectively solve the problem of particle clustering. Later, Akinci et al. [17] proposed a method of constructing cohesion and implemented on PCISPH. This method can solve the above problems. However, when the surface tension or the attraction force acting on the fluid is the main force, the time step is limited.

We propose a surface tension fluid simulation algorithm based on implicit incompressible SPH method. The experimental results show that the surface tension and adsorption force model proposed in this paper can minimize the surface area of the fluid. Furthermore, the efficiency of the simulation is significantly improved compared to the constant time-stepping.

2 Modeling of Surface Tension and Adhesion

Similar to Akinci et al.'s method [17], our surface tension model effectively solves the problem of gravitational repulsion and the minimization of the fluid surface area.

First of all, the cohesion between the particles will be computed based on the size of the distance between the particles to create gravitational and repulsive. The cohesion between the particles will produce gravitational and repulsive forces according to the distance between the particles. Similar to the force between the molecules, when the distance is too large to produce gravity, the distance is too small to produce repulsion until the gravitational and repulsive balance. The form is as follows:

$$a_i^c = -\delta \sum_j m_j(x_i - x_j) \, e(|x_j - x_i|) \tag{1}$$

where j is the neighbor particles of i, m denotes mass, x denotes the displacement of particles, and e is a spline function.

As can be seen from (1), the spline function e determines the nature of F, just like a kernel function. F should meet the following conditions: when the distance between the particles is less than a certain threshold, F is the repulsive force; when the distance between the particles is greater than the threshold, F produces gravitational force. It can be deduced that the spline function e is a piecewise function form. In this paper, we use the spline function proposed by Akinc et al. [17]:

$$e(r) = \frac{32}{\pi h^9} \begin{cases} (h-r)^3 r^3 & \frac{h}{2} r \leq h \\ 2(h-r)^3 r^3 - \frac{h^6}{64} & 0 < r \leq \frac{h}{2} \\ 0 & otherwise \end{cases} \tag{2}$$

In order to better simulate the microscopic characteristics of the fluid surface, we also need an additional force to minimize the fluid surface area.

$$a_i^k = -\chi \sum_j \left(n_i - n_j \right) \tag{3}$$

where χ is the correction factor, and n is to avoid the display of the calculated surface curvature:

$$n_i = \mu \sum_j \frac{m_j}{\rho_j} \nabla W \left(|x_i - x_j| \right) \tag{4}$$

where μ is the scaling factor.

In summary, the complete surface tension can be expressed as:

$$a_i^{st} = \psi_{ij} \left(a_i^c + a_i^k \right) \tag{5}$$

where $\psi_{ij} = \frac{2\rho_0}{\rho_i + \rho_j}$ is the control factor.

The adhesion is different from the surface tension, which is caused by the interaction between the different types of particles. The adhesion of this paper is mainly for the fluid-solid coupling problem, as following:

$$a_i^{ad} = -\gamma \sum_k \psi_{b_k} (x_i - x_k) g(|x_i - x_k|) \tag{6}$$

where γ is the adhesion coefficient, ψ_{b_k} is the volume of boundary particles, g is a spline function:

$$g(r) = \frac{0.01}{h^5} \begin{cases} -\left(r - \frac{3h}{4}\right)^2 + \frac{h^2}{16} & \frac{h}{2} \wedge r \leq h \\ 0 & otherwise \end{cases} \tag{7}$$

3 Adaptiving Time Steps

The upper bound of the time step of SPH numerical simulation is given by CFL (Courant-Friedrich-Levy). It can ensures that the velocity of the numerical propagation is faster than the velocity of the physical propagation, so that the numerical calculation is stable and convergent.

$$\Delta t_{CFL} \le \lambda_v \left(\frac{h}{v_{max}} \right) \tag{8}$$

where $v_{max} = \max_i \|v_i\|$ is the maximum of all fluid particles velocities, $\lambda_v < 1$ denotes safety factor.

In addition, the fluid simulation algorithm based on the SPH method also needs to consider the force of the fluid particle (the acceleration produced by the force):

$$\Delta t_f \le \lambda_f \left(\frac{h}{f_{max}} \right) \tag{9}$$

where $f_{max} = \max_i \|\frac{dv_i}{dt}\|$, $\lambda_f < 1$.

The final time step requires consideration of both of the above conditions:

$$\Delta t \le \min \left(\Delta t_{CFL},\ \Delta t_f \right) \tag{10}$$

Algorithm 1. Adaptiving time steps for surface tension fluid simulation

---

1: **while** *animating* **do**
2: **for** *all particles i* **do**
3:      search neighbor particle j
4: **for** *all particles i* **do**
5:      compute $\rho(i)$, $p(i)$
6:      compute a_i^{st}, a_i^{ad}
10: **for** *all particles i* **do**
11:     compute the total acceleration a_i^{total}
12: compute time step by (10)
13: **for** *all particles i* **do**
14:     update $v_i(t + \Delta t) = v_i^* + \dfrac{\Delta t F_i^p(t)}{m_i}$
15:     update $x_i(t + \Delta t) = x_i(t) + \Delta t v_i(t + \Delta t)$
16: $t = t + \Delta t$

---

4   Experimental Results

In this section, we show the capabilities of our approach. Firstly we compare the simulation results with surface tension and without surface tension. Then, we discuss the improvement of computational efficiency by adaptiving time steps. All timings are given for an Intel 3.50 GHz CPU with 4 cores. The simulation software is parallelized with OpenMP.

4.1   Surface Tension

The following figures show the flow of a water-drop on the board. First of all, the water-drop acts as a free falling body. Then the water-drop moves around on the board when it touches the board. We use the IISPH method without surface tension and adhesion firstly. The fluid particles present a loose state, which is more severe at the edge of the fluid (Fig. 1). After rendering, the grain is still very strong in the edge of the fluid (Fig. 3), which is clearly inconsistent with the actual physical scene. After using the method in this paper, the fluid particles are not in a loose state and the effect of the fluid edge has been significantly improved (Fig. 2). After rendering, the fluid surface becomes smoother and ensures surface area be minimized (Fig. 4). The fluid becomes a slightly flat water-drop shape eventually (Table 1).

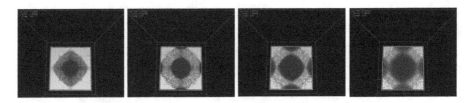

Fig. 1. Simulation without surface tension before rendering

Fig. 2. Simulation with surface tension before rendering

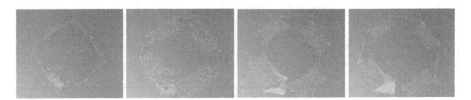

Fig. 3. Simulation without surface tension after rendering

Fig. 4. Simulation with surface tension after rendering

Table 1. The simulation parameters of experiment

Parameter	Value
The scale of simulation domain	8 m × 8 m × 8 m
The density of fluid particles	1000 kg/m^3
The smooth radii	0.2 m
The width of fluid particle	0.1 m

4.2　Adaptiving Time Steps

We designed a large 3D dam-break experiment to verify that our adaptive time-stepping algorithm improves the computational efficiency. The setting parameters of the experiment are shown in Table 2.

Table 2. The simulation parameters of 3D dam-break

Parameter	Value
The scale of simulation domain	12 m × 12 m × 8 m
The number of fluid particles	153 K
The number of boundary particles	73 K
The smooth radii	0.2 m
The width of fluid particle	0.1 m

The results of 3D dam-break experiment are shown in Table 3. In order to compare difference of the running time in different methods, we calculate the calculation time of the same experimental scenario in fixed time steps, and adaptiving time steps. Through the data in the Table 3, we can find that the adaptive time step algorithm has 4.27 times the acceleration ratio compared with the fixed time step.

Table 3. The experimental result of 3D dam-break

Method	Total calculation time	Speedup ratio
The fixed time steps	128 min	
The adaptiving time steps	30 min	4.27

5 Conclusions

We propose a surface tension fluid simulation algorithm based on implicit incompressible SPH method. The experimental results show that our method has better surface tension effect compared to IISPH without surface tension. Under the influence of the surface tension, the fluid particles will gather with each other rather than disperse without restraint. At the same time, our method realizes the minimization of the fluid surface area, which makes the fluid surface become smoother. Furthermore, we suggested an adaptive time-stepping method which reduces the overall computation time for the simulation.

Acknowledgments. This work was supported by National Natural Science Foundation of China (No. 61572075) and The National Key Research and Development Program of China (Grant Nos. 2016YFB0700502, 2016YFB1001404)

References

1. Monaghan, J.J.: Smoothed particle hydrodynamics. Ann. Rev. Astron. Astrophys. **30**, 543–574 (1992)
2. Monaghan, J.J.: Smoothed particle hydrodynamics. Rep. Prog. Phys. **68**(8), 1703–1759 (2005)
3. Desbrun, M., Gascuel, M.P.: Smoothed particles: a new paradigm for animating highly deformable bodies. In: Proceedings of Eurographics Workshop on Computer Animation and Simulation 1996, pp. 61–76 (1996)
4. Müller, M., Charypar, D., Gross, M.: Particle-based fluid simulation for interactive applications. In: ACM SIGGRAPH/Eurographics Symposium on Computer Animation, pp. 154–159 (2003)
5. Becker, M., Teschner, M.: Weakly compressible SPH for free surface flows. In: Symposium on Computer Animation 2007: ACM SIGGRAPH/Eurographics Symposium Proceedings, pp. 209–217 (2007)
6. Solenthaler, B., Pajarola, R.: Predictive-corrective incompressible SPH. ACM Trans. Graph. **28**(3), 40 (2009)
7. Solenthaler, B., Pajarola, R.: Performance comparison of parallel PCISPH and WCSPH. Technical report, IFI-2009.0, Department of Informatics, University of Zürich (2009)
8. He, X., Liu, N., Li, S., et al.: Local Poisson SPH for viscous incompressible fluids. Comput. Graph. Forum **31**(6), 1948–1958 (2012)
9. Macklin, M., Mueller, M.: Position based fluids. ACM Trans. Graph. **32**(4), 104 (2013)
10. Cummins, S.J., Rudman, M.: An SPH projection method. J. Comput. Phys. **152**(2), 584–607 (1999)
11. Premžoe, S., Tasdizen, T., Bigler, J., et al.: Particle-based simulation of fluids. In: Computer Graphics Forum. Wiley Online Library (2003)
12. Losasso, F., Talton, J.O., Kwatra, N., et al.: Two-way coupled SPH and particle level set fluid simulation. IEEE Trans. Vis. Comput. Graph. **14**(4), 797–804 (2008)
13. Ihmsen, M., Cornelis, J., Solenthaler, B., et al.: Implicit incompressible SPH. IEEE Trans. Visual. Comput. Graph. **20**(3), 426–435 (2014)

14. Cornelis, J., Ihmsen, M., Peer, A., et al.: IISPH-FLIP for incompressible fluids. In: Computer Graphics Forum. The Eurographics Association and Blackwell Publishing Ltd. (2014)
15. Tartakovsky, A., Meakin, P.: Modeling of surface tension and contact angles with smoothed particle hydrodynamics. Phys. Rev. E **72**(2), 254–271 (2005)
16. Becker, M., Teschner, M.: Weakly compressible SPH for free surface flows. In: Proceedings of 2007 ACM SIGGRAPH/Eurographics Symposium on Computer Animation, pp. 209–217 (2007)
17. Akinci, N., Akinci, G., Teschner, M.: Versatile surface tension and adhesion for SPH fluids. ACM Trans. Graph. **32**(6), 182 (2013)

USE Together, a WebRTC-Based Solution for Multi-user Presence Desktop

Laurent Lucas[1]([✉]), Hervé Deleau[1,2], Benjamin Battin[1,3],
and Julien Lehuraux[1,3]

[1] University of Reims Champagne-Ardenne, CReSTIC, Reims, France
laurent.lucas@univ-reims.fr
[2] University of Reims Champagne-Ardenne, Image Center MaSCA, Reims, France
[3] OPEXMedia, Reims, France

Abstract. Ubiquitous is one of the essential features of what should be the desktop of the future. In practice, this concept covers several issues related to multi-users collaboration, remote applications control or remote display and secure access over IP networks. With its standards and capabilities, WebRTC provides a new vision of real-time communications services that can raise these challenges. In this paper we present a WebRTC-based middleware solution for real-time multi-users remote collaboration. It allows a full desktop setup where everyone can see what other users are doing and where they position themselves in the shared workspace. In contrast to standard WebRTC's Peer-to-Peer architecture, our system supports a synchronous communication model through a star topology. It also improves network bandwidth efficiency by using hardware video compression when the GPU resource is available, though assuring a very low latency streaming. In this way, we can maintain awareness and sense of presence without changing the usual practices of the users in front of a desktop. Several use cases are provided and a comparison of advantages and drawbacks of this solution is also presented to guide users in applying this technology under real-life conditions.

Keywords: WebRTC · Remote display · Multi-users collaborative environment

1 Introduction

The requirements related to teamwork and mobility especially in corporate environments as well as in science and academic environments are becoming increasingly requested. This new way of working on spatially and temporally distributed systems has become a more commonplace practice especially with the emergence of remote collaboration tools allowing a group of people to share their resources or to create in a common effort. In this sense and for a growing range of devices, the availability of these tools has to be ensured particularly in terms of security and accessibility, for instance, from traditional computer as well as

Y. Luo (Ed.): CDVE 2017, LNCS 10451, pp. 228–235, 2017.
DOI: 10.1007/978-3-319-66805-5_29

from mobile devices like smartphones and/or tablets. Web technologies through modern capabilities of browsers enable today the development of cross-platform software systems as capable and powerful as desktop applications [1]. From this point of view, the Web has opened a new way for the development of cloud hosted Internet-based collaboration apps [2] and other means of interaction. Online collaboration tools can be classified in two categories: synchronous vs. asynchronous communication tools. Unlike asynchronous communication, synchronous communication involves an ongoing real time character and can take place face-to-face irrespective of distance. Although this distinction tends to fade, the feeling of presence has become crucial in all collaborative environments [3,4] especially with the recent development of immersive collaborative solutions [5,6]. This observation has been partly achieved by the widespread use of both HPC and graphics virtualization that has brought significant changes to corporate networks by delivering for instance an immersive, high-quality user experience for everyone [7], from designers [8] to engineers [9] and other mobile professionals or simple office workers. This technological innovation used widely in many industrial sectors is one of the most disruptive of our time.

However, if current software solutions partially and specifically address – e.g. in terms of online collaborative work, video conferencing, multi-users remote control or remote display – the issues raised by the "desktop of the future" [10], it must be noted that *(i)* there is no integrated environment today around all of these elements and *(ii)* data privacy is not always guaranteed which can be a serious problem of sovereignty for all strategic institutions.

Whether they are research projects as well as commercial systems, there are many collaborative online solutions used today in areas such as health [11], collaborative visualization [3,4,8] and learning [12,13] with specific software developments related to whiteboarding collaboration [14–16] for instance.

Regarding commercial products, software market can be segmented into three fields: *(i)* online collaborative solutions first such as those offered by Cisco with Spark or Amazon with Chime, *(ii)* multi-users remote control next with Screenhero and *(iii)* remote visualization after all through solutions like Citrix HDX 3D Pro, HP RGS or Nice DCV.

In this paper we present our solution called USE Together. This middleware is a secure multi-user collaborative system allowing professionals to share their applications and data in real time, accessible from any device, over any network. It enhances your communications in terms of *(i)* user QoE by delivering HD in real time with low latency, *(ii)* simplicity of use based on standards such as WebRTC and HTML5 with zero-client deployment *(iii)* security without data transmission but only pixel on a Peer-to-Peer architecture with encrypted streams and *(iv)* flexibility of use by supporting both SaaS, on-premises and host-to-host deployment modes. Our contribution is based on the hybridization of solutions supporting native web access, GPU encoding and multi-cursor management, summarizing the best of both world. The reminder of this paper is organized as follows: in Sect. 2 we propose a brief overview of the main functionalities of WebRTC before introducing, in Sect. 3, our contribution USE Together and its architecture. Then we present and discuss in Sects. 4 and 5 some use cases and their performance. Finally, conclusion and future works are given in Sect. 6.

2   WebRTC

WebRTC (Web Real Time Communication) [17] is a technology that allows real-time Peer-to-Peer communication between browsers without the use of additional plugins. WebRTC is designed "to enable rich, high-quality RTC applications to be developed for the browser, mobile platforms, and IoT devices, and allow them all to communicate via a common set of protocols" [18]. WebRTC was open-sourced by Google in 2011 and after that an ongoing work started to standardize the protocols associated with it by IETF and its browser APIs by W3C. Interest and support for WebRTC has been since growing steadily. Today, the most advanced WebRTC implementation is offered by Mozilla Firefox and Google Chrome and includes three APIs:

1. MediaStream, which allows an application to stream media from the users web camera and microphone or from a screen capturing.
2. DataChannel, which allows to share arbitrary data between peers. This layer is an important feature of WebRTC allowing the development of all kind of Peer-to-Peer applications and collaborative solutions.
3. PeerConnection, which represents the glue between MediaStream and DataChannel by providing a handshake mechanism for two machines to exchange necessary information so a Peer-to-Peer connection can be set up.

The architecture of WebRTC including the signaling server is shown in schematic Fig. 1. Although WebRTC aspires to enable Peer-to-Peer communication between browsers without relaying data through any intermediary, the use of a server is still required for two reasons: the first reason is the obvious one, a web server is needed to serve? the actual web application that utilizes WebRTC. The second reason is less obvious. A server is required in order to initialize sessions between the clients that need to communicate. This process is known as Signaling and is responsible for the exchange of the initial (meta) data of session descriptions (using SDP and ICE framework) which contain details on the form and nature of the data which will be transmitted. These information can include network data, such as IP addresses and ports, media metadata such as codecs and codec settings, bandwidth and media types, error messages or user and room information. PeerConnection API is used to achieve this process.

3   USE Together Overview and Implementation

Based on the native C++ APIs implementation of WebRTC by Google, USE Together is structured around two modules: USE Signaling and USE Engine. The implemented and developed solution with all its elements with respect to

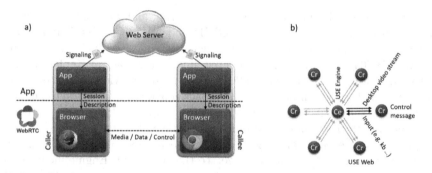

Fig. 1. (a) WebRTC system architecture and (b) peers connection topology – star – where a callee (noted Ce) sends captured media to each caller (noted Cr) which, in turn, transmit their inputs with transactions of control messages in both cases.

the architecture is illustrated in Fig. 1a. In the two following subsections, to give a better understanding of the overall architecture to the reader, we will illustrate the description of each module with a typical usage scenario: a user A starts a collaborative working session S on his desktop and a user B wants to join S.

3.1 USE Engine

The USE Engine module consists in two major sub-systems: the former, called 'USE Engine Core', acts as the central point of communication between the host (which initiates the collaborative session) and the remote users who join it. In terms of network topology (cf. Fig. 1b), one can see a collaborative session as a star where the host is located in the center and each remote user resides in a branch. Thus, the 'USE Engine Core' part is essentially dedicated to receiving and delivering data to each branch over WebRTC channels: video and audio streaming (resp. input and control messages) over Media Channels (resp. Data Channel). The latter sub-system, named 'USE Engine GUI', is an application responsible for the following tasks: *(i)* capturing an entire desktop or a specific window, *(ii)* capturing local video and/or audio data (eg. from a webcam), *(iii)* encoding the resulting streams and transmitting it to 'USE Engine Core', *(iv)* injecting keyboard and mouse input events from remote peers and *(v)* specifying multiple settings to configure the session.

When the user A wants to start a collaborative working session, he just starts USE Engine, which automatically creates a working session S and registers it on USE Signaling (described below). The session is now active and can be reachable by any remote user who knows the session name and the session password.

In order to provide the best possible experience to the user, USE Engine especially focuses on addressing two typical issues related to collaborative softwares: latency and multiple user inputs management. With traditional remote desktop visualization tools, the user generally has to deal with high latency which could be annoying while using real time applications remotely. USE Engine exploits the latest technologies in terms of screen capturing and video encoding respectively with the use of the NVIDIA's GRID and NVENC APIs. The first one, (GRID), provides direct access to video memory while NVENC makes use of a hardware H.264 encoding chip, integrated since the release of Kepler NVIDIA GPUs, to produce a low latency H.264 video stream. Obviously, if the desktop is not equipped with such hardware, a fallback mode provides a desktop capture system based on OS APIs and a CPU encoding framework delivering either an H.264 (still with a low latency profile) or a VP8 video stream. The last issue lies in the input events handling of each connected user on an operating system natively thought for a single usage. To that end, USE Engine includes two interaction modes: a synchronized one, where a user can seamlessly take the control anytime he does a specific action (mouse clicks or keyboard usage) and if nobody already did, ignoring the other users input events for the duration of those actions, and a token-based one where a user has the control as long as he keeps the token (set by the session administrator).

3.2   USE Signaling

As mentioned in Sect. 2, an auxiliary server, which acts both as a web server and as a signaling server, is required to set up the Peer-to-Peer communication between user A and user B. Firstly, user B has to log himself, then specify the session name and the associated password. USE Signaling is then able, from the session name, to identify the user who initiates the collaborative session (in our case, user A) and to relay messages between A and B during the signaling stage. Signaling can be defined as a classic handshaking phase during which the two users exchange network information (to find the best network route between them) and their session descriptions (a data structure containing streaming capabilities of a specific machine/browser couple) to negotiate a compatible way to exchange data. As soon as the negotiation is done, the peer connection (and the associated communication channels) can be created between A and B. At this point, B is now connected to S and can work collaboratively with user A.

4   USE Cases Description and Discussion

Two kind of use cases have been realized with a common objective to stay focused on what is essential to application area by centralizing data and applications for a remote multi-peer collaborative access.

For manufacturing industries case first, USE Together has been used as a project management tool to enable its users to work remotely with different CAD applications. Project review, synchronous co-design, simulation and visualization are the main functions tested in a multi-user collaborative framework. As we can see in Fig. 2, four users interact synchronously on a same 3D model during a project review phase. The second use case was carried out within a biomedical environment with different softwares visualization. Mainly based on GPU-accelerated direct volume rendering algorithms, these tests confirmed the

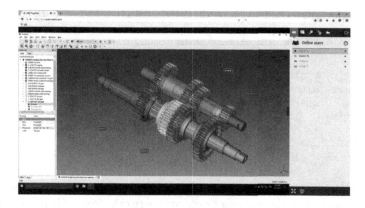

Fig. 2. Example CAD viewer application. The actual image shown on screen is being rendered remotely. The four users connected to their browsers can interact simultaneously on the 3D model.

compatibility of the system with GPU-intensive resources applications without altering facility to encode the output video stream in real time. Several scenarios have been designed to work remotely with different partners on a collegial basis in order *(i)* to jointly annotate and navigate in a set of biological data obtained through a slide scanner and *(ii)* to engage HPC resources to visualize and interact with simulations remotely.

In both cases, USE Together has received a large endorsement by:

- increasing users' productivity on load-intensive applications and complex data through remote access on centralized resources.
- enhancing performance of teams with a real time collaborative solution running on a same application instance.

5   Performance Analysis

In order to test our solution, different experiments over several hundred kilometers between the server and three simultaneously connected clients were conducted. All these results are reported on Table 1, which also includes the specifications of the various materials used. On the server side, we used a virtual machine (VM) equipped with an Intel Xeon E5-2650v2 @ 2.60 GHz (8 cores), 32 GB of RAM and a NVidia GRID K2 of 4 GB of VRAM mounted in PCI Passthrough as GPU. This VM runs on Windows 7 Pro with a desktop resolution configured in HD. We used both the Unigine Valley Benchmark and FreeCAD workload to simulate real user behavior and/or monitored the following user experience and scalability metrics in fullscreen for three kinds of image quality setting (Low/Medium/High) with NVIDIA GPU based H.264 encoding (NVENC high performance low latency preset). On the client side, three device types were used with different network accesses for each of them (see Table 1).

Table 1. Performance comparison on three terminal types and network connections.

Specs terminal	Network connection	Packets recvd (K)/lost	Bytes recvd (Mo)	Mean bitrate (Mb/s)	FPS
		L/M/H	L/M/H	L/M/H	L/M/H
#1 Desktop Quadro M4000	ADSL RJ45	64/110/258 6/96/469	63/111/280	1.81/3.12/7.88	30/30/31
#2 Laptop Intel HD4000	ADSL Wifi	75/110/265 38/551/8500	72/115/295	1.99/3.22/7.95	22/23/22
#3 Tablet Tegra K1	4G	76/150/247 11/72/394	73/157/270	1.92/4.31/7.30	21/18/14

All these elements show that USE Together has achieved to bring a smooth experience on both of the use cases over any network, from 3G/4G to Wifi and Ethernet, with a mean bitrate of about 3.2 MB/s for a full HD remote display.

6   Conclusion and Future Works

This paper proposed a WebRTC-based collaborative multi-user solution enhancing communications of a group by enabling them to share their applications and data in real time over any network. This solution called USE Together can be deployed on various hardware environments in a secure way and be accessed through a simple web browser without using any additional software nor plugin. Composed of two modules allowing *(i)* to connect two peers and *(ii)* to exchange encrypted streams between peers, USE Together is able to address many challenges in relation to pervasive computing like capabilities to offer interactive shared workspaces in a collaborative way and to maintain calculation accessibility through "invisible" resources while guaranteeing a good level of confidentiality during exchanges. Exclusively based on a web implementation today, this solution should also evolve to provide end-point devices support like specific 3D displays and VR/AR devices.

Acknowledgment. This work is supported by the French national funds (PIA2'program) under contract No. P112331-3422142 (3DNS project).

References

1. Wright, A.: Ready for a Web OS? Commun. ACM **52**(12), 16–17 (2009)
2. Nunamaker, J.F., Briggs, R.O., Romano, N.C.R.: Collaboration Systems: Concept, Value, and Use. Taylor & Francis, Routledge (2015)
3. Isenberg, P., Elmqvist, N., Scholtz, J., Cernea, D., Ma, K.-L., Hagen, H.: Collaborative visualization: definition, challenges, and research agenda. Inf. Vis. J. **10**(4), 310–326 (2011)
4. Mouton, C., Sons, K., Grimstead, I.: Collaborative visualization: current systems and future trends. In: Proceedings of the 16th International Conference on 3D Web Technology, Web3D 2011, pp. 101–110. ACM, New York (2011)

5. Childs, H., Geveci, B., Schroeder, W., Meredith, J., Moreland, K., Sewell, C., Kuhlen, T., Bethel, E.W.: Research challenges for visualization software. Computer **46**(5), 34–42 (2013)
6. Zudilova-Seinstra, E., Adriaansen, T., van Liere, R.: Trends in Interactive Visualization: State-of-the-Art Survey, 1st edn. Springer Publishing Company, Incorporated, London (2008)
7. Nicolaescu, P., Jahns, K., Derntl, M., Klamma, R.: Yjs: a framework for near real-time P2P shared editing on arbitrary data types. In: Cimiano, P., Frasincar, F., Houben, G.-J., Schwabe, D. (eds.) ICWE 2015. LNCS, vol. 9114, pp. 675–678. Springer, Cham (2015). doi:10.1007/978-3-319-19890-3_55
8. Desprat, C., Luga, H., Jessel, J.-P.: Hybrid client-server and p2p network for web-based collaborative 3d design. In: Proceedings of the 23rd International Conference in Central Europe on Computer Graphics, Visualization and Computer Vision, WSCG 2015, pp. 229–238 (2015)
9. Wang, L., Wang, J., Sun, L., Hagiwara, I.: A peer-to-peer based communication environment for synchronous collaborative product design. In: Luo, Y. (ed.) CDVE 2007. LNCS, vol. 4674, pp. 9–20. Springer, Heidelberg (2007). doi:10.1007/978-3-540-74780-2_2
10. Pizarro, R., Hall, M., Bermell-Garcia, P., Gonzalez-Franco, M.: Augmenting remote presence for interactive dashboard collaborations. In: Proceedings of the International Conference on Interactive Tabletops and Surfaces, ITS 2015, pp. 235–240. ACM, New York (2015)
11. Van Ma, L., Kim, J., Park, S., Kim, J., Jang, J.: An efficient Session_Weight load balancing and scheduling methodology for high-quality telehealth care service based on WebRTC. J. Supercomput. **72**(10), 3909–3926 (2016)
12. Xenos, M., Avouris, N., Komis, V., Stavrinoudis, D., Margaritis, M.: Synchronous collaboration in distance education: a case study on a computer science course. In: Proceedings of the IEEE International Conference on Advanced Learning Technologies, ICALT 2004, Washington, DC, USA, pp. 500–504. IEEE Computer Society (2004)
13. Osipov, I.V., Volinsky, A.A., Prasikova, A.Y.: E-learning collaborative system for practicing foreign languages with native speakers. Int. J. Adv. Comput. Sci. Appl. **7**(3), 40–45 (2016)
14. Zeidan, A., Lehmann, A., Trick, U.: WebRTC enabled multimedia conferencing and collaboration solution. In: Proceedings of the World Telecommunications Congress 2014, WTC 2014, pp. 1–6, June 2014
15. Wenzel, M., Meinel, C.: Full-body WebRTC video conferencing in a web-based real-time collaboration system. In: Proceedings of the 20th IEEE International Conference on Computer Supported Cooperative Work in Design, CSCWD 2016, pp. 334–339 (2016)
16. Pinikas, N., Panagiotakis, S., Athanasaki, D., Malamos, A.: Extension of the WebRTC data channel towards remote collaboration and control. In: Proceedings of the International Symposium on Ambient Intelligence and Embedded Systems 2016, AmiEs 2016 (2016)
17. Grigorik, I.: High Performance Browser Networking: What Every Web Developer Should Know About Networking and Browser Performance. O'Reilly Media Inc., Sebastopol (2013)
18. WebRTC. https://webrtc.org/. Accessed 07 Mar 2017

Collaboration Patterns at Scheduling in 10 Years

Xiujuan Xu[1,2], Yu Liu[1,2(✉)], Ruixin Ma[1,2], and Quan Z. Sheng[3]

[1] School of Software, Dalian University of Technology, Dalian 116620, China
{xjxu,yuliu}@dlut.edu.cn, teacher_mrx@126.com
[2] Key Laboratory for Ubiquitous Network and Service Software of Liaoning Province,
Dalian 116620, China
[3] Department of Computing, Macquarie University, Sydney, NSW 2109, Australia
michael.sheng@mq.edu.au

Abstract. Scheduling analysis, which focuses on the evaluation, testing and verification of the scheduling systems and the algorithms used in real-time operations, is critical to a number of research areas such as databases and transaction management. In order to better understand the field of scheduling, we select and investigate 9,611 papers about scheduling from five SCI journals which have published many excellent papers about scheduling. This paper presents a collaboration analysis of the scheduling field. In addition, we generate three networks to analyze collaboration patterns between scientists, including co-authorship network, keyword co-occurrence network and author co-keyword network to show the collaboration relationship between authors in the field of scheduling. The research findings from our work can help researchers understand the research status of scheduling and gain valuable insights on future technical trends in the scheduling field.

Keywords: Visualization · Scheduling · Social network analysis · Research collaboration

1 Introduction

In the field of computer science, scheduling is the methodology that assigns appropriate resources to complete certain tasks. More specifically, scheduling is about defining the sequence and time allocated to the activities of an operation. It is the construction of a detailed timetable that shows at what time or date jobs should start and when they should end [3]. For the last ten years, many scientists have shown their significant interest in scheduling problems. Scheduling is a relatively steady field of research, in which the stable interest and practice has led to thousands of publications over the years. Recently, some researchers presented the literature review for the scheduling field [2,3,19]. Those work makes us to deeply understand the field of scheduling.

Scientific publications in the scheduling field have reflected such active scientific activities. Scientists could use empirical measures to analyze scientific output of the specific field so as to better understand the dynamics and structure of the

© Springer International Publishing AG 2017
Y. Luo (Ed.): CDVE 2017, LNCS 10451, pp. 236–243, 2017.
DOI: 10.1007/978-3-319-66805-5_30

scheduling research development. For example, researchers study the development status in many subjects, including cloud computing [10], knowledge-based systems [6], intelligent transportation systems [13,14] and fuzzy sets [5] and so on. Science mapping analysis discovers conceptual structure and scientific evolution in a particular field [15]. Meanwhile, scientometrics on a particular field could find its different subtopics so as to get high-level papers and follow high-impacted researchers. Therefore, it is helpful and necessary to analyze a particular field by intelligent techniques to find the evolution directions of the field.

However, it is surprising that not much work has been done to scientometrics analysis of the scheduling research. Naturally, there are some major questions in the scheduling field which remain to be answered as the following:

(1) Who are high productive authors in the scheduling field? What are the hot topics in the field? What are the technical trend?
(2) How do the authors cooperate? Which topics do active authors focus on?

In this paper, we aim to answer the above questions from the data of published papers in the scheduling field. Although many journals have topics about scheduling, we select five top journals as our data source. The selected journals indexed by SCI are Journal of Combinatorial Optimization (JOCO), The Journal of Scheduling (JOSH), Operations Research (OR), Management Science (MS) and the European Journal of Operational Research (EJOR). We retrieve thousands of papers from these five journals to analyze collaboration pattern.

In this paper, we present a comprehensive scientometric study about bibliographic analysis related to scheduling area. To the best of our knowledge, this is the first scientometrics study that assesses the scheduling field. We collect and analyze the data published by the five journals over a 10-year period from 2006 to 2015. We present the visual pictures to show the relationship between the researchers. Based on our results, this paper makes the following main contributions:

(1) We collect the data about 9,611 papers from five top SCI journals in the scheduling field from the Web of Science. We analyze the basic statistical results for the scheduling field.
(2) We construct three networks, including co-authorship network, keyword co-occurrence network and author co-keyword network in the scheduling field to show the relationship between scientists.

The rest of this paper is organized as follows. We overview the related work in Sect. 2. Section 3 describes the details on the dataset used in the paper. In Sect. 4, we present collaboration patterns. Finally, Sect. 5 concludes the study.

2   Related Work

In this section, we first present an overview of scientometrics analysis in several subjects and then discuss some review papers about the status of the scheduling field.

In recent years, scientometrics has widespread developed in many subjects, for example, cloud computing, intelligent transportation systems (ITS), knowledge-based systems and fuzzy sets and so on. In 2011, Cobo et al. [5] presented an approach to analyze the thematic evolution of a given research field. In 2013, Cobo et al. highlighted the conceptual structure of the ITSs research field in the period 1992–2011 based on the journal of IEEE transactions on ITS. Recently, we presented an analysis framework for the ITS field [21]. In 2014, the evolution and state of cloud computing research was studied based on a large bibliographic data base [10], which provided a better understanding of publication patterns, research impact and research productivity in the area of cloud computing research. In 2015, Cobo et al. presented a bibliometric analysis about the conceptual evolution of 'knowledge-based system' journal and some of its performance bibliometric indicators based on citations, as the evolution of its impact factor, its H-index, and its most cited authors/documents [6], by using the scientific content of the journal from 1991 to 2014. In 2016, Muñoz et al. combined different biblimetric tools to analyze the evolution of the cognitive structure of e-Government field [16]. However, there are no related biblimetric work about the scheduling field.

Meanwhile, some scientists reviewed the literature on scheduling. In 2006, Zhu and Wilhelm focused on the class of scheduling problems that involved sequence-dependent setup times (costs) [22]. In 2010, Cardoen et al. provided a review of operational research on operating room planning and scheduling [3]. In the same year, Potts and Kovalyov presented an extensive literature scheduling with batching, giving details of the basic algorithms, and referencing other significant results [19]. They focused on two types of scheduling models that required batches to be formed. In 2013, Van den Bergh et al. presented a review of the literature on personnel scheduling problems [2]. Different to their work, our paper studies the status of scheduling field by the biblographic dataset from five top related journals. In this paper, we use the *GN* algorithm to study collaboration patterns in the scheduling field.

3   Overview of Dataset

In this section, we introduce the method to get our data and the property of our dataset. Meanwhile, we present the results of data statistics.

3.1   Data Source

We select five influential journals which have published many high-quality papers about the field of scheduling.

(1) Journal of Combinatorial Optimization (JOCO) (link.springer.com/journal/ volumesAndIssues/10878) promotes the theory and applications of combinatorial optimization, which is an area of research at the intersection of applied mathematics, computer science, and operations research.

(2) Journal of Scheduling (JOSH) (llink.springer.com/journal/volumesAndIs sues/10951) provides a global forum for the publication of all forms of scheduling research. JOSH is one of the top journals in the scheduling field. It focuses on the cutting-edge of the scheduling field and has the highest impact factor (1.028 in 2016) in the scheduling field. Therefore, JOSH could provide a more comprehensive view on the scheduling research area within a relevant time frame.

(3) Operations Research (OR) (pubsonline.informs.org/loi/opre) aims to publish high-quality papers that represent the true breadth of the methodologies and applications that define its field.

(4) Management Science (MS) (pubsonline.informs.org/loi/mnsc) is a cross-functional, multidisciplinary examination of advances and solutions supporting enhanced strategic planning and management science.

(5) The European Journal of Operational Research (EJOR) (www.journals. elsevier.com/european-journal-of-operational-research) publishes high quality, original papers that contribute to the methodology of operational research and to the practice of decision making.

3.2 Data Statistics

First of all, we obtain data from five journals from the website of Web of Science. We extract 10 years data from 2006 to 2015 using a web crawler. Then, we construct three collaboration networks by *GN* algorithm [8] and visualize them by Ucinet NetDraw.

Our study intends to cover a large part of peer-reviewed articles in the scheduling field published over the last decade. We aim to obtain the meta-scientific findings of the scientometric study in the scheduling field.

Our dataset includes five related journals, which are JOSH, JOCO, MS, OR and EJOR. We only retain original papers with abstracts and keywords. There are 9,611 papers in our dataset. Figure 1 shows the distribution of publications per year and presents a deeper insight into contribution patterns.

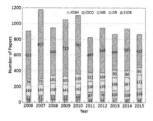

Fig. 1. Paper published per year in five journals from 2006 to 2015

Fig. 2. Largest component (size = 229) (Color figure online)

4   Analysis of Collaboration Patterns

We implement the Girvan-Newman algorithm (GN algorithm) to cluster authors. Different colors represent different clusters and the sizes denote the number of collaborators [8]. Consequently, it is interesting to visualize the collaboration patterns in layers of countries, institutions and authors.

4.1   Co-authorship Network Analysis

In order to find co-authorship effectively, we only study authors who published more than two papers. The researcher-level co-authorship network compose of 1,953 nodes and 586 components. The average degree is 1.39.

In Fig. 2, the first largest component has 229 nodes. The average degree is 2.72 and clustering coefficient is 0.37. Therefore, the cooperation time between authors is 2.72, which is a tight relationship in the average relationship of authors.

(1) In the blue cluster: Cheng, T.C.E. (Chair Professor of Management, The Hong Kong Polytechnic University, China), Ng, C.T. and Yuan, Jinjiang are three productive authors [4]. Both Cheng, T.C.E. and Ng, C.T. are from The Hong Kong Polytechnic University. Yuan, Jinjiang is from Zhengzhou University. Their main research focuses on scheduling and combinatorial optimization. (2) In the read cluster: The representative nodes in this cluster are Sethi, Suresh P [17] and Janakiraman, Ganesh [11] from The University of Texas at Dallas. They focus on scheduling and sequencing of robotic cells. (3) In the yellow cluster: Glover Fred [9] and Gendreau Michel [20] are dominated in this cluster. Glover, Fred is from University of Colorado, USA, whose research focuses on mathematical and computer optimization, applied to systems design and so on. In our dataset, Gendreau, Michel published 19 papers which is cited by 506 papers. He is interested in the research of operation research, stochastic optimization and so on.

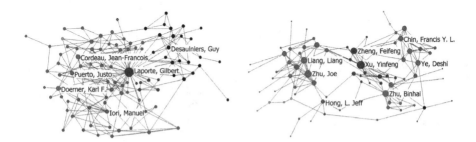

Fig. 3.   Second   largest   component (size = 95) (Color figure online)

Fig. 4.   Third   largest   component (size = 77) (Color figure online)

Figure 3 shows the second largest component with 95 nodes. The average degree is 2.42 and clustering coefficient is 0.33. In this network, Laporte, Gilbert has the largest number of collaborators (degree = 33). He is one of the productive authors and majors in operations research, distribution management and mathematical programming. Cordeau, Jean-Francois [7] and Puerto, Justo play key roles in the red cluster. Cordeau, Jean-Francois is a professor from HEC Montreal, Canada and Puerto, Justo [18] is a professor from Universidad de Sevilla, Spain. They focus on combinatorial optimization, mathematical decomposition and so on. Iori, Manuel plays a key role in the purple cluster, whose H-index is 19 from Google Scholar.

Figure 4 visualizes the third largest component with 77 nodes. The average degree is 2.69 and clustering coefficient is 0.52. Zhu, Joe in the pink clustering and Xu, Yinfeng in the blue clustering are both in the list of top ten productive authors.

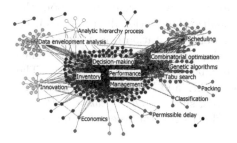

Fig. 5. Keyword co-occurrence network (Color figure online)

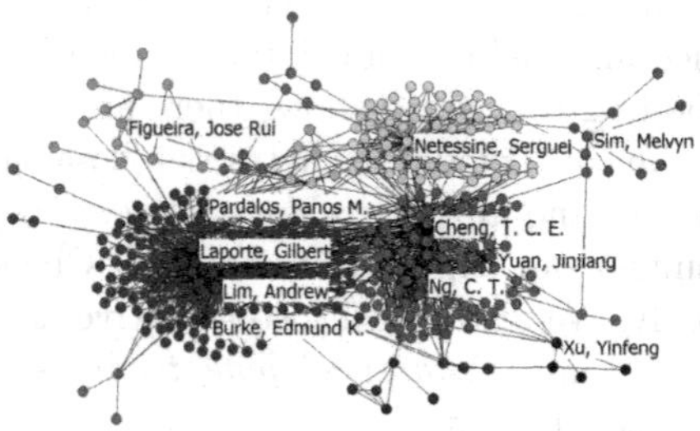

Fig. 6. Author co-keyword network (Color figure online)

4.2 Keyword Co-occurrence Network Analysis

The keyword co-occurrence network includes 324 keywords and 1,187 links. It refers to similarity between keywords. And similar keywords represent a topic. Two keywords have the closer relationship when they co-occurred more times. So we only analyze keywords that co-occurred more than ten times.

We cluster them and identify 20 topics. In Fig. 5, each cluster has its own color. We regard the largest degree node as the topic of this cluster. The nodes in Fig. 5 denotes the hot topics in the scheduling field. The blue cluster are the biggest cluster in the keyword co-occurrence network. In the blue cluster, keywords includes 'Decision-making', 'Inventory', 'Performance' and 'Management', in which there are three most frequent keywords. The red cluster as the second biggest cluster contains 'Combinatorial optimization', 'Genetic algorithms' and 'Tabu search'. 'Scheduling' in the yellow cluster represents the third biggest cluster.

4.3 Author Co-keyword Network Analysis

Author co-keyword network indicates authors' common interests. To focus on outstanding authors' common interest, we only consider authors who have published more than 5 papers and two authors' co-keywords number must be more than 30. Figure 6 has 346 nodes and 1,127 links. Authors are partitioned into common interest groups. We identify 16 clusters.

The most noticeable clustering is the red one, which includes many productive authors, such as Cheng, T.C.E. and Ng, C.T. The second cluster is the blue one, which includes Laporte, Gilbert and Lim, Andrew. Netessine, Serguei as the center of the yellow cluster focuses on operations management and supply chain management [12].

5   Conclusions

Over the recent years, the scheduling field attracts the significant interest of scientists and thousand of papers about scheduling have appeared in the literature [1]. In this paper, we collect 9,611 papers from five SCI journals' data about the scheduling field as our data source. We visualize the citation distributions from 2006 to 2015, which shows there are a long delay of citation time-window.

We construct three networks (co-authorship network, keyword co-occurrence network and author co-keyword network) to analyze collaboration patterns. The results of our experiments find that Cheng, T.C.E. and Ng, C.T. collaborate very closely. We also identify some active keywords, such as '*Optimization*', '*Performance*' and '*Data envelopment analysis*', which show the research tendency of the scheduling field.

For the further research, we intend to obtain more papers about scheduling field from other journals and conferences as well as visualize collaboration structures among authors per year in order to understand the evolution of this field better.

Acknowledgment. This work was supported in part by the Natural Science Foundation of China under Grant 61502069, by the Natural Science Foundation of Liaoning under Grant 2015020003.

References

1. Allahverdi, A., Ng, C., Cheng, T.E., Kovalyov, M.Y.: A survey of scheduling problems with setup times or costs. Eur. J. Oper. Res. **187**(3), 985–1032 (2008)
2. Van den Bergh, J., Beliën, J., De Bruecker, P., Demeulemeester, E., De Boeck, L.: Personnel scheduling: a literature review. Eur. J. Oper. Res. **226**(3), 367–385 (2013)
3. Cardoen, B., Demeulemeester, E., Beliën, J.: Operating room planning and scheduling: a literature review. Eur. J. Oper. Res. **201**(3), 921–932 (2010)
4. Cheng, T.C.E., Ng, C., Yuan, J.: A stronger complexity result for the single machine multi-operation jobs scheduling problem to minimize the number of tardy jobs. J. Sched. **6**(6), 551–555 (2003)
5. Cobo, M.J., López-Herrera, A.G., Herrera-Viedma, E., Herrera, F.: An approach for detecting, quantifying, and visualizing the evolution of a research field: a practical application to the fuzzy sets theory field. J. Informetr. **5**(1), 146–166 (2011)

6. Cobo, M.J., Martínez, M., Gutiérrez-Salcedo, M., Fujita, H., Herrera-Viedma, E.: 25 years at knowledge-based systems: a bibliometric analysis. Knowl.-Based Syst. **80**, 3–13 (2015)

7. Cordeau, J.F., Laporte, G., Moccia, L., Sorrentino, G.: Optimizing yard assignment in an automotive transshipment terminal. Eur. J. Oper. Res. **215**(1), 149–160 (2011)

8. Girvan, M., Newman, M.E.: Community structure in social and biological networks. Proc. Nat. Acad. Sci. **99**(12), 7821–7826 (2002)

9. Glover, F., Sueyoshi, T.: Contributions of Professor William W. Cooper in operations research and management science. Eur. J. Oper. Res. **197**(1), 1–16 (2009)

10. Heilig, L., Voß, S.: A scientometric analysis of cloud computing literature. IEEE Trans. Cloud Comput. **2**(3), 266–278 (2014)

11. Huh, W.T., Janakiraman, G.: (s, S) Optimality in joint inventory-pricing control: an alternate approach. Oper. Res. **56**(3), 783–790 (2008)

12. Kim, S.H., Cohen, M.A., Netessine, S.: Performance contracting in after-sales service supply chains. Manag. Sci. **53**(12), 1843–1858 (2007)

13. Li, L., Li, X., Cheng, C., Chen, C., Ke, G., Zeng, D.D., Scherer, W.T.: Research collaboration and ITS topic evolution: 10 years at T-ITS. IEEE Trans. Intell. Transp. Syst. **11**(3), 517–523 (2010)

14. Li, L., Li, X., Li, Z., Zeng, D.D., Scherer, W.T.: A bibliographic analysis of the IEEE transactions on intelligent transportation systems literature. IEEE Trans. Intell. Transp. Syst. **11**(2), 251–255 (2010)

15. Martínez, M.A., Cobo, M.J., Herrera, M., Herrera-Viedma, E.: Analyzing the scientific evolution of social work using science mapping. Res. Soc. Work Pract. **25**(2), 257–277 (2015)

16. Muñoz, L.A., Bolívar, M.P.R., Cobo, M.J., Herrera-Viedma, E.: Science mapping tools: their application to e-government field. In: Proceedings of the 17th International Digital Government Research Conference on Digital Government Research, pp. 194–201. ACM (2016)

17. Naik, P.A., Prasad, A., Sethi, S.P.: Building brand awareness in dynamic oligopoly markets. Manag. Sci. **54**(1), 129–138 (2008)

18. Perea, F., Puerto, J.: Revisiting a game theoretic framework for the robust railway network design against intentional attacks. Eur. J. Oper. Res. **226**(2), 286–292 (2013)

19. Potts, C.N., Kovalyov, M.Y.: Scheduling with batching: a review. Eur. J. Oper. Res. **120**(2), 228–249 (2000)

20. Vidal, T., Crainic, T.G., Gendreau, M., Prins, C.: Heuristics for multi-attribute vehicle routing problems: a survey and synthesis. Eur. J. Oper. Res. **231**(1), 1–21 (2013)

21. Xu, X., Wang, W., Liu, Y., Zhao, X., Xu, Z., Zhou, H.: A bibliographic analysis and collaboration patterns of IEEE transactions on intelligent transportation systems between 2000 and 2015. IEEE Trans. Intell. Transp. Syst. **17**(8), 2238–2247 (2016)

22. Zhu, X., Wilhelm, W.E.: Scheduling and lot sizing with sequence-dependent setup: a literature review. IIE Trans. **38**(11), 987–1007 (2006)

Scalable Real-Time Sharing of 3D Model Visualizations for Group Collaboration

Sven Ubik[(⊠)] and Jiří Kubišta

CESNET, Prague, Czech Republic
{ubik,Jiri.Kubista}@cesnet.cz

Abstract. Digital 3D models and their visualizations are increasingly being used in many fields of research, engineering design and humanities. They enable people to see objects in perspectives not available in 2D images. It would be useful if a group of people in a classroom, laboratory or across distances can collaboratively discuss their observations drawn using 3D models. We describe a simple system that allows a group of people to share in real-time their views of a 3D model using their devices ranging from mobile phones to large video walls. We evaluated the system performance and usability with 3D models of digitized cultural heritage objects.

Keywords: 3D models · Digital cultural heritage · Interactive visualizations · Video walls

1 Introduction

Digital 3D models are increasingly being used for research, education and presentations of objects. One field where digital representations of physical objects are used is museum collections. The Europeana[1] portal includes digital images of millions of artefacts. A small but increasing number of objects are now available also as 3D models. A Sketchfab[2] service is a popular solution for web-based access to 3D models.

Digital representations can document the current state of artefacts (which may deteriorate), allow study of artefacts without physical contact and might serve as a form of backup, to help restore precious artefacts, should a damage occur.

We foresee bigger potential of 3D models for education, research, scientific collaboration and popularization. We concentrate on tangible three-dimensional objects, because this part of cultural heritage is now less well represented in digitalized forms than flat works, such as prints or paintings.

The rest of the paper is structured as follows. We identify the main requirements in Sect. 2. We discuss design options and describe a possible solution in Sect. 3. We present an experimental evaluation in Sect. 4. Finally, we draw conclusions and propose directions for future work in Sect. 5.

---

[1] www.europeana.eu.
[2] www.sketchfab.com.

© Springer International Publishing AG 2017
Y. Luo (Ed.): CDVE 2017, LNCS 10451, pp. 244–251, 2017.
DOI: 10.1007/978-3-319-66805-5_31

2 Requirements

We wanted to provide an environment for teachers, students and researchers that would allow them to collaboratively view, discuss and compare 3D models. A widespread availability of mobile devices, such as phones and tablets, can be utilized to turn them into personal navigation and visualization devices. At the other end of the size range, video walls made from LCD panels are now commonly present in visualization facilities at universities and can be used as working interactive space. There are several requirements for 3D visualizations of objects to be more useful for education, research and collaboration:

- Requirement R1: scalability of visualizations for devices ranging from mobile phones to large video walls, which are useful for class work, research and to enliven physical exhibitions.
- Requirement R2: presenting multiple 3D models simultaneously for comparison. It is useful to see both a "big picture" for context and details, without the need to zoom or pan, allowing people to concentrate on the content.
- Requirement R3: low-latency network sharing of 3D models among multiple devices. This can enable real-time discussions and collaboration for a group of people within one room as well as for a group distributed in different places.

Museum institutions typically see two areas where 3D models can be useful. First, as a next generation of online presentations of digital cultural heritage, bringing new opportunities when compared to still photographs. Second, as an addition to physical exhibitions, providing visitors with more information, hands on feeling of the exhibited objects and making the exhibition more attractive especially for young visitors.

For distance collaboration and interactive feeling of remote object manipulation, the latency between commands and visualization changes should be as low as possible. An empirical evidence has shown that for the user to feel that a communication system is not affecting a workflow by its latency, the one-way delay should be less than approx. 150 ms [4].

3 Related Work

Europeana (see footnote 1) is a multilingual access point to Europe's cultural heritage in a digital form, allowing to search through millions of digital objects provided by European museums, galleries, archives, libraries and other institutions, whose objective is the preservation of cultural heritage. Many countries also have their national databases of digital cultural heritage.

Digital heritage is in these databases are currently represented predominantly by still photographs, audio and video samples. A small number of models can be seen in 3D PDF documents specified in the Universal 3D (U3D) format. However, the interaction possibilities in 3D PDF are limited and it cannot be seen from within a web browser, a PDF viewer needs to be started externally.

Guarnieri et al. [1] describes a complete process of creating and presenting 3D models of cultural heritage using only open-source and free software. Models can be seen in a web browser, which however requires an X3D plugin and the solution is not scaleable to allow distributed rendering such as for LCD walls and remote access.

Scopigno et al. [2] stresses importance of tools beyond pure visualizations, which would help researchers to work with digitized cultural heritage, such as fragment restoration and shape analysis.

Hermon [3] suggests a process of creating 3D models in archaeology from multiple sources of information and using them to assist research work, such as reconstructions. This was confirmed in our talks with people in archaeological institutes.

Visualisation laboratories and class rooms are now commonly equipped with walls from LCD panels of various sizes and configurations, thanks to their decreasing costs. To share such a wall by multiple visualizations and to utilize the total resolution of all LCD panels, some software for distribution of application visual output is needed. A commonly used system is the Scalable Amplified Group Environment (SAGE2) [9]. The SAGE2 system can drive LCD walls of different sizes and configurations in a scalable way. It is web-based using multiple web browsers running in a full-screen mode, stitched together to cover the LCD wall. Application functionality is divided into client and server side. The client side is implemented in JavaScript and runs inside web browsers that display the content. The server side can provide content to be streamed to the wall and exchanges synchronization messages between clients. The SAGE2 system can run on any web browser-based device, including tablets and mobile phones. SAGE2 requires two web interfaces - one for applications in a full-screen mode and one for the SAGE2 controller (for starting new applications, etc.).

4   Design

The requirements R1 for scalability and R2 for multiple 3D models to be presented simultaneously for comparisons and study can be in part satisfied by using an LCD wall in a class room or laboratory driven by the SAGE2 software. Although the wall content is displayed by multiple web browsers, they cannot be directly used to open Sketchfab web pages and interact with the 3D models. One model can span multiple web browsers and the pan and zoom done in one web browser would not be shown in a synchronized way in other web browsers.

Therefore we used the Sketchfab Viewer API to implement a SAGE2 Sketchfab Viewer application that can show a Sketchfab model across multiple web browsers. Synchronization is done by exchanging SAGE2 messages through the SAGE2 server. Multiple instances of the SAGE2 Sketchfab Viewer application can be started and presented at the same time. Each window of any application instance can be freely moved and resized, while always keeping the full resolution across any number of LCD panels. The SAGE2 Sketchfab Viewer application provides the following features:

- scalability across arbitrary number of web browsers for large LCD walls
- orbit look and zoom with adjustable speed
- presentation of Sketchfab 3D animations
- presentation of annotations
- presets for easy switching between multiple modules

The Sketchfab Viewer applications is freely available from the SAGE2 app store[3].

A user in a distant room can use a regular PC or a laptop to connect to a remote SAGE2 server and display the content of the wall on its screen. However, given the smaller size of the PC monitor or even a tablet or mobile phone display, it may be useful if a user has an option to see a selected model separately and still be able to interact with the model in a synchronized way with other users.

To satisfy the requirement R3 also for mobile devices, we have developed a Mobile extension to the SAGE2 server. It allows users to start a SAGE2 application directly in web browsers of their mobile devices. In order to utilize the smaller screen size, the browser can be switched into a full-screen mode. The user can switch between multiple application instances even in a full-screen mode by a one-touch selection of the application in the upper left corner. It eliminates the need for a separate tab for the SAGE2 control page. Presentations of multiple 3D models on an LCD wall using multiple instances of the application along with sharing a selected model on the user's mobile device is illustrated in Fig. 1.

Fig. 1. Sharing a 3D model between an LCD wall and a mobile device

Some features provided by Sketchfab web interface are missing in the Sketchfab Viewer API, such as automatic detection of the model visual centre for intuitive rotation. The Sketchfab Viewer API assumes a rotation centre at the coordinate origin, which can be anywhere, even outside the model.

Touch control and gestures recognition are implemented using the Hammer.js library. The press and release, pinch to zoom and pan events are mapped to WebSocket messages, which are exchanged through the SAGE2 server with web browsers of other users, allowing all users to see the same application content.

Message exchange between devices and SAGE2 server is illustrated in Fig. 2. When a user moves a finger on a touch screen of a mobile device, the following

---

[3] http://apps.sagecommons.org.

sequence of events takes place to change the camera position of a 3D visualization for all connected users:

- A Hammer.js library inside the user's web browser detects the user's gesture
- The application calculates an offset from the previous position
- The application sends a `pointerMove` (rotate) or `pointerScroll` (zoom) WebSocket message to the SAGE2 server to inform it about the change of the position of the user's pointer
- The SAGE2 server distributes this message to all user's web browsers
- Each application instance receives the message (including the original instance) and changes the model view accordingly. It is important that each application instance renders the model in a resolution of the user's devices, which can range from 300×200 pixels on a mobile phone to tens of megapixels on an LCD wall
- In order to change the model view, the application calculates the new position of the camera and its direction and then calls the setCameraLookAt function of the Sketchfab Viewer API:

```
api.lookat(
    [ 0, 13, 10],  // camera position
    [0, 10, 0],    // target to look at
    4.3            // duration of the animation in seconds
);
```

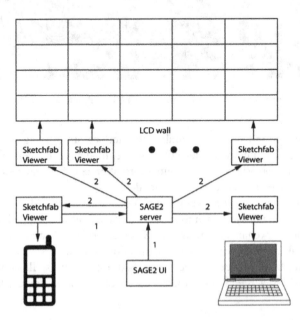

Fig. 2. Message exchange between devices and SAGE2 server

5 Evaluation

We did several experiments to check scalability (R1), multiple model ability (R2) and low-latency distance sharing (R3) for various kinds of 3D models of cultural artefacts. We used a set of models created from three sources: (a) modelling applications Blender and 3ds Max, (b) photogrammetry software (Agisoft Photoscan and custom software used for the Langweil digitization project[4]) and (c) 3D scanner Creaform Go!Scan 50. We selected several models that differ significantly in the number of faces and vertices and in the size of textures. Characteristics of the selected models are summarized in Table 1.

Table 1. Models used for evaluation

Model name	Source	Size of textures	Number of faces	Number of vertices	Visualization update time
Amphora	Blender	1.2 MB	95k	95k	193 ms
Vessel	Blender	1.41 MB	56.1k	56.1k	200 ms
Langweil - 09	Photogrammetry and modelling	35.4 MB	800	613	483 ms
Langweil - 27	Photogrammetry and modelling	264 MB	29.3k	17.1k	551 ms
Cup	3D scanner (Creaform Go!Scan 50)	48 MB	273.3k	136.6k	177 ms

The last column in Table 1 shows the time from the user's request of a change in the camera position to the actual change of visualization measured by the timeline monitoring in the Google Chrome DevTools. The used PC was a Dell 3610 with Xeon E5-1603 2.8 GHz, 8 GB RAM. We can see that the update time is more affected by the texture size than by the mesh size of the underlying 3D structure. For smaller textures, the response time is within the recommended limit (see Sect. 2). For larger textures, performance optimizations will be needed. A demonstration of synchronized interaction with a 3D model on an LCD wall, a PC and a mobile phone can be seen online[5].

We conducted a subjective usability evaluation test in order to obtain user feedback. Subjects were random students (5) from the Faculty of Information Technologies and the Faculty of Architecture. The former were supposed to have more technological background, while later tended to be more oriented towards one of the targeted application areas. Each subject used his/her mobile device while a person in the teacher's position was looking at the LCD wall. The evaluation environment is shown in Fig. 3. Each subject was asked to perform 12 tasks on 3 models. For example, to show peer students and the teacher a specific part of a model or to compare parts of two models. The subjects should then indicate their perceived level of difficulty to perform

---

[4] http://www.langweil.cz/index_en.php.

[5] https://youtu.be/Aj79dycaoYQ.

Fig. 3. Usability evaluation of SAGE mobile extension

individual tasks. Due to a low number of subjects, the results are not statistically significant, but provide useful qualitative feedback. The most important usability issues can be summarized as follows:

- Satisfaction with usability of elementary navigation functions was 75% for camera orbit look, 60% for zoom and 35% for pan
- The centre of the orbit look should preferably move along with pan and zoom to be at the centre of currently visible model part
- The sensitivity of the orbit look and pan should decrease with zoom in
- When a navigation function was initialized on an LCD wall or on one mobile device, the responsiveness of visualization changes on other devices was fully acceptable and not causing any distraction in group collaboration.

6   Conclusion

Current technologies such as WebGL, SAGE2 and Sketchfab API allow creation of applications for visualizations of 3D models scalable from mobile devices to large LCD walls. A 3D model can be accessed by multiple users concurrently, enabling real-time discussions, distance teaching and collaboration. For instance, distance access to digitized cultural heritage can contribute to the protection of collection items by minimizing physical handling for e-learning, research discussions and to enhance museum exhibitions. In our measurements, response time depended more significantly on the texture size than on the model mesh size. The technology allows embedding 3D models into current web-based portals, such as Europeana.

References

1. Guarnieri, A., Pirotti, F., Vettore, A.: Cultural heritage interactive 3D models on the web: an approach using open source and free software. J. Cult. Herit. Elsevier **11**, 350–353 (2010). doi:10.1016/j.culher.2009.11.011
2. Scopigno, R., Callieri, M., Cignoni, P., Corsini, M., Dellepiane, M., Ponchio, F., Ranzuaglia, G.: 3D models of cultural heritage: beyond plain visualization. Computer **44**(7), 48–55 (2011). doi:10.1109/MC.2011.196
3. Hermon, S.: Reasoning in 3D: a critical appraisal of the role of 3D modelling and virtual reconstructions in archaeology. In: Beyond Illustration: 2D and 3D Technologies as Tools for Discovery in Archaeology. BAR International Series, pp. 36–45
4. ITU-T Recommendation G.114: Telecommunication Standardization Section of ITU (2003)
5. WebGL Specification, Khronos WebGL Working Group. https://www.khronos.org/registry/webgl/specs/latest/
6. Sketchfab Viewer API. https://sketchfab.com/developers/viewer
7. Autodesk A360 Viewer. https://a360.autodesk.com/viewer
8. Exocortex Technologies. Clara.io. https://clara.io
9. Marrinan, T., Aurisano, J., Nishimoto, A., Bharadwaj, K., Mateevitsi, V., Renambot, L., Long, L., Johnson, A., Leigh, J.: SAGE2: a new approach for data intensive collaboration using scalable resolution shared displays. In: 10th IEEE International Conference on Collaborative Computing: Networking, Applications and Worksharing (2014)

A Tongue Image Segmentation Method Based on Enhanced HSV Convolutional Neural Network

Jiang Li, Baochuan Xu$^{(\boxtimes)}$, Xiaojuan Ban, Ping Tai, and Boyuan Ma

University of Science and Technology Beijing, Beijing, China
790966919@qq.com, xubc_2005@163.com,
banxj@ustb.edu.cn, pingkflod@sina.com, 793960328@qq.com

Abstract. In the procedure of the Chinese medical tongue diagnosis, it's necessary to carry out the original tongue image segmentation to reduce interference to the tongue feature extraction caused by the non-tongue part of the face. In this paper, we propose a new method based on enhanced HSV color model convolutional neural network for tongue image segmentation. This method can get a better in tongue image segmentation results compared with others. This method also has a great advantage over other methods in the processing speed.

Keywords: Tongue image segmentation · Convolutional neural network · Snake model

1 Introduction

Tongue diagnosis is a unique diagnosis method of the Chinese traditional medical science. Doctors can get the information of patients' illness conditions by observing their tongue features [1]. It's important to diagnose the patient's health condition and make a prescription. Modern research shows that tongue diagnosis, as a unique diagnosis method to identify the functional status of human body, has great value in diagnostics, so it's necessary to inherit and carry forward tongue diagnosis.

The automation process of tongue diagnosis based on tongue image analysis is to analyse tongue features by extracting them from tongue images captured by digital image device. So, the tongue body segmentation is the first step of tongue image analysis and accurate tongue body segmentation can reduce interference caused by non-tongue body of the face to tongue feature extraction [2, 3].

Image segmentation is the hot research field all the time, and there are several methods which can be used in tongue image segmentation. Currently the method applied to tongue body segmentation are mainly traditional image processing algorithm such as threshold segmentation method, region growing method, cluster partition method, watershed transform method, edge detection segmentation method and snake model method [4–7]. The snake model method has better performance than the others. But all of these methods of tongue segmentation still have their imperfections because it's hard to precisely divide tongue and lips as their colors are similar.

© Springer International Publishing AG 2017
Y. Luo (Ed.): CDVE 2017, LNCS 10451, pp. 252–260, 2017.
DOI: 10.1007/978-3-319-66805-5_32

In some of the collected images, the boundary of the human body's facial region and the tongue body region is not obvious, and the color of the face area and the tongue area is relatively similar. In this case, the threshold segmentation method can't obtain accurate segmentation results, and the effect of segmentation method based on snake model is bad because the energy function of snake model can't converge. Besides the snake model method can't use RGB image directly and need to convert RGB image to gray image in advance.

In recent years, deep learning has developed rapidly and deep neural network in image understanding has achieved good results. The convolutional neural network is an application of the deep learning method in image processing field [8, 9]. In this paper the enhanced HSV convolutional neural network based method for tongue body segmentation was proposed for the first time. Set the enhanced tongue image as the input of convolutional neural network and calibrate the image of tongue body as the tag of tongue, then use convolutional neural network to conduct training. The convolutional neural network finally output a binary image of the tongue body which has same size with the original tongue image. The white area of the binary image is the tongue body and the black area is the non-tongue body of the face. Merge the output binary image with the original image, the resulting image is the image of tongue body extracted by the convolutional neural network.

Specially, we did some preprocessing for the image in order to obtain more exact features. Firstly, we convert image from RGB color model to HSV color model because that the HSV color model can show the tongue edge more clearly. Then we use image enhancement to strengthen the edge. Our method which used enhanced HSV color model based on convolutional neural network obtain a good effect in the tongue image segmentation.

2   Enhanced HSV COLOR Model

2.1   HSV Color Model

Generally, the extracted image data was RGB color model. The RGB color model is an additive color model in which red, green and blue light are added together in various way to reproduce a broad array of colors. And the HSV color model is another representation of the image attribute value. HSV stands for hue, saturation, and value, and is also often called HSB (B for brightness). In our experiments, we convert image from RGB color model to HSV color model because we found that HSV color model was easy to show the tongue rough edge.

As we can see in the Fig. 1, the hue channel of the tongue image shows a distinct edge between the tongue bottom edge with the face and the saturation channel of the tongue image shows a distinct edge between the tongue top edge with the mouth.

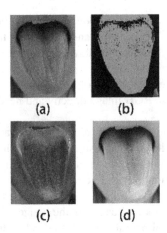

(a)   (b)

(c)   (d)

Fig. 1. Split RGB image into HSV channel (Color figure online)

2.2 Image Enhancement

After convert RGB color model to HSV color model, we Contrast Limited Adaptive histogram equalization (CLAHE) [10, 11] to enhance the tongue image in order to obtain a clearer edge.

AHE algorithm is a histogram method in order to improve image contrast locally by the cumulative distribution function. But image is often distored by AHE because the image local contrast was improved too much. In order to solve this problem, we limit the local contrast. In the histogram equalization, the relation of the mapping curve T and the cumulative distribution function (CDF) is shown as in (1).

$$T(i) = \frac{M}{N} CDF(i) \tag{1}$$

The cumulative distribution function (CDF) is the integral of the histogram of the gray scale so we can limit the slope of the CDF to limit the contrast.

$$\frac{d}{di} CDF(i) = Hist(i) \tag{2}$$

We cut the histogram obtained in the subblock so that the amplitude is lower than a certain upper limit, and the cut-off portion can't be discarded. We also distribute the cut value evenly over the whole gray interval to ensure that the total area of the histogram unchanged (Fig. 2).

Contrast Limited Adaptive histogram equalization (CLAHE) can't be applied to multi-channel image directly so we apply CLAHE to each channel of HSV image and then merge these three channels. The tongue image was enhanced obviously by this method and our result was shown in Fig. 3.

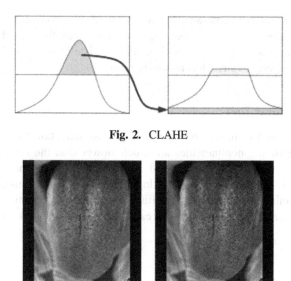

Fig. 2. CLAHE

Fig. 3. Enhance image by CLAHE

3 Convolutional Neural Network

The convolutional neural network is a multi-layer artificial neural network which can extract features from input data automatically and it was always used to classify images. In convolutional neural network, each layer is composed of many 2-dimension planes and each plane is composed of many independent neurons. Neurons in two adjacent layers were interconnected but neurons in a same layer were not connected [12]. In the convolutional layer, neurons are locally connected with the next layer's neurons and this structure can reduce the number of the weight params. But in the full-connected layer, all the features are connected to the full-connected layer neurons.

3.1 Convolutions

Natural images have the property of being stationary, meaning that the statistics of one part of the image are the same as any other part. Therefore, the features that we learn at one part of the image can also be applied to other parts of the image, and we can use the same features at all locations. Having learned features over small patches sampled randomly from the larger image, apply this learned feature detector anywhere in the image. Specifically take the learned features and convolve them with the larger image, thus obtain a different feature activation value at each location in the image [13].

3.2 Max Pooling

Features that are useful in one region are also likely to be useful for other regions because of the stationarity property of image. Pooling is an operation to aggregate statistics of these features at various locations. Divide the convolutional features of image into pooling area by defining pooling size, then obtain the pooled convolutional features by meaning pooling or max pooling. Pooling is effective to reduce dimension of the features and improve results (less over-fitting).

3.3   Rectified Linear Unit

Instead of sigmod and tanh, we choose ReLU [14] as activation to model a neurons output. These saturating nonlinearities are much slower than the non-saturating non-linearities. CNNs with ReLU are trained several times faster than with tanh on CIFAR-10 dataset. Moreover, when executing back propagation, sigmod and tanh will cause gradient vanishing because of saturating, which leads to information loss. ReLU makes some output of neurons zero that causes sparse of network, which prevents overfitting.

3.4   Dropout

Dropout [15] is a recently-introduced technique preventing overfitting when train data is not that much. Dropout sets part of the output of each hidden neuron to zero. These neurons do not contribute to the forward pass and do not participate in back propagation. Every time input is presented, parts of the hidden neurons are "deleted" randomly. The architecture trains lots of networks with some neurons and learns more robust features that are useful. Most correct subsets of networks impact on final result, but other subsets are abandoned. A 50% dropout rate is employed to discourage the co-adaption of feature detectors, which is proved better. Figure 4 shows the operation mode of dropout.

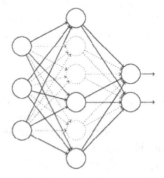

Fig. 4.   Half of hidden neurons are dropped out

3.5   Full-Connection

The last layer before output layer in the convolutional neural network is full-connected layer. Each neuron in the layer connected to all the features which was generated by the convolutional layers.

4   Enhanced HSV Convolutional Neural Network

4.1   Convolutional Neural Network Model

In the experiment, we used a ten-layer convolutional neural network to train the tongue image. The convolutional neural network structure was shown as Fig. 5.

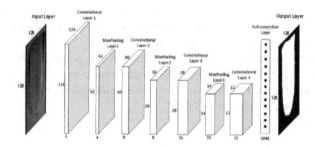

Fig. 5. Convolutional neural network structure (Color figure online)

From Fig. 5, we can see that the input layer is a marked tongue image which is a color picture. The 2, 4, 6 and 8 layer are the convolutional layers and the second lay uses 5 * 5 convolutional kernel and others use 3 * 3 convolutional kernel. The 3, 5 and 7 layer are the max pooling layers and their pooling size is 2 * 2. The 9 layer is the full-connection layer with 2048 neurons. The 10 layer is the output layer with 128 * 128 neurons and we can transform the outputs to a binary image as the tongue outline.

4.2   Dataset

The original tongue images were captured from a hospital by a digital camera. There are 264 tongue images in total and we used 211 tongue images for training and 53 images for test. We cut the training tongue images randomly (reserve at least 70% tongue body) to generate more training data. Standardize the original tongue images and make the tongue images in same size. Draw the outline of the tongue artificially in the standardized image, then blacken the tongue body. Executing the XOR operation to the marked tongue image and the original image, the resulting image is outline of the

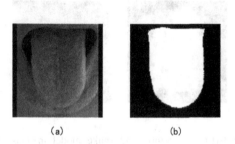

(a)   (b)

Fig. 6. Image preprocessing result (a) standardized tongue 128 image (b) marked tongue image

tongue and the tag of the original tongue image which is the training target of the convolutional neural network. The standardized tongue image and the marked tongue image were shown in Fig. 6.

5 Experiment Result

After training and testing the convolutional neural network, the tongue body segmentation result was shown in Fig. 3, we can see that the tongue body was accurately segmented by the convolutional neural method.

To validate the availability and practicability of the proposed algorithm, take a tongue image for example, we do the contrast segmentation experiment with traditional snake model algorithm and the proposed improved snake algorithm. The result image of these two methods are shown as Fig. 7.

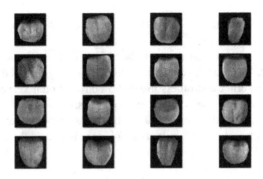

Fig. 7. Experiment result

In Fig. 8, we can see that the proposed tongue segmentation method based on convolutional neural network obtained a better result than the method based on snake model. The former tongue segmentation method kept more details of the tongue than the latter method especially in the part of the tongue edge where the color of tongue was similar to the color of face. Result by the snake model method get a poor

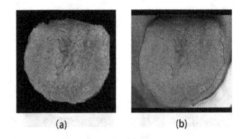

Fig. 8. Comparison of EH-CNN method and snake model method (a) result by EH-CNN (b) result by snake model (Color figure online)

performance when the edge was indistinct and in this case the tongue contour line often moves in the wrong direction. In our experiments, there are several tongue images which didn't get a convergent contour lines by using snake model method. We use the mean error pixel rate to evaluate these two segmentation algorithms, result was shown in Table 1.

Table 1. Mean error pixels rate comparison.

Method	Mean error pixel rate
EH-CNN	5.3%
Snake model method	8.7%

Our enhanced HSV convolutional neural network also has a great advantage over the snake model method in the processing speed. When apply these methods to large amounts of data, faster processing speed has more import application value. The processing speed comparison of these two method was shown in Table 2.

Table 2. Processing speed comparison.

Method	Time (second) per image
EH-CNN	0.0275
Snake model method	3.1355

6   Conclusion

The convolutional neural network is used widely in image recognition. The proposed tongue segmentation method based on enhanced HSV color model convolutional neural network obtains good results particularly performs better in this condition. That the tongue image has an indistinct edge between the tongue body and the face. Tongue image segmentation by snake model method can't get a convergent tongue contour line occasionally. However, we get lower mean error pixel rate by using our enhanced HSV convolutional neural network. Besides, the method we proposed in this paper has a great advantage over the snake model method in tongue image segmentation.

This method also has potential to get better results by increasing the number of training samples and making the artificial marks of tongue body more accurate. Our next stage is to optimize the network structure by adding more layers and fuse multi-layer data features.

References

1. Yuan, L., Liw, E., Yao, J., et al.: Research progress of information processing technology on tongue diagnosis of traditional Chinese medicine. Acta Univ. Tradit. Med. Sin. Pharmacol. Shanghai **25**(02), 80–86 (2011)

2. Guo, R., Wang, Y.-Q., Yan, J.-J., et al.: Study on the objectivity of traditional Chinese medicinal tongue inspection. Chin. J. Integr. Tradit. West. Med. **29**(07), 642–645 (2009)

3. Chiu, C.-C.: A novel approach based on computerized image analysis for traditional Chinese medical diagnosis of the tongue. Comput. Methods Programs Biomed. **61**(2), 77–89 (2000)

4. Sun, X., Pang, C.: An improved snake model method on tongue segmentation. J. Chang. Univ. Sci. Technol. **36**(5), 154–156 (2013)

5. Wang, K., Guo, Q., Zhuang, D.: An image segmentation method based on the improved snake model. In: IEEE International Conference on Mechatronics and Automation, pp. 532–536 (2006)

6. Xu, C.Y., Prince, J.L.: Snakes and gradient vector flow. IEEE Trans. Image Process. **7**(3), 359–369 (1998)

7. Kass, M., Witkin, A., Terzopoulos, D.: Snakes: active contour models. Int. J. Comput. Vis. **1**(4), 321–331 (1988)

8. Krizhevsky, A., Sutskever, I., Hinton, G.E.: ImageNet classification with deep convolutional neural networks. In: Advances in Neural Information Processing Systems, vol. 25, no. 2 (2012)

9. Sun, Y., Wang, X., Tang, X.: Deep learning face representation from predicting 10,000 classes. In: Computer Vision and Pattern Recognition, pp. 1891–1898. IEEE (2014)

10. Zuiderveld, K.: Contrast Limited Adaptive Histogram Equalization. Graphics Gems, pp. 474–485. Academic Press, San Diego (1994)

11. Zhang, L.: Contrast limited adaptive histogram equalization. Comput. Knowl. Technol. (2010)

12. Lecun, Y., Bengio, Y.: Convolutional Networks for Images, Speech, and Time Series. The Handbook of Brain Theory and Neural. MIT Press, Cambridge (1997)

13. Unsupervised Feature Learning and Deep Learning. http://ufldl.stanford.edu/

14. Glorot, X., Bordes, A., Bengio, Y.: Deep sparse rectifier neural networks. In: International Conference on Artificial Intelligence and Statistics (2011)

15. Hinton, G.E., Srivastava, N., Krizhevsky, A., et al.: Improving neural networks by preventing co-adaptation of feature detectors. Comput. Sci. **3**(4), 212–223 (2012)

Multi-faceted Visual Analysis on Tropical Cyclone

Cui Xie, Xiao Luo, Guangxiao Ma, Xiaotian Gao,
and Junyu Dong[⊠]

Ocean University of China, Qingdao 266100, Shandong, China
dongjunyu@ouc.edu.cn

Abstract. In this paper, we propose an interactive visualization system for tropical cyclone data analysis. We collect historical tropical cyclone data, clean and preprocess them into a unified form for the following visual analysis. We design several views based on direct visualization and feature visualization to facilitate user understanding of the physical characteristics of tropical cyclones. Additionally, we use Support Vector Machines (SVM) to predict the tropical cyclone trajectories for users to make a deep analysis and assessment of the cyclone's movement features. In this visual analysis process, we provide multiple linked views for physical characteristics exploration and cyclone trajectories prediction. Our system also supports multi-resolution analysis with temporal and spatial filtering. The experiments and user study demonstrate the effectiveness of our system.

Keywords: Cooperative visual analytics and communication · Tropical cyclone · SVM

1 Introduction

Tropical cyclones are often associated with severe weather conditions and can cause natural disasters. To understand and predict tropical cyclone trajectories and their destructive power is always the aim of governments, enterprises and research institutions. However, it is difficult to grasp the multi-faceted features of tropical cyclones and predict their trajectories, since they are dynamically changing with the environmental field and the local terrain that they pass by. In this paper, we propose a visual analysis system to study and explore the features of tropical cyclone and to predict their trajectories. This system combines automatic computation on historic data with the knowledge of experts in this field, which facilitates the analysis efficiency and quality.

In the interface, as shown in Fig. 1, we allow users to explore and analyze multiple attributes of cyclone in temporal and spatial domain simultaneously. We offer multiple views for visual analysis. Our main contributions are:

(1) We adopt the Similar Environmental Field method and SVM (Support Vector Machines) to predict the tropical cyclone trajectory. The combination of these two methods can provide a good result.

© Springer International Publishing AG 2017
Y. Luo (Ed.): CDVE 2017, LNCS 10451, pp. 261–269, 2017.
DOI: 10.1007/978-3-319-66805-5_33

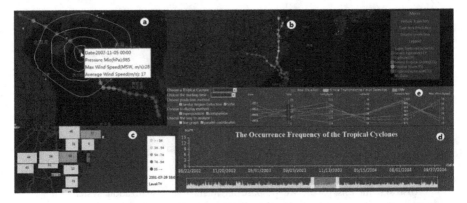

Fig. 1. An overview of our interface. (a) The spatial view, showing tropical cyclones, trajectories and nearby pressures at certain time. (b) The view of predicted trajectories, supporting comparison and analysis of various prediction algorithms. (c) The disaster assessment view, showing the influence index of tropical cyclones in different areas based on relevant historical records. (d) Time series statistics supporting zoom and filtering. (e) The parallel coordinate graphs, comparing two tropical cyclones from multiple dimensions. (Color figure online)

(2) We design a visual interface for physical characteristics visual exploring and trajectories prediction, which supports data filtering with multiple dimensions.

2 Related Work

We briefly review related work in the following areas: trajectory prediction, visual analysis of trajectories.

2.1 Trajectory Prediction

The activities of tropical cyclones are affected by various factors, e.g. bogus vortex and Monsoon Season. Liu et al. [1] adopted smooth scalar field to consider the uncertainty of tropical cyclones and calculate a set of their trajectories. Then, trajectory prediction based on similar environmental field is proposed [2]. The similarity among studied areas mainly includes two types: the first one is based on the distance (Hamming Distance and Euclidean Distance etc.) between two areas and the second is the similarity coefficient/disparity, whose absolute value is close to 1 for two similar areas and 0 for two different areas. Wan et al. [3] found that Hamming Distance produced slightly better result than other methods and was applicable for rainstorm prediction. Xue [4] claimed that the tropical cyclone is a complex weather system, which still needs human experience when in the analysis of similar environmental data.

Support Vector Machine (SVM) is adopted for trajectory prediction in recent studies [5]. The basic idea of SVM is, through the nonlinear transformation defined by kernel functions, to transform the input space to a high dimensional space, in which we can find a non-linear relationship between input and output variables. SVM has the advantage of high precision even with small amounts of sample data. SVM has been used in many research and application areas [6]. We also employ SVM in this paper, as will be presented in Sect. 4.2.

2.2   Trajectory Visual Analysis

Trajectory visual analysis has been commonly studied. Ferreira et al. [7] proposed a method for trajectory visualization and analysis of the origin-destination (OD) data, including start and end positions, as well as other attributes associated with the path. Chen et al. [8] explored the sparse trajectory data with the help of modelling the uncertainty of the Gauss mixture model. Willems et al. [9] used the method of point polymerization to deal with the problems of dense-point visualization. Hurter et al. [10] proposed how to select a particular trajectory with certain properties, without considering event interactions. Wang et al. [11] focused on the interaction between these events, and pay attention to the problem of traffic congestion. Wang and Yuan [12] studied on hurricane visualization and used a fold line to connect the path so as to highlight the hurricane's spatial locations of trajectory. Lundblad et al. [13] studied the influence of meteorological conditions on the ship sailing trajectory by using the parallel coordinates.

Different from the traffic OD tracks, tropical cyclones' trajectory has no limited activity range and change with the surrounding environmental field, which increase the complexity of visual analysis. When the number of trajectory points increase, the problem of the occlusion appears, which is pretty disadvantageous for the study of interaction and relative motion among tracks.

3   Data

3.1   Data Sources and Components

Our data mainly consists of two parts:

(1) The historical best route data of tropical cyclone comes from China Meteorological Administration [14]. It includes tropical cyclone data from 1949 to 2014 in the Northwest Pacific Ocean (including the South China Sea, north of the equator, west of longitude 180°), composed of multiple trajectory lists, each of which includes a unique international number, a cyclone name, longitude, latitude, central minimum pressure, central maximum wind speed and time stamp etc. Data in each list is arranged according to the time sequence, and its interval is 6 h.

(2) The environmental field data is from the reanalysis data sets in National Centers for Environmental Prediction (NECP) and National Center for Atmospheric Research (NCAR), which is collected at 500 hPa height every 6 h. The data includes time, latitude and longitude coordinates as well as pressure values with a spatial resolution of $2.5° \times 2.5°$.

3.2   Data Preprocessing

Firstly, data sets are constructed into a unified data format as is shown in Table 1. All the data are co-related through composite-ID of time as well as longitude and latitude. Thus, once the pressure, the wind and other parameters of a tropical cyclone at a certain moment within a certain area are known, we can easily find the corresponding environment field data of the same time within the same area. Then, only the research data within the range in [99°E, 158°E] × [3°N, 52°N] are extracted. Next, the Linear Interpolation method is used to enhance its resolution up to $1.25° \times 1.25°$. Fix the missing data due to the acquisition equipment problems by averaging the monitoring data from the Japan Meteorological Agency (JMA), the Korea Meteorological Agency (KMA) and the U.S. Joint Typhoon Warning Center (JTWC).

Table 1.   The unified data structure.

YTD	Time	Longitude	Latitude	Pressure	Wind
900101	1200	112.1	23.1	1000	10
...	...	...	...	...	...
141231	2400	113.1	25.1	999	10

4   Trajectory Prediction Methods

Tropical cyclone trajectory can be affected by many factors. Therefore we combine two prediction methods in 4.1 and 4.2, and identify the suitable application occasions for each method through visual analysis with comparison (described in Sect. 6).

4.1   Trajectory Prediction Based on Similar Environmental Field

The key to find similar tropical cyclone trajectory is to discover the movement characteristics of tropical cyclones' surrounding environmental field along with the cyclones. We use a comprehensive assessment of environmental field method [15] for judging the trajectory similarity of two tropical cyclones, and introduce 14 types of factors as criterions. These factors are shown in Table 2. Both the grid data' spatial distribution and the change trend of the tropical cyclone trajectories are considered for the similarity comparison. By similar criterions computation, the similarity index SI_i of each criterion is calculated by the Formula 1. When we predict a tropical cyclone trajectory, we query the long history data set and we can find a similar tropical cyclone ensemble based on the similarity computation of 14 types of factors of SI. The one with the most similar environmental field is taken as the candidate prediction result.

$$SI = \sum_{i=1}^{14} SI_i \tag{1}$$

Table 2. 14 types of factors of the comprehensive assessment of environmental field.

Num	Criterions	Num	Criterions
1	Time	8	Current 500 hPa height field
2	Location	9	Initial 500 hPa wind field
3	Central air pressure	10	Future 500 hPa wind field
4	Center maximum wind	11	Current 500 hPa wind filed
5	Initial velocity of cyclone	12	Initial guidance flow field
6	Initial 500 hPa height field	13	Future guidance flow filed
7	Future 500 hPa height field	14	Current guide flow field

4.2 SVM-Based Trajectory Prediction

We use the data of tropical cyclone including the central pressure, the wind speed, the moving speed, the latitude and longitude, the original place, the date and time from 1949 to 2009 as the input of SVM, and the difference value between longitude and latitude as the output.

The specific trajectory prediction is as follows. For a tropical cyclone trajectory, the input at t moment and the output at t + 6 moments are used as a set of input and output values of SVM. Assuming that each tropical cyclone has m pairs of input and output values, and there are n tropical cyclones involved in training, thus we get a total of m × n pairs of samples for training and construct the SVM model. Finally we can input the actual related test value of an interested tropical cyclone at current time and obtain its predicted trajectory position offset after 6 h by SVM. By combining the latitude and longitude of the current time, the latitude and longitude of 6 h later can be calculated. Similarly, if the input and output values at t moment and t + Δt (Δt = 6,12,···,168) moment are used for training, the position offset after Δt (Δ t = 6,12, ...,168) hours will also be obtained when inputting the testing data at current time t. After other necessary calculation, the information of location, pressure and wind power of the predicted trajectory can be obtained.

5 Physical Characteristics Visual Exploration

We design several views for the visualization of trajectories, geographical distribution and time series statistics of tropical cyclone. We also provide scalable time series analysis and interactive parallel coordinates for comparison analysis.

(1) As shown in Fig. 1a, we use different color dots to represent different intensity of a tropical cyclone. According to experts' advices, we adopt purple, pink, orange, earth yellow, lemon yellow and green to respectively represent different intensity levels from high to low, and use lines with consistent colors to connect track points according to their different intensity. (2) We use an isobar icon moving along the trajectory lines to indicate the state of tropical cyclone movement. (3) We use black dot to represent the extinction or merging of tropical cyclone. (4) In addition, we provide auxiliary information tips to facilitate the analysis. When moving the mouse to a certain point of a trajectory, information such as the time of occurrence, the central minimum pressure

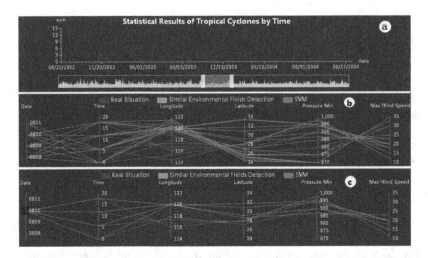

Fig. 2. (a) The statistical line chart of the occurrence frequency of the tropical cyclone appeared from august 22, 2002 to september 27, 2004. (b) Comparing the actual situation with the prediction results of multiple attributes. (c) Brushing on 1th axis and selecting of the interested data on august 10, and the parameters comparison shows that similar environmental field detection method is closer to the real situation than SVM.

and the central maximum wind speed will be shown, and the current pressure of environmental field will also be shown on the map.

We offer a time series plot to show the occurrence frequency of the tropical cyclones based on the historical data (see Fig. 2a, the number of occurrence in 2004 is the biggest and the number in 2003 is relatively small). We also provide a scalable time slider supporting for choosing any period of time while avoiding the dense and blurred drawing effect during long time intervals observation and analysis. Thus, users can interactively explore the occurrence of tropical cyclones by filtering the tropical cyclones of interested time range, and extract trajectories within these periods for further analysis.

Furthermore, users can drill down to observe the multiple parameters along with an interested tropical cyclone and study the relationships among the parameters of different trajectories by a parallel coordinate. From Fig. 2b we know that there is a deviation in latitude prediction and the prediction accuracy of minimum pressure is relatively high with a possible reason of a slight change of the pressure. Since we occasionally pay attention to the relationship of some interested cyclones, thus we also offer the brushing operation to filter the items for further analysis.

6 Visual Analysis on Trajectory Prediction

Firstly, we take the cyclone Morakot (international ID number: 0908) cross the Hualien area of Taiwan province on August 8, 2009 as our experiment object. We extract the useful data, such as shape index, center pressure, wind speed, longitude and latitude, origin place, time etc. for our trajectory prediction. Secondly, we choose two above methods for trajectory prediction with comparison and find their application occasions respectively (see Fig. 3). Similar environmental field detection method is better for the short-time trajectory prediction of tropical cyclones, while SVM is better for the long-time trajectory prediction of tropical cyclones. Then, we drill down with parallel coordinates to observe the specific differences between parameters/factors of two predicted cyclones with different prediction methods (Fig. 4). From Fig. 4, we can see that during the period of 8th to 11th of August, the prediction result of similar environmental field method is closer to the attributes of the real situation, especially on longitude and latitude prediction. However, two prediction results of minimum pressure are both with relatively high accuracy. Furthermore, our parallel coordinates view also support verifying the predicted result with real track from historical records.

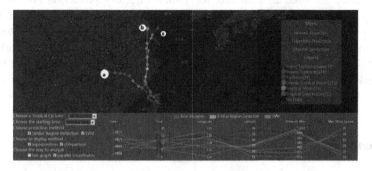

Fig. 3. The view of trajectory prediction of No. 0908 tropical cyclone. (a) The similar environmental field detection results. (b) The actual track for verification. (c) The SVM results.

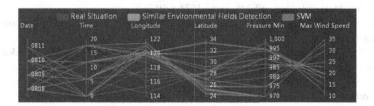

Fig. 4. Comparing the actual situation with the prediction results of multiple attributes.

7 Domain Expert's Review

We have invited three domain experts to perform several evaluation tasks for our system based on our demonstration about the system functionalities. In the first task, experts are asked to visual explore the physical characteristics of tropical cyclone. This task is similar to Sect. 5. In the second task, we ask experts to predict the trajectory of the cyclone with two different prediction methods. In the meanwhile, we ask experts themselves to perform filtering, parameter adjusting and brushing to generate a SVM model and do some comparison and statistical analysis. Finally, we discuss with the experts and collect their feedbacks when they complete the tasks with our system. Most experts consider the visual design and the functionality of our system has fulfilled its design requirements and supports the major tasks. They point out a negative review on the visual confusion in parallel coordinates. They also complained about the difficulty of interaction in the trajectory prediction for generating an appropriate prediction model. Their reviews are very helpful to our future improvement.

8 Conclusion and Future Work

In this paper, we propose a visual analysis system for tropical cyclone. The tropical cyclone trajectories, historical records and environmental field in the Pacific area from 1949 to 2014 are used as data sets for visual trajectory prediction. We show the trajectory prediction results on the map view, and add isobars around the trajectory points to visualize the cyclone's state. The system supports multiple trajectory prediction and allow parameter adjustment for higher prediction accuracy. Our work in the future will focus on optimizing prediction algorithm and developing a more friendly visual interaction interface. In addition, we will study more trajectories of tropical cyclones to extend the existing visual analysis functions.

References

1. Liu, L., Mirzangar, M., Kirby, R.M., Whitaker, R., House, D.H.: Visualizing time-specific hurricane predictions, with uncertainty, from storm path ensembles. In: Computer Graphics Forum, vol. 34, no. 3, pp. 371–380 (2015)
2. Lu, X., Yu, H., Zhao, B.: Study on similarity retrieval method for ambient field of tropical cyclones. Meteorol. Mon. **39**(12), 1609–1615 (2013)
3. Wan, R., He, X., Lin, G.: Dynamic analogue methods in experimenting regional heavy precipitation in guangdong. J. Trop. Meteorol. **22**(2), 198–202 (2006)
4. Xue, J.: Weather forecaster and numerical weather prediction. Meteorol. Mon. **33**(8), 3–11 (2007)
5. Mukherjee, S., Osuna, E., Girosi, F.: Nonlinear prediction of chaotic time series using support vector machines. In: Neural Networks for Signal Processing, pp. 511–520. IEEE (1997)
6. Sapankevych, N.I., Sankar, R.: Time series prediction using support vector machines: a survey. IEEE Comput. Intell. Mag. **4**(2), 24–38 (2009)
7. Ferreira, N., Poco, J., Vo, H.T., Freire, J., Silva, C.T.: Visual exploration of big spatio-temporal urban data: a study of New York City taxi trips. IEEE Trans. Vis. Comput. Graphics **19**(12), 2149–2158 (2013)
8. Chen, S., Yuan, X., Wang, Z., Guo, C., Liang, J., Wang, Z., Zhang, J.: Interactive visual discovering of movement patterns from sparsely sampled geo-tagged social media data. IEEE Trans. Vis. Comput. Graphics **22**(1), 270–279 (2016)
9. Willems, B.N., Wetering, H.V.D., Wijk, J.J.V.: Visualization of vessel movements. In: Computer Graphics Forum, pp. 959–966. Blackwell Publishing Ltd. (2010)

10. Hurter, C., Tissoires, B., Conversy, S.: Fromdady: spreading aircraft trajectories across views to support iterative queries. IEEE Trans. Vis. Comput. Graphics **15**(6), 1017–1024 (2009)
11. Wang, Z., Ye, T., Lu, M., Yuan, X.: Visual exploration of sparse traffic trajectory data. IEEE Trans. Vis. Comput. Graphics **20**(12), 1813–1822 (2014)
12. Wang, Z., Yuan, X.: Visual analysis of trajectory data. J. Comput. Aided Des. Comput. Graphics **27**(1), 9–25 (2015)
13. Lundblad, P., Eurenius, O., Heldring, T.: Interactive visualization of weather and ship data. In: Information Visualization, International Conference, pp. 379–386 (2013)
14. Ying, M., Zhang, W., Yu, H., Lu, X., Feng, J., Fan, Y., Zhu, Y., Chen, D.: An overview of the China meteorological administration tropical cyclone database. J. Atmos. Ocean. Technol. **31**(2), 287–301 (2014)
15. Zhong, Y., Hu, B.: The objective analogue prediction model of tropical cyclone track considering synthetical evaluation environment. J. Trop. Meteorol. **19**(2), 147–156 (2003)

An Improved Anisotropic Kernels Surface Reconstruction Method for Multiphase Fluid

Xiaojuan Ban, Lipeng Wang[(⊠)], Xiaokun Wang, and Yalan Zhang

University of Science and Technology Beijing, Beijing, China
{banxj,wangxiaokun}@ustb.edu.cn,
lipeng.wang@gmail.com, yalan.zhang920503@gmail.com

Abstract. This paper improves the anisotropic kernels surface reconstruction method and apples it to multiphase immiscible fluid surface reconstruction. An unexpected phenomenon appears when using the anisotropic kernels surface reconstruction directly (e.g. the gap and overlap at the interface of multiphase fluid surface). We eliminate the gap by considering the neighbor particles of other phase fluid in the kernels function and eliminate the overlap by signed color field in the marching cube process. The improved method will be able to reconstruct a common surface at the interface of the multiphase fluid.

Keywords: SPH · Multiphase fluid · Surface reconstruction · Simulation visualization

1 Introduction

Because the surface representation of a fluid is crucial for realistic animation, methods for reconstructing and tracking fluid surfaces have been a topic of research since fluid simulation was first introduced in computer graphics [1–3].

The blobby sphere approach was introduced by Blinn [4], which defines a scalar field that is the sum of three-dimensional Guassian kernels [5] defined at a set of points. Surface are then taken to be smooth regions of the surface are then taken to be a particular iso-contour of the scalar field. Noting this problem, Zhu and Bridson [6] defined a new implicit surface model by averaging particle locations and their radii to enhance the surface smoothness of the blobby method. Adams et al. [3], further improved upon the method of Zhu and Bridson by tracking the particle-to-surface distances across simulation time steps. Williams [7] was the first to cast the problem of generating surfaces from particle data as a constrained of optimization problem.

Later, Yu and Turk [8] demonstrate very impressive results for the particle skinning problem, which used an anisotropic kernels and Laplacian smoothed particle positions to define a smoothed implicit surface [9]. But there will meet certain problem that gap and overlap will appear at the interface of multiphase fluid surface if we use it to multiphase surface reconstruction directly (see Fig. 1).

This paper improves the anisotropic kernels surface reconstruction method. We will first discuss the reasons of the gap and overlap, and then give the method to eliminate them. The contributions of our paper are as follow

© Springer International Publishing AG 2017
Y. Luo (Ed.): CDVE 2017, LNCS 10451, pp. 270–277, 2017.
DOI: 10.1007/978-3-319-66805-5_34

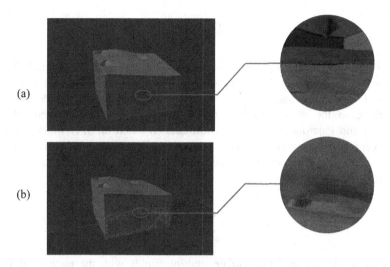

Fig. 1. Multiphase surface reconstruction. (a) using marching cube directly with overlap, (b) using anisotropic kernels directly with gap. (Color figure online)

- Consider the neighbor particles impact of other fluid in the Laplacian smoothing process and does not move the particles in the surface of multiphase fluid interface towards the inside.
- Combine the isotropic and anisotropic kernels function to eliminate the gap at the surface of multiphase fluid.
- We introduce the signed color field method to extract the surface in the marching cube process, that will eliminate the overlap.

2   SPH Framework

In SPH, fluid is discretized by particles carrying field quantities A_s. At any position r, these quantities can be evaluated by summing up the contributions of the neighboring particles j

$$A_s(\vec{r}) = \sum_j A_j \frac{m_j}{\rho_j} W(\vec{r} - \vec{r}_j, h) \tag{1}$$

where W is the smoothing kernel and h is the smoothing radius, m_j is the mass of particle, and ρ_j its density field. And then we can get the density field ρ_s

$$\rho_s(\vec{r}_i) = \sum_j \rho_j \frac{m_j}{\rho_j} W(\vec{r}_i - \vec{r}_j, h) = \sum_j m_j W(\vec{r}_i - \vec{r}_j, h) \tag{2}$$

The pressure p of particle is typically described as of the density of the fluid such as given by the Tait equation, which is

$$p_i = k\rho_0((\frac{\rho_i}{\rho_0})^\gamma - 1) \tag{3}$$

where k and γ are stiffness parameters and ρ_0 is the rest density of fluid. [10–12].

If we use the standard SPH framework to simulation multiphase fluid, a problem will arise. For particles close to the interface, the computed density is underestimated if they belong to the fluid with higher rest density, and overestimated otherwise. Solenthaler and Pajarola [13] present a formulation based on SPH which can handle this problem, and their main idea is to replace the density computation in SPH by a measure of particle densities and consequently derive new formulations for pressure and viscous forces.

They defined a particle density as

$$\delta_i = \sum_j W(\overrightarrow{r_{ij}}, h) \tag{4}$$

In this article, succeed to simulate multiple fluids with the method of Density Contrast which presented by B. Solenthaler and R. Pajarola.

3 Surface Reconstruction

3.1 Surface Field Computation

Yu and Turk made outstanding contributions to particle-based fluid surface re-modeling. Their approach used a single pass of Laplacian smoothing of particle positions, followed by defining a metaballs-like surface with anisotropic smoothing kernels. This method is perfect performed at single fluid surface reconstruction, but some gaps will arise at interface of multiphase fluid surface when used it to multiphase surface reconstruction of particle-based fluid.

We will save the particle position of each fluid when we used the method of Yu and Turk to reconstruct the multiphase fluid surface. Color field is computed by the particle position and density. This method is designed to capture the density more accurately by allowing the smoothing kernels to be anisotropic. We analysis of the causes of the gap should come from two aspects. On one hand, this method applies one step of diffusion smoothing to the location of kernel centers. The updated kernel centers are calculated by

$$\overline{x_i} = (1 - \lambda)x_i + \lambda \sum_j w_{ij}x_j / \sum_j w_{xj} \tag{5}$$

where w is a suitable finite support weighting and λ is a constant with $0 < \lambda < 1$.

The function w_{ij} is an isotropic weighting function, and formulated as

$$w_{ij} = \begin{cases} 1 - ((\|x_i - x_j\|)/r_i)^3 & if \|x_i - x_j\| < r_i \\ 0 & \text{otherwise} \end{cases} \tag{6}$$

We use λ between 0.9 and 1. According to the above two formulas, the particle position inside the fluid is relatively constant, but the particles at the surface will move towards inside. Obviously, we will not get the correct color field, because the computed fluid volume is smaller than the real color field. Shown in Fig. 2(b).

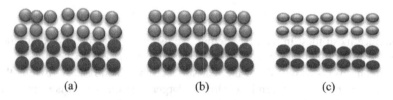

(a)   (b)   (c)

Fig. 2. (a) Particles real position, (b) After Laplacian smoothing, (c) After anisotropy (Color figure online)

On the other hand, this method used the anisotropic kernel in the surface reconstructing, and key of anisotropic kernel is to generate a spherical shape kernel in the fluid surface. The gap will be bigger at the interface of the multiphase fluid although the spherical shape kernel will make fluid surface more smoothing. Shown in Fig. 2(c).

We improved the anisotropic kernel method in multiphase surface reconstruction by considering the particle position of neighbor fluids. The improved $\overline{x}_i$ and w_{ikj} are calculated by

$$\overline{x}_i = (1-\lambda)x_i + \lambda \sum_k^n \sum_j w_{ikj}x_{kj} / \sum_j^n \sum_j w_{ikj} \tag{7}$$

$$w_{ikj} = \begin{cases} 1 - ((\|x_i - x_j\|)/r_i)^3 & if \|x_i - x_j\| < r_i \\ 0 & otherwise \end{cases} \tag{8}$$

where k is the fluid kind.

Because we have considered the neighbor particles of other fluids, the particle position in the interface of two fluids will not move towards inside. Additionally, the improved $\overline{x}_i$ and w_{ikj} can modify the anisotropic kernel function to isotropic at the interface of two fluids surface, and will not shrink fluid volume. The gap at the interface of two fluids surface will be eliminated.

3.2   Surface Extraction

Method of Marching Cube [14, 15] is usually adopted to extracting the mesh files after we computed the color field. For the reason that the different material of each fluid, we need to extract the mesh respectively. This will encounter a problem that is the overlap at the interface of the multiphase fluid. Shown in Fig. 1(a).

By analysis, the reason of overlap produce is that we used interpolation to compute the isometric surface in the marching cube. In the Fig. 3, We suppose the isometric value is 0 in mesh extracting process. we need to compute twice to get the two different

Fig. 3. Marching cube interpolation in two fluid (Color figure online)

fluid surface mesh files. In the first attempt, we use marching cube to extract the fluid which density is small (green solid). Because of the interpolation, the color field with value (green box) is in outside of the real surface (green solid). It is obvious that the extracting surface is near green box which is larger than the real. It is same when we extracting the fluid which density is large. Then we will get a large overlap at the interface of two fluids (green box and yellow box overlap).

Therefore, we propose signed color field to eliminate the overlap at the interface of the multiphase fluid. We define one fluid color field is positive and others fluid color field is negative to extract the one fluid surface mesh. successively, we extract all of the fluid surface mesh. The algorithm showing as follow (Table. 1).

Table 1. Algorithm of signed color field in the marching cube

---

compute the fluid particle position
generate grid
 for fluid i
    Compute i *positive* color field
    compute others *others positive* color field
    interpolation $x = x_1 + (isovalue - \rho_1)\dfrac{(x_2 - x_1)}{(\rho_2 - \rho_1)}$
    compute mesh file
    save mesh file of i
merge mesh files

The signed color field method in the marching cube interpolation will always generate one surface at the interface of the multiphase fluid. This is because the value 0 from negative to positive is always unique and exists.

4   Results

In this section, we describe three simulations that are used to evaluate our surface reconstruction method: three fluids interface, double dam break simulation, two fluids mixing. Our experiment running platform is Intel (R) Xeon (R) CPU E5-2687 W v4 @3.00 GHz, 64-bit Windows operating system.

In the double dam break simulation, see Fig. 4. The green fluid density is 200 kg/m3, and the gray fluid density is 1000 kg/m3. Top render result is using anisotropic kernels method and marching cube directly, and bottom render result is using our improved method. The surface reconstruction time spent shown as Table 1. Both the result is smoothing and spend time is Almost the same, but our method the gap at the interface of two fluids is thinner.

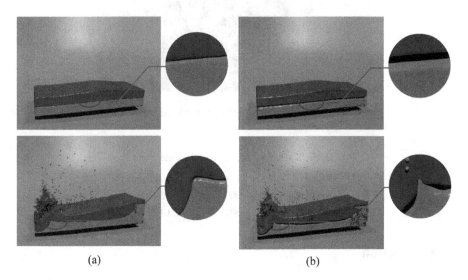

(a)   (b)

Fig. 4. Double dam break simulation, (a) our improved method, (b) using anisotropic kernels method and marching cube directly. (Color figure online)

Figure 5 shows three fluids mixing surface reconstruction results. (a) using our improved method. (b) using anisotropic kernels method and marching cube directly. Note that our result has narrow gap at the interface of multiphase surface, and without overlap in the inner interface of two fluid surface.

Figure 6 shows a frame of double dam break simulation, which rendered by the Blender (Table 2).

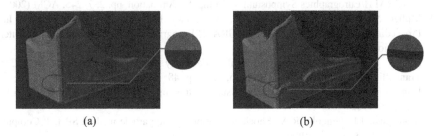

(a)   (b)

Fig. 5. Three immiscible fluid mixing, (a) our improved method, (b) using anisotropic kernels method and marching cube directly.

Fig. 6. Double dam break simulation, rendered by the Blender.

Table 2. Surface reconstruction time spent

Method	Total frame	Total time
Anisotropic kernels	600	19.091 h
Our method	600	20.197 h

5   Conclusion

We improve the anisotropic kernels surface reconstruction method then apply it to multiphase immiscible fluid. Using this method to reconstruct the surface of multiphase immiscible fluid will get smoothing surface and without gap or overlap problem. Additionally, it is easy to implement and does not require more time than the original method.

References

1. Müller, M.: Fast and robust tracking of fluid surfaces. In: Proceedings of the 2009 ACM SIGGRAPH/Eurographics Symposium on Computer Animation, pp. 237–245. ACM (2009)
2. Müller, M., Solenthaler, B., Keiser, R., et al.: Particle-based fluid-fluid interaction. In: Proceedings of the 2005 ACM SIGGRAPH/Eurographics Symposium on Computer Animation, pp. 237–244. ACM (2005)
3. Adams, B., Pauly, M., Keiser, R., et al.: Adaptively sampled particle fluids. In: ACM Transactions on Graphics (TOG), vol. 26, no. 3, p. 48. ACM (2007)
4. Blinn, J.F.: A generalization of algebraic surface drawing. ACM Trans. Graph. (TOG) **1**(3), 235–256 (1982)
5. Monaghan, J.J., Gingold, R.A.: Shock simulation by the particle method SPH. J. Comput. Phys. **52**(2), 374–389 (1983)

6. Zhu, Y., Bridson, R.: Animating sand as a fluid. ACM Trans. Graph. (TOG) **24**(3), 965–972 (2005)
7. Williams, B.W.: Fluid surface reconstruction from particles. University of British Columbia (2008)
8. Yu, J., Turk, G.: Reconstructing surfaces of particle-based fluids using anisotropic kernels. ACM Trans. Graph. (TOG) **32**(1), 5 (2013)
9. Bhatacharya, H., Gao, Y., Bargteil, A.: A level-set method for skinning animated particle data. In: Proceedings of the 2011 ACM SIGGRAPH/Eurographics Symposium on Computer Animation, pp. 17–24. ACM (2011)
10. Becker, M., Teschner, M.: Weakly compressible SPH for free surface flows. In: Proceedings of the 2007 ACM SIGGRAPH/Eurographics Symposium on Computer Animation, pp. 209–217. Eurographics Association (2007)
11. Clavet, S., Beaudoin, P., Poulin, P.: Particle-based viscoelastic fluid simulation. In: Proceedings of the 2005 ACM SIGGRAPH/Eurographics Symposium on Computer Animation, pp. 219–228. ACM (2005)
12. Premžoe, S., Tasdizen, T., Bigler, J., et al.: Particle-based simulation of fluids. In: Computer Graphics Forum, vol. 22, no. 3, pp. 401–410. Blackwell Publishing, Inc. (2003)
13. Solenthaler, B., Pajarola, R.: Density contrast SPH interfaces. In: Proceedings of the 2008 ACM SIGGRAPH/Eurographics Symposium on Computer Animation, pp. 211–218. Eurographics Association (2008)
14. Wilhelms, J., Van Gelder, A.: Topological considerations in isosurface generation extended abstract. ACM (1990)
15. Heiden, W., Goetze, T., Brickmann, J.: Fast generation of molecular surfaces from 3D data fields with an enhanced "marching cube" algorithm. J. Comput. Chem. **14**(2), 246–250 (1993)

Team Cooperation and Its Factors:
A Confirmatory Analysis

Roberto Ruiz-Barquín[1], Aurelio Olmedilla[2(✉)], Pilar Fuster-Parra[3],
Francisco Xavier Ponseti[3], Yuhua Luo[3], and Alexandre Garcia-Mas[3]

[1] Autonomous University of Madrid, Madrid, Spain
roberto.ruiz@uam.es
[2] University of Murcia, Murcia, Spain
olmedilla@um.es
[3] University of the Balearic Islands, Palma, Spain
{pilar.fuster,xponseti,y.luo,alex.garcia}@uib.es

Abstract. Recently knowledge has been obtained about the Cooperative meta-dynamics in performance teams, and also on the fit between the manager's and team member's beliefs about teamwork and performance. To obtain this, a specific instrument has been created and validated, the *Questionnaire on Cooperation in Performance Teams* (CWQ). The need for such this kind of tool is double fold: first, to combine the most relevant conceptual theories in a short and friendly usable instrument, and to obtain easily applicable knowledge addressed to managers and coaches working with performance teams. In order to accomplish fully with this aim, a confirmatory analysis of the new instrument is required too. Consequently, the CWQ was administered to 218 players of performance sports teams (Mean age = 21.12; SD = 6.72; mean years of experience = 11.42; SD = 6.33). The data analysis consisted on the study of the main components (forcing and without forcing the number of factors), with a Varimax rotation. The results confirm the validation of the CWQ both for the "A" and "B" versions of the questionnaire and the existence of four meta-factors: 1. Global cooperation with the team; 2. Cooperation for personal growth in the team; 3. Emotional cooperation, and 4. Conditional cooperation. The four factors shown factorial weights similar to those obtained in the previous exploratory study. These data confirms its transcultural and transituational invariance of the CWQ, as along with its conceptual validity and the solid theoretical conception of the abovementioned factors, and also its applicability in various performance environments. In addition, a mathematical analysis has been introduced to evaluate the symmetry between cooperative work beliefs from both coach and player views, embedded in the conceptual framework of the Cognitive Dissonance Theory.

Keywords: Cooperation · Cohesion · Sportive teams · Confirmatory analysis

© Springer International Publishing AG 2017
Y. Luo (Ed.): CDVE 2017, LNCS 10451, pp. 278–289, 2017.
DOI: 10.1007/978-3-319-66805-5_35

1 Introduction

It is demonstrated that the fit between the person and the organization (Fit Theory, FT) [1, 2] is one of the most relevant factors to analyze the effectiveness of the management style and the behaviors of the members of the work teams. However, research has long found some deficiencies in the explanatory quality of this Fit Theory when it is used for building up empirical applications in the real work teams [3].

In order to solve these deficiencies [4] used a new psychological approach based on an overall analysis of the personal relationship in a cooperative work team. Recently, knowledge about the meta-dynamics of cooperation in performance teams has been obtained, as well as on the adjustment between manager and team member beliefs about teamwork and performance [5]. This model combines the five major conceptual frameworks related to the cooperative team psychological dynamics. It is listed in an increasing order of theoretical complexity: Coordination, Cohesion, Cooperation, Integration and Identification.

Actually, these five psychological conceptual frameworks have been synthesized psychometrically, and meta-knowledge has been obtained over the psychological dynamics of the teams. Thus, through the use of the aforementioned CWQ [4] it has been possible to demonstrate the existence of four factors that are based on the conceptual validity of these five theoretical frameworks. The first of these, the Global Cooperation, covers all five concepts in an egalitarian way: all of the five contributes to this factor; the second one, Personal Growing, indicates that the team member or manager is aiming for their personal fulfillment and/or their growth professionally through their work on the team; the third is the Emotional Cooperation, whereby a person works as a team, or coaches it, because of the positive emotions that their work entails. Finally, the fourth is the Conditional Cooperation, which indicates that a member of a team or a manager considers his/her work in the team as instrumental, mainly to obtain its own objectives, whatever they were. Thus, this study respond to the need to confirm the psychometric properties and conceptual validity of a tool, also with a friendly approach (short, and with low-impact items) addressed to the evaluation of the performance team's psychological dynamics. Its purpose is also to provide clear and accurate information about the psychological characteristics of team members, so that managers and coaches can handle them in the most effective way. Considering all the previous findings, and derived from the first data found [4, 5] the objectives of the present study are:

1. Perform the confirmatory factor analyses of the "A" (team members point of view) and "B" (coaches' point of view) versions of the CWQ, with a large sample of teams, following the same procedure used [4, 5].
2. Determine the degree of convergence between the factorial structure found in the exploratory study of the CWQ (the initial theoretical proposal of four factors), in both "A" and "B" versions, as along with the level of factorial congruence between both versions using a similar approach [6].

2   Method

The study design is cross-sectional descriptive and correlational. At the level of psychological research, it would be an instrumental research based on descriptive strategy [7]. Considering a more traditional perspective [8], it would be an empirical study based on a quantitative methodology, constituting an instrumental study.

2.1   Participants

The sample studied is composed of 220 participants, of which 89.1% are football players (n = 196), and the remaining 10.9% (n = 24) are 15 Rugby players. The mean age of the sample is 21.12 years (SD = 6.72), and they have an experience of 11.42 years (SD = 6.33).

2.2   Instruments

The CWQ [4] consists of 12 Likert items with 5 points an show an internal concordance index of .89 among experts. The CWQ showed a good reliability index (alpha = .61), and is composed of four factors: Global Cooperation (alpha = .77); Personal Growth (alpha = .54); Emotional Cooperation (alpha = .34), and Conditional Cooperation (alpha = .38). The CWQ has a two-way answer for each question: one from the point of view of the team members (Version A) and the other from the coach point of view (Version B).

2.3   Procedure

The Spanish Football and Rugby Federation were contacted in order to obtain they collaboration in the development of the study. The athletes completed the questionnaire just after finishing a practice and after been briefed about the research project and also on the administration of the questionnaire. All participants signed an informed consent form.

2.4   Analysis of Data

Using the SSPS Version 21.2, the data analysis consisted in frequency data analysis; central tendency (mean) and dispersion analysis (standard deviation) [9]; Principal Component analysis was made using Varimax rotation [10] and sedimentation graphs [9]. Some of the crucial formulas used in this analysis are:

Average score (X)

$$\bar{x} = \frac{1}{n} \sum_{i=1}^{n} x_i.$$

Standard deviation (SD)

$$\sigma = \sqrt{\frac{1}{n-1}\sum_{i=1}^{n}(x_i - \bar{x})^2}$$

Kaiser-Meyer-Olkin Index (KMO)

$$KMO = \frac{\sum\sum_{j\neq k} r_{jk}^2}{\sum\sum_{j\neq k} r_{jk}^2 + \sum\sum_{j\neq k} p_{jk}^2}$$

where rjk is the Correlation Coefficient between the variables xj and xk; and pjk is the Partial Correlation Coefficient between xj and xk, given the other xs.

Principal component analysis

$$y_j = a_{j1}x_1 + a_{j2}x_2 + \ldots + a_{jp}x_p$$
$$= a_j'x$$

where:

Variables: x1, x2, ..., xp
New set of variables:: y1, y2, ..., yp.
Each y1 (where j = 1,...p) is a linear combination of original x1, x2, ... xp.
a′j is a vector of constants
a′j = (a1, a2, ..., apj)

$$x = \begin{bmatrix} x_1 \\ \vdots \\ x_p \end{bmatrix}$$

For we maintain the orthogonality of the transformation performed, it is necessary that the modulus of the vector a′j = (a1, a2, ..., apj) is 1.

$$a_j'a_j = \sum_{k=1}^{p} a_{kj}^2 = 1$$

3 Results

Versions "A" and "B" of the CWQ are analysed using the principal component procedure, following the same developed [4, 5], when performed the exploratory data (Table 1).

Table 1. The descriptive values for both "A" and "B" versions of the CWQ

Ítems	Version A		Version B	
	M	DT	M	DT
1	3.97	.92	3.85	1.03
2	2.59	1.37	2.85	1.54
3	3.83	1.13	4.05	1.05
4	3.97	1.05	4.18	.99
5	3.29	1.24	3.27	1.35
6	3.91	1.11	4.14	.96
7	4.30	.91	4.20	1.01
8	4.15	1.01	4.32	.91
9	3.31	1.43	2.93	1.38
10	3.79	1.14	3.92	1.08
11	3.83	1.20	3.78	1.23
12	3.80	1.12	3.62	1.29

3.1 Principal Components Analysis of the CWQ's Version "A"

The Kaiser-Meyer-Olkin (KMO, see above) index was applied to the sample in order to verify its adequacy for the principal component study, obtaining a value of .780 (0.500 < KMO < 1.00) and a Chi-square of 399,030.

The Barlett Sphericity Test (BST) obtains a significance of $p < .001$. The values obtained with the KMO index are satisfactory, indicating that there is an adequate sample number for conducting a Principal Component analysis (n = 220). On the other hand, the statistical significance obtained in the BST shows the adequacy of the data's matrix for to conduct an accurate the Principal Components test.

The application of the factorial analysis of main components with Varimax rotation, whether initially the four theoretical factors are forced, or if the same analysis is performed in an exploratory way without forcing them (only considering the criterion of factors with eigenvalues greater than 1), the percentage of the explained variance is the same (56.21%). According to Hair et al. [10], when these values are greater than 50%, are considered adequate. Table 2 shows how 12 factors are extracted thanks to the use of Principal Component analysis, of which only four have eigenvalues greater than 1.

In the sedimentation graph (Fig. 1) we can see how the first factor of the "A" version becomes the highest factor considering its value of explained variance (21.34%), observing how from the fourth factor appears a great downward slope when passing to the 5th factor. None of the other factors reach an eigenvalue with value 1.

The matrix of rotated components shows high factorial loads, reaching in some cases values of .800. As the criterion for to select items, and considering the sample quantity, those with a factor load higher than .30 were accepted. The performance of Principal Component analysis with Varimax rotation (see Table 3) shows high saturations in the four factors, reaching factorial loads of .800.

The varimax rotation has only required 5 iterations to achieve the final factorial matrix, which is configured as pretty congruent with the initial structure made up of the four theoretical factors.

Table 2. Eigenvalues and percentage of variance explained for each factor of the version "A" of the CWQ.

Component	Initial eigenvalues			Addition of saturations to the square of rotation		
	Total	% variance	% accumulated	Total	% variance	% accumulated
1	3.124	26.033	26.033	2.560	21.336	21.336
2	1.281	10.671	36.705	1.560	12.998	34.334
3	1.225	10.204	46.909	1.334	11.121	45.455
4	1.116	9.304	56.213	1.291	10.758	56.213
5	.908	7.569	63.782			
6	.822	6.854	70.636			
7	.707	5.895	76.531			
8	.650	5.418	81.949			
9	.626	5.220	87.169			
10	.596	4.964	92.133			
11	.511	4.256	96.389			
12	.433	3.611	100.000			

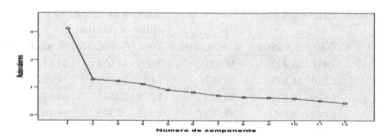

Fig. 1. The sedimentation graph (Fig. 1) we can see how the first factor of the "A" version

3.2 Principal Components Analysis of the CWQ's Version "B"

Regarding the analysis corresponding to the version "B", KMO values are shown to be significantly higher than those of version "A", since a value of .800 (Chi-square = 499,519) was obtained, and with a significance of p < .001. Therefore, the adequacy of the magnitude of the sample for the analysis is significantly greater, showing the adequacy of the data matrix for the Principal Component Analysis. The performance of Principal Components analysis with Varimax rotation, are highly convergent between both two versions, "A" and "B", of the CWQ. Like with the version "A", when we are looking for the principal components, the same four factors are extracted with both the forced Varimax rotation and without forcing them (when the selection of factors have the condition that their eigenvalue were greater than 1). In this particular case (see Table 4), the percentage of variance explained is significantly higher than the "A" questionnaire (2.50% higher), obtaining satisfactory values of explained variance [7].

Table 3. Principal component analysis with Varimax rotation of the "A" version of the CWQ.

	Component			
	1	2	3	4
c3a	*.800*			
c1a	*.743*			−.102
c4a	*.731*			
c6a	*.599*	.326		
c10a	*.417*	.412		.372
c8a	.	*.696*		−.125
c11a		*.673*	.307	
c7a	.479	*.494*		
c9a			*.760*	
c12a			*.745*	
c2a				*.746*
c5a				*.744*

Table 4. Eigenvalues and percentage of variance explained by each factor of the CWQ, "B" version

Component	Initial eigenvalues			Addition of saturations to the square of rotation		
	Total	% variance	% accumulated	Total	% variance	% accumulated
1	3.411	28.422	28.422	2.955	24.628	24.628
2	1.389	11.575	39.997	1.692	14.099	38.727
3	1.209	10.077	50.073	1.277	10.643	49.370
4	1.043	8.690	58.763	1.127	9.393	58.763
5	.862	7.185	65.948			
6	.792	6.600	72.548			
7	.717	5.977	78.525			
8	.651	5.422	83.947			
9	.580	4.829	88.777			
10	.527	4.392	93.169			
11	.442	3.685	96.854			
12	.377	3.146	100.000			

Figure 2 shows a structure of the "B" version, which is quite similar to that one obtained in version "A", although in this case the slope of the curve between factor 4 and factor 5 is lesser than in the graph corresponding to the "A" version.

The analysis of Principal Components with Varimax rotation shows high saturations in the four factors, reaching factorial loads of .802, and therefore, showing values very similar to those obtained in version "A" (see Table 5). As was done with the same analysis with version "A", it has been accepted as criterion of selection of items, those with a factorial load higher than .30.

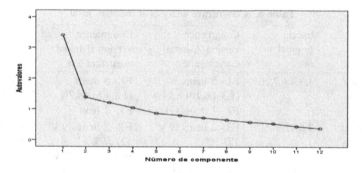

Fig. 2. Sedimentation graph of the 12 factors extracted from the version "B" of the CWQ

Table 5. Principal component analysis with Varimax rotation, version "B"

	Component			
	1	2	3	4
c3b	.802			
c1b	.753			
c7b	.727			
c4b	.691			
c6b	.644	.315		
c11b		.660		
c5b		.616		
c8b	.370	.598		
c10b	.344	.582		
c9b			.777	.345
c12b			.714	-.460
c2b				.840

As was the case with version "A", only 5 iterations were required to achieve the factor's matrix. Table 6 shows the degree of convergence - at the item level - found of the final factor structure of versions "A" and "B", in relationship with the initial exploratory and theoretical proposal made of four factors.

The results show a high concordance between the initial questionnaire structure and the final factorial solution of both "A" and "B" versions of the CWQ. This convergence is even greater when comparing the factorial structure of the two versions in the final questionnaire. We have found a high convergence among the items, especially when considering the first factor. Also, it is observed that the initial factor 3 mainly integrates factor 2 of the final questionnaire, version "A", and that the factor 2 of the initial CWQ structure is manifested now mostly in factors 1 and 3 of the final questionnaire, version "A". Moreover, the degree of agreement when the CWQ is considered factor by factor is never less than 50%. When comparing the initial CWQ structure with the "B" final

Table 6. Congruence analysis at the item level

	Escala original	Congruence version A-Initial estructura test	Congruence version B-Initial estructura test	Congruence version A with B
F1.- global cooperation (6–18)	1,3,4,6,7,10	F1.- 5 ítems (1,3,4,6,10) 83.3% F2.- 1 ítems (7)	F1.- 5 ítems (1,3,4,6) 66,7% F1.- 1 ítem	1,3,4,6 66.7%
F2.- Personal Growing (4–12)	4,6,12,9	F3.- 2 ítems (9 y 12) 50% F1.- 2 ítems (4 y 6)	F3.- 2 ítems (9 y 12) 50% F1.- 2 ítems (4 y 6)	4,5,12,9 100%
F3.- Emotional Cooperation (2–6)	2,5,8	F4.- 2 ítems (2 y 5) 50% F2.- 1 ítem (8)	F2.- 2 ítems (5 y 8) 6,7% F4.- 1 ítems (2)	2 y 8 66.7%
F4.- Conditional Cooperation (2–6)	2,11	F4.- 1 ítem (2) 50% F2.- 1 ítem (11)	F4.- 1 ítem (2) 50% F2.- 1 ítem (11)	2 y 11 100%

version, the results are similar to those obtained in "A", although the percentage of factor convergence stays closer, meaning between 50 and 66.7%. The greatest convergence is obtained between CWQ's versions "A" and "B", since in all cases it exceeds 66.7%.

4 Discussion

In this study, once the complete confirmatory statistical analysis has been performed, it can be stated that the CWQ tool behaves in a stable manner and that the four factors defined theoretically and empirically in the exploratory analysis are solidly maintained [4], with small variations due to the change of location of some of the items.

Moreover, this accuracy obtained means that this tool will be available for the sport psychologists – and others working with different performance teams – to design precise and theory-based interventions. As was discussed in the exploratory study, the basic idea and main objective was to make a synthesis of the five theoretical frameworks that currently explain the psychological dynamics of sports teams, coordination [11, 12]; cohesion [13–15], cooperation [16–18]; identification [19–21] and integration [22–24] to obtain a meta-knowledge about these dynamics, and, at the same time, design and validate a tool that should reduce the high length and impact of the tests used up to the moment.

These obtained factors fully explain an implicit and latent knowledge about the motivations of the people for to form part and/or manage performance oriented teams. The first one, the Global Cooperation, has psychometric characteristics coming from all the five theoretical frameworks on which our study has been conceptually based. That is, the people studied have internally built up a cognitive scheme that unifies and gives meaning to a global teamwork. The second of these, the Personal Growth through belonging to the team, implies that the personal motivation of realization of the person [25], can coexist with their integration with the team. Moreover, can explain perfectly the fact that managers and team members must understand their time spending working/playing in the team as a process rather than a final state.

The third factor introduces the emotional component ("feeling good in the team"), which is one of the basic components of the sports Cohesion [14]. This finding reinforces the idea that sports-based cohesion based on affection among team members has its own entity and must always be considered when analyzing and intervening in a performance-oriented team. Finally, a fourth factor has been confirmed – the Conditional Cooperation - that explains that in the mind of the components of a team there is also their own self-interest, and their possible efforts should be accommodated with the objectives of the team. The fact that this kind of "tit for tat" cooperation coexists in the minds of managers/coaches and players/team members with the other three factors gives relevance to the theoretical concept [16, 17] and raises the need for consider this motivation in any intervention addressed to work in performance teams.

Moreover, the level of correlation that has been found between the two viewpoints (manager/coach and team member) indicates that there are points of contact between the both beliefs, and it is evident that the resolution of this pretty relevant cognitive dissonance in an performance-oriented behavior may be an added value to the use of this theoretical framework and this expanded CWQ tool. The confirmation of the existence of these factors, both by the factorial and the sedimentation studies, assure us that we can use this tool with technical security and at the same time we will be able to extrapolate the data obtained, through the theoretical framework that has been acquired and consolidated. In addition, in this confirmatory study, the existence of a symmetry between the points of view of the coach/manager and the team member has been verified, using the two versions of the same CWQ questionnaire.

This conceptual approach has been based on two theories. The first one is the FIT [1, 2], which has been studied and demonstrated repeatedly about the congruence between managers and team member within a organization or team aimed to obtain performance. Secondly, is grounded on the Theory of Cognitive Dissonance [26]. This one indicates that these two points of view have to coexist in people's minds and that a resolution of the dilemma must be reached.

This "internal" solution of the dissonance will determine the positioning and disposition of each person regarding of which variables are more relevant and necessary in order to obtain performance from their teams. This last improvement [5] of the model derived from the CWQ and the conceptual framework that supports it, we believe that contributes in a relevant way to our knowledge about the underlying psychological mechanisms which determines the coaches/managers' and team members' behaviors.

Finally, we have to indicate that this tool that can be used in two very different ways. Firstly, as an instrument addressed to know the distribution of the different profiles of the people who compose an specific performance team, and, secondly, as a way for these people, through self-evaluation and psychological assisted analysis -both with the five original theoretical frames and the final four meta-dynamics- can advance in improving their abilities to lead or to be members of a team.

Acknowledgements. Authors would thank the European Union Grant, "PsyTool: Sport Psychology as a strategic tool for prevention and training on grassroots sports", Code 567199-EPP-1-2015-2-ES-SPOSCP, for to fund partially this study; and Football Project FFRM +UMU (04-0092-321B-64502-14704).

References

1. Gilbert, G.R., Myrtle, R.C., Sohi, R.S.: Relational behavior of leaders: a comparison by vocational context. J. Leadersh. Org. Stud. **22**, 149–160 (2015)
2. Round, J., Dawis, R., Lofquist, L.: Measurement of person-environment fit and prediction of satisfaction in the theory of work adjustment. J. Vocat. Behav. **31**, 297–318 (1987)
3. Edwards, J.A.: Person job-fit: a conceptual integration, literature review and methodological critique. In: Cooper, C.L., Robertson, I.T. (eds.) International Review of Industrial and Organizational Psychology, pp. 283–357. Wiley, Oxford (1991)
4. Olmedilla, A., Garcia-Mas, A., Luo, Y., Llaneras, C., Ruiz-Barquín, R., Fuster-Parra, P.: Multilevel psychological analysis for cooperative work teams. In: Luo, Y. (ed.) CDVE 2016. LNCS, vol. 9929, pp. 322–331. Springer, Cham (2016). doi:10.1007/978-3-319-46771-9_42
5. Olmedilla, A., Cantón, E., Luo, Y., Ruiz-Barquín, R., Fuster-Parra, P., García-Mas, A.: Cooperative psychological dynamics of working teams: a symmetrical meta-model. Symmetry (in review)
6. Ruiz-Barquín, R., de la Vega-Marcos, R.: Adaptación de la escala de liderazgo LSS-3 al fútbol/LSS-3 Leadership Scale Adaptation in Soccer. Revista Internacional de Medicina y Ciencias de la Actividad Física y del Deporte **15**, 677–700 (2015)
7. Ato, M., López, J.J., Benavente, A.: Un sistema de clasificación de los diseños de investigación en psicología. Anales de psicología **29**(3), 1038–1059 (2013)
8. Montero, I., León, O.G.: A guide for naming research studies in psychology. Int. J. Clin. Health Psychol. **7**(3), 847–862 (2007)
9. Pardo, A., Ruiz, M.A.: Análisis de datos con SPSS 13 Base. McGraw Hill, Madrid (2005)
10. Hair, J.F., Black, B., Babin, B., Anderson, R.E., Taham, R.L.: Multivariate Data Analysis, 7th edn. Prentice Hall, Upper Saddle River (2009)
11. Lausic, D., Razon, S., Tenenbaum, G.: Nonverbal sensitivity. Verbal communication and team coordination in tennis doubles. Int. J. Sport Exerc. Psychol. **13**, 398–414 (2015)
12. López, C.J., Mohamed, K.M., El Yousfi, M.M., Zurita, F., Martínez, A.: Communicative features in basketball coaches from different levels. A case study. Cult. Cie. Dep. **6**, 199–206 (2011)
13. Carless, S.A., De Paola, C.: The measurement of cohesion in work teams. Small Group Res. **31**, 78–88 (2000)
14. Carron, A.V., Brawley, L.R.: Cohesion. Conceptual and measurement issues. Small Group Res. **31**, 89–106 (2000)
15. Carron, A.V., Brawley, R.L., Widmeyer, W.N.: The measurement of cohesiveness in sport groups. In: Duda, J.L. (ed.) Advances in Sport and Exercise Psychology Measurement, pp. 214–226. WV. Fitness Information Technology, Morgantown (1998)
16. Garcia-Mas, A.: Cooperation and competition in sportive teams. A preliminary study. Análise Psicológica **1**, 115–130 (2001)
17. García-Mas, A., Olmedilla, A., Morilla, M., Rivas, C., García-Quinteiro, E., Ortega, E.: A new model of sportive cooperation and its evaluation with a questionnaire. Psicothema **18**, 425–432 (2006)

18. Rabbie, J.M.: Determinants of the intra-group instrumental cooperation. In: Hinde, E.H., Groebel, J. (eds.) Cooperation and Prosocial Behavior, pp. 97–131. Visor Aprendizaje, Madrid (1995)
19. Garcia-Mas, A., Palou, P., Gili, M., Ponseti, X., Borrás, P.A., Vidal, J., Cruz, J., Torregrosa, M., Villamarín, F., Sousa, C.: Commitment enjoyment and motivation in young soccer competitive players. Span. J. Psychol. 13, 609–616 (2010)
20. Rusbult, C.E., Martz, J.M., Agnew, C.R.: The investment model scale: measuring commitment level, satisfaction level, quality of alternatives and investment size. Pers. Relat. 5, 357–391 (1998)
21. Sousa, C., Torregrosa, M., Viladrich, C., Villamarín, F., Cruz, J.: The commitment of young soccer players. Psicothema 19, 256–262 (2007)
22. Rivas, C., Ponzanelli, R., De la Llave, A., Pérez-Llantada, M.C., Garcia-Mas, A.: Individualismo y colectivismo en la relación a la eficacia colectiva percibida en jugadores de fútbol (Individualism and collectivism in relationship with perceived collective efficacy in football players). Rev. Mex. Psicol. 32, 68–80 (2015)
23. Scandroglio, B., López-Martínez, J.S., La San José Sebastián, M.C.: Teoría de la Identidad Social: una síntesis crítica de sus fundamentos. evidencias y controversias (The social identity theory: a critical synthesis about its foundations and controversies). Psicothema 20, 80–89 (2008)
24. Topa-Cantisano, G., Morales-Domínguez, F.: Burnout and team identification: role of social support in a model of structural equations. Int. J. Clin. Health Psychol. 7, 337–348 (2006)
25. Maslow, A.H.: A theory of human motivation. Psychol. Rev. 50(4), 370 (1943)
26. Festinger, L.: A Theory of Cognitive Dissonance. Stanford University Press, Palo Alto (1962)

A Visualization System for Dynamic Protein Structure and Amino Acid Network

Silan You[1], Lifeng Gao[1], Yongpan Hua[1], Min Zhu[1(✉)],
and Mingzhao Li[2]

[1] College of Computer Science, Sichuan University, Chengdu 610065, China
silanyou@163.com, brendagao.lf@gmail.com,
huayp@outlook.com, zhumin@scu.edu.cn
[2] RMIT University, Melbourne, Australia
mingzhao.li@rmit.edu.au

Abstract. In this paper, we design and implement a visual analytics system to visualize dynamic protein structure and amino acid network. Specifically, we propose a mixed layout method based on Force-Directed Algorithm and Circular Layout Model to visualize protein structure. We design a dynamic visualization framework of the amino acid network with multiple coordinated views. We implement a prototype system and present case studies based on the molecular simulation data of the β2-Adrenergic receptor (β2AR, a protein) to demonstrate the usefulness and effectiveness of our system.

Keywords: Dynamic network visualization · Visual analytics · Multiple coordinated view · Protein structure · Amino acid network

1 Introduction

The studies on the changes of protein structure can be of great help for the analysis of protein functions. However, with existing experimental instruments, it is difficult to observe the dynamic behavior of a single large molecule on the atomic scale. Bioinformatics researchers also use the method of molecular dynamics [1] to simulate how protein structure changes. The simulation produces a lot of trajectory data, i.e., molecular dynamics trajectory conformation data [2]. Existing works based on such trajectory data mainly focus on studying the activation mechanism and structural changes of proteins according to how parameters (e.g. energy, density) change. However, those methods can only analyze proteins from either the global view or the local view, but fail to support how the changes of local structure affect the global view.

Several researchers have been working on analyzing protein amino acid networks, protein interactions and metabolic networks [4–6]. We have noticed some drawbacks of the existing work: (i) visualizing the process of how protein structure transforms into amino acid network can easily cause the loss of spatial information of protein; (ii) the state-of-the-art visualization is unable to provide an effective way to dynamically display the amino acid network, and it is hard for researchers to recognize and map the changes of protein structure based on the changes of amino acid network structure; (iii) existing complex network visualization tools fail to display the dynamic changes of the amino acid network data effectively.

© Springer International Publishing AG 2017
Y. Luo (Ed.): CDVE 2017, LNCS 10451, pp. 290–297, 2017.
DOI: 10.1007/978-3-319-66805-5_36

To overcome the above drawbacks, in this paper, we propose a visual analytics system to visualize dynamic protein structure and amino acid network. Specifically, we make the following contributions: (i) we design a novel visualization method to display the topology structure of the amino acid network, which reduces the loss of protein space information; (ii) we propose a dynamic visualization scheme of amino acid network topology with time series; (iii) we design and implement a visualization system with multiple coordinated interactive views to visualize the amino acid network.

2 Related Work

In this section, we first review the literature in our domain (visualization of protein structure and amino acid network). Then we discuss related visualization techniques.

2.1 Amino Acid Network Visualization

Bioinformatics is used to study the protein in the following aspects: protein sequence analysis, protein folding dynamics, protein structure analysis and prediction, protein stability analysis and protein interaction [3]. Some efforts have been made to visualize the amino acid network. Seeber et al. developed Wordom module PSN [4], which implemented the method of constructing an amino acid network. However, it lacks the function of network visualization. Vidotto et al. [5] built an amino acid network and displayed the generated network using Cytoscape. However, it only implements the construction of amino acid network defined by the nearest atomic distance. RINerator [6] is also a constructed an amino acid network which defines the edges of nodes in different ways and quantifies the intensity of interactions. However, it fails to reflect the connection between protein structure visualization and amino acid network topology visualization.

The molecular dynamic is widely used to simulate the folding and binding process of proteins which produces rich protein conformation. There is also some software specifically designed for amino acid networks. Cusack et al. developed a tool to identify important residues in proteins [7]. RINalyzer is a Cytoscape plugin that can provide analysis and visualization of amino acid networks [6]. Doncheva et al. provided a detailed workflow to compare multiple amino acid networks [8]. However, those tools cannot effectively present the dynamic changes of protein secondary structure.

2.2 Related Visualization Methods

The protein trajectory conformation data is composed of several amino acid network data in order. It has a clear hierarchical information and sequence information. We mainly discuss hierarchical visualization and dynamic visualization in this subsection.

Hierarchical Visualization. The goal of visualizing hierarchical structure data is to effectively depict the hierarchy in the data. Common layout methods of network data include node-link methods, adjacency matrix methods and mixed layout methods [9].

Node-link methods are mainly implemented using Force-directed Layout [10] and multi-dimensional scaling (MDS) layout [11]. Adjacency matrix [12] effectively presents the two associated network data. Although a single layout method can show the topology of the amino acid network, it cannot integrate the structural information of the protein itself, resulting in the defect of protein space information. In this paper, we propose a new layout to visualize amino acid networks which displays the protein secondary structure and amino acid network topology at the same time.

Dynamic Visualization. Dynamic visualization focuses on the changes of object structure [13]. Beck et al. studied dynamic graph visualization and divided it into animation technology and timeline technology [14]. Rufiange et al. proposed a mix technology DiffAni [15], integrating multiple display forms to allow users to switch among different views. Dynamic network data visualization aims to keep the continuity and consistency of the frame as far as possible. The corresponding difficulties are as follows: (i) the trade-off between the optimal layout of each time slice and the stability of different time slices; (ii) the trade-off between displaying forms and displaying effects. In this paper, the data scale is large, using multi-view interaction and displaying data statically cannot show the structural changes of the amino acid network. It is difficult to understand the changes of protein structure. The animation way can be a good solution to this problem.

3   The Proposed Visual Analysis Model

We propose a visual analysis model, which includes construction of amino acid network, protein structure analysis, amino acid network topology structure analysis and amino acid network property analysis.

3.1   Construction of Amino Acid Network

To better study the topology of proteins, network characteristics can be introduced into protein structure, amino acids can be abstracted into nodes and the interactions between amino acids can be abstracted into edges to get amino acid network [16]. Different node abstractions can be used to construct the amino acid network [17, 18]. In this paper, the amino acid network is constructed by using C_α [17] as the node. If the distance between two nodes is less than $7\,\text{Å}$, then there is an edge between the two nodes. The weight (w) of the undirected weighted graph of the amino acid network can be constructed as formula (1).

$$w(i,j) = \begin{cases} \dfrac{1}{d(i,j)}, & d(i,j) \leq 7\,\text{Å} \\ 0, & d(i,j) > 7\,\text{Å} \end{cases} \tag{1}$$

where (i,j) is the pair of amino acid nodes and $d(i,j)$ is the Euclidean distance between pairs of amino acid nodes.

3.2   Mixed Layout Visualization Method

In our visualization model, we combine Circular Layout with the Force-Directed model which can visualize both the secondary structure of the protein (which is important for the study of G Protein-Coupled Receptors [19]) and the global topology of amino acid network.

Global Structure Layout Design Based on Force-Directed. We use the following steps to optimize the process: (i) the three-dimensional coordinates of the amino acids are projected onto the two-dimensional plane by using the PCA method to obtain the corresponding amino acid initial coordinates (x, y); (ii) a virtual central node is added to ensure that the entire layout is distributed around the canvas center; (iii) a reasonable threshold is defined. When the total energy of the system in the amino acid network topology layout is less than the threshold, the iteration will be stopped.

Our Force-Directed method adopts the energy model, in which the energy involved includes the repulsive force formed by the traction between the nodes, the repulsive force between the nodes, and the attraction between the node and the center point. Each node is subjected to the traction of the edge, the repulsive force of the neighboring nodes and the attraction of the virtual center node. For the whole model, the energy to be calculated corresponds to the energy as E_s (formula (2)) of the elastic system, the gravitational system energy between the nodes as E_n (formula (3)), the gravitational system energy between the node and the center point as E_c (formula (4)), the corresponding system total energy as E (formula (5)).

$$E_s = \sum_{i=1}^{n} \sum_{j}^{n} k_s w_{ij} (d(i,j) - s(i,j)) \tag{2}$$

$$E_n = \sum_{i=1}^{n} \sum_{j=1}^{n} \frac{k_n w_i w_j}{d(i,j)^2} \tag{3}$$

$$E_c = \sum_{i=1}^{n} \frac{k_0 w_i w_0}{x_i^2 + y_i^2} \tag{4}$$

$$E = E_s + E_n + E_c \tag{5}$$

where $s(i,j)$ represents the natural length of the spring; k_n is the electrostatic force constant between the two points; w_i is the weight of the point i; k_0 represents the electrostatic force constant between the amino acid node and the "center node"; w_0 is "center node" corresponds to the weight.

We use three-dimensional coordinates of the amino acid in the protein structure to map its initial position in the plane coordinate to ensure its initial state stability. In addition, the corresponding threshold is chosen reasonably to reduce the number of iterations of the Force-Directed Algorithm.

Local Structure Layout Design Based on Circular Layout. As a whole of the secondary structure of the protein, the center coordinates (X, Y) of the secondary structure can be obtained based on the layout result of the above. In this paper, we use a circular layout to visualize the secondary structure of the protein. Assuming S is a secondary structure of the protein, the secondary structure contains the amino acid sequence $\{\alpha_1, \alpha_2, \cdots, \alpha_n\}$, where each amino acid is represented by a radius r of the circle and the amino acid is evenly distributed on the circumference of S. The coordinates of S will be determined by the global structure and the coordinates (x_i, y_i) of the corresponding amino acid α_i will be determined by (X, Y).

3.3 Dynamic Visualization Design for the Changes of Amino Acid Network Topology Structure

Dynamic Layout and Algorithm Optimization of Amino Acid Network Topology. To visualize the process of how protein structure change and to maximize user observation and understanding, it is required that the amino acid network topology layout maintains the maximum similarity between the current and next moment.

In this paper, the amino acid network topology at each time slice is called a frame. We save the current frame layout results as the initial state of the next frame and optimize the algorithm. We compare the performance of the algorithm before and after optimization in energy change (Fig. 1). We find that the energy of the optimized algorithm can stabilize earlier and reduces the number of iterations.

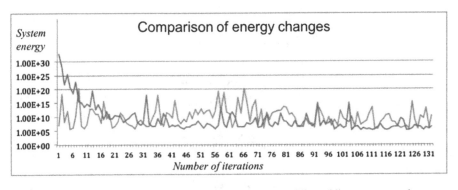

Fig. 1. Energy change graph of different initial state systems. (The red line represents the energy change before the system is optimized; the blue line represents the energy change after the optimization.) (Color figure online)

Visualization Design of Amino Acid Network Topology Structure Change. The changes of the amino acid network topological structure are caused by the changes of the edges. There are three cases about the changing edges from the previous frame to the current frame: the new edges, the edges which will disappear and the edges keeping reserved. We use green, red and the gradient color from cyan to magenta to present the different edges. Through this visual form, we can understand the relationship between the local structure and the global structure in the whole network. Therefore, it is possible to understand the changes of protein structure and the relationship between local and global. It plays an important role in the study of protein structure.

3.4   System Design

To achieve multi-aspect observation of protein structure, multiple coordinated views are designed for different aspects, which contain protein structure view, amino acid network topology view, amino acid network topology performance view and timeline view. The interaction and linkage of each module are shown in Fig. 2.

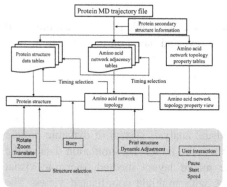

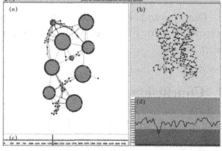

Fig. 2. System interaction design.

Fig. 3. The interface of the protein amino acid network dynamic visualization system. (a) Amino acid network topology view; (b) protein structure view; (c) timeline view; (d) amino acid network property view.

4   Case Study

In this section, we use the molecular simulation data about β2AR protein [20] to verify our proposed system. This data is based on the Amber molecular dynamics simulation software, which is obtained by applying the AMBER03 environmental force field to the β2AR protein.

Based on the mixed layout visualization method proposed in this paper, the β2AR protein amino acid network topology layout effect is shown in Fig. 3. The layout algorithm enables the observer to grasp and understand the global topology of the amino acid network and further correlate it with the secondary structure of the protein. In the process of the movement of protein, the user focuses on the changes of the local structure of the protein.

As shown in Fig. 4, we can clearly observe the dynamic changes of the amino acid network topology. Firstly, some fluctuations in the edge are obvious, which accompany with the whole process of protein structure change; secondly, compared to the whole amino acid network topology, the secondary structure is more stable in the internal, but the secondary structure also exists several edges which fluctuate frequently.

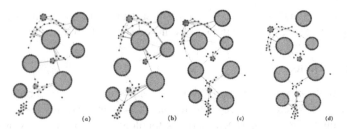

Fig. 4. Dynamic visualization of amino acid network topology. (a) Red marks edges will disappear; (b) Green marks new edges; (c) Purple shows the accumulation process of the edges; (d) Magenta shows the steady state of the edge. (Color figure online)

Our system is beneficial to understand the active and stable parts of the amino acid network topology change. More details can be revealed based on the interaction with other views.

5 Conclusion

In this paper, we design and implement a visual analysis system of dynamic protein structure and amino acid network. Then we use the molecular simulation data of the β2AR protein to do experiments with the mixed layout method, dynamic visual analysis model and visualization framework with multiple coordinated views. The experiment results show that the structure of the protein can be observed intuitively and analyzed with its multi-angle views.

References

1. Li, Y., Zhu, F., Vaidehi, N., Goddard, W.A., Sheinerman, F., Reiling, S., Morize, I., Mu, L., Harris, K., Ardati, A., Laoui, A.: Prediction of the 3D structure and dynamics of human DP G-protein coupled receptor bound to an agonist and an antagonist. J. Am. Chem. Soc. **129**(35), 10720–10731 (2007)
2. Swift, R.V., McCammon, J.A.: Catalytically requisite conformational dynamics in the mRNA-capping enzyme probed by targeted molecular dynamics. Biochemistry **47**(13), 4102–4111 (2008)
3. Gromiha, M.M.: Protein Bioinformatics: From Sequence to Function. A Division of Reed Elsevier India Pvt., Gurgaon (2010)
4. Seeber, M., Felline, A., Raimondi, F., Muff, S., Friedman, R., Rao, F., Caflisch, A., Fanelli, F.: Wordom: a user-friendly program for the analysis of molecular structures, trajectories, and free energy surfaces. J. Comput. Chem. **32**(6), 1183–1194 (2011)
5. Martin, A.J., Vidotto, M., Boscariol, F., Di Domenico, T., Walsh, I., Tosatto, S.C.: RING: networking interacting residues, evolutionary information and energetics in protein structures. Bioinformatics **27**(14), 2003–2005 (2011)
6. Doncheva, N.T., Klein, K., Domingues, F.S., Albrecht, M.: Analyzing and visualizing residue networks of protein structures. Trends Biochem. Sci. **36**(4), 179–182 (2011)

7. Cusack, M.P., Thibert, B., Bredesen, D.E., Del Rio, G.: Efficient identification of critical residues based only on protein structure by network analysis. PLoS One 2(5), e421 (2007)
8. Doncheva, N.T., Assenov, Y., Domingues, F.S., Albrecht, M.: Topological analysis and interactive visualization of biological networks and protein structures. Nat. Protoc. 7(4), 670–685 (2012)
9. Beck, F., Burch, M., Diehl, S., Weiskopf, D.: A taxonomy and survey of dynamic graph visualization. In: Computer Graphics Forum (2016)
10. Walshaw, C.: A multilevel algorithm for force-directed graph-drawing. J. Graph Algorithms Appl. 7(3), 253–285 (2006)
11. Brandes, U., Pich, C.: An experimental study on distance-based graph drawing. In: Tollis, I. G., Patrignani, M. (eds.) GD 2008. LNCS, vol. 5417, pp. 218–229. Springer, Heidelberg (2009). doi:10.1007/978-3-642-00219-9_21
12. Bach, B., Henry-Riche, N., Dwyer, T., Madhyastha, T., Fekete, J.D., Grabowski, T.: Small MultiPiles: piling time to explore temporal patterns in dynamic networks. Comput. Graph. Forum 34, 31–40 (2015)
13. Vehlow, C., Beck, F., Weiskopf, D.: Visualizing dynamic hierarchies in graph sequences. IEEE Trans. Vis. Comput. Graph. 22(10), 2343–2357 (2016)
14. Beck, F., Burch, M., Diehl, S., Weiskopf, D.: The state of the art in visualizing dynamic graphs. In: EuroVis STAR, vol. 2 (2014)
15. Rufiange, S., McGuffin, M.J.: DiffAni: visualizing dynamic graphs with a hybrid of difference maps and animation. IEEE Trans. Vis. Comput. Graph. 19(12), 2556–2565 (2013)
16. Zhou, J., Yan, W., Hu, G., Shen, B.: Amino acid network for the discrimination of native protein structures from decoys. Curr. Protein Pept. Sci. 15(6), 522–528 (2014)
17. Bartoli, L., Fariselli, P., Casadio, R.: The effect of backbone on the small-world properties of protein contact maps. Phys. Biol. 4(4), L1 (2008)
18. Estrada, E.: Universality in protein residue networks. Biophys. J. 98(5), 890–900 (2010)
19. Alves, N.A., Martinez, A.S.: Inferring topological features of proteins from amino acid residue networks. Phys. A 375(1), 336–344 (2007)
20. Xiao, X., Zeng, X., Yuan, Y., Gao, N., Guo, Y., Pu, X., Li, M.: Understanding the conformation transition in the activation pathway of β2 adrenergic receptor via a targeted molecular dynamics simulation. Phys. Chem. Chem. Phys. 17(4), 2512–2522 (2015)

Author Index

Printed in the United States
By Bookmasters